SHIPWRECKS of the IRISH COAST

1105-1993

EDWARD J. BOURKE

D1513128

Cover illustration, City of Chicago wrecked at Holeopen Bay West,
Old Head of Kinsale, 1893.
Photo for Ensor Salvage provided by Bill Swanton, Cobh.

Published in Ireland by the author 33 Rushbrook, Blanchardstown, Dublin 15.

Typeset and design Crotare Printing, 87 Jamestown Rd., Finglas Dublin 11.
8640014

Printed by Power Print, Old Barrack Road, Rush, Co. Dublin.

ISBN 0 9523027 0 5

CONTENTS

Introduction

Over 12,000 shipwrecks are estimated to have occurred on the coast of Ireland based on what are recorded, the levels of trade and estimates of missing data. This book brings together data on some 2,000 total losses between 1105 and 1993. These are in addition to the 800 mentioned in Ian Wilson's "Shipwrecks of the Ulster Coast" The information will be of interest to maritime and local historians. The book will be especially useful to divers and help them to identify underwater remains.

Sources

Information has been gleaned from Board of Trade returns and many other sources which are referenced in brackets after entries. The references form a significant list of Irish Maritime sources of information. I have tried to correct errors where they have occurred in reports. Even the official records mention only half of the wrecks which happened. Examination of locally kept lists for Tramore, Brandon, and Wexford indicate this deficiency. Generally only total losses are described but some exceptions occur. Folklore has been reliable in recording an event but inaccurate on dates.

Organisation

Information is presented by ship name and the order follows the coastline clockwise from Louth to Donegal. Items for Meath are included in Louth, the Shannon with Clare and Leitrim with Sligo. Location was considered more appropriate than chronological order. Wartime losses are listed separately. An alphabetical index by ship name is provided but the name of many wrecks is unknown. British warships and East India ships are indicated HMS and EI in the index.

A different era

Over the centuries the size of ships has greatly increased and the small local colliers beaching with 100 ton loads have been replaced by 150,000 ton bulk carriers. Small but economical cargoes once carried to forgotten harbours and piers by schooners are now transported by trucks. Fog was a deadly hazard until the civil use of radar in the 1950s. The risk was partially alleviated by the construction of fog stations such as that at Mizen in 1908. Accurate navigation was impossible if the stars could not be seen. This is hard to imagine in the present era of Global Positioning Satelites. The term "Dog Barking Skippers" was applied to captains who were reputed to sail within earshot of the land, navigating by their alleged skill in identifying the barking dogs. The term could praise their intimate knowledge of the coast or scorn their deep sea experience. The trade around the coast of Ireland was mainly coal from Britain and grain from the Continent. In addition more exotic routes touched the Irish coast. East India ships bound for Northern Europe often avoided the English Channel. The wartime traffic from the USA to Britain was particularly concentrated in the northern and western approaches.

Placenames

Throughout the book placenames applied in contemporary newspaper accounts are used. Thus Cobh succeeds Queenstown which succeeds Cove. Irish placenames give difficulty in anglicisation. Locally the use of names in Irish is quite precise, the problem arises in pronunciation and spelling. Some names changed over a period. For example Brownstown Head was called Newtown Head and also Red Head.

Wrecking

Deliberate wrecking of ships on the Irish coast to pillage the cargo seems to have been rare. Accounts allege this practice in Wexford, Kerry, Mayo and Donegal. The ancient common law directed that the cargo of a wrecked ship belonged to the King who might assign his privilege to a local landowner. Henry II ruled in 1120 that if any person survived a shipwreck, the cargo would not be deemed to be wreck. This was further modified in 1236. Edward III in 1353 ordained that four men would be appointed receivers and would try to find the owner. These decrees led to the practice of murdering survivors who would have allowed the legitimate owner claim the salvage. The number of shipwrecks in the early part of the nineteenth century led to the Merchant Shipping Acts and the modern principles of salvage. However locals in coastal areas still regarded salvaged goods as their own. This book contains several accounts of shootings which occurred as coastguards and militia fought mobs to protect wreckage.

Coastguards

The British Coastguard service was established at the time of the Napoleonic invasion threat. They had up to 200 stations and signal towers around Ireland. At each station they kept a boat which was frequently launched to rescue mariners. In addition the coastguard had rocket firing appartus (Dennets Rockets). Lines could be fired with this gear to allow rescue by breeches buoy. Many hundreds of lives were saved by the coastguards.

Among coastguard duties was the recording of wrecks and notification to the Board of Trade.

Acknowledgments

I wish to acknowledge the help of the staff of the following: National Library of Ireland, Trinity College Library, National Maritime Museum Library at Dun Laoghaire, Dublin Corporation Gilbert Library and also the Head of the Department of Folklore at University College Dublin for permission to use material from the manuscripts held there.

I am grateful for the help of the Naval Historical Association, London: the Hydrographic Office of the Royal Navy, Taunton; the Museum of Science and Industry, Newcastle; the Norwegian Maritime Museum, the Danish Maritime Institute, the French Naval Archives and the US Naval Historical Centre, Washington.

The following individuals helped me greatly with information or photographs: Bill Swanton of Cobh; Maurice and Jonathan Wigham, the late Brendan Neary of the Maritime Institute, Paddy O'Sullivan of Bandon, Dave Woosnam of Cork, Pierce Hickey of Skibbereen, Derek Paine of Greystones, Robin Leigh of Wellingtonbridge, John Gill of Ennis, John Roberts of Reanies, Michael Hall of Dalkey, Alled Eames of Wales, Richard Roche of Clontarf, Lucius Emerson of Ballyshannon, Roy Stokes, Terry Conlan and Cormac Lowth of Dublin, Michael Kirwin of Limerick, James Sherwood of Chester, James Quain of Glounthane, W. Gosset of Northampton, Nigel Kelleher of Tralee and Dave Donnan of Portavogie.

Especially I thank Annie Bourke and Paddy O'Sullivan for proofreading, Liam Killion for advice and typesetting; and Paul Power for printing. I dedicate the book to my wife Maire and thank her for her patience with my project.

LOUTH

LOUTH

Daisey
The smack Daisey of Beaumorris was wrecked on Carlingford Bar on 8-10-1844. Her master John Lewis was buried at Carlingford cemetery.

Liverpool vessel
A Liverpool vessel was wrecked on Bellagan point year unknown. Her master Nathaniel Marks is buried at Carlingford. The vessel name is inscribed (E.. bo...) but is not clear.

Jason
On 4-6-1878 the 96 ton schooner Jason of Workington ran onto Hally Hunter rocks. The vessel sank off Cranfield Point before the boats from the Bessbrook could rescue the crew. There were no survivors. She carried a cargo of rails.

Connemara
On 3-12-1916 the ferry steamer Connemara of 459 tons collided with the local ship Retriever of 500 tons. The Connemara, owned by the LNWR was built by Denny Bros in 1897 and plied between Holyhead and Greenore. In crossing Carlingford Bar against the ebb tide she was driven into the Retriever whose cargo of coal had shifted. The Retriever had been built in 1899 by the Ailsa Shipbuilding Co. and was owned by Clanrye SS Co. Both ships sunk with a total loss of 97 lives. The victims are commemorated in a stained glass in Dundalk cathedral. The ghost ship of Carlingford Lough PS Blaney a 200 ton

paddle steamer is reported to have been seen before the loss of local ships. The Blaney was wrecked near Prestatyn after sailing from Newry on 18-12-1833. She was seen locally before the loss of the schooner Robert Burns and the Connemara.

Falavee
The Falavee a coalboat was wrecked in Carlingford Lough on 14-1-1942. She was owned by Hoydens of Larne.

Stratheske
The steam collier Stratheske was wrecked at Haulbowline lighthouse in Carlingford Lough on 21-11-1889. She was bound for Newry from Glasgow.

Actur
The Dublin schooner Actur was stranded in Carlingford Lough on 28-12-1895. The wreck occurred between Greencastle pier and Carlingford Bar. She carried potatoes for Cunninghams of Millboy. Her crew were saved and the ship may have been salved.

Mourne
The steam launch Mourne was wrecked in Carlingford Lough on 15-10-1881. During a storm she broke moorings and was driven aground. She was owned by Lord Kilmory.

Crusader
The luxury 200 foot, 1300 ton yacht Crusader was built in 1929 by Comper and Nicholsons at Southampton. The owner was Mr Kingsley Maccomber, an American living in Paris. The ship was burned out and sunk at Portsmouth by German bombers in March 1941. In 1945 she was raised, repaired and

beached on mud at Northampton. In 1947 while on tow to Greencastle she sank in a NE gale off Carlingford almost in Northern Ireland waters. The position is known and the wreck which has been dived lies upright and intact except for the original bomb damage in 38 metres. Another wreck found by echo sounder lies in view of Carlingford and about 10 miles NE of Clogherhead. The remains consist of two anchors and a cargo of rails

Empire Of Peace

A 1493 ton Liverpool barque Empire of Peace was wrecked on 23-10-1881. The wreck occurred a mile north of Anagassan harbour.

Topaz

The Glasgow steamer Topaz (353 tons) en route to Dundalk with a cargo of rails struck Dunaney Reef in 1893. She backed off into deeper water and sank. A coastguard cutter sunk there on 27-6-1868.

Margaret

A stone at Dundalk's St Nicholas's Churchyard marks the resting place of Capt Robert Bryan. He died on 24-3-1810 in a gale. He was captain of the Margaret of Liverpool.

Minerva

On 12-11-1852 the 349 ton Minerva was wrecked at the lighthouse station at Drogheda. She was en route from Liverpool to Berbice. The cargo consisted of cutlery, London porter and Manchester goods. Only two including the captain survived of a total of 17 crew. Another account describes a schooner Minerva lost at Clogherhead on 6-1-1839.

Fidelity

The brig Fidelity of Dublin en route from Troon was wrecked at Clogherhead on 28-10-1852.

William Pitt

The schooner William Pitt struck a reef to the north of Clogher Head and sunk on 11-11-1852. She carried coal from Whitehaven for Dublin. A large ship was wrecked at Clogherhead on 16-11-1852.

Sherelga

The trawler Sherelga of Clogherhead was dragged under by the British submarine HMS Porpoise on a Sunday in April 1982. The crew all escaped with their lives. The owner Mr Raymond McEvoy was awarded £350,000 and his crew £20,000 each.

Troubadour

The 170 ton iron steamship Troubadour sank at Drogheda Bar on 15-11-1882. She carried coal from Garston to Drogheda. Her crew of ten were all safe.

Manly

The 165 ton brig Manly of Whitehaven was driven ashore at Bettystown Beach Co. Meath on 27-9-1871. Some of the crew were rescued by a Miss Campbell from Bettystown assisted by Mrs Fox from Kells. The Manly carried coal from Newport for Dublin.

Eilean Glas

The Scottish motor vessel Eilean Glas was driven ashore at Bettystown Beach Co. Meath near the golf club on 2-5-1980. The tug Carmelhead of the Holyhead towing company had tried to tow the vessel but was thwarted by a strong easterly gale. The Eilean Glas was carrying 450 tons of salt from Belfast to Devon. Captain Reilly and his crew of three were safe. The Carmelhead towed the beached ship 50 yards offshore and the salt was unloaded. However the Eilean Glas was damaged, took water and keeled over. Eventually the ship was written off then dismantled on the beach by a Dundalk scrap merchant. (232)

Irish Trader Baltray

Irish Trader
On 2-2-1974 the 500 ton Irish Trader went aground at Baltray Co Louth. She was carrying fertiliser from Sharpness, Glouster to Drogheda. The vessel had suffered engine failure a few weeks before and the crew were rescued by lifeboat. The vessel was taken to Rosslare, after some repairs the trip was resumed with the assistance of some Rosslare crewmen. The vessel was driven ashore and Captain Cox and the crew of five escaped on a liferaft and waded ashore. The Nigerian owned Liverpool registered ship still lies on the beach.

Louisa Jane
The 78 ton schooner Louisa Jane was wrecked at the entrance to Drogheda harbour on 27-4-1892. She was en route from Carrickfergus to Dublin with salt.

Williamson
The 126 ton Williamson was wrecked at Bettystown Co. Meath on 27-1-1873. She carried coal from Whitehaven to Cardiff. A large schooner was wrecked at Laytown on 5-12-1873. (66) A Coalboat lies off Laytown beach in under 25 metres depth.

Georgina
On 30-3-1850 the schooner Georgina White of Glasgow bound for Opporto was wrecked at Annagassan.

Gwalia
The Collier Gwalia bound for Drogheda from Garston foundered off Baltray on 4-3-1908. She carried 200 tons of coal for Murdoch's of Drogheda. She was in difficulties in a severe gale about three miles off shore when she foundered and sank in full view of a crowd of watchers. Only her mast showed. The lifeboat found no trace of Captain Smyth nor his five crewman.

Maxim
The brigantine Maxim of St John, New

Brunswick was wrecked on 25-9-1867 about two miles north of the Boyne near Termonfeckin. A SE gale drove the ship onto the beach. The lifeboat from Baltray rescued the eight crew.

Swedish barque

On 17-11-1852 a three masted barque was wrecked in the bay between Bettystown and Clogherhead. All were lost except the captain and cabin boy. She carried sugar, rum and tobacco for Liverpool. (132)

Mail

In 1859 the Malcomson's screw steamer Mail ran aground near the Dundalk light-house. She was wrecked by a storm before she could be refloated. The wreck was demolished as a danger to naviga-tion in 1893. (164)

Mistletoe

In 1910 during a southerly gale the herring steamer Mistletoe was swamped and sunk at the entrance to Dundalk Harbour. The stern had touched the bottom in the swell. All but one of the crew were rescued by ropes from the quay. (164)

King of Prussia

The King of Prussia went ashore in Dundalk Bay on 28-4-1812. The vessel was bound for Newry from Liverpool. (234)

Promenade

The Promenade was wrecked in a storm just before December 1904 on the sands in Dundalk Bay. (164)

Pilot Queen

The Carnavon smack Pilot Queen was wrecked in a gale near "Rocksbill", Clogherhead in January 1887. Her crew of only two were rescued by the coast-guard who went out in their longboat. She carried slates for Williamson's of Dundalk. (164)

Nelson

On 13-11-1874 the Nelson was wrecked on Dundalk Bar. She carried a cargo of coal from Troon bound for Dundalk. Captain Jones survived but his wife and one crewman were lost. The vessel was owned by Mr Oaks and Mr Williamson of Dundalk. (164)

Fanny Bailey

The 138 ton brig Fanny Bailey owned by Mr Oakes and Mr Cunningham of Dundalk went to pieces on the Bar at Dundalk a few days after going aground on 25-1-1879. Her crew of four were saved by the lifeboat. (164) The cargo was coal and iron from Troon for Dundalk.

Jane

On 16-4-1877 during a severe gale the Jane of Whitehaven was driven ashore at the Dundalk Bar near the lighthouse. The crew of five was rescued by the lifeboat. She carried coal from Garston to Dublin. (64)

Andromeda

On 16-4-1877 at the same time as the wreck of the Jane the Andromeda also carrying coal from Garston to Dublin was wrecked nearby. The crew of five were taken off by lifeboat as well as the master's wife and daughter. The master hoped to refloat the ship and took to the mast. He was persuaded to leave the ship by the coastguard before she went to pieces. (164)

Mary

The schooner Mary struck the wall at Drogheda Bar on 24-3-1867. She was bound for Dublin from Runcorn with salt. The crew of three were rescued by the lifeboat. (132)

Maria

The Maria of Milford was wrecked on the North Bull Wall of the Boyne in 1864. The lifeboat rescued the three crewmen.

Englishman

On 23-12-1869 the brig Englishman grounded on the South Bull of the Boyne estuary. The lifeboat took off the crew of five.

Richard Cobden

The barque Richard Cobden of Liverpool was entering the Boyne on 4-4-1870. A severe gale drove the ship ashore outside the North Bull. The lifeboat took off the crew of 16 before the ship broke up.

Delight

The 119 ton brig Delight was wrecked at the North Bull Drogheda on 5-12-1877. She carried coal from Workington for Dublin. The crew of four were safe.

Anna

The 76 ton brig Anna was wrecked at Drogheda Bar on 10-10-1884. She carried coal from Adrossan for Dublin.

Sisters

The 354 ton barque Sisters was wrecked a mile and a half SSE of Drogheda Bar on 11-1-1877. The cargo was maize from Baltimore for Drogheda. The crew of eleven survived.

Agnes

On 19-12-1853 a fine brig went ashore between Laytown and Gormanston Co. Meath. Seven of the crew climbed the rigging but three were washed away. Rockets were fired but could not reach the wreck. The local gentry assembled to render assistance. One man went to Dublin by train to obtain a lifeboat in Dublin Docks. The first attempt failed to manoeuvre the ships boat from the dock onto the train. Communication was maintained by telegraph. A boat was obtained at Kingstown and transported to Laytown. The first launching was unsuccessful but when the tide receded the boat reached the wreck. Three men were saved after 62 hours in the rigging. The brig was the Agnes of Whitehaven bound for Dublin with iron ore. (65)

Chatham

The same day 19-12-1853 the Chatham was wrecked at the mouth of the Boyne. Sixteen were lost. A collier brig sank off the lighthouse at the Boyne. She had been struck by a sea at Clogherhead and a man was washed overboard. (65)

Unknown

An unnamed vessel captained by Mr Albo was stranded and lost near Drogheda on 9-4-1749. The cargo of 20,000 deals from Drunton for Dublin were saved. (234) a large square rigged ship (name unknown) was lost on 26-1-1796 about a league north of Drogheda bar. The same day a brig was lost at the Nanny at Bettystown.

Violet

The 44 ton schooner Violet was lost on 22-12-1895 in Dundalk Bay. Her voyage was Castletown to Dublin with barley.

Frances and Mary

The 84 ton brig Frances and Mary was lost at Drogheda Bar on 22-8-1878. She was bound for Drogheda from Ayr with coal.

Parkside

The 132 ton brig Parkside was lost near Dunaney Point on 15-12-1880. She was en route from Newport to Dundalk with coal.

Erin

The 70 ton schooner Erin was wrecked at Mitchelstown, Louth on 24-12-1895. The cargo was bricks and cement from Glouster for Dublin.

Cumberland

The schooner Cumberland was lost at Annagassan on 14-10-1891. The 65 ton vessel was moored at the time. She was built in 1856.

Rocket

A 100 ton lighter the Rocket was lost in

Carlingford Lough on 7-10-1889. She carried building goods from Carlingford for Newry.

Bredalbane

A 115 ton brig the Bredalbane sank at the entrance to Carlingford Lough on 31-7-1886. She carried coal from Swansea for Newry.

Endeavour

The 50 ton sloop Endeavour was wrecked at Cooley on 8-4-1858. She carried slates.

Canada

The 281 ton barque Canada was wrecked a mile from Bettystown Co. Meath on 14-12-1868. The voyage was from Liverpool to west Africa with general cargo.

Earl Spencer

The 57 ton schooner Earl Spencer was wrecked on Drogheda bar on 12-11-1858. The cargo was coal.

Mary Stoddart

A 466 ton barque the Mary Stoddart was lost at Dundalk lighthouse on 7-4-1858. Seven of the crew of seventeen were drowned.

Lord Nelson

The Lord Nelson was lost in Dundalk Bay on 28-1-1848. The vessel was bound for Africa from Liverpool.

Margaret and Anne

On 9-12-1868 the Margaret and Anne a 75 ton schooner was wrecked near Carlingford lighthouse. The cargo was coal bound for Newry from Cardiff. One of the four abroad was lost.

Alceste

The Alceste was wrecked on Carlingford Bar on 8-12-1848.

Dart

The Dart sank in Drogheda bay on 10-1-1848. The Dart was en route from Glasgow to Drogheda.

Lady Huntley

On 20-6-1852 the Lady Huntley was wrecked at the South Bull at Dundalk.

Charlotte

The Charlotte was wrecked near Drogheda on 3-11-1835. She was en route from Glasgow to Liverpool.

Pembroke

The Pembroke was wrecked at Dunaney Point on 20-2-1833. She was bound for Dundalk from Milford.

DUBLIN

DUBLIN/ NORTH

Iron Man
The vessel is described by this name which may be local because of its pig iron cargo. The wreck lies in 17 fathoms near Rush and is well known to local fishermen who have trawled pieces of iron. The wreck lies with its funnel over to one side.

Gazelle
The mud barge Gazelle lies in the Skerries road where she sank on 26-7-1875.

Belle Hill
On 26-2-1875 the 800 ton American barque Belle Hill struck 100 yards from the shore at Balbriggan. She was en route from Liverpool to Kingstown or Valparaiso. The vessel had wandered aimlessly about the coast during the storm and hundreds gathered to watch the coastguard. Three of her crew were washed ashore but two died. (68). Locals waded out to salvage the goods on board. The ribs remained visible in the sand until the 1940s or 50s. The sole survivor was vague about what had happened and locals surmised that the vessels bizarre behaviour was explained by a mutiny during which the crew had broached the rum supply. Seven bodies were recovered and buried at the old cemetary at Balrothery. (91)

Azalee
The new 96 ton French schooner Azalee was wrecked on rocks off Skerries on 28-4-1859. She was en route from Troon to Nantes with pig iron. Two of the crew of six were washed overboard. A seaman waded out to the wreck with a line and the other four aboard were taken ashore.

Vingafjord
The trawler Vingafjord was washed up on the NE corner of St Patricks Island at a high tide. The vessel lodged 200 feet from the sea. A Ringsend boatbuilder, Joe Murphy undertook the work of freeing the trawler. Explosives were considered but damage to the Vingafjord could not be avoided. Rails were laid to a gulley to the north of the stranded trawler and rock projections were cleared. For the relaunch the engine was started to drive the vessel out to sea and she was slid sideways down the slip. During the operation two cannon from a previous wreck were seen in the gully.

Falcon
The smack Falcon of Skerries was wrecked at Skerries on 2-1-1877.

Ann Carmel
On 15-1-1988 the Skerries trawler Ann Carmel sunk just off the harbour. The crew of two were taken off by another local trawler.

Grace & Anne
This wooden smack rigged vessel was reported high and dry at Skerries on 12-11-1852. A great storm had raged for several days and Ireland had suffered aftershocks of an earthquake. Despite the position of the vessel the report expected that it might be refloated. The storm continued and it is not clear if this hope was realised.

Young Englander

Initially this vesel was reported lost at Rush on 11-11-1852. A letter to the Freemans Journal of 23-11-1852 reports the loss of an East Indiaman on Monday 22-11-1852. The 409 ton Scottish barque was en route from Singapore to Liverpool when caught by a severe storm. The storm halted mailboats and delayed troops and dignitaries on their way to the Duke of Wellington's funeral in London. The wreck occurred half a mile to the north of Balbriggan in Bremore Bay near a reef known as Cardy. The coastguard captain a Mr Barret fired rockets and made a fire to signal the crew but they retreated to the rigging. The Rev Synge, Mr Barrett, his son and local men and sailors launched Mr Hamilton's boat and brought nine of the crew ashore. The boat was launched again but the tide had ebbed and the wreck was surrounded by breakers. After much hardship the tide rose and the remaining six of the crew were taken ashore. Three dead remained on the wreck including a William Sudbury of the Royal Marines and a Mr Jackson of Chatham. The body of a lady was washed ashore at Skerries. (65)

John Patton

The 1157 ton American ship John Patton was lost on 5-3-1881 two miles south of Balbriggan lighthouse. She carried salt from Liverpool for New Orleans. The 17 crew were safe. Balbriggan local lore recalls the loss of a four masted ship on the Three Nuns Rocks.

Senhouse

The large brig Senhouse was wrecked at Balbriggan railway station on 11-11-1852. The crew were rescued by Captain Carvan of the Montaineer.

Maid of Galloway

On 30-3-1850 the paddle steamer Maid of Galloway burst her boilers in the storm while off Holyhead. She was driven across the Irish Sea and onto the rocks north of Balbriggan Harbour. She parted abaft her paddle box and there was no hope of salvage. Her cargo was brought ashore. The wreck was sold at auction on 8-4-1850 and purchased by Mr Fagan of Dublin.

Tergiste

On 14-11-1858 the Austrian coal brig Tergiste of 333 tons was wrecked on Portrane Rocks between Lambay and the mainland. She had anchored under Lambay for shelter from an easterly gale. The anchors dragged and the masts were cut off. Despite the efforts of Skerries lifeboat and a steamer it was the next day before the crew were saved.

Bower Hill

This wreck lies within 100 yards of the location of the Young Englander at Balbriggan.

Isabel

A wreck lies on the edge of the sand line near the sewer outlet at Rush. This is probably the Isabel a 209 ton brig. She was carrying railway sleepers from Ardrenoe to Dundalk when she sank on 11-11-1876. One of the eight crew was lost.

Margaret Anne

During the great easterly gale of 9-2-1861 there were many North Dublin casualties. The schooner Margaret Anne of Preston was wrecked at Skerries on 8-2-1861. Her crew of five were saved by the lifeboat. The Aurora of Belfast was also driven on the beach at Skerries in the same storm. (66)

Duke of Wellington

The 70 ton coal brig Duke of Wellington was driven ashore at Knockingar on the beach at Gormanstown 2 miles north of the railway station on 13-2-1861. Her master McCarroll was washed overboard but the crew were saved. (66) (132)

Anne

The schooner Anne went on the Caragree rocks at Newhaven Point near the tower at Balbriggan on 8-2-1861. The crew were saved. (66)

St George

The Schooner St George of Drogheda went ashore in Ballynagerath bay 3 miles north of Balbriggan 8-2-1861. The captain was drowned but the rest of the crew were rescued by the coastguards. (132) Another vessel was wrecked at the same place.

Mary of Carnavon

In 1859 the Mary of Carnavon was wrecked at Balbriggan. The crew were rescued by Peter Carton who was prominent at other rescues in the area.

Triumph

The schooner Triumph was driven ashore at Balbriggan where she was scuttled on 16-3-1857. She was en route from Wigan to Dublin with coal. A SW gale arose and drove the ship ashore. Her crew were all safe and it was thought that her cargo would be saved.

William Cardiff

On 19-10-1881 the William Cardiff went ashore at Skerries. She was en route to Ardrossan from Cardiff. Her crew were safe. (140)

Canadian vessel

A large vessel was seen in distress at Ben Head, Balbriggan during the storm of 24-10-1881. Her masts had been cut away. She was believed to be Canadian. The lifeboat was unable to go out.

Goshawk

The trawler Goshawk got into trouble when she sprang a leak SE of Clogher head on 27-3-1968. She was taken in tow by Creidhte an Duin and they made for

Skerries. She sank in 4 fathoms just off the pier at Skerries.

St Ibar

The trawler St Ibar got into difficulties in 1974 near Rockabill. Six miles off Rockabill she sunk. Despite the presence of other trawlers nearby they failed to notice the crew in the water. Skipper Brian Lonregan alone survived of the crew of five.

Agnes

The Agnes was wrecked at Ben Head Balbriggan on 20-12-1853. She went aground about quarter of a mile out from the high tide mark. Mr Hamilton a magistrate brought out a lifeboat and led a crew of five out to the rescue. The captain and two crew had lashed themselves to the mast and were saved. A boy and two seamen were lost. (Times London 10-1-1854).

Henry

The 79 ton schooner Henry was lost in Skerries roads on 4-3-1908. The lifeboat saved her five crew. The Henry carried coal from Liverpool to Wicklow. This was the occasion of a great storm and two other ships were lost in the Irish sea the Orior, of Newry with seven crew and the Wavelite of Maryport with 12 crew.

James Hamilton

The James Hamilton a collier en route from Troon to Dublin went ashore at Murphy's Bay on 28-9-1852. The crew escaped and she broke up on the next tide. The cargo of coal was purchased by Mr Hamlet of Balbriggan.

Sarah of Runcorn

The Sarah of Runcorn was wrecked on Black rock near Balbriggan on 5-2-1873. She carried coal from Garston. During efforts to rescue the crew a lifeboat was overturned and all but two of its crew lost. Three of the Sarah's crew were also lost. (91)

Fishing boat
A Loughshinny fishing boat was wrecked at Skerries on 30-11-1929. The fishermen were making for the shelter of Skerries during a storm when they were lost.

Gipsey
The smack Gipsey of Newry was wrecked on 8-2-1861. The crew were rescued by the lifeboat from the back of Skerries Island. (66)

Spanish Ship
A mound at Balrotherey cemetary marks graves of Spaniards drowned during the seventeenth century. A Skerries trawler dragged up cannonballs filled with small shot and timbers from a depth of 50 metres between Balbriggan and Howth. Six onion type wine bottles dated between 1730 and 1760 were also recovered.

Skerries trawlers
On 15-10-1881 during a WSW gale several trawlers were wrecked in the vicinity of Skerries. The 43 ton Anna Maria was wrecked off the pier head. Her master Richard Pelham and the crew were saved. The 35 ton Belle went ashore behind the pier. Her master John Burns and crew were rescued by rocket line. The 38 ton Victor went ashore half a mile SW of Skerries pier. The 42 ton Ebruna went ashore at the same place. Her master Stephen Bersey and crew were safe. (65)

Dolly Varden
The 30 ton Dolly Varden sunk near the entrance to Rush Harbour on 2-5-1900.

Star of Ulster
The motor finishing vessel Star of Ulster was wrecked on Perch rock at Skerries on 22-12-1958.

Victoria
The 77 ton schooner Victoria was wrecked in Rogerstown Bay on 5-1-1854. All five abroad were lost. The cargo was coal.

Wanderer
The 80 ton collier Wanderer was wrecked at Colt island, Skerries on 28-9-1856. All five aboard were lost.

Billow
The 51 ton schooner Billow was lost at Balbriggan on 13-4-1879. The cargo was coal from Glasgow for Balbriggan.

Lady Lifford
The 104 ton brig Lady Lifford was wrecked at Long Leg, Balbriggan on 8-1-1879. The cargo was coal from Ardrossan for Dublin.

Welsford
The 106 ton brig Wellsford was wrecked on Lowther Ledge two miles north of Balbriggan. The cargo was coal from Maryport for Dublin. The four crew escaped.

Richard and Martha
The 500 ton, 50 gun ship Richard and Martha was wrecked on Lambay in 1689. The commander was A. Condore. Cannon from a wrecked ship are reputed to be buried on Lambay. Naval activity in the area was intense with the Williamite army being ferried to northern ports from Hoylake. The galley Charles captured five gabarts loaded with provisions for the Jacobite army on 19-2-1689. Three were sunk. They were bound for Dundalk from Dublin.

Tayleur
While on route from Liverpool to Melbourne with emigrants for the goldfields of Australia the Tayleur was wrecked on 21-1-1854. She was completed in 1853 by Bankquay Foundry at a cost of £34,000 and was the largest sailing ship of her time. An idea of her size may be had by viewing the Cutty Sark preserved at Greenwich which is of similar size and type though

built of wood. She had four decks over a lower hold and could carry 4000 tons of cargo. The 1,900 ton gross iron built sailing clipper carried 660 passengers and a crew of 26 when it was towed down the Mersey by the steam tug Victory. A storm arose and the meagre crew could not handle the ship. The enquiry on 31-1-1854 observed that a normal crew would be 80 but the Tayleur carried only 26 including 11 boys. They were described as a rabble of foreigners who had difficulty in understanding orders. The ship as a result took an hour to tack around. An ordinary ship would have turned in half that time. The inquest recommended that emigrant ships should carry the same number of crew as government chartered ships. Land was seen over half an hour before she struck Lambay but no avoiding action was possible due to additional trouble with the semi mechanical steering gear. The presence of the Tayleur in that area was itself bizarre. Captain Noble was censured because he failed to take soundings. The three compasses were wrong because they had not been adjusted after loading the cargo. The owners Pilkington and Wilson's White Star Line were criticised because the ship proceeded to sea on her maiden voyage without any trials. The Tayleur ran ashore at 11.45 on the night of Saturday 21 February but the news did not reach Dublin until Tuesday 24th.

The ship's boats could not be launched because of the rough water. A passenger scrambled ashore with a line and many were saved by this. About 400 were drowned. A hundred victims are buried on Lambay, 282 survived. The wreck lies on the east side of Lambay between the Nose and Seal Hole. The remains are close to the Nose and a rock slide on shore points to the wreck. The Tayleur dropped its anchors before slipping into deeper water. Thus the location of the ship is about 100 metres to seaward of the rock fall in which spot it is possible to see past Kiln point. The wreck can also be located by following the shingle slope at 12 metres in the bay until the anchor chains are found, these lead directly to the wreck.

The wreckage is in one section and consists of the plates collapsed in on the ribs. The masts are conspicuous being about one metre in diameter and ten metres in length. The seabed is littered with fragments of willow pattern pottery from the vessel's cargo. The ship also carried 40,000 slates, tombstones, 10,000 bricks, the hull of a river steamer as deck cargo, fireplaces, lamps, linen and tinplate. Some complete items of the pottery are on display in the Maritime Museum in Dun Laoghaire. The kedge anchor of the Tayleur is on display in the main street of Rush. A half model of the Tayleur and the bell are in the Civic museum in Dublin. (65, 10, 9, 101)

Yacht
In August 1964 a 20 foot yacht was wrecked on Taylor's Rock on the NW corner of Lambay. The origin of the name Taylor's rock is not clear but it was so called on Cowans chart of 1800 which was 54 years before the Tayleur wreck.(188)

Shamrock II
The 231 foot 865 ton iron vessel Shamrock sank on 5-5-1918. The ship ran ashore at the NE corner of Lambay. The thirty aboard were taken off by a patrol boat before the Shamrock broke her back. The wreck is well scattered as the Hammond Lane Co cut the ship down to the water level and removed what they could. The wreckage includes

two boilers and a cabin structure as well as decking plates and ribs. As the loss occurred during the First World War some 4 inch shells may still be found among the debris. The wreck lies at 10 metres between a scree slope on the shore and the rocks at Carrickdoorish point. Metal fragments extend right onto the rocks at the shoreline. Horses aboard escaped by swimming ashore, one of the survivors is reputed to have won the Grand National the next year. The 1919 National was won by Poethlyn owned by Mrs H Peel. The Shamrock was built by Inglis in Scotland in 1879 for the Lairds Dublin to Glasgow service.

Grainuaile

On 14-4-1847 the steamship Grainuaile (245 tons) en route from Liverpool to Drogheda caught fire to the north of Lambay. After remaining afloat for some time while the passengers were saved the vessel foundered. This wreck may have been located recently.

Will O The Wisp

The Will O the Wisp was lost on 8-2-1855 near Lambay. The 150 foot 384 ton auxiliary schooner was en route from Newcastle to Dublin with a cargo of coal and some passengers including thirteen captains of sailing colliers windbound at Dublin. They had taken the opportunity to visit their families in England. She was built by Cookson of Newcastle in 1854. All eighteen aboard were lost as though an attempt was made to launch the boats only one containing the ships papers was found by the Portrane coast-guard. There is conflict on the exact location. Some sources suggest that it was trying to pass between the island and the mainland and was lost near Burren harbour. Local information is quite definite. On the island The Will is known as the wreck of Harp Ear. This indicates

a location on the north east corner of the island near the headland of that name. There is no evidence to support this story and scattered wreckage has been located near the Burren rock including a condenser raised from close to the marker pole. An upside down wreck off Harp Ear may be the Will O the Wisp.(65)

Rose Mystique

The Lorient trawler Rose Mystique sunk on 4-2-1957. She landed a sick crewman on Monday 3rd at Dublin and rejoined a French fleet fishing north of Lambay. A storm arose that night and she last reported her position as off Kish Light. Nothing more was heard until her punt was recovered off Rockabill by another French Trawler. An RAF Shakleton spotted wreckage off Rockabill and further debris was washed ashore at St John's Point in Co Down. A French frigate was dispatched to assist the search which was joined by the Irish corvette Cliona but no trace of the seven crew were found. There was speculation that she struck a sandbank at Rockabill. If this is correct she must have drifted four miles south as the wreck is located near caves in the cliffs on the north side of Lambay.(99)

Pioneer

A coal schooner the Pioneer was wrecked in Saltpan Bay near Taylor's rocks. Scattered coal lies between the rocks and the harbour.

Strathay

The wreck known as the number one wreck at Harp Ear was investigated and a wheel boss raised which bore the inscription Strathay, Glasgow. The remains of a French schooner are reputed to lie at the east side of Harp Ear.

Una

The 51 ton schooner Una sank when she

struck Taylor Rock, Lambay on 28-2-1881. The ship was en route from Aberdovey to Belfast with a cargo of slates. Built in 1841 she was owned by Edwards of Barmouth. The crew of four were all safe. (196)

Shamrock

The 64 ton schooner Shamrock was wrecked on the NW side of Lambay on 21-12-1878. She was en route from Glasgow to New Ross with a cargo of coal.(196)

Albion

The 146 ton iron steamship Albion was wrecked at Lambay on 11-12-1887.(196)

Tom

The Tom was wrecked on Lambay on 6-9-1849.(196)

Horatio

The Horatio was wrecked off Lambay on 17-8-1848.

Polewell

The 2013 ton collier Polewell was torpedoed by U 98 and sunk on 5 June 1918. She was carrying coal from Troon to an unknown destination in France. She went down 6 miles E by S 1/2S of Rockabill. Previously on 5-8-1917 she was attacked in the Atlantic by a submarine whose torpedo missed. The wreck is charted but the position is slightly inaccurate. Nautilus SAC are reputed to own the wreck which lies in 30 metres. The Polewell was built in 1888 as the Northumbrian at Troon. (188 vol. 9, No. 2)

Salaminia

The 4000 ton 98 metre Salaminia was torpedoed 12 miles SE of Rockabill on 30-3-1918. One of her lifeboats landed at Rockabill. She was built in 1897 by J. Readhead as the Trevilly. The name was changed to Salaminia by her new owners A.A. Embiricos of Greece. The wreck lies in 85 metres at 53.36.10N, 5.37.33W.(188)

Lancaster

The bell of a 150 foot steel coalboat at 45 metres was recovered from the wreck a mile off Lambay. The 77 ton Lancaster also described as Lancashire sank on 28-1-1910 en route from Widnes to Balbriggan. The crew of six were all safe. (196) The Lancaster was built in 1880.

Isabel

The 79 ton steel steamer Isabel sank two miles north of Lambay on 9-1-1913. She carried coal from Garston to Balbriggan. One of the crew of five was lost. A 70 foot metal wreck was discovered in 1991 between Lambay and Rockabill in 27 metres.

Hypatia

The 55 ton steam trawler Hypatia foundered 6 miles east of Lambay on 24-7-1904. The crew of nine escaped.

Slate boat

A slate boat lies about a mile east of Lambay off Seal Hole. The wreck is on a line where the Burren rock marker is just visible around the headland. There may also be a further wreck off Kiln Point. A local story tells of a baby washed ashore in a cot being the sole survivor of a wreck near this point. Bits of pipe have been found on the seabed and rust observed on lobsters.

Industry

The Arklow sailing ship Industry owned by Tyrell & Co was lost off Lambay. The 66 ton wooden ship was built at New Brunswick in 1849.

Unnamed ship

On 16-3-1857 a full rigged ship was observed by steamers in distress to the north of Lambay. The SW gale was so strong that the steamers were being driven backwards though at full speed.

Georgina

On 1-3-1873 the schooner Georgina was driven back to Lambay from Howth. She anchored off the NE corner of the island. The wind shifted eastwards, her cable parted and her kedge anchor was let go. The wind drove her on the rocks. The coastguard boat took off her crew of four. She was en route from Liverpool to Dublin with a cargo of stone setts for tramway construction. The wreck lies at the Quarry inside the Taylor's rocks. (66)

First War Wreck

A coal boat was wrecked during the First World War on the shingle bank off the SE corner of Lambay. The masts of the ship showed and a local fisherman Mr Fargey was deputed to tend warning lights on the wreck. It was later raised by the Port and Docks Board who placed barges on either side and lifted the ship with the tide.

Wrecking

In 1307 a pilot John De Colchester was imprisoned in Dublin Castle. He was accused that he had deliberately driven a ship on Lambay. (156)

Robert

The Robert foundered near Lambay on 5-2-1834. The ship was bound from Liverpool to Savannah.

Santanna

The 56 foot Howth trawler Santanna ran ashore at Lambay on 28-9-1992. The accident occurred in fog. The crew escaped onto the island. The wreck lies in 5 metres between Taylor's rock and Lambay.

Deliverer

The 79 ton drifter Deliverer on hire to the Royal Navy disappeared outside Dublin port on 3-11-1917. The vessel is thought to have foundered in the vicinity of Lambay.

William

On 10-11-1690 the packet boat William from Holyhead was wrecked at Sutton. She carried mails and eighty passengers. Among them were several persons of distinction including General Fitzpatrick who was buried at St Patrick's Cathedral. The vessel was caught by a storm on entering Dublin Bay and dashed to pieces on the shore between Sutton and Raheny. The master and a galley boy were the only survivors.(146) A Mail boat is described as lost off Howth Head in 1696. There were 80 passengers aboard.(246)

Dutch ship

On 30-11-1684 a 100 ton Dutch ship was wrecked at Howth. The vessel had been driven ashore by SE winds.

Edward & Mary

The Edward and Mary went ashore near Dublin on 12-4-1782. She was en route from Dublin to Weymouth. The ship was expected to be a total loss. Her master was Mr Cross.(234)

Packet Boat

On 30-3-1675 another packet boat was wrecked near Dublin. Fourteen women and twenty five men were drowned but the Earl of Ardglass was saved. The seamen were described as having got drunk on the dozens of wine carried by the Earl. Some of the passengers and crew escaped onto a nearby rock and were saved. (217)

Wine Wreck

In December 1464 a ship laden with a cargo of wine was wrecked at Portmarnock.(156)

Nicholas

The Nicholas of Downpatrick carrying wine, wax, copper pots and jewels was wrecked at Portmarnock in 1306. This is the earliest named shipwreck in Ireland.

(9) Various inhabitants of Portmarnock and Malahide were accused of pillage.

Cu Na Mara
At the small beach on Ireland's Eye lies the wreck of a trawler at about 6 metres. The 55 foot trawler Cu Na Mara was driven onto Ireland's Eye during a force 10 gale in 1979 or 1980. The Howth lifeboat was itself grounded in an attempt to tow the vessel off the beach.

Leinster
The pilot yawl Leinster was sunk in collision with the steamer General Lee between Howth and Lambay on 22-10-1868. The crew managed to board the General Lee because the yawl remained entangled in her bowsprit before sinking.

Dusty Millar
The 240 ton Dusty Millar of Newcastle was wrecked at the NE corner of Irelands Eye on 29-4-1859. The vessel was en route from Troon to Nantes with a cargo of pig iron. Wreckage was washed ashore at Howth which revealed her name. The master Mr Bogue and eleven crew were lost. (151) (65)

Roxane
The 124 ton Roxane was wrecked at Ireland's Eye on 19-5-1852. Her voyage was from Maryport to Dublin.

Trawler
In the channel between Howth and Ireland's Eye lies a trawler with the mast showing about a metre above high water. This vessel caught fire and sunk about 1982. The main body of the wreck is in about 10 metres. Up to five trawlers were dumped in the vicinity of Howth over years. Gear was also dumped about 50 yards off the end of the east pier. Further gear was dumped 100 yards off the stack on Ireland's Eye.

Therese Emile Yuon
On 23-2-1955 the Concarneau trawler Therese Emile Yuon suffered engine failure and was taken in tow by a Howth fishing vessel. The tow broke near Howth and she was blown on a sandbank half a mile north west of the harbour. Her crew of seven were rescued but the vessel was a total wreck.

Nelly
The Nelly foundered near Howth on 18-12-1816. She was bound for Rio from Greenock.

Isa I
On 12-8-71 or 25-7-71 the 30 foot sea angling craft Isa I leaked and went aground in fog on Claremont beach. All ten aboard were rescued by a Garda sea angling club craft. The wreck can be seen at low tide.

Queen Victoria
This paddle steamer of 337 tons and 150 ft was built in 1837. It was owned by the City of Dublin Steam Packet Company. On 14-2-1853 en route from Liverpool to Dun Laoghaire with cargo and 120 passengers the vessel struck the rocks near the Baily lighthouse. In efforts to save the ship it was backed off the rocks and sank in 30 metres just off the lighthouse. The wreck is in good condition. The site can only be dived at slack water as the currents meet at this point to form a confused and choppy sea.

Marlay
The 798 ton collier Marlay was lost a mile off the Baily on 16-12-1902. She was owned by Tedcastles and built by Workman Clarke in 1890. The 200 foot ship was en route from Liverpool to Dublin. Captain Hamilton and 15 others were lost. A seaman named McGlue was saved from a boat by the trawler Peter Johnson (Capt. Wright) near Skerries. He recounted that though the hatches were battened down they came loose. The captain ordered the boats out, McGlue boarded one but it was washed away.

The wreck lies in 20 metres on its side. (65)

Eva

The Dublin barque (117 tons) of this name sunk on 25-3-1877 in the channel between Howth and Ireland's Eye. Strong currents make this dive difficult. A figurehead was washed into Howth harbour a few years ago and may have been from this wreck.

Antelope

On the eastern beach of Bull Island lie remains of the Antelope which was stranded in only six feet of water on 13-12-1950. She had left Dublin for New Ross but a strong gale drove her across the bay. Her plight was noticed at once but she was too far out for the coast lifesaving apparatus. The lifeboats from Dun Laoghaire and Poolbeg could not come inshore. Meantime the schooner was pushed towards shore during the night and the crew managed to scramble onto the beach without loss. The Antelope must have been immortal, much of her timbers were salved when Wexford Dockyard used the remains of an American Barque of 700 tons wrecked on the Saltees in the mid 1880s. In 1923 an auxiliary engine was fitted, the schooner's topmasts were removed and a pole mizzen fitted. After the wreck her mainmast was removed and used in 1952 on the ketch Venturer. The wreck is at six metres and is marked on the Admiralty charts. (185)

Geo H Oulton

On 24-10-1881 the Geo H Oulton was wrecked on the North Bull. The 1175 ton vessel from St John NB was en route from Antwerp to Liverpool in ballast. The gale was so strong that she reached Dublin Bay only 26 hours out of Antwerp. Capt. Spriggs and his crew of 15 were rescued by Howth lifeboat. She was owned by S. Vaughan Co of Liverpool.

Unknown Vessel

On 2-11-1881 a wreck occurred on the North Bull. The tug Flying Dutchman of Kingstown went out but could not find it. The Poolbeg lifeboat found the wreck but saw no life and could not determine the name.

Blackwater

The City of Dublin Steam Packet Co vessel Blackwater sank in Dublin Bay in 1905 after collision with the Wexford.

Flying Dart

The 9 ton iron paddle tug Flying Dart of 100 tons built in 1882 was sunk in a collision with the vessel North Wall off the Baily on 12-8-1890. The tug was owned by the Clyde Company.

Gainsboro

On 6-1-1839 the Gainsboro of Ipswich was wrecked at Baldoyle strand in Gay Brook Cove. The master Daniel Jeffries and crew were saved by the coastguard under Captain Jones. The wreck is in shallow water visible at low tides. A cannon is reputed to have been found in 1986. The Corporation removed the timbers of a ship from Portmarnock beach in 1987. These may have been the remains of the Gainsboro. A cross at the top of Sea road near the cove commemorates the loss of three of the crewmen.(153) Several other vessels were wrecked on the beach. Just north of the Martello tower lie the remains of another ship. These used to be uncovered at particularly low tides. The whole wreck is described as visible 100 years ago.

Ellwood

The 91 ton, Ellwood was en route from Liverpool to her home port of St Ives in Cornwall when she encountered the great gale of 1-1-1906. She was blown across the Irish Sea and wrecked at Baldoyle Spit, on Portmarnock Strand. Her crew were rescued by the lifeboat.

Elizabeth
The 135 ton brig Elizabeth was driven on the Baldoyle Bank on 2-4-1882. The vessel was bound for Dundalk with coal.

Robert Brown
The coal schooner Robert Brown was driven ashore near the Baily at Dublin on 27-10-1880. The vessel was caught by an ENE gale and could not enter the port of Dublin. As the Ringsend coastguards were in Dun Laoghaire at drill the lifeboat was manned by soldiers to save two of the crew of four. The captain John Curran and two men were lost. The survivors described how the Flying Dutchman and a Tedcastle collier had passed without rendering assistance. (65)

Unknown ship
On 27-10-1908 wreckage was cast ashore on the North Bull. It consisted of several boxes of soap, wood, a baby's basinette, and bale goods. They did not appear to have been immersed for long.

Bydan
The trawlers Dietier and Bydan collided on 1-2-1989 about threequarters of a mile NE of Howth. The 60 foot Bydan of Greencastle sank immediately and the crew of four escaped in the trawler's liferaft. The 60 foot Dieter of Skerries was en route there from Galway and was damaged in the bow. Escorted by the lifeboat she made for Howth but sank in twelve feet of water 200 yards off the elbow of the East pier. An effort was made to raise the sunken trawler.(140)

North Sea
On 7-1-1879 the 99 ton North Sea was wrecked on the spit of Howth near the lighthouse. The schooner carried coal from Newcastle for Dublin.

Ada
The Ada was wrecked when she struck an offshore rock 600 yards from the sand hills at Portrane on 2-2-1873. She carried a cargo of palm oil and superphosphate bound for Dublin. The crew sought refuge in the masts. Though the coastguards tried to reach her with rockets six times her crew were taken off by boat.(66)

Galatee
The Galatee was wrecked near the patient's graveyard at Portrane. She carried pig iron which was looted. The looters were known locally as "Block Daniels".(153)

Mary Anne
The coalboat Mary Anne was wrecked on a sandbank off Corballis. Her timber was salved by a John Smith of Balbriggan.(153) This may be the brig Maryanne described as wrecked off Malahide on 24-10-1881. This ship's masts had been cut away. She was believed to have been Canadian. The lifeboat was unable to go out.

Mary Anne
The Mary Anne of Belfast bound for Kingstown lost her rudder on the Ravens off Ireland's Eye on 9-2-1861. She was driven ashore bottom up at Balscadden. Her crew of five were drowned.(132)

Timber ship
During the first World War a ship carrying timber was wrecked at Portrane. The coastguard permitted the removal of the planks on payment of a shilling.(153)

William & Sarah
About 1880 the crew of the William and Sarah refused to sail because her sails were rotten. The vessel was allowed to rot on Portmarnock beach for 30 years. (153)

Swansea
The Swansea was wrecked at Baldoyle

on 31-3-1812. Commanded by Mr Chapman she was en route from Chepstow to Dublin. (110)

Oona

In 1886 the new fast schooner Oona was wrecked near Malahide. She was en route from Southampton to Belfast. Captain Plunkett went down with the ship. His body was washed ashore on the Velvet Strand a year later and identified by a watch.(153)

Two Friends

The Two Friends from Whitehaven was wrecked at Malahide on 7-12-1812. Captain Connell and the crew were lost. (110)

Jamaica Packet

The Jamaica Packet went ashore on the Velvet strand in Portmarnock. Her crew lightened the ship by throwing her cargo of rum overboard. This was much appreciated by the locals. Ten years later in 1888 she was not so lucky. The vessel struck again at the same spot and was lost with all hands.

Queen Adelaide

During a severe storm on 8-2-1861 the Queen Adelaide was wrecked at Donabate.

Perseverance

In the same gale on 8-2-1861 the 97 ton schooner Perseverance from Ardrossan with coal was wrecked at Portmarnock. Three men were washed away. Two reached shore but one died.(132)

Lady Hobart

On 28-1-1865 the Lady Hobart sank off Baldoyle during a gale. Nine aboard took to a boat and the coastguards saved the others. The survivors were taken to the Jameson residence. (67)

Weiser

At the spot where the Perseverence was wrecked on the Velvet Strand Portmarnock the Weiser was wrecked two years previously.(132)

Malfilatre

On 28-12-1899 the 116 ton Malfilatre was wrecked at Portmarnock Point.

Dutch Vessel

On 13-2-1861 during a severe storm a Dutch vessel was wrecked at Portrane. At the same time 16 bodies were cast ashore from another wreck at the Velvet strand, Portmarnock.

Jameson yacht

A yacht owned by the Jameson distilling family was burned and sunk during the Troubles in 1920. The remains of charred timbers are visible at low tide behind the Country Club on the strand at Portmarnock.

Active

On 27-11-1798 the Active of Liverpool was wrecked on the North Bull. Her cargo and crew were saved. Another vessel overturned at the same place and 14 crew were lost. Two more ships had broken away from their moorings at Poolbeg and were stranded at Clontarf. The sloop of war Kangaroo narrowly missed being wrecked at the same time in the fierce easterly gale. (69)

Fisher Lass

On 1-10-1929 the motor fishing boat Fisher Lass went on fire 7 miles east of Ireland's Eye. She burned to the waterline and sank. Two of the crew were picked up by an Arklow trawler but a third was lost.

Charles Bal

The 1432 ton ship Charles Bal was lost on Clontarf strand on 8-11-1888. She was bound from St John N.B. to Barrow with timber. The 18 crew survived.

Simpson

The Simpson was lost at the Baily lighthouse on 9-10-1849. The Smyrna was described as lost with all aboard at "Dublin lighthouse" on 29-9-1852.

Mary Ann
The 91 ton brig Mary Ann was wrecked at Howth Harbour on 9-2-1861.

Hampton
The 124 ton barque Hampton was wrecked on the North Bull on 13-4-1874. The cargo was coal from Troon for Dublin. Two of the five aboard were lost.

Hope
The Hope was lost at the North Bull on 17-2-1748. She was bound for the West Indies from Dublin (234).

DUBLIN/ SOUTH

Flemish hulk
In 1570 a 700 ton Flemish hulk was wrecked between Dalkey and Bray. Some years before in 1537 a ship was lost sailing between Dalkey and Dublin due to carelessness of the pilot. (193)

Merchant Ship
During a gale a Dublin merchant ship was driven ashore in Dublin Harbour on 24-2-1668. Three others were bilged.

1693 wrecks
On 30-3-1693 a 150 ton ship was wrecked on the North Bull. The crew and her cargo of deal, pitch, and tar were saved. A 40 ton collier of Workington was wrecked in the same place the same day. A Milford vessel was lost on the Bar with all aboard. (110)

Hinde
On 8-11-1711 the sixth rate 16 gun frigate Hinde was lost in Dublin Bay. The Duke of Ormonde reported from Chester in a document preserved in Historical Manuscripts Report 11 appendix 5 1887 p308. After damage at sea the warship sunk bilged at anchor in the harbour. All her men, guns and rigging were saved. She had been captured on 21-9-1709 by the Medway. (147) (London Gaz 29-11-1711 4935)

Aldeborough
The British man of war Aldeborough sunk at Poolbeg harbour during a storm in April in 1725. The Ballast Office Committee Journals record a request from the Lord Lieutenant to the Lord Mayor desiring five of the Port gabbards to assist captain Lawrence in weighing his ship. Fifteen men in five gabbards (a kind of barge) completed the task in 12 days and in May 1725 the Ballast committee paid the men £7-14-0. (85).

Friendship
The Friendship of Bristol was stranded on the North Bull in 1726. She went ashore due to a missing buoy and was wrecked. (85)

Dublin
A ballad gives scanty information on several Dublin Bay wrecks in the gale of 1-1-1726. On the South Bull the Dublin of Bristol was wrecked and 22 passengers drowned.

Storm of 14-1-1757
In 1757 a single gale wrecked eight vessels near Dublin. These were two Scottish herring boats, the schooner Quarantine, Malaga a fruit vessel, St Pedro, Volunteer bound from Liverpool to Jamaica, Fortune from London for Lancaster commanded by Mr Fish, and Wilson commanded by Mr Hunter. (234)

William and Mary
On 1-11-1758 the William and Mary sunk at Dublin Harbour. The cargo of 250 hogsheads of tobacco from Whitehaven for London was saved. The master was captain Falcon. (234)

Robert
The Robert was overset near Dublin on 8-11-1758 en route from Dublin to Antigua. The cargo was saved but the vessel lost. Mr White was master. (234)

Friends
The Friends captained by Gifford from

Bordeaux was wrecked on 21-8-1781. She was driven ashore at Dublin bay but her cargo was saved. (234)

Anna Maria Ann

The Anna Maria Ann stranded and was lost in Killiney Bay on 1-4-1788. She bound for Dublin from New York commanded by Captain Lewis.

Storm of 16-2-1799

Dublin Bay was badly hit by a gale on 16-2-1799. Six ships were wrecked on the South Bull between the battery and Sandymount. The ships and their captains were Hero (Fleck), General Prescott (Boyd), Lowther (Scott). Also wrecked were Hero (Capt Wood) bound from the Clyde to the West Indies and the Fanny Source (Robinson) of Liverpool. A huge mob gathered to pillage the wrecks and bodies. To restore order the battery at Sandymount was fired at the crowd. A sentinel of the South Lincolnshire regiment froze to death at his post guarding a wreck at the Pigeon House.

Robinson

The Robinson of Whitehaven was wrecked on 29-11-1798 at the North Bull. Her master was Captain Atkinson.

Richmond

On 29-12-1798 several ships were driven ashore near Dublin. These included the Abbey, Active, Lee from London for Dublin, and the Richmond from Dublin for Jamaica.

Adventure

The Adventure sunk at Dublin Harbour on 26-2-1799 after striking an anchor. She was from New York for Dublin commanded by Captain Perady. (234)

Pilot

The schooner Pilot was sunk at Kingstown by the Nagpore on 9-11-1863. The Nagpore sailed on 12-7-1874 from Calcutta bound for Liverpool. As she proceeded up the Irish Sea she encountered a severe gale and the ship caught fire. It proved impossible to extinguish the blaze at sea and the captain made for the nearest harbour. A court case ensued and was heard on 18-2-1874 when the owners of the Pilot were compensated.

Jeanette

On 26-10-1880 the 23 ton trawler Jeanette was driven ashore by a severe gale. She was smashed on the rock at the coastguard station at Kingstown. There was no crew abroad. (65)

Annie Elizabth

The 80 ton Norwegian vessel was wrecked at the Loreto convent Dalkey on 28-10-1880. During a severe storm the nuns were awoken by the cries of the crew. They sent their man for the police. Though the vessel was only twenty yards offshore in a depth of four fathoms efforts to assist the crew were in vain. There were no survivors and the name was only deduced from the wreckage. (65)

Adonis

The 458 ton, iron framed screw steamer Adonis of Waterford struck the Muglins on 4-1-1862. She was built by Walker at Northumberland in 1847 and had one deck and three masts schooner rigged. She was 199 feet long and her engines were 100 horsepower. Owned by Malcomsons of Portlaw, she left Belfast on 3 January bound for Waterford, Plymouth and London. After striking the rock at full speed (9 knots) Captain George Spark Silly backed off and the ship drifted in a SE direction. The boats were manned some points east of Bray Head as she was now in a sinking condition. The first and second boats with 22 crew reached Bray and alerted the coastguard. The coastguard sent a man to Kingstown to alert the guardship Ajax. Meanwhile the captain and his family with the remaining passengers stood by the derelict until she went down. They landed at Greystones. A court of inquiry observed that no vessel had ever been known to strike the Muglins. However in 1873 Captain Hutchenson is reputed to have prepared a list of twelve ships wrecked on the Muglins. (41) A 13th wreck is alleged to have occured in 1876. The captain was on deck at the time and described seeing the various lights except the Muglins beacon but could not explain the collision. The ship had made no distress signals. There was also a mystery why he did not try to beach her at Killiney strand. A newspaper pointedly observed that the court might give some indication that Irish captains might be employed by Malcomsons.

Victoria
The 70 ton Glasgow clipper Victoria was wrecked on Dalkey Island abrest of the Muglins on 3-2-1855. Captain Brown and his crew of four men and a boy were driven ashore in a snowstorm. The sea was rough and no boat could be launched. The captain and one man were drowned the others were assisted by Maurice Scallan the man in charge of the island. The ship was engaged in the fruit trade between Lisbon, Dublin and Glasgow. She was on the return leg and was carrying a load of pig iron. Some of this was recovered. Wreckage and anchors lie between Muglins and Dalkey Island. An anchor and windlass are at the south end of the Muglins.

Favourite
The 74 ton schooner Favourite sank three quarters of a mile east of Dalkey Island on 20-3-1876. Her cargo was malt from Wexford for Dublin.

Essy
The Essy bound for Dublin stranded on Dalkey island on 7-12-1834.

Flying Hawk
The Clyde Co Tug Flying Hawk struck the Maiden Rock on the south side of Dalkey Island on 27-10-1887. She was built of iron in 1876 and was an 80 foot twin screw vessel. The crew scrambled ashore. The wreck lies in 6-10 metres.

Clyde
In the easterly storm of 11-2-1861 sixteen vessels were driven ashore at Kingstown. The schooner Clyde of Bideford had been windbound at Kingstown for two months and sailed without a pilot. She was bound for Cork with a cargo of salt. She cleared the harbour mouth but struck the rocks just outside the east pierhead. In their efforts to rescue the crew captain Boyd and sixteen crew of the guardship Ajax were drowned when their boat overturned. An obelisk commerates the event on the pier.

Guide Me II
During the First World War the anti submarine drifter Guide Me II was sunk in a collision on 29-8-1918. The 100 tón drifter was hired in 1916 by the Admiralty. The sinking occurred off the Muglins. The wreck lies in 35 metres and the gun was recovered during 1990.

Marchioness of Wellesley
The ship the Marchioness of Wellesley was wrecked in Dublin Bay in 1820 or 1825. She was sailing from Dublin to the West Indies. All abroad were lost. They were mainly Belfast traders and included the sons of several prominent families Raphael, White, Biggar and Agnew. These and other Antrim people were bound on a trading expedition. A ballad described the wreck.

Cynthia
Photo James Sherwood

Cynthia

During a gale and snowstorm on 25-2-1933 the paddle steamer Cynthia anchored at Dun Laoghaire broke adrift. She was wrecked against the west pier. The gale caused some confusion in the harbour as several vessels broke adrift including a dredger. The Cynthia was owned by Hewitts travel agency and had operated as a pleasure cruiser around the bay. Formerly she was a liner tender at Lough Swilly.

Seymour

The schooner Seymour of Bray was wrecked on the Burford Bank on 16-3-1844. She carried coal from Whitehaven. All aboard were lost. (132) Wooden beams have been found near the South Burford buoy. A charted wreck nearby is believed to be that of a yacht. A trawler lies on the east side of the bank.

Challenger

The 26 ton cutter Challenger was wrecked at Dalkey Island on 17-7-1897.

The vessel was en route from Bray to Kingstown. The nine aboard survived. The Challenger was built in 1848.

Smyrna

On 28-9-1852 the brig Smyrna of Workington went on the rocks during a gale at Poolbeg lighthouse. All of her crew were lost. The gale was so severe that the steamer Herald left Dublin and turned back when she reached Lambay. She reached Kingstown but could not berth and left the harbour before reaching safety at Dublin.

Flora

The coastguard cutter Flora was wrecked in Kingstown harbour in a storm on 12-11-1901. The 60 ton King George built in 1863 was renamed Flora on 26-5-1883 on transfer to the coastguard. She parted anchor and was dashed on the shore opposite the Royal Irish Yacht Club. Mr Simpson and his crew of ten were rescued by lines shot to the wreck. (147) (65)

Hampton
Photo Wigham Collection

Hampton

The 294 ton schooner Hampton was driven ashore half a mile from the Kingstown pier and came to rest with her bowsprit over the wall at Salthill railway station on 12-11-1901. (65)

Loch Fergus

The 874 ton Glasgow iron barque Loch Fergus was wrecked at Killiney Bay opposite the railway station on 6-2-1899. She was caught by a SE gale while on route from Glasgow to Brisbane. Three crew boarded a boat the morning after she struck and were dragged ashore by locals. Seventeen others were rescued by the lifeboat. (9) The wreck was dismantled by salvors now only a few metal plates remain. Other Dublin Bay wrecks include: Leonie 1876, Blue Vein 1868, Olympia 1808, Anne 1812, Robert 1820, Ellen 1821, Duke 1829, Mary 1861,

Inveresk 1915, Louise 1829, Price of Wales 1807, Rochdale 1807.

Gale of 1844

In a great easterly storm on 16-3-1844 the harbour of Kingstown was open to the elements. The brigs Hemer of Maryport and Mary of Whitehaven as well as the schooners Bellvue of Greystones, Bettes of Liverpool and Tom of Whitehaven were wrecked. (132).

Sarah Rooke

The trawler Sarah Rooke went ashore at the Kingstown New Quay in the same storm. The crew were saved by lines. (65)

Octopus

The 71 ton schooner Octopus broke her mooring in Kingstown harbour during the storm before she sank. The Octopus was registered at Bridgewater. The 81 ton Sarah Rourke was lost nearby. (65)

Palme
Photo: National Maritime Museum

Palme

During a storm on 24-12-1895 the Palme was lost off Seapoint. The lifeboat was upset and her crew drowned during a rescue attempt. The crew of the Palme were rescued by the Lighthouse tender Tieraght. On 25-5-89 a report in the Sunday Press suggested that her timbers were the source of the wooden fragments disturbed by a Dutch dredger working in Dublin Bay. However this is unlikely as most of the ship's timbers were purchased by a local carpenter Mr James Gaffney of Merrion and incorporated in barns built at the rear of Chesterfield and other houses on Cross Avenue.

Brig

On 4-3-1852 an alert pilot saw a brig in distress between the Kish and Burford banks. She had struck the Kisk while en route from Liverpool to Waterford with salt. The stricken ship sank within a mile of the east pier at Dun Laoghaire. Two of the crew climbed the masts which stayed above water and were saved. (132)

Jane

The Arklow schooner Jane was driven ashore at the Kingstown coastguard station on 12-11-1901. (65)

Crane Barge

In November 1987 a barge carrying a crane on caterpillar tracks overturned when it struck the rocks at Bulloch harbour Dalkey. It had been tied to the rocks while work was being conducted on an outfall. The crane and a container were thrown into the water and lie in 15 metres.

Henry Hall

On 20-3-1812 the Henry Hall foundered in Dublin Bay. The ship had come from Liverpool. The Ant was also lost. (234)

Tieraght
Photo: Wigham Collection

Tieraght

On 16-12-1917 the Irish Lights tender Tieraght broke from her moorings in Kingstown harbour during a gale. The vessel was dashed against the harbour wall and sank. The wreck was refloated by Ensor, the Cork salvage company. A fishing vessel the Granuaile met the same fate.

Duke of Leinster.

On 22-10-1883 the 60 ton collier Annie collided with, struck and sunk a dredger in Dublin Port half a mile north of the Pigeon House Fort. The dredger sunk and the Annie returned to the quay. Shortly afterwards the Dublin to Glasgow screw steamer Duke of Leinster sailed and when leaving the port she struck the sunken dredger. The dredger's anchor caused a 60 foot gash in her side. The boats were lowered and all escaped before the Duke of Leinster sank. The

rising tide covered her upperworks. About ten days later the wreck was raised and beached on the south bank of the Liffey near the Pigeon house. (65)

Jealous of Me

The hobble Jealous of Me was lost while journeying from Dublin port to Dun Laoghaire on 5-12-1934. She was last seen at the Poolbeg Light. The hobbles were once common about Dublin Bay and were powered by a mizen sail and oars. All three aboard were lost.

Kilkenny

The B&I line container ship Kilkenny sank on 21-11-1991. She collided with another container ship on charter to the B&I line, the Hasselwerder which was leaving the port. The collision occurred a mile off Poolbeg. The Kilkenny was holed amidships and sank rapidly with the loss of three of the crew. The wreck removal contract was awarded to Bugsier whose floating crane Roland commenced work in January 1992. The plan was to cut the wreck in three and remove the parts on a submersible barge. The first part was removed to North Quay Extension in late February and the midsection on 8-3-1992. The metal was cut up for scrap by the Hammond Lane company.

Dwarf
The 203 ton cutter Dwarf was wrecked on the pier in Royal Harbour at Kingstown on 3-3-1824. Lieut Gould and 59 of the 60 crew were saved. Men from the Pike claimed payment for raising her though some accounts suggest she went to pieces. (141)

Victory
The Victory sunk at the North Bull on 28-1-1812. The ship was from Honduras and her master was Mr Sterling. (234).

Maria
The Maria was lost at the same place and time. She had come from New York commanded by Mr Mara. (234)

Langston
The next day 21-3-1812 the Langston from Portsmouth was described as lost in Dublin river. Her captain was Mr Douglass. (234)

William
The William commanded by Mr Mitchell was wrecked on Dublin Bar on 23-3-1812. She had come from Chepstow. (234)

Mary
The Mary en route from Dublin to Lisbon and Cadiz was wrecked on the South Bar on 10-12-1812. She was commanded by Mr Parcells. (234)

Neptune
On 19-10-1765 the Neptune was wrecked at Dunlaoghaire. She sprung a leak in a NNE gale and filled. The cable was cut and the ship driven ashore. The hull was lost but the cargo saved. (234)

Plymouth
The packet boat Plymouth was burned at Dublin on 26-1-1765. The vessel was bound for the Leeward islands commanded by Mr Roach. (234)

Dunbar
The brig Dunbar sank at Poolbeg on 20-2-1765. Commanded by Mr Graham she was bound for the Western Isles from Dublin. (234)

Thomas and Anne
The Thomas and Anne from London sank in Dublin Harbour on 20-1-1764. Her captain was Mr Bartlett. (234)

Edith
The 208 ton brig Edith was lost at the pier at Kingstown on 1-2-1884. She was bound for Ardrossan from Waterford.

Alice Woods
The 199 ton brig Alice Woods was wrecked at Dublin Bar on 19-11-1879. She carried coal from Ardrossan to Dublin.

WiCKLOW

WICKLOW

Trusty

The Trusty became stranded on sandbanks and was lost off the Irish coast on 12-4-1782. Commanded by Mr Slow she was bound for Dublin from Swansea with a cargo of copper. (234)

Jenny

On 29-1-1799 the Jenny was wrecked on the Arklow Bank. The ship was en route from Opporto to Dublin under captain Pickering. (234)

Leinster

Built in 1897 at Lairds the Leinster was operated by the City of Dublin Steam Packet Co. The vessel maintained the mail service throughout the First World War. On the night of 10-10-1918 she left Kingstown (Dun Laoghaire) for Holyhead with 680 passengers under the command of Capt W. Birch. Only hours out she was struck by torpedoes fired by a German submarine U 123 commanded by Oberleutnant Ramm which itself was sunk probably in the Norway-Scotland mine barrage on 19-10-1918. (86) The first torpedo missed. The second hit near the bow where 22 post office sorters were at work and there was only one survivor from this area. The third penetrated the engine room and caused heavy casualties. The captain who was wounded was taken aboard a lifeboat but was lost when it was swamped alongside the destroyer Mallard. Though the weather was bad an attempt was made to take the vessel in tow. In response to an

SOS the destroyer HMS Lively came to the scene and rescued 33 persons but by this time the Leinster had foundered. Due to the rough sea and darkness there was much confusion when the sleeping passengers rushed on deck. Several of the boats were got out too hurriedly and capsized. Of the total of 757 aboard 501 were lost in the worst disaster in the Irish sea. Since over 500 soldiers were aboard a large number of the victims were buried in the military cemetary at Blackhorse avenue in Dublin. The wreck lies in 30 metres about 4 miles east of the Kish lighthouse. Lat 53.18.88, Long 5.47.47. The vessel is fairly intact and lies about 3 metres proud of the sandy bottom.

Albatross

The Kish Lightship the Albatross, a wooden vessel was sunk at her station on the Kish Bank when struck by the Leinster. The accident happened on 13-10-1902 when a dense fog descended on Dublin Bay. The crew were rescued by the Leinster. This was the third occasion that the Kish lightship was struck by the mailboat. The wreck was sold to S. Jack of Glasgow and raised by the Passage West salvor, Thomas Ensor. (188)

Bolivar

On 4-3-1947 the Bolivar a 5,320 ton Norwegian motorship of the Fred Olsen Line en route from Liverpool to Dublin in a severe snowstorm struck the north end of the Kish Bank near No 2 Kish Bank Buoy and began to disintegrate. The crew and 45 passengers were rescued by the Dun Laoghaire lifeboat.

The tug Collimore also assisted. The engine room was subsequently salvaged. A Mr Gibney of Dun Laoghaire tendered to disperse the wreck on 10-5-1948 which was an obstruction to shipping. The bow section now stands intact about 5 metres clear of the sandy seabed. (188)

Vesper

On 13-1-1876 the 620 ton steamer Vesper was grounded on the Kish bank. Captain Tolson and the thirteen crew escaped in the ship's boat and landed at Killiney. The vessel was owned by Huntley Berne and Co of Glasgow. She was bound from Glasgow to Dunkirk with sugar and coal.

Vanguard

On 1-9-1875 the reserve squadron of the Channel Fleet consisting of five ironclads and the yacht Hawke left Kingstown for Cork. The warships were Warrior, Achilles, Hector, Iron Duke, and Vanguard. The fleet encountered mist off Wicklow and slowed but Vanguard was rammed four feet below her armour belt by the next in line Iron Duke. She had turned to avoid the next ship ahead exposing her broadside to Iron Duke. She sank inside an hour. Vanguard (6010 tons) was built in 1870 at Birkenhead. The incident occurred in 18 fathoms about 8 miles ESE of the Kish Light. All the crew of 450 were rescued. The wreck is reported to lie at 42 metres upright but slightly to one side. Because of its strong armour the wreck is in very good condition. The wreck was purchased in 1987. (190)

Cameo

The MV Cameo of Glasgow grounded on the Arklow Bank 7 miles north of the South Arklow Light Vessel on 10-9-1950. The 950 ton vessel had a cargo of coal. The master expected that the vessel could be refloated at high tide. A southerly gale blew up and though a tug was in attendance it was soon clear that the vessel was in distress. On the 12-9-1950 the lifeboat took off the crew of 11.

Anna Toop

In January 1958 the 421 ton Cardiff coaster Anna Toop grounded on the bank south east of Arklow. She carried sheet steel from Port Talbot to Derry. The crew of ten were rescued by the lifeboat before she went down near the Arklow no 4 buoy. During the Summer 1958 a local trawler the Naomh Eamonn was used as a salvage boat for divers working on the wreck. During this operation a German submarine was described near the wreck. The Anna Toop was refloated on 21-9-1959.

German Submarine

The Irish Sea was an active submarine area during the First World War. Early in the morning of 21-9-1917 Kynoch's munitions factory at Arklow disintegrated in a terrific explosion. The four magazines situated at 50 yard intervals disappeared in a bang that was heard 20 miles away. Twenty eight workers were killed and many injured. Tight wartime security lowered a veil of secrecy over the event. Witnesses at the Kynoch's inquest however described a whirring sound just before the main explosions. The manager believed that the plant had been shelled from the sea. It is surmised that the submarine foundered during a crash dive following the attack after striking the Arklow bank. No official records describe a loss at this location. (218)

Lily

On 10-1-1872 the Lily of Wexford struck the extreme north end of the Kish Bank. The accident occurred in thick weather and a WSW wind. She was en route from Barrow to Cardiff with 180 tons of pig iron. Her compass was disturbed by the cargo. The master James Scallan and crew of six took to the boat and pulled for the Kish Light vessel.

Crisis

In the great storm of 16-2-1862 the Crisis a 1000 ton Liverpool vessel was lost on the Arklow Bank. One boat was launched but 9 perished.

Fanny Palmer

The 194 ton brig Fanny Palmer of Youghal was wrecked on the Arklow Bank on 29-11-1872. Captain Guest and his crew were rescued by an Arklow boat. The same day a vessel was in distress at Five Mile Point and the lifeboat went to Newcastle to assist. (66).

Dromedary

The 374 ton irons screw collier Dromedary sank on 10-4-1873 off the Arklow Lightship. She carried coal from Newport to Dublin. The stern pipe broke flooding the vessel. The crew were picked up by the Pernambuco.

Lord Mulgrave

The naval sloop Lord Mulgrave was wrecked on the "Wicklow Bank" in a severe gale on 10-4-1799. Captain Hawkins was in command. (141).

Maggie

The Howth fishing yawl Maggie sank in a choppy sea near the Kish Lightship on 24-3-1898. Her crew of four were drowned.

Peter

The barque Peter of Sundswell struck the Arklow Bank on 29-3-1880. A steamer assisted but the ship was a total wreck. The Arklow lifeboat took off the crew of fifteen. The Peter was en route from London to New York, (67) (132)

Alhambra and Holyhead

On 30-10-1885 the Holyhead struck and sank the German barque Alhambra. The 2 screw 842 ton London and North Western Railway Co cattle ship Holyhead was en route from Dublin to Holyhead with 27 crew and 4 passengers as well as a full cargo of cattle. The Alhambra was en route from Liverpool to New York with 700 tons coal as ballast. The collision occurred within 25 miles of the South Stack lighthouse. The mate of the Alhambra mistook the Holyhead's mast light for a fixed light and veered away. The Holyhead struck the Alhambra amidships. The Alhambra sunk within five minutes. Captain Hicks ordered the Holyhead's boats to be lowered. Two boats picked up the Alhambra survivors but captain Seivitty, his daughter and eleven crew were lost. Meanwhile the other two boats were lowered from the Holyhead and Captain Hicks and all but two of the Holyhead compliment escaped. She sank 20 minutes after the collision. When the Holyhead was overdue Admiral Dent at Holyhead sent out the Edith which soon found the lifeboats. (65)

Irwell

The 1000 ton bucket dredger Irwell overturned whilst on tow from Liverpool to the Shannon on 28-10-1989. The capsize occurred in a gale about seven miles south of Tramore. The bucket chain protruded sixty feet below the upturned vessel and prevented efforts by the tug Lady Alma to right the dredger. For five days the tugs Lady Alma and Brandon towed the dredger towards the Arklow Bank where it was hoped to right the Irwell on the bank. After snagging a French trawler the tow parted. A decision was made to sink her as a she was a hazard to shipping. The L.E. Ciara which had accompanied the tow sank the Irwell by gunfire on 2-11-1989 at position 53.01.17N, 05.24.04W. (67) (191)

Agnes Craig
Photo: Derek Paine

Agnes Craig

The Agnes Craig went aground on the Arklow Bank in August 1952. The vessel was a total loss.

Firth of Solway

The barque Firth of Solway was en route from the Clyde to Dunedin when she was struck by the steamer Marsden near the Kish lightship. The Marsden of Newcastle on Tyne was en route from London to Greenock. The barque sank fast with the loss of 15 of the 22 aboard including the captain's wife and child. (65)

W.M. Barkley

The 569 ton W.M. Barkley a former collier was purchased by Guinness in 1913. On 12-10-1917 she was torpedoed and sunk by a German submarine while en route from Dublin to Liverpool with a cargo of beer. Four of the crew were lost. The wreck lies in 45 metres just on the east side of the Kish bank.

Scotia Queen

The 423 ton three masted barque Scotia Queen was wrecked on the Arklow Bank in 1867. She was built in Nova Scotia in 1865 and owned by William Murphy at Wexford. (192)

Trustful, Pulteny

A chart marks wrecks on the Arklow Bank. These include Trustful N 53 10 00, W 5 56 00. The Pulteny was sunk in a collision on 18-8-1934 in position 52.27, 5.5.

Exchange

The 563 ton New York vessel Exchange struck the Blackwater Bank on 5-4-1858. She was washed off as the tide rose and blown towards Wicklow Head. Captain Jones and ten of the crew of thirteen survived when the ship was wrecked on Wicklow Head. She was bound from Liverpool to Savanah with railway iron. (132) (55)

Trifylia
Photo: Derek Paine

Trifylia

Just off the beach at Newcastle about 2 miles south of Greystones lies the coalboat Trifylia. An iron screw steamer of 1336 tons and 258 feet in length the Trifylia was en route from Ayr to Rouen with 2,000 tons of coal. A gale drove the ship ashore on 12-11-1915. The ship was Greek owned and the translation of the name means shamrock. The wreck lies in 10 metres and has been scattered by storms. Wicklow SAC raised the three anchors and they are now on a plinth on Wicklow beach.

Julia

The Julia was wrecked on 19-2-1931 at the North Arklow Bank. Captain George Kearon and all four crew were lost. The ship was bound from Glasgow to Newhaven with pig iron. A storm arose after she passed the Codling light vessel. The following morning the Cymric spotted the wreck. It is believed that the

Julia had turned and tried to run for shelter in Dun Laoghaire. The 179 ton ship was built in 1879 at Padstow.

Fleck

The 99 ton steel steam ketch Fleck was lost on 1-2-1935 at the north end of the Arklow bank near the No 2 buoy. She was from Milford.

Burford

Bligh in his survey of the Port of Dublin refers to the loss of the Burford. He describes the mast being washed ashore at Howth. The Burford Bank seems to be the place of the loss. Though described as a man of war the Burford does not seem to figure in RN losses.

Eliza

The Eliza was wrecked on the Arklow Bank on 14-12-1812. Commanded by Mr Caitehorn she was en route from Liverpool to Waterford. (234)

Charles

The Wexford schooner Charles was

carrying barley from Dundalk to Wexford on 10-8-1873 when she was wrecked on the Arklow Bank. She had been windbound at Kingstown and left in the company of four schooners. The steamer Contessa of Dublin stood by but could not help as she had no hawser long enough. Captain James Devreux and six crew were lost. (66)

Aid

The most publicised wreck of Wicklow Head is the Aid. This wreck was described in Lord Cloncurry's papers as having occurred in Killiney Bay But newspapers put the wreck at Wicklow Head. The barque was carrying classical art from Rome to Dublin and sank in a storm in April 1804. Lord Cloncurry of Lyons House Celbridge was a collector of Roman material as was the fashion of the time. His house was furnished with much of his collection. The Aid was carrying 13 crates including portrait busts and a statue of Venus as well as material which he described as more valuable owned by a Mr Moore. All that is found so far is a wooden brig of the right period in 20 feet of water.

Nestorian

The 790 ton Nestorian of Liverpool bound for Baltimore with salt foundered on 14-11-1858. The incident happened off Jacks Hole near Arklow. All but one of the crew were saved.

Hottinguer

On 12-1-1850 the 1050 ton Hottinguer en route from Liverpool to New York struck the Blackwater Bank seven miles from the Wexford coast. Built in 1843 she was owned by the Fieldens Line. In 1848 she had been sold to Swallow Tail Line by the Liverpool firm Woodhull & Minturn's. Nineteen sailors abandoned the ship along with fourteen passengers and landed at Morris Castle. Captain

Bursley and fourteen stayed aboard. Mr John Agar the coastguard commander and the Zephyr of Ballinourlart went out to the wreck. The screw vessel Rose piloted the Hottinguer through the banks after a high tide allowed her escape. The ship was damaged and the Rose took off a further eight passengers. The Hottingeur then headed for Kingstown. She must have been difficult to control for the next night she struck the Glasgorman Bank a mile off shore at Arklow Bay. A storm was raging and no help was possible. The crew clung to the rigging but after sixty hours only one survivor was taken ashore.

Armenian

The South African steamer Armenian struck the Arklow Bank on 24-2-1865. The 763 ton Royal Mail vessel had 300 hp engines. She was bound for Madeira and West Africa from Liverpool. When she struck she was proceeding under full sail and steam. A fire broke out and Captain Thomas Leaman ordered the boats out. These reached the Arklow lightship. A further 31 of the crew had fled to the rigging. The Lightship crew went to assist the wreck but their boat was overturned and four were drowned. The steamer Montague under Capt Clarke rescued all 60 passengers and the crew except for four. The wreck went down bearing Wicklow Head N by E 1/2 E, Arklow Light SW by W. Fishermen from Arklow had to be assisted by the coastguard when they consumed a cask of rum found near Arklow. The rum was of a special strong strength to the taste of the South Africans and overcame the fishermen.

Endeavour

The collier Endeavour of Drogheda was wrecked on Bray strand at Cumings coal yard in the gale on 11-2-1861. The crew of five were rescued from the rigging by ropes thrown from the shore. During the same gale three vessels were seen to go on the rocks at Bray Head. Among them was the Industry from which seaman King was drowned.

Mary
The 88 ton schooner Mary of Warrenpoint was lost at Greystones on 11-2-1861. Her crew of four were drowned. She carried coal.

Robert Seamour
This coal brig was wrecked on 11-2-1861. A further coal brig was wrecked at Kilclougher on the same day. Four of the crew of five survived.

Eliza
At Wicklow town on 11-2-1861 the Eliza of Maryport a coal schooner was wrecked with the loss of two of the crew of four. Also at Wicklow town the Whitehaven coal brigs Roland Hill and Mary Drapers were wrecked in the storm. Three of the crew of four died in the Roland Hill. Eight survived the Mary Drapers. All the crew were saved from the coal brig William Moorecambe, the fifth Arklow casualty of the storm.

Champion of the Seas.
The 73 ton Ardrossan registered schooner Champion of the Seas was wrecked at North Beach, Arklow on 21-10-1911. She was built at Sunderland in 1877. The coast guard rescued captain Tyrell and two others by rocket apparatus. She was undermanned as two crew had deserted at Liverpool.

Forest Deer
The 68 ton Forest Deer was wrecked a mile south of Five Mile Point on 12-11-1901.

Hematite
The 84 schooner Hematite was wrecked near the pier on Arklow south Beach on 2-6-1902. She was en route to Llanelly

with a cargo of macadam when a strong NE gale drove her ashore. All five aboard were saved.

John Morrison
The 202 ton barquentine foundered off Wicklow Head on 26-12-1925. She had been damaged when she struck Wicklow pier leaving the harbour. Constructed by Tracy's in 1874, she was the largest vessel built at Arklow. She carried a cargo of pit props and after sinking, the ship was neutrally buoyant and moved about the seabed. The Irish Lights eventually dispersed the remains by dropping a large weight on the wreck.

Pacific
The 95 ton schooner Pacific was wrecked on Wolf Rock near Wicklow Head on 25-7-1932. She was built at Prince Edward Island in 1864 and bought by J. Tyrrell in 1870.

Seabank
The 365 ton motor ship Seabank was driven ashore at Brittas Bay on 5-3-1963. Two salvage companies attempted to refloat the ship. A local man used fire pumps to scour a channel and she was refloated a year later, towed to Dublin and later scrapped in Scotland. She was built in 1935 at Poole by Carter as Jolly Nights. Renamed Cranborne in 1946 and renamed Seabank when bought by Arklow owners in 1954.

Packet Boat
On 6-12-1670 the Irish Packet boat developed a leak en route from Britain. She was driven ashore and struck a rock about 50 yards offshore at a point between Arklow and Wexford. Three sailors made for the shore in the ships cock boat. Many notables were aboard. Fourteen women and 25 men were drowned among them the Earl of Meath, Earl of Ardglass, Dean Tate, Capt Knowles a servant of the Duke of York

and Capt Cartwright of the Clonmel garison. While the captain was drowned most of the crew survived. The survivors included Alderman Forrest, Quartermaster Lloyd and Lord Ardee. A previous packet yacht Mary lost near Holyhead on 12-8-1660 has been discovered recently. She was en route from Dublin to Chester. (217)

Brackley
The Wexford shooner Brackley was wrecked at Wicklow in the storm of 27-2-1903. She was owned by J.S. Davis of Wexford. Her captain and crew of three men and a boy were saved by the lifeboat.

Amanda
On 20-1-1973 the Amanda went ashore near Mizen Head. She was carrying stone to the Kish lighthouse. At low water two of her crew escaped ashore onto the rocks. The others stayed with the ship.

Confido
On 9-1-1908 the ketch Confido was torn from her anchorage and driven on the sand on the north of Arklow harbour. She carried a cargo of coal for Kynochs. The owner was Mr Dunne of Greystones. The Alnwick and Agnes Glover were damaged by the same gale in the harbour. (67)

Amethyst
On 6-10-1908 the Steamship Amethyst of Glasgow collided with the Steamship Daisy of Liverpool off Wicklow Head. The Amethyst sunk.

Speranza
On 3-1-1906 the 200 ton French schooner Speranza was wrecked one and a half miles SW of Wicklow Head. She carried coal from Swansea. The crew escaped ashore by means of a rope. Except for the cook who was drowned. (67)

Speedwell
The cutter Speedwell of Newry went ashore at Pennycomequick two miles north of Arklow in January 1789. Captain Veacock and his crew scrambled ashore by means of a rope. The captain asked the crowd of 150 assembled to help the crew with the salvage of the cargo. He offered to split the value of the goods between them and the crew. The crowd refused all aid and even stole the clothing of the crew who barely escaped with their lives. (89)

Penryn
The schooner Penryn of Liverpool was wrecked at Arklow on 16-3-1844. All her crew were saved. The Brothers of Arklow was wrecked 300 yards offshore on the Bar at Arklow at the same time. She carried copper ore bound for Bristol.

County of Lancaster
On 12-11-1901 the railway workers noticed signals of distress out sea off Greystones. The next morning dead men and a boat were found on the beach. Glasgow papers indicated that the wreck had been the County of Lancaster bound for Carnlough. Her captain was Henry Murray. (65)

Leonie
On 30-9-1876 the Leonie struck the shore NE of the former site of a Martello tower. She capsised at the mouth of the Bray river. (149)

Roman Vessel
A grave with Roman burials from the time of the Emperor Hadrian was discovered at Bray in 1835. Since it was believed that there was no Roman settlement in Ireland and the graves were near the shore it was speculated that a Roman vessel had been wrecked at Bray Head. This supposition is disputed. (171) Further Roman burials occurred on Lambay.

Reciprocity
Photo:Derek Paine

Reciprocity

During a storm in 1913 three local colliers were driven well aground at Greystones. The "flats" owned at Greystones were accustomed to discharge by beaching on the strand. They were the Reciprocity, Velinheli and Federation. The ships were eventually refloated but the landing of coal on the beach became an uninsurable risk. The local Greystones coal importer was Mr Dann. Arthur Evans owned the Velinheli which was built in 1878 by Ree Jones at Port Dinorvic in Wales.

Osage

On 18-12-1940 the Osage was attacked and sunk near the Arklow light vessel. The crew of 21 were saved by the Crewhill of Belfast. (149)

Orphan Girl

The Arklow schooner Orphan Girl was in difficulties outside Wicklow harbour on 28-10-1916. Her crew were taken off by the lifeboat. Her anchor was dragging. (161)

Seaflower

The schooner Seaflower went ashore at Arklow on 17-11-1852. She was en route from Wexford to Glasgow. All her crew were safe and her cargo was salvaged and sold at auction at Wicklow. (132). A large schooner was reported lost on the Arklow Bank at the same time.

Eumaeus

On 11-12-1939 the Liverpool steamer Eumaeus was in a convoy which was attacked. She ran aground near the No 3 Kish buoy. (149)

Blanch

The 112 ton schooner Blanch of Belfast was wrecked at Ennerilly two miles north of Arklow on 9-2-1861. Patrick Foy the master and two crew dived into the sea and were snatched from the water by Pat McDonnell. The cook was lost. (132)

William

The 167 ton coal schooner William from Maryport for Dublin went ashore at Wicklow on 9-2-1861. The crew ascended the rigging and the coastguard attempted to reach them by boat. The boat overshot the wreck and was blown upwind. Fishermen took a line and towed the lifeboat along the beach for a mile to allow a rescue. (132)

Neptune

The square rigged brig Neptune was wrecked on the Wicklow coast on 2-2-1788. She was bound for Dublin and struck the Wicklow bank. The Wicklow lighthouse was not seen. The disabled vessel came ashore at the south cave on Wicklow Head. She was owned by Mr Somers and captained by Richard Cully. Her cargo was porter, hops and sugar. The Neptune was built in Wales in 1776. (188)

Storm of 1853

On 19-12-1853 a severe storm struck the east coast. A barque was wrecked at Wicklow head. There were also two wrecks at Greystones. (65)

Mersey

On 5-10-1892 two men were lost when they were washed off the Greystones pier in an effort to let the Mersey loose and beach her. The storm was so fierce that they reckoned that the ship would be beaten to bits on the pier.

Mountain Ash

The Mountain Ash was driven ashore at Kilcoole in the Winter of 1950-1. The wreck was dismantled on the beach by the Hammond Lane company.

Pensiero

On 27-1-1873 the 428 ton Pensiero went ashore north of the Bray River. The voyage was Barletta to Dublin with wheat. The crew were taken to Dublin by tug. The vessel was a total wreck.

Don Antiocho

The 522 ton barque Don Antiocho en route from Dublin to Baltimore in ballast was wrecked at Mizen Head, Wicklow on 18-10-1882.

Lady Harriet

Three vessels were wrecked in the storm of 12-11-1852 at Bray. The Lady Harriet of Chester with a cargo of coal was discovered by the Greystones coast-guards with the five crew lashed to the masts. Four were lost when the mainmast fell overboard. The captain miraculously held on for a time but was washed overboard and all thought he was lost. He reached the shore only to be washed back by a wave. One of the crew was picked up but died later. A mile away another collier Betsey of Maryport was wrecked but the crew escaped. The New Valliant of Portmadoc carrying grain was washed ashore. There was no word of her crew.

Marie Celine

On 31-1-1926 the 75 ton ketch Marie Celine of Drogheda was wrecked at Bray Harbour. The coast lifesaving service towed their rocket cart by truck from Greystones. The rocket line was made fast quickly and Captain Chamber and the crew brought ashore. (99)

Erne

The sloop Erne was driven ashore on the seafront at Bray on 17-10-1936.

Mary

Captain Hopton Scott lost his ship on Ballygannon Point off Kilcoole. He was given hospitality by the O'Byrne family and fell in love with Thady O'Byrne's daughter Randelia. They agreed on condition that he would reside in Ireland. They were married in 1692. It is likely that the ship was the Mary a fourth rate 48 gun ship. The Mary was lost in Wicklow bay in 1690 but her commander is recorded as Captain Wise. A Mary was used as the Royal Yacht at this time and transported William of Orange on several Irish Sea trips.

Drake
A further 234 ton 6th rate warship Drake with 24 guns was wrecked on the "coast of Ireland" on 20-12-1694. The 93 foot vessel was built by Fowlers of Rotherhithe and launched on 26-9-1786.

Sarah Jane
The 46 ton schooner Sarah Jane was wrecked at Greystones on 23-10-1886. She had come from Troon with coal for Greystones.

Paragon
On 8-11-1918 the Paragon was wrecked at Mizen Head Co Wicklow. The ship was en route from Swansea to Belfast with a cargo of coal.

Rover
On 11-12-1914 the 152 ton iron tug Rover was wrecked 200 yards north of Arklow.

John Scott
The 222 ton brig John Scott was wrecked at Kilcoole on 1-2-1873. The vessel was en route from Whitehaven to Newport with iron ore. Six of the seven crew were lost. A yacht became entangled in wreckage described as the John Scott off Killoughter on 26-10-1963. This John Scott was described as having run aground during the first world war. The plight of those aboard was observed by a train driver from the railway which runs along the shore at this point.

Hector
The Hector was lost near Arklow on 24-3-1812. She was en route from Guernsey to Dublin commanded by Mr Brown. The crew were rescued. (234)

St Peter
On 30-9-1765 the St Peter went to pieces at "Ardinary" Bay, Wicklow.

Commanded by Mr Eyres she was en route from Dublin to Maderia and Tenerife. (234)

Duncan
The Duncan was en route from Chester to Dublin when she was lost near Wicklow on 16-3-1812. (234)

Giorgina
On 28-1-1885 the 558 ton Italian barque Giorgina was wrecked at Killoughter. The ship was bound for Cardiff from Dublin in ballast. The crew of eight survived.

Guerrera
The 406 ton Italian brig was wrecked the same day at Newcastle. The brig was on the same voyage as the Giorgina and the crew of eight survived.

Elaine
On 9-1-1882 the 233 ton brig Elaine was wrecked three miles north of Wicklow harbour. The brig was en route from Liverpool to Paraguay with a cargo of salt. All eight aboard were lost.

Kestrel
The 555 ton iron steamship Kestrel was lost at Brittas Bay on 29-6-1883. She was on a voyage from Hamburg to Dublin with general cargo. All twenty aboard escaped.

Tonquin
The 475 ton American barque Tonquin was wrecked at Wicklow Head on 9-2-1861. The cargo was iron. The same gale wrecked the coalboats Eliza nearby, Margaret Mortimer at Resil Strand, Roland Hill and William Campbell at Wicklow Head and Blanche 3 miles offshore. Altogether 32 crewmen were lost.

Wilson
The 245 ton barque Wilson was wrecked at Five Mile Point station on 15-1-1851. Four of the eight crew were lost. The cargo was rum and sugar.

Wanderer
On 7-12-1849 the Wanderer was wrecked at Greystones. She was en route from Liverpool to Stetin.

Breeze
The 144 ton brigantine Breeze was wrecked at the Arklow Light on 28-5-1860. The cargo was pig iron. One of the crew was lost.

Higgeson
The 453 ton barque Higgeson was wrecked at Wicklow pier on 28-9-1856. She carried a cargo of timber. Ten of the crew of fourteen were lost.

Emma
The Emma was lost at Kilmichael point on 23-11-1852.

Patriot
The 199 ton Patriot was wrecked at Kilmichael on 20-2-1892. The barque carried a cargo of phosphate from Dunkirk to Garston. Three of the five crew were lost.

Edouard Marie
The Edouard Marie was wrecked at Rockfield Bay in April 1850. The ship was bound for Batavia from Liverpool.

Entreprise
The Entreprise was wrecked at Arklow lighthouse on 22-12-1848. The 113 ton brig came from Poole.

Fame
The Fame from Workington was lost in Arklow roads in September 1851.

Pilgrim
The Pilgrim was wrecked near Arklow in December 1851. She carried cargo for Arklow.

Britannia
The Britannia was wrecked on Arklow Bar in January 1849. She was bound for Preston from Wexford.

WEXFORD

WEXFORD

Talbot

On 15-12-1694 the Talbot a ten gun naval vessel was wrecked. The location is described as Glascarmen Sand and is probably Glasgorman Banks off Castletown. A pilot error was blamed for the loss.

Glasgow

The Glasgow a 423 ton American ship sunk after striking the Barrells on 14-2-1837. She was en route from Liverpool to New York with 90 passengers and a cargo of iron, salt, copper and bale goods. When the ship struck she lost her rudder and drove over the rocks. Confusion and panic occurred and the lifeboats were found to have no oars. Captain Robinson sounded the bell as a sign of distress as the ship could not be seen due to fog. Captain Walsh in the Alacia came to assist. A pinnace was let out on a rope and reached the Alacia with four crew who collected oars and rowed back. After three trips the majority of passengers had been saved. Five hours after the ship struck Captain Robinson boarded the pinnance and the Glasgow sank suddenly. The twelve left aboard were thrown in the water and six were picked up. Altogether 82 were rescued by the Alacia at considerable risk. Captain Walsh had sailed around the crippled Glasgow in high seas and dangerous water for several hours. (58) (66)

Niobe

The Niobe en route from New York to Cork carrying Indian corn for famine relief was wrecked on 26-1-1847 on the Keeraghs near Cullenstown. The corn was a great relief to the inhabitants and was attributed with saving this part of Wexford from the worst effects of the Famine. (58, 107p95)

Georgina

The Georgina en route from Liverpool to Valparaiso struck the Blackwater Bank on 17-3-1844. When she struck the Bank her rudder was lost and Captain Wilson dropped the anchor. The first anchor was lost and as the position was not clear a second anchor was dropped. When daylight came the ship was quarter of a mile off Curracloe. The crew could not cut the anchor chain to allow the ship drift ashore at high tide. They abandoned ship and the boats were overturned in the surf. Twelve of the fourteen crew were drowned. The Georgina was swamped and sank in seven fathoms. Her masts showed at low water. The general cargo was valuable as one bill of lading washed ashore with the captains gear valued a portion at £10,000. (132)

Shark

The 125 ton iron screw steamer Shark was wrecked at Ballymurray, Tacumshane on 26-12-1872. Owned by Munn Millar she had been built at Dublin in 1866. She was bound for Liverpool from Dunkerque in water ballast. In a storm and heavy seas her compass may have failed and she went ashore. Though high and dry she was wrecked. Her master was Charles St John. (132)

Belfast Harbour dredger No. 2
Photo: Colm Mahady

Dredger No 2

The Belfast Harbour Commissioners suction dredger was being towed by the tug Empire Demon when the tow snapped near the Blackwater LV. The 213 ton ship was en route to Cork to be scrapped. She drifted ashore at Ballymoney on 17-2-1966. The wreck was described as on "Orphan Girl" beach.

Orphan Girl

The 77 ton schooner Orphan Girl was en route from Rochester to Liverpool with a cargo of cement. The crew were rescued by coastguard rocket lines. She was wrecked at Ballymoney on 22-10-1881. (58)

Macao

The cargo of the wrecked Macao was auctioned at Kilmore on 23-1-1847. She was en route from New York to Belfast with 2000 barrels of corn and 500 barrels of meat. Her captain was Mr Scott of Coleraine. (132)

Mutlah

The 714 ton Mutlah was en route from Liverpool to Bombay with coal when she struck rocks near Tuskar on 16-4-1877. Owned by Henderson of North Shields she had been built at Southbank, Durham in 1856. The surviving crew described striking the rocks and the captain turned and passed the Blackwater lightship so close they could read her name. They presumed he was making for Kingstown despite the damage. The ship went ashore at Glynn Point, Poulshone near Courtown. Captain Farquahar, one passenger and ten of fourteen crew were drowned. At the court of inquiry the survivors described the captain as drunk since they sailed. (58) (132)

Saltee

On 16-3-1888 the Wexford barque Saltee was wrecked. The lifeboat saved the crew of thirteen.

Mary Anne & Eliza

This Plymouth ship was en route to

Wexford with super phosphate. On 25-4-1877 she struck the Dogger Bank and struck fast. No tug was available, the weather worsened and the ship was wrecked. (132)

Isallt

The two masted (134 ton) auxiliary schooner owned by the South of Ireland Shipping Company was wrecked on rocks at Ballymoney strand on 5-12-1947. Built at Portmadoc in 1909 the vessel had been used as a training schooner by the Department of Defence during the war. She had been purchased for film work and was en route to the Caribbean. Five of the seven aboard were lost. (140) (133)

Michelle

The 200 ton Greek brig Michelle was wrecked on rocks at Carne on 17-9-1852. She carried coal from Liverpool to Constantinople. Captain G Callare and his crew were saved. (66)

Bhurtpoor

The Bhurtpoor struck Holden's Bed part of the Long Bank off Wexford on 17-9-1852. The 1500 ton emigrant ship was bound for New Orleans from Liverpool. A NE breeze arose and the masts were prudently cut off. Lifeboats were launched and reached Wexford. The cutter Rapid under Capt Devreux set out from Rosslare Fort and supervised the rescue. Pilot boats and fishing craft took off 360 passengers safely. Rosslare and Kilmore lifeboats assisted. The master George Bainbridge was drowned when leaving the ship. He became entangled on the bower anchor ropes. A further 5 passengers were drowned. The rescue work was completed with great difficulty as a gale arose and hampered the rescuers. (66)

Speedwell V

The minesweeping drifter Speedwell V struck the North Splaugh Rock inside the Carricks near the pier at Greenore on 28-10-1916. The incident happened during a SE gale. A distress signal was seen and reported to the coastguard but no help was possible. The distress was confirmed when another drifter reported at the pier that one of her number was in distress but she could not assist. It appears that the red light on Long Bank was extinguished by the storm and the Speedwell lost her bearings. All ten of her crew were drowned and are buried in the Kilscoran Church of Ireland. The ship sank until only her masts and funnell showed. She had been built at Aberdeen. (160) (161)

Elsie Annie

This 250 ton steamer was wrecked when she struck the Wexford Bar on 6-2-1936. She was en route from Ayr to Wexford with 300 tons of coal for the Wexford Gas Co. Captain R. O'Neill and the crew were taken off by the Wexford pilot boat. The vessel became a total loss when she shifted and listed. (160) (161)

Wexfordian

The 807 ton Wexfordian was also wrecked on the Wexford Bar on 29-2-1936. She carried coal for the Wexford Gas Company. Nine of her crew of 13 were rescued by the lifeboat. Captain Peter McGrath and the others abandoned ship a few days later. The vessel was a total loss. She was owned by Staffords Wexford SS Co. (160) (161)

Svanen

The Danish four masted auxillary schooner ran ashore on Raven Point on 23-11-1933. She had unloaded timber at Rosslare and struck at the N entrance to Wexford harbour during a NE gale. Captain Ramussen and the crew of seven eventually abandoned ship on 30-12-1936. (160) (161)

Crest
The three masted auxillary schooner Crest formerly the Vigilant went ashore on the beach at Rosslare harbour on 9-3-1936. She was bound from Wexford to Dublin with salt. She was owned by Mr Rochford of Kilmore. Captain Bent and his crew were safe. The vessel was accessible on foot at low tide. (161)

Szarpey
The 746 ton Austrian steamer of Fiume was wrecked at the Randal rock at Bannow on 27-12-1882. She had no sight of land since Cape Finisterre and struck during a southerly wind and thick weather. Her crew of 23 were saved by coastguard rocket line. She was en route to Dublin with a cargo of flour. (2) (161).

Liffey
The 845 ton Liffey of and from St John NB grounded on St Patrick's Bridge on 2-11-1881. She drifted off and stranded 500 yards south of the pier at Kilmore. She carried 1000 tons of cargo bound for Liverpool. Her captain mistook Coningbeg for Tuskar. (132)

Clementina
The Clementina of Cardiff was carrying a cargo of rum and sugar from Demerara to Greenock when she was wrecked on 22-2-1883 three miles west of the pier at Kilmore. Her crew of 11 were rescued by coastguards. Her cargo was salvaged. (132)

Regalia
The Ketch Regalia of Jersey went ashore at Ballyhealy on 12-1-1882. She was owned by F.J. Picot and carried 104 tons of barley. She had been built in 1872 and was expected to be refloated. (132)

Louisa
The river steamer Louisa sank at Morris Castle on 9-2-1861. Her shallow draught allowed her to cross the sandbanks driven by the easterly gale but she filled and sank before the steamer Firefly could reach the scene. (132)

Thomas Patrick
The smack Thomas Patrick of Arklow was seen to founder by the Rosslare coastguard near Carrig rocks on 29-1-1882. She carried manure from Dublin to Wexford. (132)

Sir Allen McNab
On 9-2-1861 was driven ashore at Ballymoney. The four crew were in a bad way three were numb and the fourth dying. A large crowd gathered and Lt Bolger stripped and swam out with a line. The three men were saved. (132)

Florentine Glenville
On 6-4-1858 the Florentine Glenville of Regniville sank at Curracloe a short distance from Raven Point. She was in ballast from Llanelly. Her mast showed and could be seen from the quay (132)

Edward Phelan
The Edward Phelan drove ashore at Wexford on 7-4-1858. Her cables had parted while she tried to ride to the gale. She sank opposite the White house. (132)

Iris
The Iris sunk in the North Bay between the coastguard station at Curracloe and Raven Point on 6-4-1858. Captain George Harrisson and his crew ascended the masts. One jumped and reached shore another jumped and was lost. The reminder were rescued by coastguard rocket. She was bound from Liverpool to Belfast with coal. (132)

Jenny Lind
The Wexford collier Jenny Lind was en route from Newport when she grounded at the entrance to Hantoon channel on 30-1-1861. Her crew were saved by lifeboat. (132)

Vivid
The 83 ton schooner Vivid owned by

Allen's of Wexford was discharging cargo at Cahore on 15-9-1868. Her anchor dragged and she grounded quarter of a mile offshore. Her master James Storey and the crew of four were saved by lifeboat. (132)

Sorcier
The fruit clipper Sorcier of Guernsey was wrecked on Dogger Bank on 18-12-1855. She was en route from Liverpool to St Michaels captained by John Henry. (132) The same day two ships came ashore near the pilot station at Rosslare.

Brandiwine
The American ship Brandiwine was stranded at Carne early in January 1861. The wreck broke up in the storm of 30-1-1861. (132)

Vulcan
The remains of the Vulcan wrecked at Tacumshane were disposed by auction on 12-4-1833. They consisted of 15 tons of Swedish iron as well as ropes rigging and timber. Her master was Mr Bunker. (174)

Priory
The Priory of Milford struck the north end of the Dogger bank on 30-3-1871. She was owned by Mr Williams and only a year old. The voyage was from Dublin to Wexford with 60 tons of manure captained by James Cullen. (132)

City of London
On 13-1-1875 the 1700 ton City of London mistook Hook light for a steamer masthead and went ashore 5 miles west of Carnsore point. She had sailed from San Francisco on 1-11-1875 with wheat and 68 tons of pressed salmon. The ship came to rest on a steeply sloping sandy beach. Captain James Browne and the crew of 25 were safe. A compass fault was blamed for the accident. (132)

Girl Arline
The 70 foot Clogherhead trawler Girl Arline sank in 26 metres of water SW of Baginbun Head on 13-11-1989. She was struck during fog by another trawler. Both were fishing a shoal of herring. (140)

Vigilant
The Liverpool to Pigeon House Dock, Dublin cargo and passenger vessel Vigilant was wrecked on the Wexford coast on 18-12-1764. The ship left Liverpool during a lull in a storm on 15 December commanded by Captain Mullen and carrying 22 passengers. About 20 miles from the Irish coast the wind intensified to a gale. The sails were split and three crewmen were washed overboard. Two women were killed when they were dashed against the cabin walls. During the night the ship struck reefs on the Wexford coast and sank within a half hour. Two of the crew the mate Joe Dillon and a cabin boy survived by holding onto a crate and drifting ashore. (177)

Jacob Pennell
The 547 ton Jacob Pennell of Brunswick, Maine ran ashore and was wrecked at Carnsore during fog on 21-2-1846. The master Mr Martin and 15 crew were rescued by Dennets rockets. Her cargo was cotton bound for Liverpool. (132)

Iride
The 158 ton Iride went ashore at Tacumshane on 22-2-1846 and was dashed to pieces. The master Carmello Agracta and crew of 8 were saved. She was bound from Messina to London with fruit. (132) There were reputed to have been eight Wexford wrecks that Winter.

Achroite
The 314 ton trawler Achroite was en route from Fleetwood to Passage West to be scrapped. During a storm on 5-2-1963 the vessel was driven ashore at Rosslare.

Helga/Muirchu

the 166 ft steel twin screw Helga was built in 1908 by the Dublin Dockyard Co for fisheries protection work (131). At the outbreak of war she was transferred to the Royal Navy. during the 1916 Easter Rising she was used to shell several sites in Dublin. She sank a German submarine in the Irish Sea in April 1918. In 1922 the vessel was transferred to the Irish Government and served as a fisheries protection vessel until replaced by flower class corvettes in the late 1940s. She sank on 8-5-1947 eight miles south of the Coninbeg light vessel under tow from Haulbowline to Hammond Lane shipbreakers in Dublin. Her crew were taken off by a Welsh trawler. (133)

Eliza Taylor

The sloop Eliza Taylor of Cork struck Hore Rock off Ballygeary on 7-4-1850 and sunk in four fathoms. She was en route from Liverpool to Youghal with salt. The captain Philip McDonnell and crew came ashore in their jolly boat.

John R Skiddy

On 1-4-1850 Captain Shipley the master of the John R Skiddy mistook the Arklow Bank Light for the Tuskar. He sailed his vessel ashore on Glascarrick beach and she struck 200 yards offshore. In his account of the event he described the locals as "the most abandoned set of villains that he had encountered". They pillaged the wreck and anything brought ashore by the ship's boats in defiance of both coastguard and police.

Les Bussionnets

The Lorient trawler les Bussionnets was smashed on the rocks at Roastoonstown 3 miles west of Carnsore on 28-1-1958. She went ashore in fog and stormy conditions while fishing offshore.

Captain Gaultier and one crewman were lost. The six saved were pulled from the surf by farmers who were attracted to the scene by the trawler's siren. Yves Dantec who was captain of the Auguste Maurice wrecked on 28-12-1957 was among those saved from this his second shipwreck in a few months. The wreck caught fire on the beach soon after the rescue. Her nameboard marked L'Orient L5076 is in the County Museum at Enniscorthy. (99)

St Kevin

The 35 foot trawler St Kevin was driven ashore and wrecked on 10-12-1958. The crew were able to wade ashore onto the sandy beach at Reedstown. The wreck was only half a mile from where Les Bussionets came ashore. The crew had to walk to a nearby farmhouse for assistance as nobody saw them come ashore among the sandhills.

Stockton

The privateer Stockton of Stockton was lost during a gale as she entered Wexford Harbour in January 1780. Her crew were all saved. (101)

Akme Phal

The 500 ton Akme Phal went ashore at Raven point in December 1971. She was given up as lost but 43 days later on 1-2-1972 a local salvor Mr James Doyle of Forth Rock, Coolballow managed to refloat the stranded ship. He towed her into Roslare Harbour.

Idaho

The 3356 ton, Liverpool and Great Western SS Co vessel Idaho struck Coningmore Rock on 1-6-1878. She left New York on 21 May for Liverpool via Queenstown with 63 passengers and 82 crew. Fog occurred on nine out of the eleven day voyage. The vessel left Queenstown on 1 June and quickly ran into haze. Thinking that only banks of mist were about Captain Holmes posted lookouts and maintained speed. The Idaho struck Coningmore Rock quickly after the order to stop had been given due to the sighting of smaller rocks. Good order prevailed and all aboard reached the boats safely before the Idaho sank 22 minutes after striking the rock. The only causalities were 54 horses. The survivors spent a cold night on the Saltees until they were rescued. At an inquiry on 26-6-1878 the captain was censured for faulty navigation and maintaining speed. The wreck was located about 17-2-1976 by the Guiding Star trawler of Kilmore. A local diver James Kehoe recovered some portholes. Her anchor was raised in 1988 and adorns the bow of the Guillemot Museum ship at Kilmore Quay. The Idaho was built at Palmer's of Newcastle on Tyne in 1869. (2) (132)

Mary Grace

During the First World War the sailing ship Mary Grace had bombs placed on her by a submarine prize crew. Her crew abandoned ship and rowed to the Coninbeg lightship. The ship drifted ashore onto Ring Ban beach. (135,1399, p237) This was probably the same 58 ton vessel attacked by submarine on 24-9-1917.

Chervil

The French vessel Chereval, Chevreux or Chevreul of Harvre struck Kilkeen rock a mile north of Carnsore Point on 27-12-1879. She carried a cargo of logwood to Grascon via Queenstown. She mistook the Coninbeg light for Tuskar. Thirteen crew were rescued by Fethard lifeboat. The wreck occurred a mile from where the Lonsdale was lost a few months previously with the loss of nine lives. A Norwegian barque was lost at the same place a week after the Lonsdale (Langdale). The newspaper

remarked that all wrecks had occurred on Saturday nights. (66)

Langdale

The 1237 ton Langdale of Liverpool struck the Barrels Rocks, drifted towards shore and sank off Tacumshane after she struck the Combe rocks on 27-9-1879. She was en route from San Francisco to Liverpool. Captain Jenkenson, his wife, the mate and bosun were drowned when their gig overturned. Three men were washed ashore from this boat. The 23 remaining crew survived in the other boat and landed at Carne. The ship was a total wreck but some of her cargo of wheat was saved. She was owned by J.D. Newton of Liverpool. (135, 1399, p134) (66).

William and John

The schooner William & John carrying butter and bacon was wrecked at Carne in November c1850. (1399, p237) A barque carrying ice was wrecked at Ballyhealy about 1890. The crew were saved by the coastguards rocket apparatus.

John Calvin

The four masted American ship John Calvin was wrecked on a rock off Carne. Other ships lost nearby include Meridien and Industry. (135, 1399, p237)

Sea Rest

The steamer Sea Rest was wrecked in the hole in the forlorn Rocks in Winter 1870 (2). Most of those aboard were lost including 32 passengers. One survivor was a Dublin Fusilier who was so drunk that he did not know of the incident until he awoke ashore. (135, 1399, p 237)

Jessie

The three masted schooner Jessie of Lowes was wrecked at Carne on 8-10-1896. Another Jessy was lost on 24-3-1897 at Fundale Rock. She carried 3000 bags of cement. (135, 1399, p237)

Wreck at Ballyteigue

Fourteen Norwegians were buried with one Spaniard on the burrow at Ballytiegue after a wreck, year unknown. among the cargo were barrels of rum. This was drunk by the locals out of hard hats. (135, 514, p211)

Success

The 75 foot timber trawler Success was sunk by the ferry Inisfallen on 2-8-1982. She was struck during fog about a mile from Rosslare harbour. The bow sank almost immediately and the remainder sank in half an hour. Of the six aboard the trawler Brigit Carmel picked up four. (67)

Isabella Davidson

On 19-1-1861 the Isabella Davidson of Inverness was driven ashore at Rosslare. She was in ballast on route from Falmouth to Troon. (73)

Versailles

The 620 ton Versailles was en route from Liverpool to Shanghai when she was driven ashore in the South Bay under Hill of Sea at Ballygeary on 19-1-1861. The tug Erin towed a schooner from Wexford to lighten her and hoped to tow her off. The cargo was unshipped and the tugs Fire Fly, Mars and Erin tried to tow her off on 23-1-1861. The Liverpool towing company lost a valuable steam pump which the Erin had placed aboard her. (73) (132)

Montagu

On 25-4-1878 the Liverpool steamship Montagu went ashore. She struck the bar at Wexford in an ENE gale. Those aboard four men, eight women and six children were rescued by the Rosslare Fort Lifeboat. (124)

May Lily

On 3-4-1878 the iron built trawler May Lily of St Mary, Penzance was wrecked on the Barrels. She was returning form fishing off Kinsale. Four of the crew were lost, the other four reached the shore at Carne by their boat. (132)

Debonair

The Debonair of Greenock was wrecked at Kilmore durng a storm on 8-1-1879. She was en route from Bilbao to Glasgow with a cargo of iron ore and sardines. The coastguards fired their rocket and one crew member was taken ashore. The others waited for the storm to abate. (66)

Aberfeldy

The Aberfeldy of Aberfeldy went ashore at Tinnebarna two miles from Blackwater Head on 12-10-1870. She carried copper ore from Spain. Four of her crew were lost. (66)

Vittorioso G

On 20-1-1875 the Italian Brig Vittorioso G of Venice ran onto the Selskar rock in Bannow Bay. She was en route from Cardiff to Constantinople with 420 tons of coal when she was caught in a gale off Cape Clear. She was blown back along the south coast and could not enter Cork harbour. When she was driven onto the rock the coastguard could not reach her with their lines. The lifeboat was transported from Duncannon to Fethard and launched. Captain Angelo Scaipa and the crew of nine were rescued. (132)

Maud Anne

On 12-2-1870 the Maud Anne of Wexford was wrecked at Ballygeary. The Fort Coastguard travelled ten miles in the storm and rescued the crew. A wreck auction was held at Balygrangans to dispose of some birch timber part of the cargo of the wrecked Robert Hastie. She had been on route from Dalhousie to Liverpool when she was wrecked. (132)

Zorilla

The 951 ton iron steamer Zorilla was wrecked at Tara Hill on 1-1-1875. The ship was bound for Palermo from Liverpool. She struck the Glasgorman Bank near Kilmaloe coastguard station. (58)

Amelia

On 30-12-1872 the Amelia wreck was auctioned near Courtown. John Thomas and his crew were drowned. (66)

Fishing disasters

The Wexford fishermen were no strangers to disaster. A local superstition forbade sailing on St Martin's Eve. This was as a result of the loss of 70 in Wexford Bay on 10-11-1762. On 19-12-1833 the Faythe fishing craft were capsised by a gale. About 1850 Clone fishermen were lost on 3 December. The Tinnabarna fishermen were blown over to Wales and wrecked. The Glenrose of Courtown was lost off Courtown on 9 June year unknown. Six men were drowned. Arklow men were criticised and accused of passing the craft in distress. Poulduff fishermen were lost on 1-7-1880 when their craft struck the wreck of the Perseverance. (58)

Eliza

The Eliza was lost at Cahore point on 24-12-1895. Rockets were tried. Eventually the lifeboat rescued three men lashed to the shrouds. (58)

Rambler

The Wexford schooner Rambler was bound for Wexford from Liverpool with salt. She ran aground on 24-8-1873 in the North Bay at Wexford driven by a south wind. The crew were saved by the lifeboat. (66)

Garryowen

The Garryowen was wrecked on the Patch a sandbank off Balinoulart. She was an American trader and carried clothing material among her cargo. (58)

Curiana

The schooner Curiana of Ulverston was

wrecked in the South Bay at Wexford on 17-11-1852. Two of her three crew were drowned when their boat was swamped. She carried iron ore from Barrow to Cardiff. The vessel was driven high on the beach. There she joined another wreck the Briget of Liverpool. (132)

Gem

The 114 ton Gem struck the Dogger Bank and sunk in the North Bay at Wexford on 10-9-1873. She was en route from Ayr to Wexford with coal. She was owned by Kearns of Wexford. (66)

Adili

The lugger Adili was en route from Nantes to Liverpool carrying wheat and flour. On 13-1-1850 she was wrecked on the shore ten miles south of Wexford. Her master, M. Borgot and two crew, were lost.

Calcutta

The iron ship Calcutta struck the rocks off Kilmore in Ballyteigue Bay during fog on 17-1-1874. She was owned by F.A. Clint & Co of Liverpool. The ship was bound for Liverpool from Surinam. Captain Hamilton and his crew were lost. She was the third wreck in the neighbourhood in three weeks.

Demararay

On 16-12-1819 the Demararay was wrecked on the Keeraghs. She carried gold bullion in her strongroom. The tomb of a Scotsman named Hugh Munro Robertson A.M. and the sixteen crew lies flat at the disused cemetary in a field called Cill Park opposite Cullenstown Castle near Cullenstown Strand. (2)

Alcibidos

The Alcibidos of Andros was wrecked on 26-12-1852 at Cullenstown. She carried Indian corn. The crew of 8 were all lost.

Mexico

On 20-2-1914 nine members of the

Fethard lifeboat were drowned when going to the assistance of the Norwegian steamer Mexico. A SSW gale blew the steamer into Bannow Bay and on to the one acre South Keeragh Island about 220 yards from the main Keeragh Island. During the attempted rescue the lifeboat Helen Blake was smashed on the rocks. Eight of the Mexico's crew were saved by the five lifeboat survivors. All but one of the stranded survivors were saved with great difficulty the next day. A memorial in Fethard commemorates the disaster. The Mexico sailors were the last of many victims of the sea buried at the ruin of the old chapel at Cullenstown. (2) 107, p111)

Porteus
The brig Porteus was wrecked in Bannow Bay on 20-3-1869. She carried coal from Cardiff. (2)

Foxwell
In 1801 (9) the schooner Foxwell struck a rock near Carnsore. The vessel was en route to Wexford with a cargo of cotton bales. One crew member was in a cabin when the ship broke and his portion was kept afloat by the cotton bales. When this portion of the ship was washed ashore on the Burrow he was able to describe the circumstances of the wreck. The crew were rescued from the Saltees the following day by Kilmore fishermen. The location of the wreck is thought to be at the Fundale rock. Her rudder is on display in Kehoe's pub at Kilmore Quay. (2)

William
The Weymouth sloop William with all her crew was lost at Carnsore on 21-2-1818. A tombstone at St Vauxs Church Carnsore commemorates Charles & William Langrish and their crew. (2)

Carrie Davis
The barque Carrie Davis was wrecked at Carnsore point on 2-2-1866.

Guyana
The 330 ton Guyana of Glasgow was wrecked at Carnsore on 13-2-1861. She was en route from Greenock to St Kitts with coal and bricks when she went on Carron rocks at Carnsore point. The Carron lifeboat took off her Master, Mr Pledge, and crew of 19, but one died later. (73). The same day a small vessel with coal was wrecked at Courtown. Her crew were rescued from the rigging but one died.

Ceres
On 10-11-1866 the 382 ton Ceres owned by the Waterford firm of Malcomson went ashore at Carnsore point. She called at Falmouth and other ports on route as part of a regular service. A gale blew up and the ship passed the Tuskar light, but did not notice it. Despite the storm and poor visibility she pressed on under sail and steam. Of 42 passengers 29 were lost along with 9 crew. Twenty six passengers and crew escaped ashore in a boat. Captain Pascoe was censured for his carelessness at the inquiry on 15-11-1866.

Jane and Sarah
The schooner Jane and Sarah was wrecked at Carnsore on 26-3-1872. (82)

Hollyhock (Holyoke)
On 11-1-1855 the Hollyhock of Boston was wrecked on rocks at Churchtown a mile NE of Carnsore. The 500 ton copper fastened ship under Captain Parker was en route from St Johns NB to Dublin. She struck on rocks south of Tuskar and the captain went to Carne for assistance. The steamer Shamrock towed her towards Waterford but on meeting a headwind and the tide between the Saltees and Tuskar they ran her ashore. She carried timber for Martin's of Kingstown. The remains of the vessel were advertised for auction on 12-2-1855 (132)

Laparay

The Austrian barque Laparay was wrecked near Carnsore on 1-1-1882. She was carrying flour to Liverpool. Her home port was Rijka in Yugoslavia. The crew were taken ashore by breeches buoy.

Sem

The Sem of Sabronella carrying coal was wrecked a mile west of Carnsore on 12-2-1884. The wooden Austrian vessel of 500 tons was carrying coal from Swansea on to Cape Verde. Ten bodies were washed ashore at Carne and Tacumshane.

Ariadne

On 25-11-1838 the Ariadne carrying timber was wrecked on the beach between Raven Point and Curracloe. She was en route from Quebec to Belfast with timber. She struck Tuskar Rock and some of her crew were washed overboard. The vessel worked over the rocks and drifted on to the North Bar at Wexford. The crew retreated to the masts where they held on overnight. Lt Lett of the coastguard rescued eight by fishing boat. Lt Lett was awarded a medal for his gallantry on 9-1-1839.

Jadestar Glory

On 16-1-1974 the 300 ton Trawler Jadestar Glory was wrecked on Roney rock half a mile north of Poldoff Pier near Cahore Point. The crew of six were rescued from liferafts by the lifeboat. On 12-3-74 four salvors were rescued as they worked on the wreck.

Elisabeth Alida

The Sailing ship Elisabeth Alida was wrecked at Carne on 8-3-1859. She was en route from Amsterdam to Liverpool. Her remains were for auction on 12-3-1859.

Mountblairey

The Schooner Mountblairey of Plymouth went ashore on rocks at Carne five miles from Rosslare harbour on 20-10-1930. The crew of five were rescued.

Barge

A barge towing a second barge lost power and drifted aground inside Laweesh Rock on 4-10-1960. The lifeboat rescued the crew of two.

Halronell

On 22-10-1962 the 350 ton 140 foot Arklow coaster Halronell was wrecked on Black Rock two miles SW of Carnsore. She was carrying sheet steel from Newport to Haulbowline. The vessel was built at Thorne, Yorkshire in 1944. She was purchased in 1950 and named Halronnell by James Tyrrell. After striking the rock the mast was carried away which prevented radio communication. Rockets were seen by the Barrells lightship and the lifeboats from Rosslare and Kilmore quay were assisted by a helicopter from Wales. Two of the crew were washed from the forepart of the ship while a third boarded a liferaft which was blown northwards. The Arklow fishing fleet searched for the liferaft but when it was found by the aircraft carrier HMS Centaur the occupant, 15 year old Brian O'Neill, had died. The ship was built in 1943 as the Empire Laird by Dunston Thorne and the name changed to Mockton before she became the Halronnel.

Empress

The 1315 ton steamer Empress was wrecked on Black Rock near Carnsore on 21-3-1897. She was owned by Curiven Brothers and built at Grangemouth Dockyard in 1889. She was en route fron Seville to Ayr with iron ore.

John A Harvie

On 26-11-1880 the three masted barque John A Harvie of Winsor, Nova Scotia was driven aground at Ballyhealy three miles from Kilmore. Commander Elkeneh Curry was confused by the new revolving light of the Barrels Lightship and thought he was at Cardigan. She was carrying 1555 tons of loose and bagged maize from New York. Those aboard retreated to the single remaining mast and the Carne lifeboat was launched by a substitute crew assembled by local priest, Fr Browne. The sea prevented a rescue until the next day when the regular crew completed the rescue of Capain Lockhart, his wife, his sister and 14 crew This incident may have promoted the establishment of Kilmore lifeboat. (20 (132)

Brigand
Captain R.M. Hunt died at Castletown House on 4-3-1852. His vessel was wrecked at Carne.

Paquet de Terranova
The Spanish brig Paquet de Terranova was wrecked in a bay at Tacumshane on 25-9-1875. Carnsore lifeboat rescued her crew of ten. Her foremast was blown away and the rocket could not reach her. Her cargo was sugar. (58) A vessel known as the Spanish packet is described as wrecked in 1867 but may be the same.

Neptune
The Greek training ship Neptune was wrecked in April 1860 at Ballyteigue Bay near Kilmore Quay. The only survivors were eight apprentices whose cabin was washed up intact on the rocks. The other eight aboard were lost when the aft portion sank. The deck house was manhandled along a road and used at the Wooden House restaurant at Kilmore Quay The Wooden House itself is described in 1846 in a newspaper item on Kilmore. (132)

Shancaddie
On 24-1-1837 the Shancaddie (or

Subernacadie) of Liverpool was wrecked at Kilmore. She carried a cargo of cotton. Her crew were saved. The crew were alleged to have set fire to salvaged bales of cotton. (2)

Horatio
The Horatio of Sunderland was wrecked at Kilmore on 1-2-1850. She carried wheat.

Mary
On 6-2-1837 the Mary was wrecked at Kilmore

Exile
This vessel was wrecked at Kilmore in 1856.

La Touche
On 11-3-1868 the French ship La Touche was wrecked in Ballyteigue Bay. All the crew died. On 2-12-1843 a French brig with wine was wrecked at Ballyteigue.

Maria
On 5-2-1837 the Maria was wrecked at Ballyteigue Bay. (2)

Fairfax
On 30-1-1850 the brig Fairfax of Jersey carrying a cargo of palm oil was wrecked at Ballyteigue Bay. (2)

James Calder
On 18-1-1854 the James Calder bound from New Orleans to Liverpool with cotton was wrecked at Ballyteigue Bay. (2)

Emma of Scilly
On 1-2-1873 the ship Emma of Scilly was wrecked on the shore near Carnsore Pt. Captain Pendon and his crew were all lost. A stone in the small churchyard near the pier records the tragedy. A rock off shore is named after Capt Pendon.

Chattanoochee
The 1115 ton Chattanoochee was wrecked at Greenore on 15-2-1857. She was en route from Liverpool to Savannah. Her crew of 27 were saved. (55)

Magoline

The Magoline of Plymouth was en route from Liverpool to Constantinople with bale goods when she went ashore at Curracloe in hazy weather during the storm of 19-2-1850. The Lloyds agent at Waterford, Francis Harper, estimated the value of her cargo at £20,000 and expected that she would be refloated. Her master Mr Frazier and the crew were all safe.

Henry

The schooner Henry of Wexford was wrecked on the Barrells on 28-10-1874. She carried a cargo of oats. (55)

Faithful

The three masted 132 ton Arklow schooner Faithful was wrecked on Splaugh Rock in 1921. She was built in 1887 by Ferguson and Baird at Connah's Quay. She was owned by Tyrrells who bought her in 1919. (2)

Balla

The Jersey vessel Balla was lost at Bar O Lough on 22-11-1880. She carried salted fish. Her crew were saved.

Ullswater

The Ullswater was wrecked at Courtown on 13-1-1868. She carried general cargo from Liverpool. Five of her six crew were lost. (9)

Idalia

The Idalia en route from New Orleans to Liverpool was wrecked at Courtown on 13-1-1873. (55)

Orinoco

The Orinoco was wrecked at South Bay Wexford on 12-11-1876. She was en route from St Johns New Brunswick to Liverpool with timber. Three of her crew were drowned.

Torrance

The coal boat Torrance was wrecked at the fort of Rosslare on 1-2-1855. Captain Shiel had sheltered her in the bay for a few days before her anchor cables broke

and she went ashore. Mr R. Devereaux of Wexford was the owner.

Mary

The schooner Mary of Bangor with slates for Wexford was wrecked at Rosslare on 22-12-1870 (or 1869). Her crew were saved by a fishing boat.

Rose

On 15-10-1881 the Rose of Milford dragged her anchors and went aground at Holden's Bed at Wexford. She was en route from Bangor with a cargo of slates. There were no survivors. (140) The tug Ruby went to her assistance. The same day an abandoned large barque went on the rocks at Balinavaloona near Stradbally. (65)

Spanish Ship

In 1549 a Spanish ship laden with wine was wrecked on the south Wexford coast (146)

William & Michael

The smack William and Michael was wrecked on the south of Wexford Bar on 28-6-1917. She had been caught in a ENE gale. Her crew of three were rescued by the lifeboat. (149)

Northern Lights

The schooner Northern Lights of Wexford lost her sails in an easterly gale on 21-12-1917. She was wrecked at Wexford. Her crew of four were rescued by the lifeboat. (149)

Thomas Booth

The Milford steam trawler Thomas Booth was wrecked on Wilkeen rocks off Carne pier on 16-3-1941. Her eleven crew abandoned ship and reached safety. (149)

Sheila

The yacht Sheila was wrecked on the North Dogger Bank on 9-7-1941. Her crew of three escaped. (149)

Geister Hdolph

The 200 ton Danish vessel from Berth was wrecked at Ballygeary on 13-1-1850.

She was en route from Koinsberg to Liverpool with a cargo of wheat, barley and peas. Her master was J.S. Kraift. (66)

Stag
The 100 ton schooner Stag was wrecked at Blackwater on 18-12-1853. Her master J. Veneer and crew were saved by the Curracloe coastguard. She was en route from Penzance to Liverpool with china clay and tin blocks. (65)

Caravane
The French vessel Caravane of Bordeaux was wrecked on 18-12-1853 at the same place as the Stag. Captain Possioner and all the crew were lost. (65)

William and Mary
The smack William and Mary was wrecked at Rosslare on 18-12-1853. She had come from Port Gain with a cargo of slates. (65)

Niagra
The 800 ton US ship Niagra ran on to the beach at Greenore Point near Ballygeary on 18-12-1853. She carried 220 passengers and railway iron from New York to Liverpool. The passengers disembarked safely. (65)

L. Furlong
The 68 ton L. Furlong was wrecked on Collough Rock near Carnsore on 13-10-1900.

Ocean Maid
The Ocean Maid was wrecked at Rosslare on 7-3-1908. Thomas Kehoe, her captain, was drowned. The coastguards saved the three crew. The 74 ton 2 masted schooner was built at Fraserburgh in 1861 and owned by Pat Byrne of Wexford. (192)

Margaret & Mary
The 97 ton two masted schooner Margaret and Mary was wrecked at Raven Point on 19-11-1915. She was built at Perth in 1867 and was owned by James Sinnot of Wexford. (192)

John Butler
The sloop John Butler from St Martin's was lost on 10-1-1753. The wreck occurred near St Margaret's in South Wexford. The crew were saved. (69)

Deolocos
In a SSW gale on 19-1-1852 the Greek brig Deolocos was wrecked on the Burrow at Ballyteigue. The brig from the Isle of Syra was en route from Alexandria to Liverpool with a cargo of wheat. Jean Dramians, the master, and his crew of 13 were saved. The wheat was salvaged. (132)

Thotoeko
The Greek brig Thotoeko was wrecked early in 1852 at Ballyteigue. Her cargo of 190 barrels of wheat was auctioned on 30-1-1852. (132)

Loddon
The Lowestoft steam trawler Loddon struck a rock near the Saltees on 27-1-1941. Despite assistance being near at hand skipper Gilmartin and his crew stayed aboard and drove her ashore at Rosslare where they hoped she could be repaired. (99)

Galeon
The mayor of Limerick complained to Lord Deputy Bellingham on 10-1-1549 that locals had plundered a Limerick ship recently cast ashore at Wexford. (16)

Garthloch
The SS Garthloch foundered off Cahore on 15-3-1928. She was bound from Bristol to Liverpool with flour.

Lismore
The new ship Lismore of the City of Cork Steam Packet Company capsized on 10-7-1924 en route from Cork to Manchester and Birkenhead. The ship was on her third voyage and carried 200 cattle and sheep and goods for Ford Motor company. The only survivor of the 19 aboard was John Carley. He stated

that the ship developed a list and water was seen in the cattle hold. As the crew prepared the lifeboats the vessel suddenly capsized and he managed to cling to a hatch cover. He was washed past Hook and Baginbun and came ashore near Fethard. Because of the political troubles he was refused admittance to several houses before he obtained assistance. Captain Sayle and 18 crew were lost. There was speculation as to the cause of the loss of a new ship. A derrick which had been in the sea some time but was freshly broken was washed ashore at Guileen, east of Roches Point. It was presumed that the Lismore had struck this and had been holed. The survivor thought that the ship sank 15 miles from Tramore but the wreck was discovered some years ago by Wexford divers. (67)

Peace

The Peace stranded near Wexford on 27-1-1812. Captained by Mr Edmondson the vessel was en route from Swansea to Dublin. On 5-1-1812 an unknown sloop foundered off Carne with the loss of all aboard. (234)

Adventure

The French schooner Brestois, a privateer with 14 guns and 130 men, captured and sunk the Adventure on 12-11-1812 off Wexford. The Adventure was en route from Limerick to Liverpool captained by Mr Blair. (234)

Emmanuel

The Emmanuel commanded by Mr Graham was wrecked near Wexford on 7-12-1812. The cargo was driven ashore. The vessel was en route from London to Dundalk. (234)

Ann

The Ann commanded by Mr Roach went to pieces at "Ballyneshar", Wexford on 11-11-1812. Her voyage was from Bristol to Dublin. (234)

Recovery

The Recovery en route from London to Dublin was wrecked near Wexford on 3-1-1765. The master and three aboard were lost. The cargo was sugar and porter. (234)

Nancy

The Nancy was lost near Wexford on 20-1-1764. The master, Mr Hanson, was en route from Lisbon to Cork. (234)

Limington

The Limington was lost near Wexford on 17-3-1749. The crew were saved. Her voyage was London to Dublin. (234)

Wellwood

The Wellwood was wrecked near Wexford on 20-3-1812. The crew and passengers were saved. Captain Hazlehurst was bound from Liverpool to Brazil. (234)

Hawker

The Hawker was lost at the entrance to Wexford on 15-4-1812. Captain Phillips was en route from Liverpool to Jamaica. (234)

Thomas

On 14-1-1865 the 60 ton schooner Thomas was wrecked on Dogger Bank off Wexford Harbour. The incident was seen from Rosslare Fort and the Pilots took the lifeboat out to her assistance. The master Mr Owens was safely transferred with the crew to the tug Ruby. The Lloyds agent Mr Jasper arranged for the salvage of the cargo of wheat but the vessel was a total loss.

Desert Flower

The 1216 ton Desert Flower was wrecked on the Long Bank 3 miles SW of Greenore Point on 4-3-1864. The tug Ruby towed out the Rosslare lifeboat and some of the crew were picked up by a brigantine. The mate and carpenter were drowned. The ship was en route from Liverpool to Calcutta.

The list of Wexford wrecks to 1-1-1846 was compiled by William Powell a local Lloyds agent or salvor. It was first published in 1846 in the Independent Wexford but this list was not found. It was referred to in the Wexford Guardian on 19-7-1851 in an item supporting the case for a harbour of refuge at Rosslare and is part of the Tidal Harbour Commissioners Report. This item listed wrecks between 1846 and 1851. It referred to the list which was published in the Independent Wexford on 12-7-1851.

The list describes wrecks and strandings from the Bar of Bannow to Courtown Harbour a distance of 10 leagues. The list had no dates and it seems by the grouping in localities that it is not in chronological order. Dates were subsequently added where they are known. Another list is published in Tales of the Wexford Coast (36). This information serves to illustrate the scale of shipping losses in the last century.

* = Mentioned in main text

Name Date(added)	Origin	Type	Loss	Cargo	Location	Lost
Foxwell 1801*	UK	ship	Total	Sugar Rum	Bar of Bannow	
Neptune*	UK	ship	Total	wine cotton	Connoy, Saltee	
America*	US	ship	Cargo	Cotton wine	Saltee Is	33
Demerera 16-12-1819*	UK	ship	Total	coffee	Carew Is	26
Tiger	UK	ship	Total	Sugar	Black Rock	
Prince Royal	UK	brig	Total	Madder Root	Ballyteique	
Aimwell	UK	brig	Part	Fruit	Kilmore	
Anon	UK	sch	Part	oil fish	Bannow	
La Bonne Julia 16-12-1831	French	brig	Part	Oil Fish	Bannow	9
Anon	UK	brig	Part	wine brandy	Bridge of Saltees	
Britannia	UK	sch	Total	fruit	Ballyteigue	
Brilliant Star 1806?	UK	brig	Total	wheat	Ballyteigue	
Caledonia 9-4-1818	UK	ship	Total	ballast	Ballyteigue	3
Anon	UK	sch	total	fruit	Ballyteigue	
Argo	UK	brig	part	barilla	Ballyteigue	
Anon	Swedish	brig	part	barilla	Ballyteigue	3
Ecord	UK	brig	Total	ballast	Ballyteigue	
Surry	UK	cutter	part	fruit	Ballyteigue	
Progress	UK	brig	part	timber	Saltee Is	
Royal George	UK	cutter	total	grain	Saltee Is	
Lively Kate	UK	sch	total	timber	Saltee Is	
Anon	UK	sloop	total	grain	Saltee Is	
Eliza & Abbey	US	ship	total	grain	Saltee Is	
Belisle	UK	brig	part	potatoes	Ballyteigue	
Anon	UK	sch	total	turpentine	Ballyteigue	
Margaret*	UK	ship	part	timber	Ballyteigue	
Hero	UK	ship	part	cotton	Ballyteigue	
Vermot	UK	ship	part	cotton	Kilmore	
Santon	UK	ship	total	sugar	Ballyteigue	
Subernacadie 24-1-1837/1834	UK	brig	part	cotton wool	Ballyteigue	
Robert Nobel	UK	sch	part	butter	Kilmore	
Frances 9-1-1818	UK	brig	total	grain	Saltee Is	
Water Witch 19-12-1833*	UK	Stmr	total	general cargo	Near Saltees	
Fly	UK	brig	total	salt fruit	Bridge of Saltee	
Anon	UK	brig	total	coal	Bridge of Saltee	
Ann	UK	brig	part	general cargo	Ballyhealy	

Name Date(added)	Origin	Type	Loss	Cargo	Location	Lost
Waldo	UK	sch	total	earthenware	Ballyhealy	
Victorine	French	sch	total	wine	Tacumshane	
Sarah	UK	brig	part	timber	Ballyhealy	
Vulcan 12-4-1833*	US	ship	part	iron	Tacumshane	
Thomas Peel	UK	brig	part	grain	Tacumshane	
Prince Of Wales	UK	brig	part	pipeclay	Kilmore	
Anon	US	ship	part	timber	Bannow	
Anon	Maltese	ship	total	grain	Saltees	9
Rebecca	UK	ship	total	general cargo	Nr Saltee	9
James Hadden	UK	brig	part	logwood	Ballyteigue	
Maria 5-2-1837*	UK	brig	part	wine	Ballyteigue	
Maid of the Mill	UK	brig	total	sulphur	Ballyteigue	
Wellwood 20-3-1812*	UK	ship	total	general cargo	Long Bank	
Anon	UK	brig	part	wine	Splough Rock	
Anon	UK	brig	total	lumber	Splough Rock	
Honour	UK	brig	total	fruit	Tacumshane	4
Indian Lass 13-3-1816	UK	brig	part	cotton	Carnsore	4
Brunet	UK	sch	part	iron	Rostoonstown	
Sam	UK	sloop	part	General cargo	rostoonstown	
Anon	UK	sloop	part	iron	Tacumshane	8
Anon	Spanish	brig	total	beans	Tacumshane	14
Anon	UK	ship	total	coffee sugar	Tacumshane	
St Patrick 29-11-1831	UK	sloop	total	coal	Tacumshane	
Sally	UK	sloop	part	ballast	Tacumshane	
William 20-2-1818*	UK	cutter	total	grain	Carnsore	5
Ruby	UK	Brig	part	provisions	Carnsore	
Nargery & Mary	UK	brig	part	general cargo	Wilkeen rock	
Zephyr 9-10-1833	UK	cutter	total	general cargo	Tuskar	
Irlam 10-5-1812*	UK	ship	total	coffee	Tuskar	6
Mary	UK	cutter	total	grain	South Bay	
New Friendship	UK	sloop	total	grain	South Bay	
Sultana	UK	ship	total	cotton	Long Bank	
Mary	UK	sloop	part	flour, malt	Tuskar	
Brothers	UK	sch	total	salt	Tuskar	
George	UK	brig	total	General cargo	Carnsore	
Anon	UK	ship	part	coal	Tuskar	
Thistle	UK	sch	total	ballast	South Bay	
Erin	UK	sch	part	iron	Sploough Rock	
Michael Wickham	UK	sch	total	grain	Bar of Wexford	
Esther	UK	sloop	total	grain	Bar of Wexford	
Ellen	UK	sch	part	coal	South Bay	
Shilmalier	UK	ship	part	timber	South Shoals	
Brothers	UK	brig	total	coal	South Bay	
Britannia	UK	sch	total	coal	South Bay	
Tubbermurray	UK	sloop	total	coal	Splough Rock	
Native	UK	sloop	total	coal	Splough Rock	
Anon	UK	brig	total	barilla	Carnsore	
Marchioness of Wellesley	UK	steamer	part	general cargo	Bar Of Wexford	
Marchioness of Wellesley	UK	steamer	part	general cargo	Bar Of Wexford	
John & Esther	UK	brig	total	malt	South Bay	10
Sally	UK	brig	part	general cargo	Carnsore	
Anon	UK	sch	total	general cargo	off Tuskar	8

Name Date(added)	Origin	Type	Loss	Cargo	Location	Lost
Anon	UK	brig	total	general cargo	off Tacumshane	
Anon	UK	brig	total	lumber	South Bay	
Ponsonby	UK	sch	part	cattle	South Bay	
Star	UK	sch	part	coal	South Bay	
Maria	UK	sch	part	coal	South Bay	
Clonmel	UK	steamer	got off	general cargo	South Bay	
John & Samuel	UK	sloop	part	potatoes	South Bay	
Brothers	UK	sloop	part	grain	South Bay	
Anon	UK	sloop	total	grain	Bar of Wexford	6
Anon	UK	sloop	total	grain	Bar of Wexford	6
Chance	UK	cutter	total	coal	Bar of Wexford	5
Edward	UK	sloop	total	grain	Swanton Bank	
Sea Flower	UK	brig	total	grain	Swanton Bank	
Fame	UK	smack	part	coal	South Shoal	
Fame	UK	brig	part	timber	North Bay	
Subernacadie*	UK	brig	part	timber	South Bay	
Thomas Farell	UK	brig	part	timber	South Bay	
Shilleagh 4-4-1818	UK	brig	total	general cargo	Bar of Wexford	
General Moore	UK	brig	part	coal	Bar of Wexford	
Anon	Danish	brig	part	timber	Bar of Wexford	
Anon	Portugese	brig	total	ballast	South Bay	
Hector	UK	brig	total	ballast	Bar of Wexford	10
Hector	UK	brig	total	wine	Blackwater Bank	10
Swallow	UK	sloop	part	grain	South Bay	2
Calcutta	UK	ship	part	general cargo	Blackwater Bank	
Wild Irish girl	UK	sch	part	general cargo	Blackwater Bank	
Fair Reaper 10-4-1816	UK	cutter	total	general cargo	Blackwater Bank	
Abionia	US	ship	total	general cargo	Blackwater Bank	
Sochol	Russian	ship	total	glass & delph	North Bay	
Peggy	UK	brig	total	general cargo	North Bay	
Hunter	UK	ship	total	general cargo	North Banks	
Twilight	UK	sch	part	potash	North Bay	
Ann	UK	brig	part	general cargo	North Bay	
Eliza	UK	sloop	part	copper ore	North Bay	
Maryanne	UK	sch	part	grain	North Bay	3
Coquetea	UK	brig	total	sugar	Blackwater Bank	
Hawk	French	sch	part	grain	Blackwater Bank	15
Flora	UK	ship	total	sugar	Blackwater Bank	
Georgina 17-3-1844*	UK	ship	total	general cargo	Blackwater Bank	
Ariadne 25-11-1838*	UK	ship	part	timber	Blackwater Bank	
Paragon	UK	brig	total	general cargo	North Bay	
James Mathison	UK	ship	total	general cargo	Blackwater Bank	6
Jeager	UK	ship	total	general cargo	Blackwater Bank	
Albert	UK	ship	total	ballast	Blackwater Bank	
Julianna	UK	ship	total	cotton wool	Long Bank	
Indian Chief	UK	ship	total	general cargo	Blackwater Bank	
Betsey	UK	ship	total	ballast	Blackwater Bank	9
Baron Ardrossan	UK	ship	total	copper ore	Blackwater Bank	4
Hudlah	UK	sch	part	grain	Blackwater Bank	
Arnan	UK	ship	total	general cargo	Blackwater Bank	
zeno	UK	ship	total	general cargo	Blackwater Bank	
St Salvatore	Italian	ship	total	general cargo	Blackwater Bank	

Name Date(added)	Origin	Type	Loss	Cargo	Location	Lost
Water Witch*	UK	brig	total	general cargo	Blackwater Bank	4
Anon	Swedish	brig	total	steam engines	Blackwater Bank	
Merchant 11-5-1835	UK	brig	total	mahogony	Blackwater Bank	
Margaret*	US	ship	total	iron	Blackwater Bank	
Minerva	UK	ship	total	general cargo	Blackwater Bank	
Margaret	UK	sch	total	coal	Blackwater Bank	
Argyle 30-1-1834	UK	brig	total	sugar	Blackwater Bank	
Margaret	US	ship	part	lumber	Blackwater Bank	
Horatio	UK	brig	part	general	Blackwater Bank	
Crown	UK	ship	total	ballast	Blackwater Bank	10
Barrack	UK	brig	part	timber	Blackwater Bank	
Wellington	UK	brig	total	general cargo	Blackwater Bank	12
Neptune	UK	sloop	part	grain	Blackwater Bank	
Perseverance	UK	sch	total	grain	Blackwater Bank	6
Mercury	UK	sch	total	coal	Blackwater Bank	
Expendition	UK	sch	total	slates	Blackwater Bank	
Blackbird	UK	sloop	total	grain & bales	Blackwater Bank	
Sprightly	UK	sloop	total	salt	Blackwater Bank	
Laura	UK	brig	total	ballast	Blackwater Bank	
Anon	US	brig	part	salt	Blackwater Bank	
Venus	UK	steamer	total	general cargo	Blackwater Bank	
Shilmalier	UK	ship	part	timber	Long Bank	
Vine	UK	sch	total	malt	Ballyhealy	
Ilyacinth	UK	brig	total	coal	Blackwater Bank	
Slaney	UK	brig	part	timber	Bar of Wexford	
Elizabeth	UK	smack	part	genral cargo	Carew Island	
Mary 6-2-1837*	UK	sloop	total	salt	Kilmore	

Additional list from the Wexford Guardian of 19-7-1851 supplementing 1846 list.
Wrecks from 1846-1850.

Name Date(added)	Origin	Type	Cargo	Location
Jacob Pennell 21-2-1846*	US	ship	cotton	Carnsore
Iride 22-2-1846*	Spanish	ship	fruit	Tacumshane
Templeman	UK	ship	specie, copper tobacco	Kilmore
Macao 23-1-1847*	UK	ship	grain flour	
Maria*	Spanish	ship	sugar	Carnsore
Niobe 26-1-1847*	US	ship	Indian corn	Bannow
Rochester	UK		Passengers	Blackwater
Tribune 27-10-1847	UK	sc steamer		Tacumshane
Leventine (Laventeen)	UK	sc steamer	general cargo	Ballygeary
L'Active	French		Wheat	Tacumshane
St James	US		Cotton	Kilmore
Morca	Spanish		Wheat	Kilmore
Rambler	UK		General cargo	Tacumshane
Amelia	Greek		Indian corn	Bannow
Brittannia	UK		General cargo	Ballyhack
Invincible	Austrain		Indian corn	Cullenstown
Seagull	UK		wheat	Tacumshane
Gazelle	UK		timber	Ballinoulart
Adile 13-1-1850*	French		flour	White Hole
Guster Udolph 13-1-1850*	Danish		Indian corn	Ballyhire
Fairfax 30-1-1850*	Uk		Palm oil	Ballyteigue

Name Date(added)	Origin	Type	Cargo	Location
Horatio 1-2-1850*	UK		Wheat	Kilmore
Otto	German		Flour	Ballytrent
John R Skiddy 1-4-1850*	US		Passengers	Glascarrig
Adeline 19-11-1850*	US		Passengers	Blackwater
Strabane 19-11-1850*	UK	ship	general cargo	Blackwater
Magoline 19-2-1850*	UK	ship	general cargo	Curracloe
Shamrock	UK	ship	general cargo	Morris Castle
Veloz	Spanish		general cargo	Ballyhealy
Leipa Zaritza	Austrian	ship	guano	Kilmore
Anon	UK			Long Bank
Hottingeur 12-1-1850*	US		passengers	Blackwater
Agenoria	UK	coaster	Indian corn	Long Bank
Anon	UK	smack	salt	Ballyhire
Anon	UK	sch	wheat	Ballyhire
Anon	UK	sch	coal	Tacumshane
Amon	UK	sch	coal	Ballyvaloo

WEXFORD/SALTEES

Antelope

The American ship Antelope was wrecked on the Saltees about 1885. Her timbers were salvaged and constructed into a new schooner by Wexford Dockyard Co. Later she was wrecked at Dollymount.

Privateer

A merchantman was pursued into Ballyteigue Bay by a pirate vessel according to local legend. The pirate anchored for the night confident that the merchantman was at his mercy. But the wily captain prepared a raft with lights and doused the ship's lights. The raft was carried by the strong tide towards the northern end of the little Saltee. The pirate followed lest his prey should escape. The raft floated over the rocks of St Patrick's Bridge but the pirate ship struck a submerged rock and foundered. Many pirates were drowned and buried on the island. This was regarded as a tale until about 1970 when Mr Devreux, a local fisherman, trawled guns and cutlasses from the reputed location of the wreck. One of the cutlasses is in Aidan Kelly's pub in Wexford Town. A pirate ship was also wrecked at Slade.

Water Witch

The Water Witch rock east of St Patrick's Bridge is named after the steamer lost there in a storm on 21-12-1833. The Water Witch was built at Liverpool in 1833 and wrecked after only six months in service. Captain Stacey was in command. She left Bristol for Waterford with 42 aboard but suffered damage which was repaired at Tenby. The compass was four points out and this caused the error in navigation. When the vessel struck (a mile from the shore) at St Patrick's Bridge the longboat was damaged. The jollyboat reached shore with the passengers and fishing boats rescued the crew from rafts. In the same storm two fishing boats were wrecked in Wexford harbour. (68, 2)

Victory

The paddle steamer Victory was built in 1832 at Liverpool for the St George Co. The 256 ton, 152 foot ship had three masts schooner rigged as well as steam engines. Her figurehead represented a lion. She was sold to a Waterford Co in 1846. On 30-9-1853 she sunk after striking the Barrels rock en route from Liverpool to Waterford. Captain Stacey backed off and the pumps were started. After three hours journey towards Waterford she sank in 20 fathoms near St Patrick's Bridge. Her crew took to the boats and one man was drowned coming ashore. The Victory was returning empty from Liverpool having carried troops there from Waterford. Her Captain was a nephew of the captain of the Water Witch lost nearby 20 years previously. (68,2)

Goacuetta
This French barquentine was wrecked on 28-11-1908 on St Patrick's Bridge. She was carrying general cargo. (2) (NF161)

Brackley
The Wicklow schooner Brackley was wrecked on the Blue Rocks or Mageen Rocks east of St Patrick's Bridge on 28-9-1928. She carried coal from Garston to Glandore. During a storm she sprang a leak off the Lucifer lightship. While difficult to control she ran onto the rocks. The master, John Wall, and her crew of three were rescued by Kilmore Quay lifeboat. (161)

Cluny
This Milford steam trawler was wrecked on St Patrick's Bridge. After refusing to leave the stricken vessel for some days the crew were rescued on 2-5-1927. The wreck could be boarded at low tide after she drifted onto the beach. (161)

Citizen of Youghal
On 25-12-1895 this 184 ton brigantine carrying coal was wrecked at the tip of the Little Saltee. Captain Lynch and one of a crew of six were lost. The lifeboat saved four. She was en route from Newport to Youghal.

Lennox
On 18-1-1917 the 6,500 ton SS Lennox was wrecked on the Collough rocks south of the Great Saltee. Her crew of 45 were saved by the Kilmore lifeboat. Among her crew were 34 Chinamen who sold their watches in local pubs and shops. Boiler lining bricks marked Lennox are still found at the spot.

Monmouth
The 49 ton Milford steam trawler Monmouth was wrecked on the Saltees on 22-12-1895.

Grace
The Preston ship Grace was wrecked at St Patrick's Bridge on 16-1-1851. Two of her crew were lost. The figurehead at the Wexford museum at Enniscorthy attributed to Mary Grace may be from this ship

Lady Rebow
On 7-1-1860 the 86 ton Lady Rebow of London was wrecked at St Patrick's Bridge. She was caught by a storm en route from St Michael's with a cargo of oranges. The same day another wreck occurred at Kilmore. (68)(73)

Faerie Queen
The 183 ton schooner Faerie Queen was wrecked on rocks at the Little Saltee Island on 21-12-1867. She was en route from Liverpool to Liberia with general cargo which included muskets and gunpowder. A fire broke out which caused alarm due to the danger from the cargo. Captain Pearson was censured as despite the wind and thick weather he had neglected to take soundings which would have revealed the danger. The vessel was owned by Hatton and Cookson of Liverpool.

Valdura
On 12-1-1926 the Valdura ran aground on The Forlorn. She carried a cargo of 4,500 tons of maize. When this was washed ashore farmers from miles around assembled to gather up this "yellow meal" for cattle food. Photos of

the wreck high and dry are in the Wooden House, Kilmore Quay.

Brother Jonathan
The 280 ton, 250 hp tug Brother Jonathan was wrecked on the Saltees on 30-1-1879. She was built at Preston in 1857. She sunk in the Mersey but was raised and sold to the Queenstown Towing Company. She left Queenstown on 29-12-1879 towing the barque Kate Kearney to London. The barque was en route from Boston to London with peas and flour. The Brother Jonathan developed leaks and put in to Queenstown where she took on extra hands to help with the pumps. In a WSW gale the tow was slipped. The tug was in some distress at this stage and she steered for the Coningbeg light vessel. She grounded at the point of one of the Saltees and quickly broke up. The Coningbeg fired rockets but otherwise gave no help. A sailor named Hurley and the second engineer were washed ashore astride a paddle box but no others survived. The engineer died later. The captain Thomas Griffiths is buried at the cemetery at Grange. (67)

Haaswater
This 838 ton vessel grounded on the Forlorn point on 7-4-1898 in fog. The tug Wexford failed to refloat her and the tug Ida also tried to assist. The vessel was full of water and developed a list before breaking up. She was en route from Liverpool to Natal in ballast. (161)

Isabella
The 131 ton Cork schooner Isabella was wrecked at the Saltees (Lavender Rk) on 18-12-1855. She was bound for Cork from Newport with 130 tons of coal. She struck St Patrick's Bridge and went to pieces. Captain McNamara and the crew got ashore on some wreckage. One man was crushed by a spar but the coastguard saved the others. A bell dated 1841 Baltimore, at the Enniscorthy museum may be from this ship. (55)(132)

Isabella
On 3-1-1869 the 172 ton brig Isabella foundered 2 miles S of the Saltees. She carried coal from Newport to Waterford. Of the crew of 7 two were lost.

Isabella
On 29-12-1873 the Isabella of Waterford was wrecked near Greenore. The voyage was from Troon to Waterford with 280 tons of coal. Captain Whelan and the crew escaped in the ship's boats.

Bon Accord
The 600 ton Bon Accord en route from Penang to London was wrecked at the Saltees on 19-12-1855. She was observed from the mainland sinking at anchor. Only her main royal masts showed. Captain Sayer and the crew of 25 were saved by Mr Parle the tenant of the island. A court case occurred on 31-1-1856. Mr Parle's award for salvage of £760 by the Wexford court was reduced to £60 on appeal at the Admiralty court in Dublin. Her cargo was 350 puncheons of rum, hides, sugar and spices. (132) On 19-12-1885 a 60 ton schooner also sank off Ballyteigue.

Bubona
The brig Bubona of Hartlepool was sank near the Saltees on 21-12-1860. She carried pig iron from Ardrossan to Havre. About nine miles SSW of Tuskar the crew realised that they could not pump out water fast enough to save the vessel. The Gleaner answered their flags of distress and stood by. Captain Chudleigh and the crew were saved by the Gleaner of Glouster and landed at Warrenpoint. (55)(132)

Auguste Maurice
The 96 foot French trawler Auguste Maurice of L'Orient was wrecked on the

Saltees on 28-12-1957. She struck Ebba reef NW of the Great Saltee and was observed from the shore. The Kilmore Quay lifeboat was launched with great difficulty and located the stricken trawler in Ballyteigue Bay. In three runs past the wreck, she rescued the captain and crew of 11, Two were snatched from the sea. The remains of the trawler were washed ashore at Kilmore Quay.

Goelta
The bell of the Goelta, Swansea dated 24-12-1877 is on display at the Wooden House, Kilmore Quay. The 2473 ton Goelta ran ashore in fog near Rosslare on 1-12-1929. On 14-12-1929 she was refloated and brought to Dublin for repair. (99)

Palmer
On 26-12-1823 the new schooner Palmer of Whitehaven was wrecked at St Patrick's Bridge. The cargo of oats and flour were bound for Liverpool from Wexford. Captain Wolf and his crew were lost. (60)

Wayfarer
The 1321 ton, 212 foot iron sailing ship Wayfarer went ashore at the Haven between Kilmore and St Patrick's Bridge in 1871. She carried a ballast of flint. The wreck was auctioned on 30-3-1871. She was en route from London to Liverpool and had been built at Chester in 1860. (132)

Glide
The Waterford ship Glide was wrecked off Kilmore on 20-2-1874. Her crew were saved.

La Vifrido
The Spanish screw steamer La Vifrido sank after striking the East Brandie rock on the Saltees on 23-5-1863. The ship was bound for Liverpool with a cargo of fruit, wine and cattle. The ship ran on the rocks and became wedged. A local vessel went to assist manned by Msrs Rochford and Kehoe. The engineer of the Vifrido was a Scotsman and he asked them to stand by overnight. A fee of a hundred pounds was demanded and negotiations reduced this to forty pounds. The vessel suddenly broke in two. Captain Arnot, the crew of 31 and two passengers were rescued by the Petrel of Kilmore which towed the ships boats ashore.

Irlam
The Irlam captained by Mr Keyser was wrecked near the Saltees on 10-5-1812. The ship was en route from Barbados to Liverpool with troops. One report says four were lost but the local papers say over 100 troops were drowned. (110)

Invercauld
The 1416 ton sailing ship Invercauld was discovered at a depth of 40 metres half a mile west of Conningmore rocks. The ship was believed to have been captured and torpedoed on 22-1-1917 by a German submarine. The crew survived. Local opinion believes that the Invercauld struck the Coningbeg rocks. The Invercauld was built in 1891 and owned by George Milne & Co.

Machaevelli
The 485 ton barque Machaevelli was wrecked between the Saltees on 31-12-1881. The twelve aboard were saved. The cargo was boxwood from Tangrog for Liverpool.

Victory
On 28-9-1853 the steamship Victory was lost off Tuskar Rock.

Theressa
The Theressa of Venice was wrecked on Tuskar on 4-10-1852. The Captain, mate and owner's son as well as a Cork pilot were drowned.

Euphemia
The barque Euphemia was wrecked at

Tuskar on 13-12-1872. She was en route from Quebec to Scotland.

River Krishna

On 7-1-1874 the River Krishna was wrecked at Tuskar Rock. The 1068 ton iron vessel struck the South rock three quarters of a mile from the lighthouse. The steam tugs Erin and Thomas Petty went out to assist but could not pull the ship off. Her crew took to the boats and were picked up. The cargo consisted of wheat in bags and boxes of borax. The ship was built in 1868. (132)

Shields

The brig Shields of Cork was wrecked on the South Chicken rock at Tuskar on 18-6-1875. The lifeboat was towed out by the tug Thomas Petley and the crew taken off. The steam tugs Captain Blake, Ruby and Captain Ennis lightened the vessel and towed her off. (132)

Dante

The steamship Dante foundered between Tuskar and the Smalls on 30-12-1875. She had been run down by a Norwegian barque. The crew of 22 were lost. The vessel was worth £35,000 and her cargo was valued at £80,000.

Langrigg Hall

On 14-12-1882 the iron barque Langrigg Hall sailed from Liverpool for Calcutta. She was being towed against the wind down St George's Channel when on the 15th; off Tuskar, the tow parted. The barque made sail but struck on the South Rock when wearing off. She broke in two and the captain and 23 crew was lost. Two rowed ashore near Wexford.

Eurclydon

This large ship ran onto Tuskar Rock on 7-11-1864. None of her crew was lost.

Elanor Todd

The Elanor Todd struck the Baillies on 22-1-1836 and became waterlogged. On 9-2-1861 the Grace Evans of Alnwich

struck the Baillies. She was en route from Barrow to Port Talbot with iron ore. Captain Price and the crew survived. Later she was towed to Waterford. (132)

Stirlingshire

The barque Stirlingshire (365 tons) struck a mile south of Tuskar Rock lighthouse on 30-1-1865. She was en route from West Indies to Liverpool or London with a cargo of sugar, molasses, brandy and rum. The captain and thirteen crew took to the boats. The captain and six crew were lost when their boat was swamped. Though the other boat capsized the crew were saved. Under the supervision of Mr Williams the Lloyds agent the Wexford steam tug Ruby towed the ship to the beach at Ballygeary where she was lightened. The Stirlingshire was eventually brought to Waterford.

Tripoli

The Cunard liner Tripoli struck the South Rock a reef about half a mile SW of Tuskar lighthouse on 17-5-1872 during fog. She was en route from Liverpool to Boston with 328 aboard. She was travelling at full speed and had two pilots aboard. On striking the engineer reversed engines. It was clear that she would sink and all took to the boats. Luckily several steamers were nearby. The Naid took 146 passengers to Dunmore. The Glasgow steamer took 150 German emigrants to Dublin. The Cork steamer Halycon took 28. Her cargo was taken off by two tugs.

White Star

The 2098 ton Liverpool ship White Star was wrecked on 24-12-1883 near Tuskar. Her crew landed on the Tuskar Rock. Her salvage was auctioned on 18-1-1884. (132)

Manchester Market

The British steamship Manchester

Market (4091 tons gross 361 feet) was wrecked on Gipsey Rock off Tuskar on 27-4-1903. Owned by Manchester Liners, she was built by Furness Withy in 1902. She was en route from Manchester to Philadelphia with general cargo. The wreck lies in 8 metres on the west side of the rock pointing SSE. Only 10 feet of water covers the two main boilers of her triple expansion engines. (10)

Fanny

On 31-10-1878 the 153 ton coastguard cutter Fanny was run down by the National steamer Helvetia three miles NE of the Tuskar. Only seven of the 24 crew were saved. The Fanny commissioned in December 1860 was a tender to the Belisle. (132)

Mermiss

On 24-6-1895 the Turkish ship Mermiss was wrecked on Tuskar Rock. She was en route from Glasgow to Constantinople when she struck in fog. Captain Field and the crew were saved by scrambling ashore on the rock. The vessel keeled to port and sank in deeper water despite the work of a diver and the tug Wexford. (132)

Halcyon

The Halcyon (215 feet, 466 tons) was built at Cork in 1860 by George Robinson for the Cork SS Co. The vessel was wrecked on the Tuskar rocks in 1872. the crew and passengers were saved.

Sheerness

The 1273 ton Clyde company Sheerness was wrecked on Tuskar Rock on 3-2-1927. She was en route from Glasgow via Dublin to Waterford for the Clyde company. At 4 a.m. near Tuskar she sprang a leak and began to settle. The crew took to the boats. The first boat lowered badly upsetting the boat and

causing the death of the first officer. The other two boats were filled with the 30 crew. One landed with captain McClean at Ballinoulart. The other was picked up by the Kingston off Arklow. She was built in 1903 by Caledon Shipbuilding Co at Dundee. Her cargo was stout, whiskey and a valuable hunter horse. (159)(10)

Finn MacCoull

In June 1848 the wooden 220 h.p. paddle steamer Finn MacCoull was wrecked on the Tuskar Rock. She was launched at Dumbarton in 1838 for the Dundalk Steampacket Co. She was commanded by Captain John Williams and was on the Portrush to Liverpool run under charter to the Portrush Steampacket Co. (164)

Kincora

On 8-8-1901 the Cunard liner Oceanic ran down and sank the 944 ton Kincora in fog off Tuskar. Seven of the Kincora's crew were drowned. The Kincora was built in 1895 for the Waterford SS Co. The Oceanic herself was lost on 8-9-1914 off the Orkney Islands.

George Bewley

The SS Cormorant collided with the Liverpool coal barque George Bewley off Tuskar on 9-5-1884. The barque was bound for Chile. Capt. Hammond of the George Bewley was injured in the collision and two of the crew were drowned when she sank almost immediately. The Avoca of Dublin and the Minna of Cork rescued the passengers and crew of the Cormorant.

Garrydock

The Garrydock caught fire en route from England to Waterford, year unknown. Captain Cullen of Ballyhack and his crew escaped by boat to Tuskar lighthouse where they were assisted by the lightkeepers. (543, p588)

Covanenter

The schooner Covanenter of Dundee struck a derelict ship at Tuskar on 8-3-1878. Though she sank rapidly the crew were saved. (132)

Topaz

The Wexford schooner Topaz was run down and sunk by the steamer Karina near Tuskar on 3-8-1907. The steamer was identified by its deck housing which the seamen saw receding into the fog. When the Karina returned from its voyage to Africa an inquiry was held. The steamer captain was judged negligent at the inquiry on 3-3-1908.

Ripple

The brig Ripple of Wexford owned by Messrs Allen struck the Tuskar in fog on 16-1-1870. She carried Indian corn from Ibrael in Galletz near Constantinople. She saw Ballycotton and kept off the coast. When she approached Tuskar the bell was not ringing and she struck the rock. The crew escaped into the jolly boat and rowed the 16 miles to Wexford. (132)

St Patrick

The Rosslare to Fishguard ferry St Patrick was bombed and sunk east of Tuskar on 13-6-1941. Captain Fardy and 23 of those aboard were lost. (58)

Gertie

The Liverpool ship Gertie was mined and sunk near Tuskar rock on 8-12-1941. Her crew were picked up by lifeboat from the ship's boat. The Tuskar lighthouse itself was struck by a drifting mine on 3-12-1941. Two of the keepers were killed. (149)

Dream

The 18 ton steam yacht Dream en route from Kingstown to Cowes suffered a burst pipe on 23-2-1883. She was between Tuskar and the Long Bank when the explosion occurred and a piece was blown out of the yacht below the water line. Captain Woodcock and the two crew tried to pump the water out but the vessel sank. The crew escaped in a punt which was being towed. The yacht was owned by Mr Duckett of Carlow and was eight years old. (132)

Mellary

On 15-10-1886 the 1036 ton iron ship Mellary was wrecked on Tuskar Rock. The Captain, Hugh Richards, and all aboard were lost. The Mellary was built in 1869 on the Clyde. (10)

Witch

The 50 foot screw steamer Witch was on passage on 13-7-1851. It was found to be impossible to pass between the Baillies. After a period out of control she ran on Tuskar Rock. Thomas Smith was captain and the owner John Leslie was engineer. They were saved by a rope thrown from the rock. (189)

WEXFORD/BLACKWATER BANK

Irrawaddy

On 13-10-1856 the Irrawaddy was wrecked opposite Cahore Point on the Blackwater Bank. A fleet of local fishing boats was organised by the local coastguards and rescued the crew and passengers as she rapidly broke up. The teak from her hull was used to form the pews at Ballyragget Church. As a result of the near catastrophe a lightship was positioned on the Blackwater Bank the following year.

R.H. Tucker

On 7-9-1868 the R.H. Tucker struck on the Blackwater Bank and caught fire. The crew of 27 were rescued by the lifeboats from Cahore and Courtown. Four of the Curracloe coastguard were drowned in the operation.

Lanarkshire

On the 15-1-1882 the 929 ton

Lanarkshire was lost on the Codling Bank off Wexford. She was en route from the Clyde to Lisbon with coal. The ship was built by Burrell & Son in 1871

Assaye

On 1-6-1867 the Assaye was wrecked near the Blackwater Light. The 783 ton iron ship was owned by J&W Steward of Greenock. She was en route from Demerara to Liverpool with a cargo of rum and sugar when she struck the south point of Tuskar about a mile and a half from the lighthouse. She veered off and kept running in an attempt to reach a port. After eight hours struggle she went down by the bow a quarter of a mile outside the Blackwater lightship. Her crew who had taken to the boats were assisted by the lightship tender. (65)

Somnauth

On 10-12-1860 the Somnauth was wrecked on the Blackwater Bank. (55)

L'Amiable Eliza

This French vessel from St Voast was wrecked on the Blackwater Bank on 6-4-1858. She mistook the Blackwater Lightship for the Saltees and struck the bank. She drove over and sank suddenly. The captain and crew rowed ashore to Morriscastle. (55) (132)

Adoline

The Adoline of New Orleans, an emigrant ship en route from Liverpool to New Orleans, ran aground on the south end of the Blackwater Bank on 19-11-1850 during a storm. The passengers aboard were saved. Initial reports said she carried 500 but this was later denied. The vessel went to pieces rapidly.

Strabane

The Glasgow ship Strabane, master Alexander Browne, was wrecked on the Blackwater Bank at the same time as the Adoline. She was carrying coal and machinery to Aden and Bombay. The

crew were saved but the vessel was thought to be a complete wreck by the Lloyds agent.

Pomona

The emigrant ship Pomona (1181 tons) built in New York by Howland & Frothingham in 1856 was wrecked on a sandbank off Ballyconigar on 28-4-1859. There was a huge number of people seeking passage to America in 1859. The Pomona happened to be at Liverpool and was pressed into service. She left Liverpool for New York on 27th but was off course when the following morning she struck a sandbank seven miles off Ballyconigar. The captain had failed to sight the Tuskar light and ran on the Blackwater Bank. The gale prevented launching boats that night. In the morning her masts were cut away and another vain attempt to launch boats was made. No help came from the shore. Just before dark the ship began to slip off the sandbank. The bower anchor did not hold and the pumps were inadequate. The crew abandoned ship in a whaler. The Pomona sank after a short time with the loss of 388 persons including Captain Merrihew. Meantime the whaler with 18 crew and three passengers reached the coast and raised the alarm. The steam tug Erin set out from Wexford but was too late. Some relics of the Pomona were raised by divers of the Liverpool Salvage Association and are in Enniscorthy museum. Tombs of the victims are in graveyards along a 30 mile stretch of the Wexford coast. Her anchor was raised and placed on the pier at Kilmore Quay.

Freia

The Danish brig Freia grounded on the Dogger Bank on 20-12-1860. She had been en route from Konigsberg to Dublin. A pilot boat and a fishing boat tried to tow her off without success. By this time the seas has worsened and the crew were in danger. The Rosslare lifeboat was towed out by a steam tug and the six crew were taken off. (68)

Timber Shipper

The Timber Shipper went ashore on the Blackwater bank 15 miles north of Rosslare on 18-1-1975. The 369 ton vessel was owned by Nielsen's of London. Her crew were rescued by an Air Corps Helicopter.

Vivandiere

The new sailing ship Vivandiere struck the Blackwater Bank in 1885. She was abandoned by her crew. A local group from Tinnabearna put out and boarded her. They succeeded in bringing her into Wexford with the aid of a tug. (68)

Mobile

The new 1000 ton American ship Mobile of Bath, en route from Liverpool to New Orleans, struck the Blackwater bank on 29-9-1852. She carried 55 passengers and 30 crew. An ENE hurricane blew most of the crew and passengers overboard. Eight seamen and one passenger who were lashed to the mast were rescued when two schooners approached. The Rebecca took five to Glasgow while four more were taken to Wexford. The survivors reported that a large steamer had passed close by, but had not rendered any assistance.

America

The brig America was en route from Quebec to Wexford with timber when she struck the Dogger Bank in a SSE gale on 29-11-1882. The lifeboat was brought out by the steam tug Ruby and effected the rescue with difficulty. The America was built at Prince Edward Island in 1867. (132)

Lydia

The 433 ton Lydia stranded on the Blackwater Bank on 26-11-1860. She was bound for Montevideo from Liverpool with general cargo worth £30,000. Captain Bowler complained that he was ashore only a few days and had not been informed of changes to the Lighthouse signals. Cahore lifeboat tried to put out but the vessel ran towards the beach and the 18 crew were rescued by the coastguards. She was owned by Shand & Co and built in Liverpool in 1841. (132)

Test

The brig Test of Harwich struck the ridge between the Blackwater Bank and Morriscastle on 15-1-1861. This was the spot where the Lydia foundered. The lifeboats from Morriscastle and Cahore were brought on their carriages but the coastguard succeeded in taking off the master John Ellwood and thirteen crew by the rocket apparatus. The Test had been en route from Mauritius to Glasgow with 450 tons of sugar. She broke up in the storm of 30-1-1861. Five or six ships were lost here in a few years. (132) (73)

Racer

The 1696 ton 200 foot, Racer of the Red Cross Line or St George Cross Line was built at Donald McKay & Pickett at Newburyport about 1850. The line was owned by American financiers Govenor Morgan, Francis Cutting and David Ogden. She struck the Blackwater Bank about 1850 and was wrecked. (136)

Cavavile

The French ship Cavavile was wrecked on the Blackwater Bank on 18-12-1768. Captain Ormsby and 27 crew were lost. She was returning to France from Tahiti (58) (158)

Clara

The Clara sank two and a half miles SE of Blackwater Head inside Blackwater Bank on 4-3-1936. The Gronigen ship was en route from Hamburg to Wexford with artificial manure when she struck a sandbank and began to leak. The British steam trawler Encore stood by and eventually began a tow. The Irish Lights tender Ierne arrived and Captain Nairn lowered a boat. The Clara began to sink and in the nick of time Captain Sap, his wife and the crew of five were rescued. (161)

Fame

The 78 ton two masted schooner Fame was wrecked on the Blackwater bank on 18-4-1881. The Fame was built at Banff in 1874 and owned by William Armstrong at Wexford. (192)

WEXFORD/HOOK

Great Lewis

The Great Lewis, flagship of a British fleet, was lost at Hook Head on 24-1-1645. She was engaged in assisting the besieged at the fort at Duncannon. The fort was in the possession of Confederate forces. Preston in charge of 1,500 Royalists had surrounded the fort. They were strongly equipped with artillery and had undermined the fort. Thomas Preston undertook to recapture the fort for a fee of £8000. Captain Beale with four ships, Magdalen, Mayflower, Elizabeth and Great Lewis arrived to assist the besieged Parliamentary forces. He moored his ships under the fort but out of range of the besiegers guns. Beale landed sailors and supplies and concentrated heavy gunfire on the Royalists. During the night a battery of guns were moved by the Royalists and they fired on the ships at first light. The ships cut their cables and escaped. The flagship was caught by adverse tide and wind and suffered heavy mortar fire. Her masts were shot down. The ship drifted out of range but was so damaged that it sank

with the loss of most of the crew near the Hook. Beale sailed in another ship to Milford. The fort was captured after a fierce fight on 19-3-1645. (76) Duncannon was again besieged by General Kirk in 1690. It was garrisoned by troops of King James under Capt. Burke. Sir Cloudsley Shovel with 16 frigates forced the surrender of the fort. (76) (145)

Caroline

On 8-1-1852 the barque Caroline went ashore two miles east of Hook lighthouse. She was en route from Galetz to Waterford with Indian corn. The ship broke up in two hours but the crew escaped in the longboat. (132)

Royal Arthur

The Royal Arthur was wrecked at Bannow in February 1864. She carried a cargo of copper and silver ore and ivory as walrus tusks.

King Arthur

On 31-12-1878 the 1211 ton King Arthur was wrecked at Ballymadder after striking a rock at Bannow. She was bound for Liverpool from Charleston with cotton. The mate was described as having swum ashore with his cat upon his head in a bundle of clothes. The wreck lay visible on the beach until the early 1950s. (66) (2) Two other ships barely survived the storm. The Swedish Nanny got off the Bannow Bank which she struck en route from Charleston to Fleetwood. The Sarah and Susannah from Rangoon to Liverpool with rice reached Passage demasted and leaking.

Jean Gildis

The trawler Jean Gildis sprang a leak, lost power and drifted ashore on rocks 300 yards from Baginbun Head on 1-1-1964. Three of those aboard swam ashore and the other six were assisted ashore.

Croghan
Photo: Robin Leigh

Croghan

The 900 ton Croghan commanded by Capt. Kearns of Arklow was en route from Waterford to Sharpness when she struck the rocks at Hook on 1-3-1973. The vessel was badly holed and abandoned. She was refloated on 20-3-1973 by Mr Doyle of Coolbarrow but the pumps were inadequate and she went down 100 yards from the shore. Of the salvage crew of six one was lost.

Emma C Beale

The Emma C Beale was driven on rocks near the Hook tower on 14-4-1879. She was bound for Boston from Liverpool. The pilot and eight crew were rescued by the Liverpool tug Kingfisher. (66)

Shadinsay

The 158 ton Scottish coaster Shadinsay en route to the West Indies sunk at Hook Head on 9-11-1967. Captain Henderson had converted an Icelandic trawler and intended to use her in the West Indies for coastal trading. She was en route from the Clyde to St Vincent when she was driven on the rocks at Hook Lighthouse. The captain swam ashore with a line and the four crew followed safely.

Schlesien

The 303 ton German trawler Schlesien was wrecked at Hook Head on 19-2-1966. The crew of 15 swam ashore without assistance. Built in 1955 the ship was owned at Bremen. She went ashore in fog about 400 yards from Hook lighthouse. The German tug Atlantic tried to salvage the trawler but she sank.

Polynxa

The Polynxa was wrecked at Baginbun on 13-1-1873 (55)

St Margaret

The Heiton's collier St Margaret built in 1889 by McIlwaine, Lewis & Co at Belfast was lost off Hook Point. On 7-12-1919 all the crew were lost she carried coal from Troon for Waterford.

Alfred D Snow

The Alfred D Snow was wrecked at Broomhill on 4-1-1888. She was driven ashore on sandbanks at Broomhill. She had sailed from San Francisco for Liverpool with grain and was 140 days at sea. The coastguard considered it too dangerous to put out their boat. Assistance was rendered by the Dauntless but Captain Willie and 24 crew were drowned. (58)

Turtledove or Turtur

In December 1559 a Dutch ship the Turtledove was driven ashore on rocks at Fethard. She was en route from Spain to Antwerp. The captain made a deal with Alexander Bishop of Ferns and New Ross, merchants, to salvage the cargo of merchandise for a fee of a third of the profits. Her home port was Purmaren in Zeeland. (156)

Glenmalure

The 56 foot trawler Glenmalure (skipper Bates) of Kilmore Quay was wrecked on 26-11-1970. She left Kilmore to escape the storm at Duncannon. She was washed onto the rocks at Hook and struck at the same spot as the trawler Naomh Seosamh 14 years previously.

Jack Buchan

The trawler Jack Buchan capsized 300 yards off Ballyhack on 11-2-1958. She struck rocks not long after leaving Dunmore East. Five crew were lost.

Arethusa

On 7-1-1860 the Arethusa of Glasgow was wrecked at Bannow. The 322 ton vessel was built at Greenock in 1828 and owned by Dunlop & Co. She was en route from Zarza in Cuba to Hall's of Liverpool with tobacco, mahogany and lancewood. Captain Thomas Martin and his crew of 15 had a difficult voyage. They grounded on leaving port on October 10th and encountered rough

weather on 19 November. The vessel started making water and continuous pumping was necessary. Provisions ran short and were augmented by passing vessels. They reached the Irish coast and could not weather the Hook. They let go their port anchor in Fethard Bay off Baginbun and signalled for a pilot. The captain went ashore to Waterford for tow from a steamer. The anchor dragged and the second anchor was dropped. The vessel ran ashore onto rocks. One seaman who could not swim was drowned. The coastguard assembled to protect the cargo as 200 bales of tobacco were washed ashore. The duty alone on the tobacco was £7,000. The locals however were not short of a smoke despite the efforts of the authorities. (68) (73)

Sally

The Sally of Aberdovy went ashore at St Margaret's Bay near Carne Point on 28-12-1822. No crew were left aboard when she struck and there was no news of them. She had sailed from Liverpool in November according to her manifest with timber, linen, window glass, and iron. The goods were removed to the King's store as salvaged wreck.

Ankair

The Ankair was wrecked between Bannow church and Bannow Island in a storm about 1838. Fourteen of her crew were drowned. Three Greeks survived. (135, 481,p334)

Columbus

On 6-1-1852 the 1849 ton Columbus was wrecked by a storm at Killoggan Bay a half mile west of the Hook tower. She carried 3800 bales of cotton and 5000 bushels of Indian corn from New Orleans to Liverpool. The incident occurred during an eclipse(135, 591, pl35). Of 33 aboard thirteen were lost. The ship had not been met by the Waterford Pilots and ran aground while signalling for their assistance. Later in 1852 the Glenville Bay ran ashore at the Hook allegedly due to lack of a pilot. (119) (132)

Watchet

In a gale on 18-7-1873 the schooner Watchet stranded at the Hook Tower. The crew were saved by the Fethard coastguard. She was en route from Ilfracomb to Waterford. (66)

Kinsale

The Clyde Shipping Co sail and steam ship Kinsale broke its engine shaft on 21-11-1872. She left Waterford for Glasgow via Cork on 19-11-1872 with nine passengers and a cargo of ale, bacon and biscuits. She lost her rudder off Mine Head and a jury rudder was fitted. Driven back by the gale she made for Waterford. As she reached Duncannon the strain on the engine shaft caused it to snap. Captain Anderson made for Passage and anchored. When the anchors dragged she was driven ashore at the cliffs inside Hook. The ship came to rest with Hell Hole at her bow and Cotton Hole at the stern. The mate was the first ashore by the coastguards rocket apparatus but the line snapped. Only two more of the nineteen crew were saved when they scaled the cliffs aided by the strong wind which kept them pressed against the cliff face. One of the passengers, a girl named Dunphy also made her way ashore. The cargo was plundered by the crowd which gathered. The bell of the Kinsale hung above the entrance to Duncannon school yard. (66) (58)

Re di Spagna

The 502 ton Italian ship Re di Spagna was wrecked on the rocks at Duncannon on 23-11-1872. She was bound for Queenstown for orders and carried 750 tons of wheat from Borletta. Captain Nicolich and 14 of his 17 crew were eventually rescued after some initial confusion when they did not understand the operation of the coastguard apparatus. Three men were drowned when they were dropped in the sea as the rope on a breeches buoy broke. (66)

Panope

The Panope of Foway sank off Hook tower on 30-1-1865. Captain Walter Bull was saved by a pilot boat and landed at Dunmore. (66)

Victory

The Cork brig Victory was wrecked at Dollar Bay near Duncannon on 13-2-1881. She carried a cargo of coal bound for her home port of Cork. (66)

Sarah H Bell

On 7-2-1861 the Halifax barque Sarah H Bell was wrecked in Fethard Bay inside the bar of Bannow. The six crew were saved and sent home by the Shipwrecked Mariners Society. She was en route from Boston to Liverpool with logwood. (132)

Margaret

On 17-3-1911 the ketch Margaret of Glouster struck inside the Hook. She carried a cargo of coal from Newport for Waterford and was a total loss.

Golden Star

The Golden Star struck rocks half a mile from the Coninbeg on 29-12-1860. She travelled for two miles and dropped anchors. Captain Staples cut away the masts. The anchor chains parted and she drifted ashore at Carravane between Fethard and Hook. The coastguard tried to assist but 18 of the crew were drowned. Five survived by drifting ashore on bales of cotton. She carried 4030 bales of cotton from Mobile from where she sailed at the end of November for Liverpool. (132) (135,1399 p580)

WATERFORD

Unknown 1890-1900
Wigham Collection via Bill Swanton

WATERFORD

Morning Star

The schooner Morning Star of Wick was wrecked on 9-2-1874 under Ballymacarthy. She was bound for Dungarvan with a cargo of salt. Her crew were four men and a boy. The mate swam ashore and raised the alarm but the lifeboat could not go out due to the storm. The only survivors, the mate and the boy, were assisted by the lighthouse keeper, Mr Kennedy.

Seahorse

The transport Seahorse built in 1784 was wrecked in Tramore Bay on 30-1-1816. The vessel sailed from Ramsgate for Cork on 25-1-1816 carrying 15 sailors, 74 women and children and 279 soldiers of the 2nd/59 Regiment. The troops were recently returned from the Napoleonic wars in the Peninsula and the Continent. The convoy consisted of the Seahorse and two other ships Boadecia and Lord Melville, which were wrecked near Kinsale. An easterly gale arose while the ships crossed the Irish Sea and the only sailor who knew the coast fell from the rigging and broke his legs. The ship was unable to weather Brownstown Head and soon lost her masts and rudder. Though her anchors were let out she struck about a mile out in Tramore Bay. Only 30 survived and there is a memorial in

Christ Church Drumcannon. A memorial plaque is set into the cliff face on the Doneraile walk opposite the site of the disaster. The Waterford Ballast Board built pillars as navigation markers between 1820 and 1823. Two columns were placed on Brownstown head and three on Newtown Head because of the number of ships lost in the area. (186)

Henry

The brig Henry was wrecked on the rocks at Ballinacourty lighthouse on 8-2-1874. Captain Evans and the four crew were rescued. The cargo was coal bound for Youghal. (67)

Morning Star

The Morning Star was wrecked on a reef at Dunabrattain strand on 7-10-1915. She was built at Aberystwyth by Jones & Co in 1877 and owned by Fitzpatricks of Cork. She was en route to Cork from Cardiff with coal. Captain Christopher and three of the four crew were lost. (102)

San Spheredione

The 200 ton Spanish brig San Spheredione was wrecked at the eastern end of Tramore bay half a mile from Rhine shark on 11-2-1861. She had taken grain from Taganrog to London and was returning from Swansea to Barcelona with coal. One seaman tried to get ashore with a line but perished. The lifeboat was launched in treacherous conditions with an amateur crew. It overturned but righted and the crew were saved by their cork belts. The ships crew escaped to the rigging and the lifeboat was launched a second time. The master Ephemus Cazzulie and four seamen were saved but six were lost.

Galexede

The Greek ship Galexede of Patras was wrecked at Tramore on 9-2-1861. She had been blown 100 miles west of Cape

Clear then the SSW gale blew her back to Tramore. She was owned by Mr Carpatha of Constantinople and was built in 1847.

Oasis

The large iron ship Oasis went aground on the rocks west of the metal man near Newtown Head, Tramore on 11-1-1868. Twenty of the crew were rescued. One crewman was left on the mast overnight and taken off the following day. It was not clear if this crewman was alive as all attempts to attract his attention had failed until the crowd of 1500 onlookers were organised to cheer together. The seaman immediately took notice and secured the line fired to him allowing his rescue. A further seven crew had put off in a boat and were lucky to be found and rescued by fishermen from Slade near St Patrick's Bridge. (67) (66)

Jeune Austerlitz

The Jeune Austerlitz of Cardiff went on the rocks in Ardmore bay on 14-2-1895. She was carrying coal from Cardiff to New Ross. Her captain mistook Mine Head for the Hook during a southerly gale. Captain Cremin and his crew of four were taken ashore by the coastguards rocket rescue apparatus but one died afterwards.

Dunvegan

On 19-1-1898 the 778 ton three masted sailing barque Dunvegan went ashore at the cliff at Ballymacart, Old Parish. She was en route from Barry Dock to New Orleans with coal and general cargo. The ship went ashore in fog. Members of the Nugent family descended the cliff and helped rescue Captain George Bell and his crew. The wreck was purchased by Mr Fuge of Glencorran House and the cargo and furnishings taken off. (102)

Swift

The Swift was stranded near Dungarvan

on 30-12-1822. She was en route from Banff to Bristol with oranges from St Michaels. All the crew were saved. The preventive water guard from Helvic prevented the plunder of the cargo.

Moresby

On 1-1-1896 the recriminations concerning the wreck of the Moresby reached a peak when a local public meeting called for an inquiry into the behaviour of the lifeboat crews. Built by Whitehaven Shipbuilding Company in 1882 the 1259 ton iron vessel was wrecked at Dungarvan on 24-12-1895. She left Cardiff for South America with 1778 tons of coal, a crew of 23 and the captain's wife and child. The next day a storm arose and she sought shelter. She followed the Mary Sinclair into the bay thinking it was Cork. The Mary Sinclair ran aground at Clonea Castle two miles from Ballinacourty lighthouse. Her crew were rescued by the Bunmahon coast-guard rockets. As the Moresby was heading into danger at Carrickapane rock the lighthouse keepers instructed her to anchor. The crew thought themselves safe and refused the assistance of Ballinacourty lifeboat who apparently did not appraise them of their perilous position. The wind rose and the crew of the Moresby realising their danger fired distress signals. Mr Cullinan, the lifeboat secretary, signalled the lifeboat crew to launch but the crew did not respond. The coastguard made unsuccessful efforts with their rockets and then tried unsuccessfully to recruit a volunteer crew from over 100 spectators. By this time the Moresby had keeled over on the Whitehouse Bank. The surviving crew took to the rigging and some swam for the shore. Eventually a Dungarvan crew launched and took seven survivors from the water. Two of these died along with

eighteen others. It was not clear why the lifeboat crew behaved as they did but the secretary resigned. (66) (102)

Twin Brothers

On 5-4-1909 the 83 foot two masted schooner Twin Brothers was wrecked at the mouth of Dungarvan Harbour. Built at Liverpool in 1865 she was owned by Mr Hereford of Barrow in Furness. She was en route from Newport to Dungarvan with coal and was caught by SE squalls. Captain Patrick Whelan and the crew of three survived.

Folia

On 11-3-1917 the 6705 ton four masted two funnel Cunard liner Folia was torpedoed four miles ESE of Rams Head near Ardmore. She was en route from the US to Southampton with trench digging machines, empty shell cases and general cargo. Seven of her 103 officers and crew were missing when the captain called the roll on the pier at Ardmore. The wreck was depth charged by a torpedo boat a few days later when bubbles were observed rising from the sunken ship. Two salvage vessels worked on the wreck in Summer 1977; these were Taurus of Hamburg and Risdon Beazley's salvage ship Twyford of Southampton. (118) (102)

Sara Dixon

Before the turn of the century the Sara Dixon disappeared while at anchor between Ballynacourty Point and Gainor rocks. One theory proposed that the pounding of the seas tore off her bow. Another theory was that she struck under the cliffs at Ballyvoile and was buried by the rocks which then fell down on her.

Scotland

In 1875 the Scotland was wrecked at Ballymacart. She carried a load of flint stone. Much of this was used by local farmers. (102)

Marechal de Noailles
Photo: Horgan via James Quain.

Marechal de Noailles

The 2166 ton steel barque Marechal De Noailles was wrecked on rocks 200 yards west of Mine Head lighthouse on 14-1-1913. She was en route from Glasgow to New Caledonia with a cargo of coal. The Helvick Lifeboat could not approach the wreck and the 24 crew were saved by breeches buoy on lines sent out by rockets. (102)

Ary

On 14-2-1947 the SS Ary sank near Tuskar. She was en route from Port Talbot to Waterford with coal for the railway to alleviate the desperate shortage. In severe weather her coal shifted and the vessel sank. Though the crew took to the boats there was only one survivor. Several died in an open boat and are buried at St Declans Cemetery at Ardmore. (102)

Cirilo Amoros

On 15-2-1926 the 1600 ton Cirilo Amoros struck the coast between Stradbally and Ballyvooney Coves and became wedged under the cliffs at Gull Island. She was en route from Spain to Liverpool with rice, oranges, china clay and tinned goods. The Hook light was mistaken for Wales due to the bad weather. The rudder was smashed and she drove on the cliffs. At the time of the collision she was going full astern as indicated by a gash in her side. The Stradbally villagers went to assist and Wm O'Brien and Jack O'Keefe bravely took a lifebuoy ashore. This line was followed by a rope and a cable. A sailor brought a line along the rope and the breeches buoy brought the 30 crew ashore safely. The wreck was scrapped on site and a section of the hull is still visible at low tide. (102)

Teaser
Photo: James Quain.

Teaser
The schooner Teaser of Montrose was wrecked at Curragh, Ardmore on 18-3-1911. She was en route from Swansea to Killorglin. Rockets could not reach the three men seen in the rigging. Launching a boat presented difficulties. Despite the heroism of Fr O'Shea and coastguard Barry, Captain Hughes and all hands were lost. (102)

Nellie Fleming
On 18-12-1913 the collier Nellie Fleming bound for Youghal with 250 tons of coal went aground on the Black rock off Curragh in Ardmore bay. Captain Donovan and the crew stayed aboard though lifeboats and coastguards were at hand. They came ashore the next day. The ship was badly holed and the wind rose before the vessel could be lightened and refloated. The coal was purchased by locals and sold by the cartload. The ship floated in the Spring tides and was washed onto the strand at the Ardmore end of the Curragh beach. She lies half buried in the sand. (62)

Pretender's Ship
On 23-7-1497 Perkin Warbeck pretender to the throne of England and Maurice Earl of Desmond besieged Waterford with 2400 men. Waterford was held by forces loyal to the King. Eleven ships arrived at Passage East and two landed men at Lombard's Weir. One enemy ship was bulged and sunk by the ordinance from Dundory. Warbeck escaped to Cork and thence to Kinsale pursued by four ships. He then went to Cornwall still followed by ships loyal to the throne. (76). A cannon with reinforcing rings typical of the period was dredged from

the Suir and is on display at the Reginald's Tower museum in Waterford.

Noel Rhiwan

The sailing ship Noel Rhiwan was assisted by the Upupa during a storm on 10-12-1884. The Upupa took the ship in tow but the tow parted off the Waterford coast. She was en route from Newport to Valparaiso and was dismasted. Contact was lost with the stricken ship. Great concern was caused at Cork by the two day delay in the arrival of the Upupa. A vessel was assisted at Waterford by the Coastguard rockets the next day.

Cornelia Maria

The Dutch vessel Cornelia Maria was sunk in a collision by the German vessel Gustav Borgens off Waterford on 6-1-1959.

Hope

The Youghal sloop Hope bound for Youghal was wrecked off Ardmore Head on 1-1-1823. Captain Clarke and his crew were drowned when their boat overturned as they made for shore.

Kerick

The 150 ton Lorient trawler Kerick was driven aground on 8-12-1969 at Brownstown Head. Seven of the crew escaped onto the rocks while the captain and one other were rescued by the lifeboat.

Peri

The 160 ton Waterford coal schooner Peri was wrecked at Seaview between Helvick and Mine Head on 2-11-1907. She was en route from Newport via Milford to Ballinacurra with a cargo of coal. During a severe storm she was driven ashore. The lookout at Mine Head did not see her and the lifeboat was not called. Her crew of four jumped overboard, two were washed ashore safely but two were dashed on the rocks. Captain Hally was rescued clinging to a

bush on the sheer cliff face. The Peri was built at Sunderland in 1872. The Tregumel also owned by Captain Molony of Cork en route to Dungarvan was lost in the same storm. (102) (161)

Zeus

On 4-1-1875 the brig Zeus of Aberdeen was wrecked near Tramore. She carried a cargo of iron ore from Lisbon to Ardrossan. Captain Wall and his crew with the exception of the mate escaped. (67)

La Capricieuse

The French barque La Capricieuse was driven up on the strand at Rineshark Point at Tramore on 13-2-1858. The Tramore lifeboat was called but meanwhile a yawl put out and took the seven crew aboard. The yawl was overloaded and capsized. The coastguard who were standing by rescued six from the capsized boat and made for shore with a full load. They returned for the others and saved all but two of the gallant fishermen and one seaman. (66)

Peig Thrampton

The three masted ship Peig Thrampton was wrecked during a gale on the rocks at Ardmore. Year is unknown. The captain was lashed to the mast with a purse of gold in his hand. He beseeched the onlookers to save him offering them a reward. No lifeboat could have survived in the seas and all were lost. (135, 84,p9)

Montcalm

The Montcalm of Swansea lost her sails off Credan head and drove on the rocks on 12-10-1870. She was owned by Morgan and Drysdale of Swansea. She was en route from Swansea to Wexford with a cargo of coal. The crew took to the boats just before she sank and landed safely at Waterford. (66)

Fee des Ondes
Photo: James Quinn

Fee des Ondes

On 27-10-1963 the 300 ton French trawler Fee des Ondes was wrecked 300 metres from Ardmore Head in Ardmore Bay east of Youghal. Despite the efforts of the tug Utrecht, and the Youghal and Helvick lifeboats to tow her clear, the trawler went aground. Most of the crew escaped in their boat and two were rescued by the lifeboat.

Fanny

On 3-1-1875 the collier Fanny was stranded in Tramore Bay. The vessel was en route from Cardiff to Bermuda with a cargo of coal. The crew reported that the captain was in the horrors from drink and had steered towards land. The mate wanted to signal distress but had been prevented from doing so. Eventually the crew tied the captain to a door and

signalled for help. The lifeboat took off the mate and five crew as well as the captain.

Harriet Collins

The brig Harriet Collins was wrecked at Woodstown Strand on 1-1-1823. She carried timber from St Johns NB to Liverpool. The pilot went out to take the vessel to safety but her anchor cable parted. A second anchor did not hold her in time to prevent her beaching.

Submarine UC 44

The German minelaying submarine UC 44 was operating with her relief off the Waterford coast during 1917. She was mine laying before her return to base when she failed to rendezvous with her sister submarine. This missed meeting was fatal as she struck a mine laid by the other submarine off Dunmore. Captain

Tibbenjohann and two others were blown out of the conning tower while the other 18 crew went down with the ship. The captain was picked up by a local boat which went out to the scene of the explosion. The two other bodies were found at Slade and Garrarus. The submarine was raised by the British and examined for some time. Documents revealed the operating methods of the submarines in the Dover strait. As a result shallow mines were laid to counter the submarines on the surface at night. The raid on Zeebrugge which placed blockships in the harbour was organised to finally inactivate the submarine base at Bruges. Afterwards UC-44 was taken out and dumped a mile outside Dunmore. In 1930 there were complaints of the obstruction on the seabed and a diver was sent out to inspect the wreck. He reported that there was 20 feet of water over the wreck at low tides and the main portion was covered in mud. Nevertheless a decision was made to remove the submarine. (127, 221)

Ibis

The Belgian motor trawler Ibis was lost on Green Island near Dunmore East in a SSW gale on 28-2-1941.

Johannah Matilda

The barque Johannah Matilda was a casualty of the gale of February 1874. She was driven ashore and became a complete wreck near Waterford. Barrels of tallow were washed ashore near Waterford on 28-2-1874 presumably from yet another loss. (66)

Stowell Brown

On 13-2-1884 Captain Pearson of the steamer Waterford brought news that a large four masted ship was flying distress signals near the Saltees. The next day the Stowell Brown a 1300 ton barque reached the mouth of Waterford harbour

firing distress rockets. She was en route from Cardiff to Rio De Janeiro with coal. While following the pilot cutter up the river for shelter she ran aground a little below the bar and sunk in mid channel. The crew of 23 were saved and landed at Passage. Captain Smith reported that they encountered SW gales and waves were sweeping the deck. They had made two feet of water per day. This extra draught may have explained the grounding. (66)

Earl of Beaconsfield

On 14-2-1884 the Earl of Beaconsfield was abandoned by her crew east of Waterford when she was in imminent danger of going ashore in the gale. This was a new ship of 3000 tons. The Waterford Steamship Co secretary wasted no time sending their tugs Rossa and Dauntless to the scene. The river steamers of the company Ida and Tintern followed. Their joint efforts managed to salve the derelict to the considerable advantage of the company. (66)

Active

The schooner Active of Cork was wrecked at Annestown about four miles from Tramore during the storm of 22-1-1862. She was en route from Liverpool to Cork with coal under the command of James Lewis. The ship was seen in distress and was unlucky to be washed into a miniature bay surrounded by 150 feet cliffs. The Lloyds sub agent observed the wrecking of the schooner after keeping it under observation from midday. Five sailors were seen clinging to the bulwarks but the entire crew of nine were lost. She went to pieces within an hour of striking the rocks. (66)

Indian Ocean

While the coastguards were trying to assist the Active a messenger was sent to the headland to ascertain if other ships required assistance. He observed the Indian Ocean ashore at Benvoy Strand and the coastguards diverted their attention to her. She had left Liverpool on 21-1-1862 bound for Sydney with cargo and emigrants. The captain realised that he was in danger of being caught on a lee shore. He cut away the masts and dropped anchors. The crew were taken off by the Europa. Eventually the anchors dragged and the vessel was dashed on the beach. Her cargo included casks of ale and brandy which along with the wreckage were stripped by the local population. (66)

Queen of Commerce
Also on the same day 22-1-1862 the Queen of Commerce was wrecked at Ballymacaw just west of Dunmore. She was en route from Antwerp to Liverpool to pick up passengers. The ship struck close to the shore and the captain made efforts to land a line. First a chicken coop was floated off but this provided excessive windage and was not a success. Then a lifebuoy with the line attached was floated ashore. this was quickly taken by the coastguards and made fast to the cliff. The crew of 23 were all taken ashore. The 1242 ton vessel was built at St John, New Brunswick. She became a total loss as her bottom bulged severely. (66)

Nairne
The same day 22-1-1862 the Nairne of Leith en route to Havannah with coal struck rocks at Brownstown Head. The man at the wheel was washed overboard and the crew lost control. Luckily her masts fell onto the cliff face. Captain Ness and the crew were able to get ashore unscathed. (66)

Tiger
The ship Tiger of Bath N.S. was wrecked

at Credan Head on the Waterford side between Broomhill and the Hook on 22-1-1862. She was en route from Boston to Liverpool. Two sailors attempted to get ashore with a line using a small boat but it was swamped. The remaining crew of 23 were saved by Mr Boyse in his vessel Tintern . A letter to the Waterford News noted that two steamers, one a paddle vessel and the other a screw steamer had passed but rendered no assistance. The writer believed that either could have towed the ship out of danger. (66)

Sophia
The Sophia of Waterford was destroyed in the same gale on 22-1-1862 when she went ashore inside Credan Head. The wheel was broken and the vessel became unmanageable. The pilot cutter Gannett rescued Captain Barry and his crew and took them to Passage. (66)

Angelica
The day after the Sophia was wrecked the Angelica of Genoa was wrecked beside her on Credan Bay Bank. She had called at Queenstown for orders for the cargo of grain. She took on a pilot for Newcastle but was driven in by the gale. The Duncannon and the City of Paris tried to tow her off. Master Domina and his crew were saved. (66)

Sarah Anne
The schooner Sarah Anne captained by her owner was lost with all hands on 22-1-1862 at Ballynacourty in Dungarvan Bay. She carried coal from Cardiff to Waterford. The ferocity of the storm of 22-1-1862 was such that the Coningbeg lightship dragged her anchors for four and a half miles. An Austrian ship was seen from Dunmore inside the Hook tower. She was struck by a surge and lost with all hands. A schooner was lost in Waterford Harbour. A wave struck her

on the quarter. This was followed by another wave which capsized her. The stern portion of the Martha of Wexford was washed ashore near Waterford. There was no news of her crew. A large vessel was reported ashore at Passage under the Barracks. In the gale of 16-2-1862 a large vessel was lost at Brownstown Head. An American ship went down at the mouth of Waterford Harbour. A Bristol ship struck the rocks near Dunmore.

Thomas

The 60 ton schooner Thomas struck the Dogger Bank off Waterford Harbour on 14-1-1865. The incident was seen from Rosslare Fort. The pilots manned the lifeboat and transferred the crew and master, William Owens, to the steam tug Ruby. The Lloyds agent Jaspar Walsh took off the cargo of wheat but the vessel was a total wreck. (66)

Kate

On 14-2-1880 while making for Waterford in high seas the fishing boat Kate filled and capsized. The accident happened at the Hanton bar at the harbour mouth. The lifeboat picked up one man and landed him at Tramore but he only survived an hour. There was no trace of the other three. The fishing had been slack and an amateur crew had taken out the boat belonging to a Mr Carroll. (66)

Polly Pinkham

On 13-2-1881 the seven year old brig Polly Pinkham owned by Pinkham's of Liverpool was wrecked at Annstown. She struck the shore in a southerly wind in heavy mist. She was en route from Rio Grande to Liverpool with a cargo of buffalo horns and dried bones. The captain Edward Bennnet was washed ashore on a lifebuoy, the mate clung to a beam but the ship broke up before the remaining four men and a boy plucked up the courage to follow. Only the captain and mate survived. (66)

Elizabeth

On 27-10-1881 the Elizabeth of Whitehaven was driven into Whiting Bay and struck the rocks about a quarter mile from the shore. She was shorthanded as three men and the mate had been washed overboard, thus the pumps were not effective. She was carrying coal from Newport to Cork. The coastguards rocket apparatus could not reach her. The lifeboat was taken to the beach at the instigation of Sir J. N. McKenna M.P. The crew however refused to launch. Three coastguards and three brothers named Smith took out the boat and rescued the surviving crew. This was the second occasion this lifeboat crew failed a ship in distress. Observers noted that if assistance had been given in time the ship might have been saved. (66)

Kate

On 3-2-1873 the schooner Kate of Troon went ashore between Dunmore and Tramore. The same day the schooner Anne Jones went ashore below Passage. She carried coal to Dungarvan. (66)

Kincora

The small collier Kincora was wrecked on 10-12-1919 at the Whitehorse Bank. The crew had been tossed about for four days before they abandoned ship and came ashore in a small boat. The Kincora carried coal to Cork or Youghal. Captain Smith and all three crew were safe. The ship was total loss. (102) (67)

Susan

On 19-2-1861 the brig Susan of Cork was wrecked at Ballynacourty station. She carried a cargo of coal. Four of her crew of six perished. (66)

Sampson

The Maltese owned 180 foot crane barge

Sampson was driven ashore on Ram Head near Ardmore beach during a south easterly gale on 12-12-1987. The barge was being towed by the Zamtug from Liverpool to Malta when the tow parted and could not be reconnected due to the gale. The crew of two were rescued by RAF helicopter from Brawdy. The 150 foot crane jib allowed a local publican Jim Mooney to board the barge from the cliffs and claim salvage. Rough weather in the following days drove the wreck harder on the rocks holing the hull and preventing tugs from pulling the barge clear. (140) A large propeller from the Sampson was mounted outside the Commodore Hotel in Cobh in 1991.

Ann & Margaret

On 23-1-1753 the Ann and Margaret was wrecked near Waterford.

Grace

On 30-3-1850 the brig Grace of Newcastle was wrecked in Ardmore Bay. An ESE gale blew her from her anchorage in the bay and drove her ashore. She carried corn from Cork for Alexandria. Captain Thompson and eight of his crew died, two were rescued. A heavily laden sloop was wrecked in the same place at the same time. The captain and crew were taken off. (66)

Gwenissa

In January 1875 the Gwenissa en route from Falmouth to Glasgow struck the coast a mile east of Stradbally. A local farmer, John Roynane, of Killeton Farm assisted the 9 crew up the cliffs. Five more were pulled up the shore. A further man was trapped on the rocks. The farmer obtained help from the coastguard at Bonmahon who prepared their rocket. The sailor was however washed ashore safely. The farmer's work was not yet finished. He rode to Tramore to inform the Lloyds agent and collect the 8 shillings reward which was payable for such information. (82)

Gladonia

In the storm of 13-1-1989 the British 850 ton bulk carrier Gladonia was driven ashore at Tramore. She was en route from Avonmouth to New Ross with a cargo of grain. Three of her crew were taken off by Air Corps helicopter while her captain remained aboard. She was high on the beach and broadside to the shore. (During the same gale the crew of the Yarrawanga were rescued by American helicopters 300 miles west of Ireland). The vessel was refloated by the tugs Sea Alert of Cork and the Fair Play 9, a 5000 ton ocean going tug. The cargo of grain was unloaded by trucks at low tide and excavators dug a channel to allow the vessel float. After a struggle during which the tow snapped the bow was pulled to seaward and the Gladonia freed to sail to Dunmore for inspection. (143)

James Buchanan

About 1836 the James Buchanan was wrecked at Rinn near Dungarvan. (135, 259.p449).

Michael

On 14-1-1975 the 500 ton MV Michael a collier was driven ashore on Tramore beach by a SW gale. After engine failure she was driven before the gale past Mine Head and Helvick. Captain Wolf in the Bell Venture attempted a tow but failed. Captain Suliman and his crew were taken off by lifeboat. This was described as the first wreck at Tramore since the First World War. The Michael was owned by Alex Shipping of Hamburg and registered at Famagusta. The wreck of the Michael remained on the beach for several years before it was broken and transported away. (143)

Silkstone

An attempt was made to blow up the wreck of the steamer Silkstone on 13-12-1882. She had sunk in the River Suir off the Quay at Waterford. (132)

Ocean Searcher

On 28-1-1975 the 85 foot trawler Ocean Searcher suffered engine failure near Tramore. The master Wm Gunnip and three crew abandoned her when she drifted. The trawler was washed ashore on Tramore beach half a mile from the Michael. (143)

John Bull

The 120 ton schooner John Bull sank at the bar of Dungarvan on 21-12-1855. She carried coal from Newport for Youghal. (174)

John Webb

The John Webb was wrecked inside the Dungarvan bar on 21-12-1855. She carried iron ore. (174)

Margaret

The Margaret was lost at Hall bay at the entrance to Waterford Harbour on 17-3-1911. The 73 ton ketch carried coal from Newport for Waterford.

Castleton

The Castleton stranded at Dunmore 10 leagues from Cork on 9-12-1758. She was en route from Lancaster to Barbados via Cork, captained by Mackrill. (234)

Earl of Sandwich

The brig Earl of Sandwich of London sailed in June 1765 with bale goods and hardware to Santa Cruz and thence to the Canary Islands. At Oratoira she loaded wine, Spanish milled dollars, gold dust and jewels for London. On board were Captain Cocherman, Charles Pinchent, his brother, three sailors, a cook and a boy along with a passenger, Captain Glass, his wife, daughter, and a servant boy. Four of the crew conspired to take over the ship and on 30th November they murdered the captain and loyal crew as well as the passengers. The boys survived this massacre but were left to drown as the pirates abandoned the vessel. The Earl of Sandwich was reported in Bantry Bay on 10-12-1765 and sailed eastwards. The four left the ship in a sinking condition and took with them two tons of dollars in a boat. They landed at Fishertown four miles from Ross and within two miles of Duncannon and buried 250 bags of dollars on the beach. The area is since known as Dollar Bay. They then travelled to Ross where 1200 dollars were stolen from them at an alehouse where they were reported spending money freely. They then travelled to Dublin where they stayed at the Black Bull Inn at Thomas Street on 6th December. Meanwhile Capt. Honeywell of Newfoundland encountered a large three masted vessel up to her rails in water. This ship was washed ashore shortly afterwards at Islandikeem near Ardmore. The legal authorities sought arrest warrants and apprehended Gidley the cook at Carlow en route to Cork. The Duncannon garrison found the buried gold and lodged the 250 bags at the custom house at Ross. After a trial the three pirates were executed at St Stephen's Green on 31-3-1776. The three St Quentin, McKinlie and Zecherman were hung on the Muglins at the entrance to the port of Dublin. This was the traditional place where East Coast pirates were left as warning to others. The treasure was given to the receiver of treasure trove Lord Viscount Loftus of Ely. (56)

Jubilee

The 700 ton New York vessel Jubilee was wrecked on the bar at Dungarvan on 21-2-1838. She was bound for Mobile from Liverpool with a cargo of coal, salt and window glass. One of her crew was lost. (66)

Glangarry
The Glasgow sloop Glangarry was also wrecked at Dungarvan on 21-2-1838. She was en route from Cork to Dublin. Her crew were saved. (66)

Santa Justina
The Dutch ship Santa Justina on hire to Venetians was wrecked at Muggets Bay near Helvick Head in April 1620. Thirty of her crew were lost. The Venetians had contracted to pay for or replace her canon. A Dutch diver Jacob Johnson worked on the wreck for a year from August 1620 and recovered some cannon. These were loaded aboard the Fedeta at Bantry in December 1621 for transport to the Mediterranean. (170)

Dennis
The Dennis went ashore in Dungarvan bay on 16-2-1799. The Captain's name was Griffith. (234)

Betty
On 17-11-1758 the Betty was lost near Waterford. Captain Moore was en route from Glasgow to Jamaica. (234)

Certes
The Certes of Malta was wrecked at Ardmore on 28-1-1865. Nine of her seventeen crew were lost. (65)

Sextus
The 400 ton Maltese barque Sextus from Sulina Lemaze bound for Queenstown for orders was wrecked at Ardmore on 28-1-1865. The coastguard were soon on the scene and fired their rockets onto the remaining rigging. Captain Capiori and ten of the crew were saved, six were lost. (65)

Comita
The Comita of Glasgow was mined and sank five miles from Ardmore on 13-8-1917. The crew were rescued by lifeboat. (149)

Loves Increase
On 5-4-1643 the Bristol ship, Loves Increase was lost in the river of Rosse. She had taken provisions to the fort at Duncannon and then had come under the orders of the Marquis of Ormonde. While supporting the army she was lost in an unspecified manner. The owner, John Moodey, master, John Webb, and 13 crewmen sought compensation for their losses. (22)

Bomb vessel
A Royal Navy bomb vessel was wrecked in shallow water at Brownstown Head on 20-11-1703. Locals recovered an eight foot cannon, 56 pounder bombs and iron. They reported that hundreds of bombs and some more cannon were visible. The name of the ship is not known.
The bomb ship Mortar was lost on the Dutch coast on that date in an easterly gale.

Hastings
The fifth rate 32 gun frigate Hastings was wrecked on 10-12-1697 near Waterford. After serving for some time on the Irish Coast she was about to return home to be paid off. While anchored in the mouth of Waterford Harbour a storm arose. The ship drove ashore and was staved. Captain Draper and most of the crew were lost. The purser and five men survived. The 384 ton 109 foot ship was built by Ellis of Shoreham in 1695. (147).

Swan
The 18 gun, 272 ton, naval sloop Swan capsized off Waterford on 16-8-1782. The vessel formerly called Bonelta was purchased in November 1781 and named Roebuck. She was renamed Swan on 2-3-1782. The ship sailed from Waterford for Plymouth with the Artois and ten transports carrying troops. During a squall the ship was overturned

and foundered in under three minutes. Captain McBride and sixteen of the 110 aboard escaped in a boat with few oars and were saved when they came ashore at Castletown, Co Wexford after 14 hours afloat. (35).

Post

Two Tudor cannon from the reign of Henry VIII (1491-1547) and Edward VI (1547-1553) are in the Tower of London and the Museum of London. They were raised in 1972. They were made by Owens Bros the Royal gunmakers. The inscription on one reads "EDWARDVS SEX ROBERT AND IO IN BRETHER THIS PEC AN 154?" Another gun of the same period was sold in the south of England more recently. The guns are two sakers measuring 9 ft and 9ft 9inches and a falcon measuring 7 ft. A ship would have been of some importance to carry such rare guns. They are believed to have come from a wreck on the headland next to the Metal Man at Tramore. The only recorded loss of the period is the brigantine Post "lost off the Irish coast" in 1566. The Post was built in 1563.

Mary Jane

The Mary Jane of New Ross was run over by an 800 ton ship on 15-12-1852. She was formerly the D'Artangan of France one of four French ships wrecked at Tramore in December 1848. She was purchased by Howlett of New Ross and was en route from Chester to her home port. Captain Spelicy and crew took to the boats and landed at Dunmore East. (132)

Wild Horse

On 24-3-1867 the barque Wild Horse of Winsor, Nova Scotia went ashore at Tramore bay. She carried a cargo of oil from New York to Liverpool. Her crew of ten were rescued by lifeboat. (65)

Anne Sophie

On 13-1-1984 the Anne Sophie, a French trawler, was wrecked on rocks just SW of Mine Head. The eight crewmen were lifted off by RAF helicopter while Ballycotton lifeboat stood by. The wreck was under a cliff upright on the rocks. (99)

Newfoundland ship

In a severe storm on 31-12-1762 a ship from Newfoundland was wrecked two miles from the Quay at Dungarvan. Many hands were lost and only 12 of 74 passengers survived.

A 100 ton Virginian vessel was also ashore and expected to go to pieces. She was bound for Bristol with tobacco. (69).

Self Reliance

The 24 ton ketch Self Reliance was wrecked on 27-5-1902 at the entrance to Dungarvan Harbour.

Duntzfelt

On 1-11-1798 a 924 ton Danish East Indiaman was wrecked 20 miles below Waterford and four miles from Dungarvan at Dungarvan Bay. A letter from A. McGuire in the London Times of 14-11-1798 described the circumstances. The ship had been captured by a French frigate but retaken by the HMS Diana on 24-10-1798. A lieutenant, a midshipman and twenty crew were put aboard. The ship struck the shore and the masts were cut away. Six sailors tried to reach the shore on a raft of spars, two were lost but a line was taken ashore. The cargo from Calcutta consisted of sugar, silk, 667 bales of muslin and indigo worth £100,000. Though pierced for 50 guns she only carried 2 X 24 pounders. The militia were called out to protect the cargo. A huge crowd gathered and three were killed and 10 wounded when the troops opened fire to prevent plunder. A few days later the wreck was driven further up the shore and there was no hope of getting the ship off. (69) The Duntzfelt was commanded by Peter Nissen Goeg and left Bengal in March 1798. She was one of the largest East Indiamen under the Danish flag. The ship was launched in 1797 as the Fame for the Calcutta firm Hamilton and Aberdeen. It had been sold to P. Hermansen at the Danish Bengal factory Serampore. He acted for the Copenhagen merchant Christian Vilhelm Duntzfelt.

Lily
The Courtown smack Lily was wrecked at Ardmine on 18-11-1882.

Clareen
The ketch Clareen was wrecked on the rocks at Churchpoint during a south westerly gale on 17-9-1924. The vessel was en route from Kinsale to Newport in ballast. She sheltered in Waterford harbour anchoring off Arthurstown. The three crew went ashore. The anchor dragged and the Clareen was driven ashore. (67)

Metrica
The Norwegian coaster Metrica en route from Waterford to Cork in ballast was driven ashore on 30-10-1991. The six crew were lifted off by an RAF helicopter. The wreck occurred on a beach under the 200 foot cliffs between Bunmahon and Tramore. The ship was registered in the Bahamas but owned in Guernsey. Though badly damaged and a constructive loss, the ship was towed off the beach by the Irish Lights ship, Gray Seal at the end of November 1991.

Venus B
On 21-2-1885 the 707 ton Austrian barque Venus B was wrecked at Ballymacaw. The ship was en route from Liverpool to Buenos Aires with general cargo. The crew of 13 all escaped. The vessel was built in 1868.

Eliza O'Keefe
The 112 ton brig Eliza O'Keefe was wrecked abreast of Wise's Point Ballinacourty on 15-2-1900. She carried coal for Dungarvan from Newport.

Hansa
The 1198 ton barque Hansa was wrecked abreast of Credan Head on 2-11-1899. The ship carried deals from St John, New Brunswick for Waterford.

Scott Harley
On 17-11-1894 the Scott Harley was driven ashore on Tramore Beach, her cargo of coal was offloaded onto carts and the ship was successfully refloated.

Mary
The Mary was wrecked on 1-1-1795 at the entrance to Waterford Harbour. She was bound for Waterford from London commanded by Captain Glascott.

Active
The Active en route from Dublin to Martinique was wrecked at Waterford on 5-12-1798. Her master was captain Stanton.

Sta Rota
On 15-1-1782 the Sta Rota went ashore near Waterford. She was en route from Opporto to Cork. The cargo was saved but the ship was lost. (234)

Felicity
The Felicity was bound for the West Indies via Cork from Newry. She was driven ashore in Dungarvan Bay on 18-6-1782. The captain was Mr Forrest. (234)

Vrow Christina
The Vrow Christina was bound for the West Indies from Cork. She was driven ashore near Waterford on 13-12-1782. The ship went to pieces and little cargo was saved. The master was Mr Shea. (234)

Good Intent
On 27-7-1749 the Good Intent captained

by Mr Kadie was lost near Waterford. The ship was en route from Cette to the Isle of Man. The cargo was saved. (234)

Neptune
Six lives were lost when the Neptune sank in the Waterford river on 2-3-1749. The ship was bound for Lisbon commanded by Mr Cole. (234)

Friends
The Friends was wrecked on a rock in the Waterford river on 26-6-1812. The vessel was en route from Liverpool to Waterford commanded by Mr Cook. The cargo was saved. (234)

George
The Waterford vessel George misstayed and ran on rocks at Waterford on 28-2-1765. She was bound for Plymouth and Falmouth commanded by Mr Smith. The cargo of butter and tallow was saved but the vessel was lost. (234)

Uomo Graziata
The Uomo Graziata was wrecked at the Dromore Bank Waterford on 20-12-1848. The ship was en route from Galetz to Waterford.
Another unknown ship was lost at the same place and time with all aboard.

Emma
The 83 ton Emma sank in Waterford Harbour in February 1849. She was bound for Cork.

Hebron
The Hebron sank near Waterford on 22-11-1835. She was en route from St Andrews to Dublin.

St Patrick
The St Patrick of Dungarvan sank near her home port on 13-6-1834.

Commerce
The Commerce of Bideford sank near Waterford on 6-2-1834.

Industry
On 27-8-1817 the Industry sank off Mine Head. The vessel was bound for Dungarvan from Wales.

Anne Gales
On 7-12-1849 the 303 ton Anne Gales from London was lost at Credan Head.

Hibernia
The Hibernia was bound for Youghal when she was lost at Dungarvan beach on 29-3-1850.

Echo
The 170 ton brig Echo was wrecked at Mine Head lighthouse on 16-2-1860. The brig was built in 1836 and carried logwood.

Susan
The coal brig Susan was wrecked at Ballymacart on 19-2-1861. Four of the six aboard were lost.

Betsey
The 72 ton schooner Betsey was lost at Ballymacaw on 29-11-1868. She carried coal for Crosshaven from Cardiff. Three of four aboard were lost.

Egira
The 641 ton barque Egira was wrecked at Ballymacaw on 21-11-1871. The cargo was flour en route from Boston to Liverpool. Five of the fourteen crew were lost.

Fatima
The 381 ton barque Fatima sank following a collision off Waterford on 16-1-1875. She was bound for Kingston from Liverpool.

Donegal
On 12-12-1876 the 142 ton brig Donegal was wrecked near Credan Head. The brig was bound from Cardiff from Dublin. All six aboard were lost.

Scott Harley
Photo: Maurice Wigham

Tramore

The following wrecks occurred at Tramore according Maurice Wigham. (100)
The exact dates have been added where known. Wrecks from other sources have
been added and some ambiguous data altered. Those marked * are more fully
described in the text. Including these Mr Edward Jacob the Lloyds agent at Tramore
recorded 83 wrecks in 84 years. The Ringarona, Italia, Petrel and a tug were also
lost but further details are unknown.

Date	Ship Name	Type	Cargo	Origin	Lost Crew
1-3-1799	Three Brothers	ship	unknown	Cork to Liverpool	
30-1-1816	Sea Horse*	ship	troops	England 11/374	
31-1-1816	Apollonia	brig	clothes		0/7
29-9-1816	New St Patrick			Cork - Dublin.	
1816	Fanny	schooner	salt		5/5
1817	Agnes	brig	cotton		0
17-12-1817	Oscar	ship	flour	Baltimore	0
1817	Fox	brig	fruit		0
1818	Shamrock	brig	ballast		0/5
1818	Enna	brig	fish	Newfoundland	0/5
1818	Rose	sloop	potatoes		3/3
1819	Active	schooner	barley	Dungarvan	0
1819	James & Henry	brig	cotton	Brazil	0
1820	Eliza	brig	flax		0

Date	Ship Name	Type	Cargo	Origin	Lost Crew
1820	Dart		ballast		5/5
1823	Harmony	brig	timber	Aberdeen	all
1824	Bridget	brig	ballast		5/5
1825	Flora	schooner	ballast		3/3
1825	Mary	sloop	furniture	Youghal	0
1825	Ellen	smack	potatoes	Glendon	4/4
1825	???	lugger	wine & fruit	Spain	0
1825	Kitty	sloop	flour	Cork	0
1828	William & Mary	brig	ballast	Bideford	0
1829	James	smack	ballast	Rose	all
1830	Maud	brig	wine	Sunderland	0
1830	???	brig	coal	N Shield	0
1830	Diana	brig	coal	Newport	0
1830	Hound	sloop		Swansea	0
1832	???	sloop	ballast		3/3
1835	Two Sisters	schooner	tallow	Nantes	0
24-11-1835	Cuba	brig	cotton	Liverpool	0
1836	Grecian	brig	cotton	Mobile	0
1837	Sir Edward	brig	coal	Liverpool	0
1837	???	yacht		Cork	0
1838	Active	brig	wood	Poole	0
1838	Swan	brig	ballast	Ross	0
1838	Breeze	yacht			3/3
1838	Brothers	schooner	coal	Newport	0
1838	Speculator	brig	ballast	St Malo	7/7
1839	Letitia	smack	culm	Cardigan	0
1839	Prince Regent	braque	passengers	L'Pool	41/41
1839	Jane	brig	coal	Swansea	0
1842	William	smack		S Wales	0
1842	Abraham	brig	cotton	Mobile	3 lost
1844	Kate	smack	potatoes	Glendon	0
1845	Dove	sloop	brick	Ross	0
1845	Elizabeth	brig	ballast	Newport	1 lsot
1846	Joseph	smack	fish	Dungarvan	0
1847	Casket	sloop	ballast	Cork	0
1847	Mystery	brig	Maize	Portmadoc	1/14
13-12-1848	Dartagnan	lugger	corn	Nantes	0
14-12-1848	Petit/Jeune Alexandre	lugger	corn	Nantes	0
15-12-1848	Lomville/Tourville	lugger	corn	Nantes	0
17-12-1848	St Vincent	brig	corn	Nantes	0
1852	Achilles	barque	ballast	New Ross	0
29-12-1852	Anne	brig	corn	Odessa-Shields	0
1856	Eliza	brig	coal	Cardigan	0
1/1858	La Capricieuse*	brig	coal	St Malo	1/7
1858	Neptunus	schooner	ice	Norway	0/6
24-1-1861	Tycoon	barque	cotton		
11/2/1861	San Spiridion brig*		coal	Swansea-Barcelona	4
20-2-1861	Voyadore du Voga	schooner	155t maize	Viarrina-Cork	
12/1861	Nancy	brig	salt	Marsailles	0/6
22-1-1862	Nairn*	brig	Railway Iron	Leith	1/6
29-10-1863	Marinatta/Marnalto	brig	350t ballast		0/10

Date	Ship Name	Type	Cargo	Origin	Lost Crew
1863	Westock	schooner		Dungarvan	0/4
18-11-1864	Sarah	schooner	90t hay & turnips		0/6
3-1-1865	Stefarria	brig	coal	Palermo	0/12
1866	Jane	brig		Cork	0/5
6/1/1867	Anemone*	schooner	100t Iron	Nantes	0/5
24-3-1867	Wild Horse*	barque 368t	Petroleum	Nova Scott	0/10
12/1/1868	Oasis*	ship	Linseed	Liverpool	2/29
24/11/1868	Mea*	barque	600t maize	Trieste	0/10
12-2-1871	Stranger	schooner	73t salt	Newfoundland	0/3
23-11-1878					
(1871)	Adelaide	brig	210t coal	Waterford	0/8
3-1-1875	Fanny*	schooner	142t coal	Salcomb	0/7
8-3-1876	Aurora Austrailis	barque	457t sugar	Sunderland	0/13
15-1-1880	Pevieur/Pieuvre	34t cutter	trawler	Tenby	0/5
21-2-1885	Camilla	brig	coal	Cork	0/5
25-8-1891	Albert	brig	coal	Youghal	0/7
15-9-1881	Garland	38t Cutter			
22-2-1892	Paul	brig	pit wood	Newport	
11-1-1894	Monmouthshrie	1162t barque	coal & machinery	Ladcove	0/20
17-11-1894	Scott Harley	steamer	coal		0/12
10-12-1899	Unicorn	70t schooner	coal		0/4
28-1-1908	St Anthony	13t fishing lugger			
21-8-1908	Oceola	5t cutter			
5-3-1911	Christianna Davis	schooner			

Monmouthshire

Photo: Maurice Wigham

CORK

CORK EAST

Slieve na mBan

A converted collier operating as gunboat for the Free State forces went ashore at Ballycotton on 13-2-1923. She struck Brian's Rocks at Ardnahinch. The crew were rescued by the Ballycotton lifeboat which made three passes before all the thirteen crew were saved. The wreck was floated and removed to Haulbowline docks by Ensors salvage ship, the Safeguarder. The dockyard had just been taken in charge from the British and the work was the first under the new administration. The Safeguarder itself was a former naval trawler sunk at Portmagee and salved by Ensor's.

Irish Plane

The 7000 ton Irish Plane was driven ashore in shallow water off Ballyshane near Ballycotton on 1-2-1947. She struck at Kelly's Cove six miles East of Roche Point, Ballycotton. She was en route from Philadelphia to Dublin. Because of the desperate fuel shortage she called to Swansea for bunker oil. The steering had failed during a storm. Captain Hickman and the crew of 30 were rescued by the Ballyguleen rocket team. Formerly called the Arena the ship was built at Spooter's Isle, New York in 1917. She was purchased by Irish Shipping in September 1941. The wreck was broken up and removed by the Hammond Lane scrap company. The cargo was motor cars and typewriters. (67) (188)

Gin Ship

In 1856 a ship with a cargo of gin was wrecked at Baile Macaoda in Cork. The local populace looted the cargo and there followed scenes of great drunkenness. The gin was concealed in caves, the Red cave and Cabha Gleann a Muilleann near the beach where the wreck occurred. The coastguard took charge but to no avail. Eventually after death due to drinking the priest exhorted the people to surrender some of their concealed stocks. (135, 50, p260 53, p299, p263)

Upupa

The Upupa was built at Jarrow for the City of Cork SS Co in 1871. The 568 ton 235 foot vessel had three masts and schooner rig. In January 1903 she was lost at Ballycotton. She was carrying coal from Cardiff to Cork when a hurricane arose. The ship was driven on the shore after engine failure. Captain Kearney and all hands were lost.

Sirius

The paddle steamer Sirius (703 tons, 178 ft) was built at Leith in 1837 by Menzies & Co for the St George Steamship Company Co of Cork. In 1838 the company was approached by the British American Steam navigation Co for a voyage to New York as their vessel, the British Queen, was not ready. On March 28 1838 she left London for New York via Cork. She arrived at New York on April 23rd a few hours before the Great Western thus becoming the first steamship to cross the Atlantic. The Sirius was transferred to the Cork Steamship Co. On 15 January 1847 she sailed from Dublin for Cork under Capt. Moffett with 91 persons. The weather thickened and by 3 am on 16th there was dense fog. The Sirius struck a reef in Ballycotton Bay. The Captain reversed engines, backed off from the rocks and made for the shore. Though making water fast the ship was able to steam when she again crashed on a group known as Smiths rocks about half a mile from Ballycotton. The only boat was launched and swamped. Altogether 20 were lost, the rest were rescued by a rope passed from the ship to shore. The metal of the ship was salvaged by Masons of Birmingham in 1898 and many souvenirs were distributed. The drive shaft of the Sirius is on display at the pier at Passage West. Other items are on display at the hotel in Glenbrook. The wreck was dived in 1908 by the British navy. Ensor dived her in the 1900s but may have been mistaken about the location of the real Sirius wreck. The ships bell is in a pub at Ballycotton. The wreck is part covered by portions of the cliff which have fallen. The Queen Victoria which was wrecked off the Bailey was a sister ship of the Sirius.

Eugenie

The sailing ship Eugenie (1194 tons 189 feet long) built by Martin & Son in 1855 was lost in Ballycotton Bay on January 7th 1866. The ship left Liverpool in mid December. Under the command of Captain W.M. Neily bound for America She met several gales and could not escape the Irish coast. At the Old Head of Kinsale she cut away the mainmast and followed a pilot boat but this guidance was lost in thick weather. The vessel made Ballycotton Bay where both remaining masts were cut and the anchors dropped. The cables parted and Eugenie drifted ashore and went to pieces. Of a crew of 17 only Mr Russel, the first officer, survived.

Tadorna

The Tadorna (1643 tons) owned by the Cork Steam Ship Co. was wrecked under the Castle at Warrens Strand Ballycrenane some miles east of Ballycotton on 15-11-1911. She was built in 1910 by Swan Hunter and Wigham Richardson. The ship was 275 feet long. She was en route from Rotterdam to Cork carrying general cargo, when she broke her main shaft during a gale. The Clyde Co sent tugs from Queenstown to assist but the wind delayed their progress. The Tadorna drove over the first reef and became wedged between the outer and inner reefs. Though the vessel appeared intact and spectators boarded the wreck Mr Ensor of the Passage salvage company was unable to refloat her before she broke in two a few days later.

Earl of Roden

This 227 ton Steamer was built at Liverpool in 1826 for the City of Dublin Steam Packet Co. In 1831 she was purchased by the St George Company for the Cork to London route. On 27-3-1843 her engines failed off Ballycotton and she began to leak. Captain Keay strove all night to keep her off the rocks and at dawn he decided to run her ashore on the sandy spot at Ballylanders where a small creek is surrounded by rocks between Ballycotton and Poor Head. The passengers were all safely landed but the cargo was pillaged by locals until prevented by the military from Spike Island. The cargo was live pigs and sheep as well as bacon from the firms of Gamble, Burke Bros and Martins. The ship became a total wreck.

Ibis

The Ibis (605 tons) was built in 1860 by Ebenezer Pike for the Cork SS Co. During a gale she suffered a machinery breakdown, while en route from London to Cork on 21-12-1865 carrying a cargo of wine, brandy, tallow and feathers. This happened two miles east of Ballycotton in Ballycroneen Bay. Captain Holland dropped anchor to ride out the storm. Another company steamer, the Sabrina, and the tug Cormorant attempted a tow but the ropes broke. The Cormorant went to Queenstown for help and returned with the tugs, Lord Clyde and United States. The helpless vessel drifted onto Julien Rock about 300 yards from the mainland near Cork. Seven of the crew launched a spar but were all drowned in an attempt to reach the shore. Captain Holland and one crewman tried to reach shore in a boat but it capsized and the captain was washed ashore clinging to an oar. The funnel fell onto the deck obstructing rescue. In about two hours the vessel parted in two at the paddle box. The after portion sank in deep water while the forepart, consisting of the main and forehold, drifted in and sank 100 feet from the shore. The Inman steamer, City of London (Capt. Mirehouse) bound from Queenstown assisted with her lifeboats. The tug, Lord Clyde saved 21. Six of the 25 crew and eight of the 15 passengers were lost.

James Duckett
On 9-2-1872 a Kinsale coaster arriving at Waterford reported that two vessels were ashore at Ballycotton and all hands were lost. The barque James Duckett went ashore at Ballymacotter between Poor Head and Ballycotton on 31-2-1872. She was en route from Lagos to Queenstown with palm kernels. She was caught by a SW gale. The crew remained in the cabin until she had struck three times and the ship broke up. Five of the crew of eleven were drowned including Captain Naylor.

The wreck occurred in the same spot as the Eugenie and not far from the wreck of the Ibis. Numerous wrecks occurred further to the west in the previous years. (66)

William Gilmore
The 119 ton schooner William Gilmore grounded at Smith Rock near Ballycotton in February 1922. The Burns and Laird SS Puma towed her off and into Kinsale but she was broken up at Kinsale. She was owned by Richard Kearon of Arklow and built at Troon in 1871.

Helga
The 1668 ton steam ship Helga was driven ashore at Ballycroneen in February 1903 and smashed by the storm of the 27-2-1903. She carried wheat for Halls of Cork from Portland, Oregon. The crew of 21 were all saved.

Joseph and Dorethea
In 1828 the Hull vessel Joseph and Dorethea was wrecked in Inch bay to the east of Poor Head.

Mary Jane
The collier Mary Jane was lost with all hands in 1860. The wreck also occurred in Ballycroneen Bay.

Cherub
The collier Cherub was also wrecked at Ballycroneen on 16-2-1874.

Primrose
The steamer Primrose of Liverpool was wrecked at Ballycotton in 1941. The crew of eight were rescued by the lifeboat. Ballycotton was unusually affected by the second world war. On 27-1-41 drifting mines entered Ballycotton Bay, four exploded causing damage to the town. Germans landed in November 1944 at Ballycotton after the sinking of their U-boat just offshore.

Anne

The Anne of Cork was driven ashore at Ballycotton on 28-4-1849. She was endangered when her cargo of coal shifted during a gale. She was en route from Newport to Cork. Some of her crew were washed overboard before she gained shelter in the bay. Her anchor dragged after her crew escaped ashore and she was driven on rocks.

Annetta

The Dungarvan schooner Annetta en route to Youghal with coal went ashore on 17-12-1905 opposite the railway station at Youghal. The collier struck the bar and drifted ashore, waterlogged. Captain Kirby and three men were rescued from the rigging.

Eliza & Anne

The Eliza and Anne was wrecked at Youghal on 26-11-1833 during a gale. She had come from Quebec in ballast. Captain Wright and the crew were saved. (74)

Medora

In 1840 the British brig Medora was lost at Youghal

Orleans

The schooner Orleans was wrecked at Youghal on 13-2-1881. She was en route from Sydney to Cork. Three of the crew were taken off by the coastguard's rocket apparatus. Youghal lifeboat went out and saved the rest of the crew. The vessel went to pieces. Three years before, the Youghal lifeboat saved 14 from the Galatea of Norway.

Helen Mar

On 27-12-1894 the Helen Mar, owned by Farrell & Sons of Youghal, was driven ashore. The wreck occurred under the residence of Sir J.N. McKenna at Ardoghena, a few miles from Youghal. She was en route from Waterford to Youghal. Three were drowned but her captain, Pat Nagle, escaped.

Duncannon

During the Confederate wars the frigate Duncannon was sunk at Youghal on 19-8-1645. Lord Castlehaven took castles on the Blackwater and on 29 June arrived before Youghal with 8,000 men. Batteries were erected on 12-7-1645, two on the east side of the harbour and one at the South Abbey. In a sortie the battery at the South Abbey was attacked, a culverin was dismounted and thrown down the rocks. A shot fired from the ferry point sank the frigate Duncannon. These events are described in a letter from Percy Smith to Sir Philip Percival (231)

Confidence

The schooner Confidence of Swansea was stranded at Youghal on 24-12-1878. She was bound for New Ross with coal but her compass was faulty. She mistook Youghal for Waterford. The crew were all rescued by coastguard rocket line.

Blue Whale

The fishing boat Blue Whale sunk near Horse rock 3.5 cables off Barrys Point near Courtmacsharry on 19-9-81. Though the incident was observed from the shore the lifeboat was unable to find any survivors.

Latona

In 1842 the brig Latona was lost at Courtmacsharry.

Hope

The Hope bound from Waterford to London went ashore at Youghal harbour on 27-12-1787. The vessel went to pieces but the cargo and crew were saved. (234)

Galathea

On 10-2-1858 a large barque was observed in distress off Youghal. She was the five year old Norwegian ship Galathea of Tvesestrand. She carried 650 tons of guano from Callao bound for Queenstown for orders. A local pilot tried to board her with the intention of taking her into Cork; however his boat was not swift enough to catch the barque. Watched by 2000 spectators the lifeboat put out and saved the 16 crew who clambered over the bowsprit. The vessel was driven ashore and wrecked on the Bar at Youghal. (67) The barque was built by A&F Smith of Norway in 1853.

Helen
On 9-2-1858 the English schooner, Helen, with coal from Cardiff for Waterford was driven ashore on the beach at Knockadoon at the end of the strand. She was discharged where she lay. The crew of four were taken off safely. (67)

Forester
The Kinsale schooner Forester was wrecked within the bar at Youghal on 16-3-1844. She carried coal from Newport. The Youghal lifeboat was thrown ashore in an attempt to reach the stricken ship. The crew were all saved. (132)

Milford Packet
The packet boat from Milford to Waterford was wrecked on 21-2-1838 at Youghal Bar.

Capprichio
The Spanish brig Capprichio was wrecked at Youghal. An RNLI medal was awarded to a coastguard for his part in the rescue.

Iodes
On 5-5-1917 the Iodes of Middlesboro was mined and sunk off Ballycotton. The captain and seven of the nine crew were lost. (149)

Joseph Michael
The 176 foot, 900 ton iron collier Joseph Michael was lost at Ballyandreen on 8-2-1950. The steamer was en route from Garston to Cork with coal. She struck Wheaten rock about a mile off shore and five miles SW of Ballycotton. Built in 1918 as the Tirydail she was owned by Duff, Herbert and Mitchell of London. The 13 crew were rescued by the Ballycotton lifeboat. (67)

Oswego
On 9-12-1758 the Oswego was lost off Youghal. The ship was en route from Bristol to New York. Part of her cargo was saved. (234)

Winst Furlost
The Stockholm ship, Winst Furlost, was stranded at Youghal in 1766. Later the Master, Andrew Rossenious, and mate, Jonas Backman, were accused of having injured and done mischief to the ship. (155)

Patience
The brig Patience of St Johns, Newfoundland was driven ashore at Donaghmore, west of Ring on 1-1-1806. The crew were safe. The ship was en route from Newfoundland to Cork with a cargo of fish oil.

Thuringia
The 297 ton trawler Thuringia blew up on 11-11-1917 off Youghal. The vessel was on hire to the Admiralty. It is presumed that she was torpedoed. (77)

Annie
The 151 ton brigantine Annie was lost at Youghal on 25-11-1860. Six of the crew were lost. The cargo was porter and peas.

Erin
On 3-4-1874 the Erin was lost in Youghal bay.

Countess of Durham
The 298 ton barque Countess of Durham was lost at Maughans Bay near Youghal on 20-1-1878. She carried coal from Portcawl to Youghal.

Ballycotton

The following list of shipwrecks at Ballycotton is compiled from two booklets prepared by Fr B Troy. (52)

Those marked * are more fully described in the text.

Date	Ship Name	Cargo	Origin	Lost Crew
23-12-1803	Sovereign*	Sugar/coffee	Trinidad	27/35
1-1-1823	Weare		Bristol	25/38
20-12-1825	Britannia		brig Padstow	5/6
25-1-1829	Caprichio*		brig Bilbao	1/10 3
0-1-1830	Speedwell	flour	Clonakilty	0
20-10-1830	Briget			
20-11-1830	Matilda	culm	schooner Neath	
25-11-1835	? ? ?		schooner Portugal	
18-3-1836	Magnificent	arms	Liverpool	
11-9-1837	John Geo Elphinstone	coal	schooner Newcastle.	
27-11-1838	Clementson	copper	brig La Guyra	0
27-3-1843	Earl of Roden*	general	cargo steamer Cork	0
20-11-1846	Susquehana	timber	ship	0
16-1-1847	Sirius*	general	cargo steamer Cork	15/80
14-11-1848	Jessey		sloop	0
1-12-1848	Henrietta		barque U.S.	0
13-12-1848	Falcon	Indian corn	schooner Glasgow	1/5
14-12-1848	Valiant		brig Sunderland	
15-12-1848	Pandora		brig Wexford	all lost
16-12-1853	Porto Novo	Indian corn	schooner Terciera	0
16-2-1855	Choice	barley	barque N Shields	0
23-1-1862	Venus		schooner Cork	all lost
21-10-1862	Industry	salt	brig Runcorn	0/5
1862	Lisette		barque	
29-1-1865	Hants	grain	brig Odessa	0
8-10-1865	Matanzas	grain	barque	0
21-12-1865	Ibis*	general cargo	steamer Cork	14/41
29-12-1865	Eugenie*	iron & general cargo	barque Liverpool	13/25
30-12-1869	Edwardino	wheat	brig Genoa	0/13
30-12-1869	Lahaina		brig	9/9
31-1-1872	James Duckett*	Palm nuts	Iron Barque	5/11
11-2-1874	Cherub*	coal		3/3
????	Rosina		schooner	0
24-9-1874	John		ship Truro	0
22-10-1881	Gustava	coal	barque Norway	0
28-1-1883	Argo	oil	barque U.S.	0
17-10-1883	Daring	fishing	yawl	0
8-1-1894	Cooleen	wheat	iron barque	11/15
16-2-1895	Saga	derilect	brig Swedish	all
8-4-1899	Rival	timber	schooner	0/4

Florida
The 1432 ton steamship Florida sank off Ballycotton in March 1867. The ship was bound from Liverpool to Alexandria with a cargo of coal.

Entreprise
The 99 ton brig Entreprise foundered near Ballycotton on 5-1-1867. Her voyage was from Newport to Kinsale with coal. All five aboard were lost.

St Louis
The 194 ton St Louis was wrecked at Ballycotton bay on 24-10-1878. She was bound for Trinidad from Glasgow with coal. The crew of seven escaped.

Nameless
The Nameless, a 143 ton brig, was lost at the east entrance to Youghal on 7-2-1897. She carried coal and iron from Cardiff for Youghal.

Celestina
The 563 ton barque Celestina was lost at Ballycroneen bay on 18-12-1889. The cargo was maize for Queenstown from Buenos Aires. The crew of thirteen survived.

Queen
The 65 ton ketch Queen was wrecked a quarter of a mile south of Youghal lighthouse on 24-11-1911. The cargo was coal for Youghal from Lydney.

Victoria
On 28-11-1849 the Victoria was lost at Ballycotton. She was bound for Cork.

Speculator
The 271 ton Speculator was wrecked at Youghal on 24-12-1848. The vessel was from Swansea.

17 Mai Norway
The 354 ton barque 17 Mai Norway was wrecked at Ballycroneen Bay on 6-1-1874. The vessel carried timber and was drifting a derelict.

Sovereign
On 23-12-1803 the Sovereign was lost at Ballycotton Island. She carried a valuable cargo of sugar & coffee from Trinidad for London. Captain Richardson and 26 of the 30 aboard were lost.

Etna
On 31-3-1849 the Etna was wrecked at Youghal. She was bound for Palermo from Liverpool.

Warwick
The 99 ton schooner Warwick sank at the Barrells rocks at Youghal on 7-5-1898. She carried coal from Workington for Clarecastle.

John Munro
The 113 ton schooner John Munro was wrecked at Clerys bank at Youghal on 18-1-1875. The cargo was coal from Cardiff for Cork.

CORK HARBOUR

Gorilla
During the civil war in the Summer and Autumn of 1922 there was heavy fighting in the Cork area between the new Free State Army and those who did not accept the treaty. Many bridges were destroyed and Cobh and Cork were isolated. Two blockships were sunk in the river just half a mile below Blackrock castle. These were the harbour board hopper and dredge, and the corn steamer Gorilla. Troops were transported to Cork by sea from Dublin in the Arvin and Lady Wicklow on 8-8-1922. They landed at Passage West since they could not go upstream. The blockships were removed toward the end of August at a cost of £20,000 to the harbour board. (67)

Alice and Elanor
The ketch, Alice and Elanor, of Youghal was moored at the deepwater quay at Queenstown on 22-3-1906 when she sank suddenly. She carried 60 tons of gravel and was owned by Mr Ml Aherne. (67)

Celtic
Photo: Cork Examiner

Celtic

The White Star liner Celtic ran aground at Roches Point at the entrance to Cork Harbour on 10-12-1928. The wreck occurred when the vessel was washed broadside onto the rocks during a gale. The 20,000 ton liner was built for T.H. Ismay at Harland & Wolf in Belfast between 1899 and 1901. She was the first of four sisters. The Cedric, Baltic and Adriatic were the others. They were the largest liners in the world at the time. The circumstances of the wreck are not clear. She had come from New York and Boston and was destined for Liverpool. The captain stopped the ship at 2.15 and attempted to back out. The vessel grounded at 5.10 according to the pilot Mr Donovan. It was speculated that she struck the Pollock Rock and the captain was concerned about damage.

He turned towards land and was blown onto the lee shore. It was to have been Capt. G Berry's last voyage and the vessel had been sold to Italian shipbreakers. She carried machinery for Ford's and refrigerated cargo as well as passengers. Little trace of the ship remains as the fittings were removed and auctioned and the metal removed by Haulbowline Industries. Her boilers remain on the beach. The Celtic's bell adorns the bar at the Helm Hotel, Cross Haven. The wreck was bought by Petersen & Albek of Copenhagen. Some of the work was allotted to Cox and Danks who had salvaged the German warships at Scapa Flow. In efforts to refloat her they cut away the upper-works and sealed the openings. Arrangements had been made to bring the refloated ship into Cork Harbour.

The coal was removed but the grain cargo began to putrefy due to wetting in a gale. A discharge pipe burst on 30-11-1929 and an enclosed area of the No 4 hold was filled with hydrogen sulphide from the grain. Sixteen were gassed and four died in attempts to rescue the workers. (96) She was almost ready to refloat when a gale on 10-12-1929 smashed the wreck.

La Suffisante

At the height of the Napoleonic invasion scare there were daily reports of French fleets near the south coast. The British fleet were suffering severely at their station blockading the French ports. The British Caribbean fleet had arrived at Cork to allow stragglers to catch up. Robert Emmet's trial and execution had just occurred. A Captain Maguire of the Royal Navy arrived at Cork to supervise the erection of the signalling system on the Irish coast. The sloop La Suffisante with 14 guns commanded by Capt. Heathcoate went ashore between the Spit and Spike Island on 27-12-1803. The anchors had dragged in what was described as a hurricane. The vessel fired guns as a distress signal. Soon she went over on her beam end. The crew continued to fire muskets to attract assistance but none dared to launch a boat. The following day a Mr Fitzpatrick launched a whale boat at considerable risk and rescued some of the crew and some equipment. Seven of the crew were drowned and three killed by a falling mast. The wreck went entirely to pieces. About 1980 dredging work was done on the Bar and channel around the Spit. A considerable amount of naval debris was raised, some of which was deposited in the Cobh museum. The Suffisante had been captured at Texel on 31-8-1795. (147)

Bredah

On 12-10-1690 the 1055 ton 151 foot Bredah was blown up by accident and sank in Cork Harbour. The ship was anchored at Spike island with a full compliment of 400 aboard. She carried troops and 160 Jacobite prisoners. A gunpowder explosion is presumed to have occurred. Captain Tenet survived the explosion but died of injuries. Col Barret and nine men were the only survivors. She was a third rate 70 gun ship built at Harwich by Betts in 1679. (146) (147)

Water Lily

On 11-2-1895 the 99 ton coasting steamer Water Lily was sunk by the St. Finbar of the Cork SP Co leaving Cork for Liverpool. The Water Lily was at anchor sheltering from a storm. She had been en route from Schull to Liverpool with 70 tons of barytes. She was struck on the port stern and sank in fifteen minutes. Captain Driscoll and his crew escaped. The St. Finbar backed off and grounded on the Spit but was floated later. The wreck occurred immediately inside the Spit in three fathoms, where her masts showed above water. (67)

Henry & Anne

The Newcastle vessel Henry and Anne sailed with corn from Constantinople to Cork for orders concerning her final destination. While leaving Cork Harbour she was caught in a gale and went aground under Fort Camden on 19-11-1850. Her master Thomas and crew were saved when she broke up.

Ivernia

Another Cunard liner, the Ivernia, en route from Boston to Liverpool struck the Daunt Rock on 24-5-1911. Built by Swan Hunter at Newcastle in 1900 the 14,000 ton 600 foot liner was carrying 728 passengers. She passed the Old Head of Kinsale in clear weather and passed signals but encountered localised fog which stretched from Roberts Head to Poor Head. When she struck the engines were reversed and it was found that she was punctured fore on the starboard side. The liners Cymric and Coronia were close by and all the available tenders went to assist as a result of Captain Potter's signals. The passengers and 2,500 items of baggage were taken off. The proximity of sophisticated equipment now saved the vessel. Admiral Coke arrive from Haulbowline Naval Docks in a tender and dispatched the Hellespont with pumps. Messrs Ensor and sons, salvors, of Passage Docks, provided more pumps. With the assistance of the Clyde Co tugs the Ivernia was beached on the Spit. The Ivernia sunk somewhat deeper in the following days. There was a ten foot hole 120 feet from her stem. The Liverpool Salvage Association salvage ship, Ranger, joined the same company's Linnet with 200 crew to remove the cargo on 26th May. The spectacle was enjoyed by tourists who took advertised boat trips to see the Ivernia and the Falls of Garry wreck at the Soverign rocks. The Ivernia was refloated and back on the Boston run in November. (67)

City of New York
The City of New York struck the Daunt Rock on 29-3-1864. The Inman liner was entering Cork harbour after a voyage from New York. She left New York on the 19th and had a good passage. The night was clear and there was a bright moon and a NW wind. Captain Kennedy choose the inner threequarter mile wide passage between Roberts Head and Daunt Rock keeping the rock to the windward. At 2.30am he altered course away from the Head because he thought

it too close and drove onto the centre of the ridge within 20 yards of the Daunt buoy at 15 knots. The ship experienced a series of shocks as she passed over ledges. The boiler room was holed, extinguishing the fires and the stokers had a narrow escape. Flares were launched and guns fired. The tug waiting at Roches Point went to assist. HMS Advice and Magpie were joined by the tugs, Aran Castle, Brunel and Robert Bruce and they removed the 153 passengers and 120 crew. The captain supervised the removal of $186,000 in specie. She had struck on the ebb tide and at high water she filled to the main deck. The owner, William Inman, arrived by a series of special trains from Chester in 36 hours. The Liverpool tug Cruiser arrived with salvage gear and 300 labourers were brought out on the Robert Bruce. A further party of Liverpool labourers were sent for. The lower deck was caulked to form a temporary bottom. A thousand casks brought from Liverpool were packed in the damaged holds. A massive sail treated with oakum was prepared to be drawn over the ship's bottom as she was pulled clear. On 7-4-1864 seven tugs attempted a tow but her bow was firmly aground. Hawsers snapped and the casks imploded on the inrush of water. The damage was severe and a gale arose. Being straddled on the rock she broke and sank within a few days, despite intense efforts to refloat her. (67).

Westwick
During the First World War on 7-3-1917 the Westwick sank in Ringabella Bay. The 5694 ton ship was mined a mile south of Roches Point. No lives were lost. She was heading for the harbour inside the lightship and was apparently abandoned. Two pilots boarded her but

could not drop her anchor as the devil claws held it tightly. Before the dockyard tug could reach her she went ashore at Fish point on the south of Ringabella bay. Her coal was washed ashore for years in any E or SE strong wind. It was never clear why her crew abandoned ship as it was broad daylight but she may have been threatened by a submarine. She carried a cargo of grain some of which was salvaged and stored at Brideford House. The rest was rotten and stank the town with it's bad smell. (77). A First World war wreck lies in a gully at Nohaval. It is believed that she sank after being mined.

Magnificent

The schooner Magnificent was wrecked on the Cork coast in Summer 1835. She was bound for Bonney or New Calabar near Benin. Among the cargo was some brass and iron rings which were to be used as money to trade there. These rings were the currency of the people of Eboe and Brass country. The rings were exhibited at the Royal Irish Academy.

Neptunia

The 10,519 ton Greek liner Neptunia struck Daunt Rock on 4-11-1957. She was built in Holland in 1920 and lengthened in 1933 to 506 feet. She should have taken the normal easterly route on entering the harbour. However she passed west between the Lightship and the land. The pilot promptly boarded her and she was beached on the eastern bank. She carried 31 passengers and 215 crew. Her passengers were disembarked. The ship was refloated and scrapped.

Corsewall

The Clyde Company's 924 ton coaster Corsewall was lost at Roches Point on 5-12-1876. The 150 hp iron screw steamer was built in 1876 by R.Steele and Co. The two month old ship was en route from Glasgow and Dublin for Cork. The chain plates of her rudder failed as she approached Cork Harbour and she went on the Cow and Calf reef. She carried 800 tons of cargo including porter and whiskey valued at £30,000. Captain Crawford and all the crew were saved. The cargo was salvaged by throwing the barrels overboard as lighters could not approach the reef. On 9 December two salvage ships with pumps and divers arrived. The divers reported a 60 foot gash under the engine room which made refloating impossible. The wind then changed and the wreck was soon smashed to pieces. (67)

Dronning Sophie

The Dronning Sophie was built of teak as a full rigged ship, Sir George Pollock, in 1847. After a career in the Indian and Australian trade she was sold to French owners as the Marius and to Norwegians as the Dronning Sophie. In 1892 she was wrecked and was unserviceable. The Clyde Company purchased her and she was employed as a coal hulk at Queenstown Harbour. The Admiralty used her during the First World War. When the Clyde company left Queenstown she was sold to Colemans for £300. A year later on 19-11-1930 she overturned and sank in Monkstown Bay during a gale, with the loss of two lives. She was later raised and broken. (67)

MV Celtic Lee

The 501 ton tanker MV Celtic Lee capsized at the ESB power station at Marina in the inner Harbour of Cork on 3-12-1979. She had carried oil from Whitegate. Though declared a total loss and upside down, she was salvaged by Scotts of Cork. (67). Refloated on 14-1-1980 repairs were conducted at Cork. The ship was sold in 1982 as the Maldea. (201)

Puffin

Puffin

The lightship, Puffin, was built at Newcastle on Tyne in 1883. After a refit she was stationed at Daunt Rock on 1-8-1896. Daunt Rock is covered by eight or nine feet of water and the lightship was anchored in 16 fathoms. Only eight weeks later on 8-10-1896 during a storm she was lost without trace. On November 5 divers from the Cork salvors, Ensors, located the wreck at 15 fathoms sitting upright on the bottom near her station. They raised the Puffin and she was beached at Ringaskiddy. The wreck was sold to Ensor's on 27-10-1897 as scrap. (188) (67)

Daunt Lightship

In February 1936 the Daunt Lightship was again in trouble. During a storm she dragged her anchor and was soon off her station. A destroyer, H.M.S. Tenedos, stood by as did the ferry Inisfallen. The crew refused to abandon the lightship.

The Irish Lights Tender, Isolda, came from Dublin and tried to tow the lightship. The wind freshened and shifted to SSE. The tow could not be commenced and there was a danger that the stricken vessel would be dashed on the Daunt Rocks. The crew were rescued by the lifeboat which had stood by for the duration of the two day ordeal. (83).

Merion

The Dominion Liner, Merion, grounded at Roches Point on 2-3-1903. She landed passengers from Boston and ran aground at Whites bay on leaving the harbour. She struck twice; first she hit near Chicago Knoll, was refloated, and struck again. Two tugs, Flying Fish, and Flying Fox, failed to refloat her the next day. After the removal of her cargo the tugs, assisted by the Admiralty tug, Stormcock, succeeded in freeing her three days later. (67)

Fleswick
Photo: for Ensor via Bill Swanton

Fleswick

The 647 ton steamer Fleswick carrying 700 tons of coal from Garston to Cork for Suttons was struck by the Cork steamer, Killarney, on 17-10-1908. The Killarney collided with the Fleswick's port side cutting into her. The Fleswick sunk in two minutes on the north side of the channel in Monkstown Bay. Most of the crew of twelve remained with the wreck and were rescued by a cutter from the HMS Emerald but two tried to swim for the shore and one drowned as the naval craft reached them. An inquiry ensued and there was conflicting evidence. Mr Ensor, a diver of the salvage company reported that the engine room telegraph was at stop, and not astern, as the captain alleged. Despite this the Killarney was found to blame for the incident. (67) Ensors raised the wreck clearing the channel.

Amiral Coubert

The 2223 ton French steel three masted sailing ship, Amiral Coubert, arrived at Queenstown on 25-8-1915. She had discharged her cargo at Cork. She then went to Pasage West dockyard for painting and bottom cleaning. On 18-11-1915 she was towed out by a Clyde company paddle tug. A strong southerly gale endangered the vessel which was in ballast bound for Albany USA. It was assumed that she would anchor but she carried on. The tow parted between Roches Point and the Daunt Light Vessel. Despite the tug's efforts she grounded on the Carrig Rocks close to Fennels Bay near Myrtleville. Her forecastle survived until 1940-41 when it was removed by Haulbowline Industries for scrap.

Aud

The Castro was captured by Germany

during the 1914-1918 war. Renamed the Libeau she was then disguised as the Norwegian vessel Aud. On 20-21 April 1916 she brought munitions to Banna Strand on the Kerry coast for the Easter Rising. Roger Casement had previously been landed by the German submarine U19 (Captain Wisbach) and was arrested. The Aud was intercepted by a British destroyer, HMS Bluebell, and accompanied to Cork. As she approached the harbour she was scuttled by the crew off Roches Point. Mauser rifles have been recovered from the wreck by divers. The ship lies fairly broken in 42 metres. The seabed is strewn with ammunition boxes. During the Second World War the wreck was depth charged. (178)

Saima

The 300 ton wooden Russian barque Saima was wrecked at Curlew Gulley at Roches Point on 12-10-1908. She had discharged timber at Cork and was beating out of the harbour in ballast. She seemed to mis-stay and went ashore on a falling tide. The Clyde Company tugs attempted to tow her off but the stricken vessel was dashed back. The salvage firm of Ensors were engaged to save property before the vessel broke up a few days later. All the crew survived. (67)

Pluvier

After the storm of 31-12-1905 a correspondent to the Cork Examiner reported the probable loss of a two masted ship at Flat Head at the east end of Rennies Bay. He pursued his enquiries in other newspapers and meantime wreckage surfaced and bodies were washed ashore and buried at Nohaval. Finally in February the firm of Ebenezer Parry contacted him. They thought that the ship was their two masted, 310 ton Pluvier. She had sailed from Figueira in

Portugal on 24 December and from the voyage times of other vessels she would have been near Cork at the time of the wreck. Their fears were confirmed when a watch and the ships figurehead were identified. (67) The schooner was built at Fowey.

Jessie

The Jessie was wrecked at Nohaval cove on 8-2-1858. The Cork collier was en route from Newport to Cork when caught by the storm. The vessel was driven ashore at Nohaval. Captain Nicholas Hurley and his crew were saved by clinging to a portion of the wreckage which was washed up on a shelving rock. The coastguard found them at daybreak after a night on the rocks. The spot is near where the Killarney was lost. (67)

Isabella

The Isabella went ashore at Cove on 4-11-1782. She was en route from Liverpool to St Lucia, commanded by Mr Robinson. (234)

York

The 74 gun ship of the line, York, struck Daunt Rock in February 1815. She was commanded by Captain Schomberg. On 13-2-1815 she arrived at Cove. She sailed on 3-3-1815 in the company of Tigris and Tartatus. The York survived hitting the rock and became a convict ship in 1819 and was broken up in 1854. (147). Another Royal Navy ship, the Research, had a narrow escape on Daunt rock. She struck the wreck of the City of New York in 1867. The Research was in pursuit of the fast barque Alaska during a Fenian gunrunning attempt. The Research got off the rock and reached a repair yard in Haulbowline.

Morococola

The 265 ton Morococola was mined and sunk off Daunt LV on 19-11-1917. She also was a hired trawler. (77)

Clifton

The 242 ton trawler, Clifton, was hired by the Admiralty during the First World War. On 18-2-1917 she sank after striking a mine off the Daunt LV. (77)

Lord Hardinge

The 212 ton hired trawler, Lord Hardinge, sank after a collision off Daunt LV on 9-4-1918. (77)

Owencurra

On 25-11-1930 the hopper and dredger, Owencurra, overturned at the pumping station pier at Tivoli. She had loaded mud from the river. An engineer aboard had a lucky escape when he was heard tapping on the hull. Firemen and dock workers cut a hole in the side and released the man unharmed. The vessel was raised about a month later. (67)

Lee

The coaster, Lee, went aground at Cusquinny in Cork Harbour in 1870. She was raised and docked on 3-10-1870. The damage was much less than expected and was easily repaired.

Fortuna

In April 1858 the barque, General Sale, en route from Sunderland to New York came upon the Fortuna sinking off Roberts Head. Captain Wilton of the Fortuna and his crew took to the longboat and were picked up. A pilot persuaded the crew to reboard and the derelict made for Cork. However no further trace of her was found and it is assumed that she sank with the pilot and crew. The Fortuna was bound for Montevideo from Liverpool. (67)

Sarah Jane

The Sunderland barque, Sarah Jane, sank after striking the rocks at the mouth of Cork Harbour on 13-12-1872. She had brought wheat to Cork and was leaving in ballast. Efforts to tow her off were futile and she heeled over and went down. Captain Humble and the crew survived. (66)

City of Cork

The City of Cork sank in the harbour in 1821. She was raised but sank again in 1832. She was built at Passage.

Chicago

On 12-1-1868 the 3000 ton Guion Line liner, Chicago, sank at the Chicago Knoll a mile SE of Roches point lighthouse. She was en route from New York to Queenstown commanded by Captain McNay. Due to dense fog the Fastnet Telegraph station was not signalled and no tender awaited the liner. The Old Head was sighted in fog and a semicircular course steered to avoid the Daunt Rock. Though soundings were taken the ship ran onto a reef 100 feet off shore at Guleen. The reef extends out from eighty foot cliffs and is surrounded by 15 fathoms of water. The Chicago stuck fast and good order prevailed. All 130 aboard took to the boats and reached safety. The Power Head coastguard removed the passengers luggage by line. Fifty marines were dispatched from the guardship, Clyde, to prevent looting. The agents Scotts sent out the tug, Lord Clyde, and removed £60,000 in specie for dispatch by rail. A storm three days later broke up the wreck. The cargo of grain and cotton along with the ship were insured for £200,000. The marines shot and wounded a looter who refused to leave a cotton bale washed ashore. (67)

Santo

The stern dredger, Santo, sank near the Daunt Lightship on 25-12-1900. The vessel was newly built by Lobunta and Co at Renfrew and was en route to Formosa. The crew consisted of seven Britons and ten Japanese. She encountered heavy seas when travelling down the channel and found herself in distress in the severe SW gale off Cork. Her lifeboat was launched when a list developed. It was towed astern with some of the crew. The dredger was swamped and went down. The pilot boat, Maid of Erin, rescued some of the crew but Capt. Jameson and three others drowned. (67)

Vanda

On 16-1-1868 the Vanda went ashore near Power Head. In thick fog Captain Lacouteur mistook a coastguard beacon for the light at Roches point. The coastguard rescued all 14 aboard in 20 minutes, by line. The vessel broke up in the gale. The Vanda was 91 days out of Iquque bound for Glasgow with nitrate of soda and borax. (67)

Maria

The Cork lighter Maria also succumbed to the storm on 29-12-1900. The owner, Henry Gould, and his children were aboard en route to Croshaven with 40 tons of coal. The children were put into the punt when the danger became apparent. The vessel went down in shallow water south of Rocky Island. The master clung to the rigging and all were rescued. (67)

Submarines lost off Cork

The German submarine, UC 42, sank at the mouth of Cork harbour on 10-9-1917. She was laying mines when one of her own mines exploded. Captain Muller and his crew of 26 were lost. The wreck was located by Captain Connell while on a survey trip near the wreck of the Aud. The ballast of the submarine was reputed to be mercury to facilitate handling. U-49 was sunk by gunfire on 11-9-1917 after being rammed by the steamship, British Transport. UC 19 was sunk off Cork on 6-12-1916 by a destroyer trailing an explosive. U-81 (Commander Rymand) was lost west of Fastnet when torpedoed by British submarine E-54 (Commander

Riggs) It had surfaced to read the name of a ship. UC-29 was sunk off Cork by the Q ship Pargos. UB-65 sunk at N 51.07,W 9.42. She blew up when in action with the American submarine L-2 on 10-7-1918.

Submarine

In April 1945 the Courtmacsharry coastwatch called out the lifeboat to rescue the crew of a German submarine. The crew scuttled their vessel rather than surrender and took to their dingy. A revolver remains from the event in a pub at Courtmacsharry. The remains of a submarine are reputed to be near the rocks at Courtmacsharry.

A German submarine U-260, also sank off Galley Head on 13-3-1945. Position 51.15N, 9.05W. Two of the crew were buried at Nohaval and later reinterred at the German graveyard at Glencree.

Premier

On 30-1-1865 the barque, Premier, which had sunk at White Bay a short while previously was raised. Capt. Beatty of Queenstown lifted the hull off the rocks using casks and cassions. She was then towed by the tug, Lord Clyde, around to Wheelers dock. (67)

Wildding

The Wildding ran ashore at Cove in April 1773. She was bound from Cork to Guinea with wool and general cargo. (155)

Robert

The brig, Robert, was wrecked at Crab bay near Roberts Cove in April 1805. She was bound for Galway with porter from the Lee Brewery, and also with rum and sugar. The crew, passengers and some cargo were rescued by Captain Roberts and the local Yeomanry. (155)

British Queen

The Bristol ship, British Queen, ran ashore at Ringabella Bay about 13-12-1798. (155)

El Zorro
Photo: Jack Roberts

El Zorro
The 5,989 ton El Zorro was torpedoed near the Old Head of Kinsale on 28-12-1915. Two were killed and the rest of the crew of 33 abandoned ship but reboarded when help arrived. A tow was commenced but in the early hours of 29-12-1915 the tow parted and she was washed ashore at Man O War Cove. Shortly afterwards she broke in two. A Liverpool firm sent a crew of eight Chinese who worked with locals on the salvage. The copper and brass was removed, stored in an old mill near the strand and shipped to Cork in a small ship, the Nautilus. On one occasion carriers arrived with four horsedrawn dray carts to collect scrap. The Chinese were unaware of the arrangement and the engineer Mr "Chip" Watkins was not about. When the draymen attempted to load the carts the Chinese defended their horde with drawn knives. The Corkmen retreated emptyhanded. The El Zorro was built at Newcastle on Tyne in 1903. (243)

Brothers
The transport ship, Brothers, was destroyed by fire at Passage West on 11-1-1809. (155)

Ardbuckle
The brig, Ardbuckle, also described as Ambuscade of Whitehaven went ashore at Rocky Bay on 11-3-1805. (155)

Britannia
The 600 ton, Britannia, was badly damaged by an explosion at Cove on 11-2-1806. The wreck was removed to the bar and in 1889 the remains were removed by the Passage West salvor, Thomas Ensor. (155)

Victoria Cross

The 669 ton Liverpool ship, Victoria Cross, struck the Daunt Rock on 17-9-1886. She was towed off by steam tug and beached at Rocky Bay where she broke up. She had sailed from San Francisco in March with a cargo of flour and entered Queenstown for orders. She was towed out of the harbour bound for Galway. When the tug parted there was confusion over markers for the Daunt rock and she went aground. The Victoria Cross was built in 1863. (174)

Bulldog

The Passage Dock Company tug, Bulldog, foundered after a collision with the tender Queenstown on 12-7-1898. A party of children were on board the Queenstown on an excursion down the harbour and had a narrow escape. The tug sank in two minutes near Horsehead Buoy with the loss of one crewman. (67)

Cornubia

The 144 ton collier, Cornubia, of Courtmacsharry sank a quarter of a mile SE of Roches point on 20-10-1881. The owner and captain Thomas Driscoll and his crew were lost. She carried coal from Newport to Cork for Suttons. When the storm abated her masts showed above water. (67)

Idomea

The large Austrian vessel, Idomea, sank at Rocky Bay near Roberts Cove on 20-10-1881. She was outward bound from Liverpool. Two of her crew were saved. (67)

Vanguard

The Dublin and Glasgow Steam Packet company ship, Vanguard, ran ashore at Roches Point in 1844. The crew and passengers were rescued by the Queen.

Commodore

The 52 ton tug, Commodore, owned by the Queenstown Towing Company was wrecked at Morris Head near Robert's Cove on 10-9-1885. The Commodore was built at South Shields in 1876 and was 117 feet long. (186)

Primrose

The Primrose, en route from Dublin to Cork developed a list at the entrance to Cork Harbour on 28-1-1941. The mate was washed overboard. As the funnel touched the water the crew of eight escaped in the boat. They were picked up by Ballycotton lifeboat. (99)

Killarney

The paddle steamer, Killarney, sailed on Friday 19-1-1838 from Penrose quay in Cork commanded by Captain Bailey. The ship carried 50 passengers and 650 pigs. She sheltered at Queenstown to allow a snowstorm abate and after a time sailed only to return to anchor. Though badly trimmed the vessel left the harbour a second time. After a period at sea, water washed in and smothered the fires, because the engine room had not been covered with a suitable tarpaulin. The engines were restarted and an effort made to beach the ship at Roberts Cove. However she drifted nearer the rocks and struck a pinnacle at Rennies Bay near Nohaval about 3 p.m. on Saturday. Survivors were clinging to the rock on Sunday afternoon but locals were working on the beach removing the remains of the pigs. Eventually some of the survivors were saved by stringing a rope between two headlands and bringing them ashore onto the cliff. Some were not rescued until Monday. Altogether only 14 survived the disaster. The pinnacle of rock has since broken and does not show as prominently today. (183)

Rockingham

The 758 ton Rockingham, a former East India ship was wrecked on the same rock pinnacle as the Killarney in December 1775. The troopship was en route from Portsmouth to Cork carrying the 32nd regiment bound for the American War of Independence. One hundred and fifty men and the regimental pay chest were lost. (87)

Pembroke

On 9-12-1758 the Pembroke sank off Roberts Cove. Twelve of the crew were lost. The vessel was on a voyage from Bristol to New York. (234)

Mercury

The Mercury was wrecked near Cork on 15-9-1758. She was bound for Hamburg from New York. None of the cargo of clayed sugars was saved. (234)

NS de la Conception

The Nostra Senora de la Conception alias Mary of Waterford was lost near Cork on 14-11-1758. The master and another were drowned. (234)

Carrie

The 74 ton ketch, Carrie, was lost at Camden Fort on 15-10-1897. She was en route from Cardiff to Cork with coal. The crew of four survived.

Septimus

The 150 ton Septimus was wrecked at Ram Point Queenstown on 12-3-1883. The brig carried manure from Cork to Swansea.

Chiapas

The 996 ton steel steamer Chiapas foundered 7 miles off Roches Point on 30-12-1882. One of the 34 aboard was lost. The ship carried general cargo from Glasgow for Trinidad.

Princess Royal

The 121 ton brig, Princess Royal, sank off Camden 24-12-1878. She was bound for Cork from Rochester with cement.

Annie McJennet

On 8-3-1875 the 219 ton brig, Annie McJennet, was wrecked at Haggs Bay,

Queenstown. She was in ballast from Queenstown to Troon.

Petrel

The 82 ton pilot schooner, Petrel, was lost at Black Head on 26-2-1897. She had come from Kinsale seeking pilotage.

Rietta

The 370 ton brig, Rietta, was wrecked at Church Bay Queenstown on 8-3-1875. She was carrying maize from Baltimore to Queenstown.

Agapinori Adelfo

This vessel was lost at Queenstown lighthouse on 12-12-1849.

August

The 78 ton Danish schooner, August, was wrecked at Nohaval Cove on 16-1-1903. The August was dismasted before she struck the reef during a force 10 gale. Captain Clausen died but four crewmen were rescued by a local man, Denis Collins. The vessel carried horse beans from Morish in Morocco to Queenstown.

Helmi

The Russian 278 ton barque, Helmi, was wrecked near Roches Point on 3-3-1881. She carried coal from Cardiff for Naples.

Dorethea

The 150 ton Dorethea sank off Myross Island on 15-2-1861. All six aboard were lost.

Cape Packet

The Cape Packet was lost near Cork in December 1849. She was en route from Antwerp to Cork.

Phoenix

The Phoenix sank in Cork harbour on 5-2-1848. She was bound for the Clyde from Bahia. In January the Archiduca Frederica was lost near Cork.

Advocate

On 14-4-1852 the Advocate was lost at Roberts Head near Queenstown.

Start

The 222 ton Start was lost at Rennies Bay on 15-11-1852. She was bound for Newcastle from Ibraiel.

Allison

The iron steamer Allison sank north of Haulbowline on 22-11-1928. The ship had collided with the SS Lilah.

Shannon Lass

The motor Fishing vessel, Shannon Lass, sank at the wharf at Haulbowline on 1-2-1935. She had collided with SS Lissa at the piles.

CORK KINSALE

Providence

During a storm in 1668 four ships ran ashore in the harbour of Kinsale. The Providence of Kinsale sank in 6 fathoms. An eight gun ship of Matigoe sank on the harbour side of the Old Head of Kinsale. On 17-3-1634 three French corn and wine ships were lost at the harbour mouth while a Liverpool bound ship was lost in Kinsale. (29)

Swallow

The frigate Swallow was forced into Kinsale harbour on 9-2-1692 by a severe gale. The ship ran aground on a bank near Charles Fort but sank the next night. All the crew were saved. Swallow was a 4th rate 40 gun ship of 550 tons. She was built by Taylor of Portsmouth in 1653 as the Gainsboro and renamed Swallow on the Restoration in 1660. The Swallow was one of the three ships which broke the boom on the Foyle thus raising the siege of Derry. (147) (110)

Adventure

The Adventure of London was wrecked near Kinsale in a storm on 11-2-1691. The same gale wrecked a corn vessel in the harbour and several other ships in the vicinity. (110)

St Albans

The British fourth rate 50 gun ship HMS St Albans was wrecked at Kinsale on 8-12-1693. Late in the afternoon the frigate St Albans commanded by Captain Gullam, the Virgins, a prize commanded by Captain Hales and the galley Sheerness (Captain Lace) anchored a little outside the harbour of Kinsale. The wind was slight and from the NW. Captains Gullam and Lace went ashore. That night they returned in the St Albans' pinnance. The wind was now strong and from the east. The pinnance was rowed under the bow of the ship. It was staved and the two captains and 11 of the 13 crew drowned. The St Albans then drove from her anchors and ran upon rocks at the point of Sandy Cove. All but one or two men were saved. It was hoped that the guns and rigging would be saved. (110) The wreck has been dived and three large cannon lifted. These are now undergoing restoration at Charles Fort. The wreck was broken by explosives in recent years. The 615 ton vessel was built at Deptford in 1687. Material from the ship is on display at Kinsale museum. The wreck was located during work to place a chemical factory effluent pipe beyond Sandy Island.

Galiot

The Galiot was wrecked on the Old Head of Kinsale on 19-1-1797. She was commanded by Captain Stettin and bound for Liverpool from Opporto.

Stillorgan

On 16-6-1778 the British 90 gun warship Stillorgan was buffeted by a storm off Kinsale. The ship went to pieces at the Great Seal (now possibly called Bream Rock) attempting to enter the harbour. (155) The ship is somewhat enigmatic as RN lists do not record the name.

City of Chicago
Photo: O'Keefe Queenstown via Bill Swanton

City of Chicago

The Inman liner City of Chicago a steamer of 3364 tons ran aground at the Old Head of Kinsale on 22-6-1892. The ship struck under the 190 foot cliffs at the point at Ringcurteen on the west side of the headland. The ship became wedged by rocks forward. Her propeller was kept running for some days to prevent her slipping into deeper water as her stern was in 11 fathoms. The 360 passengers were transferred to Kinsale in the ship's boats or helped up the cliffs by the coastguards. Their baggage was taken to Queenstown by the tender Ireland. The tugs Flying Fish, Flying Fox, Stormcock and Jackal stood by. Three steamer's and a wrecking steamer attended the wreck. Captain Chisolm of the Liverpool Salvage Association supervised the salvage efforts. A diver observed that the damage to the bow were severe. Three days later she listed to seaward though her engines were still going slow ahead. A gale frustrated salvage efforts and she broke up rapidly. The first officer thought that an indraft between Galley Head and Old Head had pushed the ship towards land. The captain had experienced 160 previous crossings. Redfern was suspended for nine months for proceedings too fast in fog and not checking his depth with the lead line. Due to the exposed site the remains are well broken up. The wreck lies in 20 metres of water scattered about an area 120 metres by 20 metres. The City of Chicago was built by C.O'Connell of Glasgow in 1883. (67)

Trompeuse

On 15-7-1796 the 16 gun 342 ton brig sloop Trompeuse was wrecked at Farmer

Rock on Dudley Point in the lower cove of Kinsale. Captain Watson and the crew of 106 survived the wreck. She had been captured from the French off Cape Clear on 12-1-1794 by HMS Sphinx. (141) A two masted vessel from Bideford was wrecked at Farmer rock on 23-12-1787. (155)

Albion

On 1-4-1822 the Albion en route from New York to Liverpool went ashore about a mile west of the Old Head of Kinsale at a place since known as Cuis Albion. O'Neills hotel stands there now. This is about three quarters of a mile from where the Balinaspittle road reaches Garretstown Strand. The cliffs are 60 feet high and a steep path leads down to the strand. The Albion struck the westmost of a group of rocks close to the cliff. A southerly gale had broken the hatches and washed them overboard. The main mast was broken and she came ashore in fog. There were no survivors. Many of those aboard were buried at the church of Templetrine. It was believed that four tons of gold were aboard and an attempt was made to salvage this in the early 1900s. At low tide some stones foreign to that area are visible. These probably constituted the ballast. (67)

Boadicea

The brig Boadicea which accompanied the Seahorse lost at Tramore was herself lost on Curlane rocks on 30-1-1816. They separate Garrettstown and Garrylucas beaches just west of the Old Head. The gale forced the ship into the deadly lee shore of Courtmacsharry Bay. The vessel carried the 2/59 Regiment returning from the battle of Waterloo to garrison duty at Cork. Most of the crew and complement numbering 255 were drowned. They were buried in a mound on the beach. In 1900 the remains were

exhumed and reburied at Old Court churchyard at the base of the Old Head. (194)

Lord Melville

The 818 ton Lord Melville also of the same ill fated convoy carrying the 82nd regiment struck the rocks 300 yards off the Old Head on the evening of 30-1-1816. The vessel remained intact and a boat was launched but swamped and its crew of twelve drowned. Eventually the shipwrecked were saved by the men of Kinsale Head lighthouse. The Lord Melville was a former East India ship. (195)

Stonewall Jackson

This American ship was wrecked in Bullens Bay possibly while smuggling. Some crew may be buried at Belgooley cemetary.

Fishing Yawl

In August 1877 five local men were drowned when their yawl was wrecked on Minnane Rock off Black Head. This is at the northern end of Holeopen Bay East. They were returning from a fishing trip. Another Kinsale yawl was wrecked on 10-10-1909 at Bullens Bay. She was owned by Flynn & Co and skippered by Mr Kiely. She went aground when she misstayed. The crew were saved by another boat.

Ardent

On 18-11-1984 the wooden Castletownbere trawler Ardent II struck the Old Head of Kinsale just below the lighthouse. The crew were rescued by the trawler Orion. Another trawler from the same port was lost in the same storm.

Santissima Anunciada St Nicholas

The Santissima Anunciada St Nicholas San Spiriden was lost on a rock near Kinsale on 21-11-1758. The ship was on a voyage from Bristol to Venice captained by Demetrio Ulasopula. (234)

Falls of Garry
Photo: O' Mahony Cobh

Falls of Garry

On 22-4-1911 the 2026 ton steel four masted barque. The Falls of Garry went ashore at Quay Rock at the Prince's Bed at Ballymacus point near the Soverign Islands at the entrance to Oysterhaven. She was en route from Adelaide in Australia to England via the Cape of Good Hope. She sheltered in the lee of the Scilly Isles off Cornwall in a SE gale. The Captain tried to run for Queenstown (Cobh). He failed to make Roches Point at the mouth of the harbour and was driven stern first on a lee shore. The boats were launched and some escaped by this means while the others were rescued by breeches buoy. Several souvenirs of the ship are in the museum at Kinsale. The Falls of Garry was supplied with food by HMS Adventure at 50N 6W on 20-4-1911. On 22-2-1898

the Falls of Garry had been driven onto a coral reef at Ichino, New Caledonia and was sold for £47 being considered a total loss. The ship was salvaged by Mr Thompson of Sydney who blasted away the coral reef and refloated her a year later with a false bottom. The Falls of Garry had been sold again to Copen, Craig and Walker of Glasgow and was en route to the new owners. Captain Roberts was suspended for six months as a result of the loss. (67)

Lusitania

The most famous wreck off Kinsale is the 750 foot, 30,000 ton Cunard liner Lusitania. She sailed from New York on 1-5-1915 for Liverpool. Though fitted as an auxiliary cruiser during construction the gun turrets had not been placed on the rings on the deck. The cargo included explosives and shells. An escort was due to meet her but despite the sinking of the Centurion and Candidate nearby no destroyers materialised. At lunchtime on 7-5-1915 a torpedo from U-20 struck the Lusitania. A further explosion rent the ship and she sank in two hours with the loss of 1,200 lives. Despite the proximity of vessels at Queenstown and Kinsale confusion among the naval authorities hampered the rescue and only a few hundred were saved mostly by local fishermen. The wreck lies in 100 metres 11.8 miles south of the Old Head of Kinsale.

The Admiralty are reputed to have dived clandestinely on the wreck in the 1950s. In 1983 the bell was recovered by the Archimides. The propellers were raised and landed in the U.K. The ship's bell is on display at the Imperial War Museum in London. The Archimedes expedition concentrated on entering the specie room. They recovered 9000 Lord Kitchener spoons and 3000 unarmed brass detonators marked BSC (Bethlehem Steel Corp.)

The ship Orphir worked on the Luisitania in 1937. After a three month search the Hydrographic survey ship located the wreck by echo sounding. Despite rumours the Lusitania did not carry gold. A film crew visited the wreck just before the Second World War. The Ranger worked out of Kinsale to origi-nally locate the wreck after the First war. After some unsuccessful work a chance meeting with a farm worker led to a useful mark. The labourer recalled that he observed the sinking from his doorstep through the piers of a gate in a field. The next night a fire was lit on the doorstep and observed through the gate piers. Grappling hooks located the wreck as the salvors traversed the transit. The wreck was originally found by a British

and American expedition in 1923. Further work was done over four months in 1927. SORIMA the Italian group are reputed to have found the safes during their expedition in the Artiglio in 1939.

Glaramara

The 678 ton iron barque Glaramara moored between the Soverigns and Oysterhaven on 22-2-1883. Captain Moreton had dropped anchor during fog when breakers were heard. The anchors dragged and though the tug Mount Etna tried to assist, the vessel was driven ashore. The crew were all rescued by the coastguards using rockets. The Glaramara was built in 1877. She carried wheat from San Francisco bound for Cork for orders. (67)

Nelly

The 213 ton Dutch trawler Nelly ran onto the south side of the Great Soverign on 21-11-1966. She had sailed from Kinsale where the crew had been on leave ashore. All twelve aboard were taken off by a sister ship. Despite the efforts of the tug Utrecht the steel trawler remained hard ashore by the stern. A local skipper placed two men aboard to claim salvage. The vessel was built in 1959 and owned by N.J. Jaczon of Scheveningen.

Sylvan

On 11-11-1818 the Sylvan was driven ashore between the two rocks of the big Soverign. Several efforts were made by officers of the fort to rescue the crew. The gales prevented any success. After three days an Oysterhaven man, Jack Carthy swam to the wreck from a small boat. A boy who was the sole survivor was rescued.

Commodore

The Queenstown Towing Co steam tug Commodore (52 tons) was lost at Robert's Cove on 10-9-1885. The vessel was built at South Shields in 1876 and was 117 feet in length. Several wrecks occurred at Roberts Cove including coal boats and grain ships. One ship, name unknown went down at Roberts Cove on 20-11-1850

Hercules

The 500 ton German barque Hercules was wrecked at Bogstown on Garretstown strand on 12-2-1874. She was en route from Barrow to Cardiff in ballast when she was caught by a SE gale. She sprang a leak off Holyhead and became unmanageable. Driven by the gale she struck the shore near a large cave. The mate who was strong swimmer tried to get ashore with a line but failed. The vessel broke up and the Captain and eleven hands were lost. The sole survivor was a German named Carl Kooks. (65) (67)

Lovely Betty

On 23-1-1753 the Lovely Betty was lost off Kinsale. None of her crew survived.

Alligator

On 16-2-1799 the Alligator of Portsmouth, New Hampshire went ashore near Kinsale. The captain was Harris. (234)

Fils de La Tempete

The trawler Fils de la Tempete went aground on the west side of the Old Head of Kinsale on 25-3-1958. Her crew of 7 were saved.

Genoan barque

On 1-9-1857 a large American ship the Western Star from Boston reached Queenstown in a sinking state. While en route from Rio to Falmouth she had collided with and run right over another vessel which sank. The incident happened off the Old Head Of Kinsale. No survivors were picked up and the vessels name was not determined. An Italian captain at Queenstown believed the lost vessel to be an Italian barque from Genoa.

Bonnie Maggie

The 30 ton Bonnie Maggie was wrecked on Farmer Rock at the entrance to Kinsale on 6-3-1902.

Pearl of Glouster

The schooner Pearl of Glouster was wrecked at Garretstown on 19-12-1827.

Gipsey Rose

A vessel was lured ashore by a false light at Bullens Bay about 1750. The name of the ship is in doubt as a story tells that the ship carried the son of a Gipsey who cursed the Bullen family for their deed. All aboard were lost. The curse had sufficient influence that the timbers were not touched for fifty years.

Corn vessels

Corn smuggling was prevalent in Kinsale and a mill was constructed at Sandy Cove to store the cargoes. One of these smuggling ships was wrecked on the Old Head when she came too close inshore while avoiding two patrol ships. On 30-3-1850 a corn vessel thought to be from Liverpool was wrecked at Sandy Cove. Part of the wreck floated into Kinsale Harbour.

Emerald

The Emerald or Emerald Isle is believed to have foundered about 11 miles west of Kinsale in 1798. The American ship from Galveston in Texas is believed to have been carrying supplies for the 1798 insurgents from America. A story tells that casks of coins were among the cargo landed at Garretstown.

Worsley

The Worsley was lost near Kinsale on 8-12-1812. She carried coal from Workington. (234)

Lord Sandon

The 407 ton Lord Sandon was burned at Kinsale on 21-2-1849.

Ghazee
Photo: Murphy via D. Woosnam

Ghazee
The 5084 ton Ghazee was torpedoed 2 miles SSW of Galley Head on 4-2-1917. The vessel was beached and the remains lie at the reef on Garretstown beach and break at low water. The crew all escaped.

Gulf of Quebec
The Gulf of Quebec and the Conloughrey were wrecked at Garretstown year unknown (216).

Ruby
The 80 ton schooner Ruby was wrecked on 30-3-1850 at Sandy Cove, Kinsale. All five aboard were lost.

Neptune
The Swansea coal brig Neptune was wrecked near Sandy Cove on 10-3-1774. Only the captain survived. (155)

Friendship
The Friendship from Cork bound for Gibralter was lost near the Old Head of Kinsale on 14-4-1749. The captain was Mr Robinson. (234)

Bradford
The 163 ton Admiralty hired trawler Bradford sunk during a gale near the Old Head of Kinsale on 28-10-1916.

Bacchus
The Bacchus was lost at Kinsale on 24-11-1835. The vessel was en route from Bathurst to Bideford.

Try Again
The Try Again was wrecked at Kinsale on 26-11-1835. She was on a voyage from Quebec to Cork.

Flora
The Flora was wrecked at Kinsale Strand on 9-1-1818. She was en route from Quebec to London.

Santa Trinidad
In December 1849 the Santa Trinidad was wrecked in Kinsale harbour. The

vessel was bound for Dublin from Queenstown. The pair of candlesticks in the Kinsale museum may have been salvaged from this ship.

St Amaro
The St Amaro was wrecked at the Old Head of Kinsale on 4-12-1848. The voyage was from Tercia to Cork.

Voyageur
In November 1851 the Voyageur was lost at the Old Head of Kinsale. The vessel was en route from Galetz to Tralee.

Dispatch
The Dispatch was lost at Kinsale on 1-12-1798. The master was Mr Squire. The voyage was Barnstaple to Cork.

Boyd
The Boyd was wrecked at the Old Head of Kinsale on 1-12-1798. The master, Mr Leighton, and 11 of those aboard were saved. She was en route from Bristol to Cork.

CORK WEST

Abraham Lincoln
The 361 ton Italian barque, Abraham Lincoln, was a casualty of the storm of 13-2-1874. She struck Clout Rocks and was wrecked at Dunny Cove between Gramphine and Horse Strands near Galley Tower at Galley Head. Of her crew of 13 Captain Benfante and two others survived (67)

Harriet Williams
The same storm on 13-2-1874 saw the wreck of the collier, Harriet Williams, on the Island in Clonakilty Bay. She was bound for Huelva with coal from Llanelli. Her crew were all saved. The hull was sold by auction on 7-3-1874. (67)

Assaye
On 28-1-1865 the former East Indiaman, Assaye, was driven aground in Ross Bay near Galley Head. The ship had been built at Bombay Dockyard in 1854 and was owned by C De Bourke. After the voyage around the Cape she encountered heavy gales and due to fog she was unsure of her position. The promontary of Glandore was seen ahead but it was too late. Sail was shortened and an anchor dropped. Despite this she went ashore at Ross Bay, three miles NW of Galley Head. The captain volunteered to swim ashore with a line but drowned half way to the shore. A line was launched by rocket and the remaining 48 aboard were saved. Her cargo (valued at £300,000) of cotton, wool, linseed and jute was mostly washed ashore when the vessel broke up. The 1800 ton vessel built of teak was originally a paddle frigate and had been sold out of the Royal Navy as a sailing vessel two years previously. (65,67,141) A Spanish vessel also loaded with cotton was wrecked at the same time at Dunowen Head.

Kingston
On 29-4-1849 the 431 ton Kingston was wrecked at Castletownsend. She was en route from New Orleans to Liverpool.

Dolphin
The pilot schooner, Dolphin, was wrecked on Castle Island on 12-2-1874. The pilots were trying to enter Castletownsend during the storm. The pilots were saved. (67)

Caledonia
In February 1849 the Caledonia was wrecked at Horse Island Castletownsend. The ship was en route from Liverpool to Derry.

Briget
The Briget was driven from her moorings at Castletown and wrecked in 1788. The captain and seven men survived from a total crew of twelve. (155)

Two Friends
The cutter, Two Friends, which had been abandoned, was wrecked at Castletownsend on 8-5-1788. The vessel carried ballast. (155)

Philla
The Waterford ship Philla was en route from Lisbon to her home port on 25-1-1780 when she was wrecked at Castletownsend. The cargo was salt wine and fruit. (35)

Dutch Ship
A place called Dutchman's Cove in Castlehaven Harbour derives it's name from a wreck about 1823. The bookcases in the library of Drishane House were made from the timbers. The figurehead was in the yard of the house. (213)

Catherine
The Catherine, a troop transport, was wrecked at Castletownsend on 25-1-1780. She was en route for New York. The ship was part of a fleet with troops for the American War of Independence. (35)

Cisne Camillo and Maria Francesca
Prior to the battle of Kinsale the main body of the Spanish fleet landed in September 1601 at Kinsale harbour under Don Juan D'Aquila. On 28-11-1601 a smaller group of six ships equipped with stores, ordinance and ammunition commanded by Don Pedro De Zuibar were guided into Castlehaven by the O'Driscolls, who gave them their castle. On 16-12-1601 a British squadron under Sir Richard Levison reached Castlehaven. He immediately fired on the Spanish ships. As they were transports they offered little resistance. One was sunk and two others driven on the rocks. Cannon were removed from the wrecks and placed in a redoubt at Reen Point at the east of the harbour. The British fleet were now trapped because

of the SW wind. After two days bombardment Levison limped out of the harbour. Cannon balls from the action are displayed in the museum at Ceim hill. The graves of 24 Spaniards who died in the action are at Reen (Spanish) point. (167). A Cork brig was lost with all but three of her crew at Castlehaven on 11-1-1694. At the same time a London pink bound for Youghal was lost. (110)

Santa Anna Maria
A Spanish Galleon, the Santa Anna Maria, was captured by a vessel of the West India Company of United Pioneers of Holland. She was wrecked at Castlehaven in December 1628. The wreck occurred in the shallows at the western side. She carried no treasure but had thirty brass and twelve iron guns. These were cast overboard in efforts to save the ship. Jacob Johnson, a noted salvor, dived the site in summer 1630. The Dutch owners objected to his looting the wreck as they had a treaty with Britain. The State papers 16-1-1629 record (16) that Captain Peter Fransey took cannon to Castlehaven where they were broken up. James Salmon sold anchors, sails rigging, arms, gingerbread, Spanish bedsteads and silvester (a dye) from the wreck. In 1970 some bronze and iron cannon were discovered on the site of the Santa Ana Maria. They were initially thought to belong to the Spanish ship lost in 1601. One demi culverine had a crest and date which indicated that it belonged to Don Pacheco, Sargent of the Spanish Silver fleet which was captured by the Dutch. (170)

Gerda
The 136 ton Arklow brig, Gerda, registered in Dublin sank after a collision with the barque, Inchcape Rock, off Galley Head on 20-7-1895. She was built

at Prince Edward Island in 1855. All her crew were rescued.

Crescent City

The silver dollar wreck as it is known occurred on 8-2-1871. The Crescent City with the St Louis were the only vessels of the Liverpool and Missippi SS Co. The 2105 ton two masted brig rigged vessel Crescent City was built by McMillans of Dumbarton in 1870. She sailed from New Orleans for Liverpool with a cargo of 4,100 bales cotton, 3000 bags Indian corn and 40 boxes containing $240,000 Mexican silver dollars. These were valued at £101,000. After steaming out of port she called at Fayall before commencing her 26 day passage. She had resumed steam propulsion as Captain Williams calculated his position as 20 miles from Kinsale. Despite the fog he proceeded at high speed until striking Dhulic Rock off Galley Head lighthouse. The flat topped rock is visible at low tide. The 41 crew and four passengers took to the four boats which landed at Dirk Cove. The captain managed to take six boxes of specie with him from where it was stored in the lazarette. This was about a seventh of the total. The next day she slipped off the rock and sunk in 25 fathoms. Only 20 feet of her masts showed. Divers of the Liverpool Salvage Association under Captain Cawkit, surveyor, recovered about 40% of the coins shortly after the accident. A London syndicate conducted diving operations in July 1889 and recovered several hundred dollars. They reported the wreck as lying in 16-18 fathoms scattered over two acres. The wreck was also worked in the mid 1970s. (67)

Elisa Anne

The Elisa Anne was bound for Ballinacurra from Newport with coal on 16-1-1868. She was caught by a gale and

driven ashore on Long Strand near Castlefreake about a mile and a half from Galley Head lighthouse. Captain Clarke and the two crew were saved. (67)

Gudron

The 487 ton Norwegian barque, Gudron, narrowly missed the Stags Rocks as she ran before a gale but was wrecked at Rabbit Island, Glandore on 26-12-1900. It was thought that she had suffered damage at sea in the terrible storm. Masses of low quality timber were washed into Glandore Harbour. She was en route from Dalhousie to Conway with deals. There were no survivors. (67,135)

Annie

The 76 ton schooner, Annie, was wrecked near Brow Head on 31-7-1903. She was bound for Bantry from Newport with coal. The four aboard survived.

Anglesey

The 52 ton iron steam trawler, Anglesey, was wrecked at Yokane Point on 24-9-1903. She was fishing in the area.

Dewi Lass

The 85 ton schooner, Dewi Lass, was lost at Long Strand, Galley Head on 7-5-1904. She carried coal from Newport for Clonakilty.

Joseph Sprott

The 556 ton iron framed barque, Joseph Sprott, was lost with all hands on 21-2-1871. The wreck occured at Long Strand west of Galley Head. The vessel struck Hidden Reef, half a mile from where she sank. She carried sugar from Manila for London. Her foremast and yards were of iron. (165)

Nancy

The Nancy was lost in Clonakilty bay on 16-10-1849. She had come from Nantes.

Salterbeake

On 14-1-1900 the 174 ton barque, Salterbeake, was wrecked on Long Strand Castlefreake. She carried coal from Barry for Kilrush. The six crew escaped.

Emily and Louisa
On 13-1-1850 the Emily and Louisa was lost at Long Strand Ross bay. Six were lost. She was en route from Galetz for Cork.

Fanny
The 211 ton Fanny was wrecked at Long Strand Castlefreake on 24-10-1849. She was from St Domingo for Cork.

Jeffrow Neeltie
The abandoned Dutch galliot, Jeffrow Neeltie, drifted ashore onto rocks at Little Island Strand, Castlefreake on 1-4-1794. The cargo was thought to be of Spanish origin and included indigo, Spanish wool and jallop. (155)

Maria
The Maria of Plymouth was wrecked at Little Island Strand on 15-3-1810. The crew were all lost. The cargo was hops, staves, hemp and mustard. (155)

Fanny
The Crookhaven ship, Fanny, was wrecked at Ballyrizzard on 28-2-1794. She was en route from Dublin to Limerick with iron bedsteads and bedding for soldiers. The master, Richard Notter, and his crew of two were lost. (155)

Mary
The American ship, Mary, of Boston was wrecked at Glandore in January 1804. The vessel was en route from Bristol to Charleston. The crew and passengers were all saved. (155)

Mary
The Mary, of Liverpool was wrecked at Red Strand, Clonakilty on 17-11-1802. The ship carried hides, butter and uniforms to England from Limerick. Bodies from the wreck came ashore at Roscarberry. (155)

Neptune
The coal brig, Neptune, was wrecked at Courtmacsharry on 4-11-1804. Captain John Wilson lost one of his crew. (155)

Dutch Ship
A large Dutch ship was wrecked on Rathbarry Strand on 26-11-1693. All aboard were lost and buried by the Freakes at Rathbarry churchyard. (155)

Tayside
The steamer, Tayside, sank at 4 a.m. on 16-1-1921. The ship went down 5 miles ESE of Galley lighthouse. The reason for the loss is not clear.

Margaret
The Margaret was wrecked in Ross Bay on 29-3-1812. The crew were saved. She was en route to Limerick from Newport. (234)

Corinth
On 2-8-1874 the 610 ton iron steamship Corinth was wrecked at Galley head. She carried grain from New York to Liverpool.

Windan
The 271 ton barque, Windan, struck Cow Rock in Clonakilty Bay on 15-8-1886. The cargo was deals from St John NB for Clonakilty.

Hercules
The Hercules, a 365 ton barque, was wrecked at Courtmacsharry on 12-2-1874. Eleven of the twelve aboard were lost. She was en route from Barrow to Cardiff in ballast.

Santee
The 1078 ton ship, Santee, was wrecked at Toe Head on 30-12-1869. All twelve aboard were lost. The cargo was guano from Callo for Cork.

Thenea
The Thenea was wrecked at Prison Cove Skibbereen on 26-12-1848. Four of those aboard were lost.

Ceylon
The Ceylon was lost at Ross Bay on 8-1-1849. She was en route from the Clyde to New York. Thirteen were lost.

Endeavour
The Endeavour was lost at Galley Head on 4-9-1848. She was en route from Ardrossan to Dundalk.

Amy
The Amy was wrecked at the Seven Heads near Barrys Cove. Three survived. She was from Honduras for London.

Edna
The Edna was wrecked at Barrys Cove on 30-12-1869. The 730 ton barque was en route from Montreal to Glasgow with general cargo. Nine of the twenty crew were lost.

Ann
The 450 ton barque, Ann, was wrecked at Barrys Cove on 22-3-1852. She carried timber. Sixteen of the crew of eighteen were lost. An unnamed schooner was lost there on 15-12-1848 while en route from Rochelle to Waterford.

Severn
The Severn was lost in a great storm on 15-12-1848 at Courtmacsharry. She was en route from Shediac to London. At the same time the Duquet was lost. Two days later the Bernice bound from Havre to Genoa was lost with four of her crew.

Free Trade
In the same storm on 15-12-1848 the Free Trade was lost at Clonakilty Bay. She was en route from Ibrail to Sligo. The David from Bayonne for Waterford was also lost at Clonakilty.

Fitzroy
The Fitzroy, of Newcastle was lost at Skibbereen on 9-3-1835. Three of nine aboard were drowned.

Lark
The frigate, Lark, was damaged after striking rocks in Timoleague Bay on 23-11-1682. The bay is also described as Dunworley Bay two miles from Timoleague and eight miles west of the Old Head Of Kinsale. The Captain, John Moyle, had engaged the services of a William Hendly who had been recommended as a reliable pilot. Having rounded Seven Heads or perhaps Galley Head he was confident that he was past the Old Head of Kinsale and entering Kinsale Harbour. He steered close to the northmost shore in a strong SSW wind. When six fathoms were sounded he remained confidant and professed that this was the Meade Bank at Kinsale. At four fathoms the captain was uneasy and the vessel soon struck. The anchor was let out and dropped in 16 feet of water. The vessel was further damaged by the SSE wind and strongly ebbing tide. The captain ordered the masts cut but to no avail. The crew escaped in four boats leaving a small party on the stranded vessel to prevent looting. Much of the goods aboard were salvaged and the vessel was later salvaged.

Rover
An Algerian pirate ship described as the Rover was wrecked in Dunworley Bay. She was one of the vessels which were involved in the raid on Baltimore in 1631 when 200 inhabitants were seized by the Algerians.

African ship
A ship with gold dust was scuttled in Dunworley Bay during the reign of William III. The captain sank his vessel by holing her because of his fear of pirates ashore. The date was ascertained by the presence of coins from the reign of William III. (1650-1702)

Amity
The slave trader, Amity, was wrecked about 1700 on Carraig na gCun in

Dunworley Bay. Her cannon were scattered in the shallows. A Mr Bennet in 1895 described swimming down and seeing cannon which he thought were from the Lark. (67) Twelve cannon were salvaged by the Collins brothers in 1898 working for the Cork merchants, Holland and Mulcahy. (155)

Cardiff Hall

On the south tip of Courtmacsharry Bay lies the small strand of Travarra Bay surrounded by rocky headlands. At the western mouth of this bay lies Shoota rock about 30 yards from the shore. On 13-1-1925 the Cardiff Hall was wrecked on this rock and the crew of 28 drowned. She carried a cargo of 6000 tons of maize destined for R&H Hall of Cork. She had come from Rosario near Buenos Aires but encountered the strong gale which also endangered the Daunt Rock lightship. She seems to have been blown back from the Old Head of Kinsale. Captain John Bowen and his crew of 28 were drowned. Maize was thrown to the top of 150 foot cliffs by the force of the storm. The 2 ton keel of the ship landed on a ledge 40 feet over the sea. Wrecks abound in this area and the timber in Barryroe church is reputed to have come from wrecks. (67)

Ciampha

The 1498 ton Ciampha of Castle Marie was wrecked in a severe storm on 18-2-1910. The wreck occurred on the rocks of Bird Island, a 100 yard long 20 foot high rock only 50 yards from Crow Head at Dunworley Bay near Courtmacsharry. Captain Ostellone and all 26 crew were lost despite the efforts of the lifeboat who battled in vain for seven hours. Eleven bodies were recovered and buried at Lislee graveyard. Wreckage was scattered for miles along the shore and much was recovered by the local people.

The Ciampha was bound from Merriliones to Queenstown for orders with a cargo of nitrate. (67)

Pulchinella

The Italian barque, Pulchinella, was wrecked during a storm on 9-2-1874 at Blind Harbour near Union Hall. She carried Indian corn from New York. Of 13 aboard only the captain's son survived. (67)

Cecil

The 300 ton brig, Cecil, owned by C.L. Clear & Co of Liverpool encountered the same fog on 8-2-1871 as caused the wreck of the Crescent City. She was en route from Lagos to Liverpool with wine and nuts. She anchored at Ross Bay but the anchors dragged and she went ashore. Coastguards from Dirk Cove, Doney Cove and Mill Cove used their rockets to bring Captain Clements and his crew ashore. (67)

Bessie Wilkinson

The collier, Bessie Wilkinson, owned by Messrs Wilkinson was wrecked off Seven Heads on 13-2-1884. She carried coal from Newport for Glandore. Captain Pettaway and his crew were lost.

Two Brothers

The troopship, Two Brothers, sailed from Kinsale in 1656. She was bound for Jamaica with 241 officers and men and three women. She was driven ashore in the Bay of Timoleague and dashed on rocks. Only 30 of those aboard survived.

Mignonette

The 1250 ton British Flower or Arabis class sloop, Mignonette, was mined and sunk outside Sands Cove in Clonakilty Bay near Galley Head on 17-3-1917. The sloop was part of the naval anti submarine force based at Cork Harbour. The 1250 ton vessel was built in 1916 by Dunlop, Bremner. A six pounder gun was recovered in July 1982 by Messrs

Paddy O Sullivan and Ray White and is displayed at Kinsale museum. The wreck lies in 40 metres and is very broken up. (147) (77)

Alyssum

A sister ship of the Mignonette, the Alyssum was mined and sunk nearby off Galley Head the next day 18-3-1917. She was built by Earle in November 1915. The wreck lies in 60 metres. (147) (77)

Prospect

On 23-1-1924 the oak built steamer, Prospect, of Schull sank four miles south of High Island near Caraigavily. She broke her main shaft near the stern tube and took water aboard. Captain O Driscoll set sail for safety but she sank. The crew rowed ashore at Union Hall. The cargo was empty porter barrels and flour. The Prospect was engaged in local coasting. (168)

Sarah

The Sarah of London, homeward bound from Barbados was wrecked on the Stags on 11-1-1694. All the crew were saved. (110)

Asian

The British steamship, Asian, was wrecked on 17-9-1924 on the Stags Rocks in fog during a severe gale. She was en route from New Orleans to Liverpool. She carried 54 crew and six passengers. The wireless operator had time to transmit only one message before the mast fell. The message was answered by the destroyer, Seawolf, based at Berehaven which went to assist. Those aboard escaped to the ship's boats. Five crew were tossed into the sea and one man was lost when two boats overturned. The Seawolf picked up the boats and conveyed the survivors to Bantry. The Dutch tug Wittersee went to the scene but was unable to assist as the Asian

broke forward at the no 2 hatch. Owned by F. Leyland & Co she was built by Caird & Co at Greenock in 1898. The vessel measured 5514 tons and was 420 feet in length. The wreck lies in about 20 metres, is well broken and is in the entrance to the gulley between the rocks on the south side. (10) (67)

Spes Nova, Joan Patricia

The two Galway trawlers Spes Nova and Joan Patricia ran aground on the Stags on 7-11-1983. The wooden 80 foot 106 ton Spes Nova was built in 1970 at Buckie in Scotland. The Joan Patricia was a 60 foot vessel. The latter fouled her nets and drifted on the rocks while fishing for herring. The Spes Nova struck the rocks while assisting her. One crewman of the Joan Patricia, Martin Jennings was lost when he jumped for an overturned liferaft. The Crystal River took the survivors. (67)

Fox

The six gun naval sloop, Fox, was wrecked on 2-12-1699 on the NE corner of the Stags. She dragged her anchors during a storm and the cables parted. An anchor is believed to have been found and raised. Local legend alleges that the vessel was chasing pirates.

Rona

On 14-10-1893 the barque, Rona, also called Arona, ran aground during fog on the Stags. She carried a cargo of mahogany and rum. The lookouts failed to see the rocks until it was too late. The ship was badly holed and water rose to eight feet inside in three hours. The vessel heeled and Captain Oppenheim ordered the crew to the boats. One boat was smashed and a crew man injured. Three other men took another boat to assist him and eventually saved the injured man a mile and a half out to sea. The crew of ten landed safely. (67)

Kowloon Bridge
Photo: Pierce Hickey Skibereen

Kowloon Bridge

On 22-11-1986 the iron ore carrier, Kowloon Bridge, was wrecked on the Stags Rocks off Toe Head. The ship had put to sea after spending some days at shelter in Bantry Bay. The crew left the vessel by RAF helicopter and left the engines running to take her out to sea. A SW gale drove the vessel towards the coast and she ran on the rocks. Efforts by the Dutch tug, Smit Rotterdam, and others failed to free the wreck. The ship broke in three parts in Spring gales spilling her 165,000 tons of ore and 2000 tons of oil. The remains of the wreck were washed off the rocks and into 30 metres of water. The position is 51.27.08N, 9.13.07W. The crew of 44 were all lost when her sister ship, the Derbyshire, sank without trace in the Pacific on 7-9-1980. There was conjecture that she broke her back during a typhoon because of a structural fault in her hull. The exact time and place of her loss are unknown. Six sister ships were built by Swan Hunter's in the early 1970's. It is suggested that the original design was not adhered to causing a fatal weakness at frame 65 which adjoins the bridge. Another sister, the Tyne Bridge, suffered cracks so serious that her crew were evacuated by helicopter in March 1982. She was repaired and renamed the East Bridge. Another sister, the Furness Bridge, was renamed the Marconia Pathfinder then the World Pathfinder. Another sister, the Kittywake, developed cracks in bulkhead 65 because the girders did not run through the bulkhead.

Friendship

The 80 ton schooner, Friendship, was wrecked on the Stags on 13-8-1893. She was bound from Newport to Schull with a cargo of coal. The crew of 4 survived.

Carnavonshire
Photo: O' Mahony Cobh

Carnavonshire

The 1274 ton, three masted barque, Carnavonshire, was wrecked at Yokane Point near Lough Ine on 11-4-1896. She was bound from San Francisco for Queenstown for orders with a cargo of wheat. The ship struck Thige Mor Rock just off the mainland east of Barlogue coastguard station. Captain Williams and the 20 crew rowed ashore landing at Tralagogh. The Carnavonshire was built in 1876 and owned by Hughes of Liverpool. (67)

Crystal River

The 70 foot trawler, Crystal River, of Castletownbere sunk on 11-10-1984 after going on rocks near Stags Head. The skipper, Denis O Driscoll, believed that the rising tide would float the vessel but it was badly holed and sank almost immediately. The skipper and crew escaped by liferaft. (67)

Unknown vessel

On 29-12-1895 a large four masted ship was lost near Toe Head. She was thought to be English, as documents in English were recovered. The coastguards assembled timbers with the letters AONE..........H and also MAG.M but no sense was made of this information. The tops of 14 yards were floating on the surface indicating the size of the vessel. The coastguard boat went out to the scene but no survivors were found. It is thought that she sank between the Stags and Toe Head. Wreckage was examined by lowering a man down the cliffs to a point 12 yards west of Scullane Point. (67)

Ecclefechan with Ensor Co. salvage vessels
Photo: O'Keefe Queenstown from Ensor Collection via Bill Swanton

Ecclefechan

On 5-8-1898, the Ecclefechan ran ashore during fog inside Bird Island in Dunworley Bay. She was in a precarious position as while aground forward the stern was in deep water. The gunboat, Gossamer, put men aboard and tried to tow the ship off but the hawser snapped and fouled her propeller. The tugs Flying Fish, Mona and Flying Fox towed off the ship and as there was eight feet of water in her hold she was beached in the SW portion of Dunworley Bay. Ensors firm went to work on the ship. The divers, John and Pat Collins who had recently worked on the sunken lightship Puffin inspected the damage. The repairs were urgent as the bottom consisted of large boulders. She was beached just where cannon from the Amity had been found shortly before. The Ecclefechan was owned by C.T. Gutherie of Glasgow and carried 4000 tons of grain. (67)

Alondra

The 2,244 tons British Steamer, Alondra, was wrecked during fog on the SW corner of the Kedge Rocks near Baltimore on 29-12-1916. She was en route from Las Palmas to Liverpool. She was owned by Yeoward Bros and built in 1899 by D.J. Dunlop. She measured 298 feet in length. Of her crew 16 were rescued by a team led by JRH Beecher, a Church of Ireland deacon who was awarded an R.N.L.I. medal in recognition of his efforts. Six crewmen left by one lifeboat and fifteen in another, leaving fourteen aboard. After a great struggle the survivors were rescued by a ladder from the cliffs. One body and four men were landed at Union Hall. The Alondra was previously the Don Hugo. The wreck lies at about 30 metres. (10) (67)

Dido

The 695 ton iron barque Dido was wrecked a mile east of Kedge Island on 26-8-1883. The location was between the Island and Carraigathorna. She was bound from Liverpool to New York with salt. The fourteen aboard survived. The barque was built in 1859.

Charles Eliza

The 145 ton Charles Eliza sank off Galley Head on 10-1-1901. Captain La Touche and his five crew took to the boat when the situation looked desperate and landed safely at Dirk Cove near Galley Head. They had sailed from Wales but the vessel began to leak and they put back to Newport. They sailed again but were caught by a severe gale. The pumps were faulty. (71)

French vessel

A small sailing ship entered Glandore Harbour during a hailstorm, year unknown. She struck Carraig a Bhotallaig and broke in two. The captain, his wife and child and the crew were drowned. Another French ship with her went ashore at Myross. They both carried cargoes of yellow meal. (166).

Vivid

The ketch, Vivid, was wrecked on 25-9-1897 at the entrance to Glandore. The dandy, Peep O Day, was wrecked in the same place on 12-10-1898.

Faulconnier

On 1-1-1904 the 1708 ton French barque, Faulconnier, was wrecked on rocks at Seven Heads. The exact position is near Cotton Rock at Travera. The crew escaped ashore without casualty. The tug, Flying Sportsman, went to assist but the Faulconnier was well up on the rocks

pointing NE. She carried barley from San Francisco bound for Queenstown for orders. (168)

Spanish Galleons

In the time of Queen Elizabeth a Spanish galleon is reputed to have been wrecked near Dunworley according to "Finnerty" writing in the Cork Examiner. Local legend indicates that a Spanish galleon was wrecked in the South Harbour on Cape Clear Island in 1620. The name "Cuasin na Loinge Doite", i.e. the cove of the burnt ship, is in the South Harbour. Near Carraigleamore on Cape Clear a mid 17th century anchor was found. A Spanish Cove near the entrance to Crookhaven is reputed to record the place where a Spanish ship was repaired.

Norwegian

The British 6327 ton steamer Norwegian was torpedoed 4 miles south of Galley Head on 13-3-1917. An effort was made to strand the ship. She ran aground on Carraigduff Rock in Dirk Bay. After a year she settled into deeper water. Many salvage operations took place, one as recently as 1982.

Gafsa

The 3974 ton British steamer, Gafsa, was torpedoed 10 miles SE of Kinsale Head on 28-3-1917. The escort, Zinna, saw no sign of the submarine but rescued the survivors.

Spectator

The 3808 ton British steamer Spectator was torpedoed by a German submarine on 19-8-1917. The position was 11 miles SE of Galley Head. The Italian salvage ship Artiglio found the wreck 6.25 miles SW of Seven Heads. Copper was salvaged from the wreck in 1934-35.

John D Williams

The wreck of a West Indiaman is described by Edith Sommerville (214). The three masted American barque was wrecked on a reef at the edge of Tralough bay near Yokane point. The cargo contained rum, bacon and butter. This was recovered by locals and hidden on Toe Head. The hiding place was forgotten and the rum remains buried.

Isabella
The barque, Isabella, was wrecked at Yokane point. She carried a cargo of brandy. Only the carpenter was saved. (214)

Saga
The brig Saga was washed ashore in Feb. 1883. There was nobody aboard and the bloody state of the ship indicated the probability that a mutiny had occurred. A coastguard was thrown over a cliff by a woman in the melee to get at the copper which lined the ship's bottom. (216)

Coromandel
The Coromandel was wrecked east of Power Head with a cargo of paraffin. A coastguard showed the locals how to use paraffin oil in lights using a wick. Previously only rush lights were used in the locality. (216)

Kerry Head
The coaster, Kerry Head, was bombed and sunk 4 miles S of Black Ball Head in sight of Cape Clear on 21-10-1940. On 1-8-1940 the ship was attacked 4 miles ESE of the Old Head of Kinsale.

Lucy
The Lucy was wrecked near Crookhaven on 25-1-1811. She was en route from Malta to London captained by Mr Frist. Two passengers and some crew were lost. (110)

Magnet
The 74 ton schooner, Magnet, was wrecked at Scullane point on 28-12-1895. She was en route from Swansea to Truro with coal.

Dorethea
The Dorethea, en route from Charente to

Dublin went ashore near Clonakilty on 26-12-1763. The cargo was saved but the ship was destroyed. The captain was Mr Boyle. (234)

James Livsey
On 15-2-1896 the 992 ton iron barque, James Livsey, sank 12 miles south of Bull Rock. The ship was bound from Cardiff to Santos with coal.

Slateland
The London steamer, Slateland, foundered a mile off Cape Clear on 18-4-1932. She sailed from Crookhaven with a cargo of stone from the local quarry. The ship started to leak badly and Captain Douglas and the crew of nine took to two boats. They landed safely at Cape Clear Island. (67)

Isaac Wright
The ship, Isaac Wright, struck Cape Clear on 4-10-1853. Twenty of the crew of thirty were lost.

Savonia
On 17-1-1909 the wooden Nova Scotian schooner, Savonia, was wrecked on the north side of the Middle Calf Island in Roaringwater Bay. She carried £15,000 worth of pine, deal, mahogany and hickory from Liscomb to England. She was encountered during a gale by the Dominion about four miles north of the Fastnet in a waterlogged condition. The crew were taken off and the derelict reported at Queenstown. The Clyde Co Tugs, Flying Fox, and Flying Sportsman, went to sea accompanied by the Joliffe tug, Jane Joliffe. They failed to find her due to the gale and returned to port. Meantime the Savonia drifted into Roaringwater Bay. The tugs put out again when the Savonia was reported ashore but she broke up rapidly. They were only in time to see scores of local boats reap the rich harvest of timber. (67)

Malmanger
Photo: Di Silva via D. Woosnam.

Malmanger

The Malmanger sank three miles off the Beacon at Baltimore on 12-3-1917. The 5671 ton Norwegian tanker was en route from New York to Avonmouth with petroleum. Just after her escort, the Zinna, left her she was torpedoed 20 miles off Fastnet. The Zinna returned and towed the Malmanger towards shore but she sank in sight of land. The bow of the 300 foot ship struck the bottom and the stern remained fifty feet above water for an hour. A series of photographs of the sinking were taken by a young girl, Baroness de Silva who was rowed around the sinking ship by her chauffeur. The crew were rescued by the sloops, Mignonette, and Alyssum. Both sunk within a few days.

Illyrian

The Leyland steamer Illyrian was wrecked at Faill Ui Chathail under the old Cape Clear lighthouse on 15-5-1884. The 2967 ton iron screw steamer was built at Belfast in 1867. She left Liverpool en route to Boston on Wednesday afternoon but encountered dense fog. Captain Farqueson reduced speed to seven knots but believed that they were past Cape Clear. On Thursday night the Illyrian struck Cape Clear. The impact was so severe that a 16 foot section of perpendicular rock fell from the cliff. There was confusion among the cattlemen among the crew of 68. Guns and rockets were fired to attract attention and all were rescued. Though the steamer was not insured as she was quite old her cargo was covered and Mr Swanton, the Lloyds agent, rushed to the scene to secure the load of wool, whiskey and brandy. The ship heeled over and her cargo was spilled into the sea. A diver, Mr Barry, of Togher in Cork was retained by Mr Midgley of Manchester and worked on the wreck raising thousands of pounds worth of goods. The same diver was engaged by the Lloyds agent to work on the Iberian which sank in Dunmanus Bay only three years before. Several items from the Illyrian are on display at the Cape Clear museum. (67) Position 51 26 10N, 09 28 42W.

Weerit

Mr Barry also raised the pilot cutter, Weerit, of Queenstown which sunk on 26-1-1886 on the rocks at the garrison at the Sherkin side of Baltimore harbour. The owner, Mr O'Sullivan, had arranged an auction to dispose of the wreck as he had presumed the cutter lost.

Hazleside

The Hazleside, a 4646 ton steamer was torpedoed, shelled and sunk on 24-9-1940 off Baltimore. The position was given as 51.17 N, 09.22 W but she drifted before sinking. Her crew were rescued by the St Ultan owned by Con Regan of Cape Clear.

Sarah

The 267 ton Sarah sank off Cape Clear on 22-9-1852. She was bound for Queenstown from Ibrail.

Stephen Whitney

On 10-11-1847 the Stephen Whitney, a 1034 ton American liner was wrecked on West Calf Island and 92 were drowned. Captain Popham sailed from New York on 18 October for Liverpool with 27 crew and 83 passengers. In dull and hazy weather Crookhaven was seen. The vessel slowed down and the depth was found to be 50 fathoms. With some diffi-culty the ship weathered the point and a light was observed. This was thought to be the Old Head of Kinsale. However it

was Rock Island near Crookhaven. Though the light was in place for two years the crew were unaware of its existence. The ship crashed into a 30 foot high rock in the inlet at the west tip of West Calf Island. The entire side of the ship was stove in and she went to pieces in half an hour. Only 18 of those aboard managed to scramble up the rock and survive. The cargo was corn, cotton, cheese, rosin and 20 boxes of clocks. Though the disaster occurred on Wednesday night news only reached Skibereen 10 miles away on Friday evening. Conditions in that area were very bad as the famine was at its worst. As a result of this tragedy the decision to construct the Fastnet lighthouse was taken. (67)

Trial

In 1934, the Trial, carrying a cargo of timber ran onto Cape Clear Island. The vessel had been abandoned by her crew at Mizen Head and the vessel drifted on the shore. Her cargo of timber was salvaged.

England

On 16-2-1695 the 5th rate, 40 gun vessel, England, sank off Cape Clear. She had been in action with a French man of war.

Portuguese ship

A Portuguese vessel was wrecked and lost on the southern side of Carrigvuar between Cape Clear and Sherkin "in olden times". The crew survived and attributed the loss to leaving a large anchor ashore when they sailed. (208) The small bronze cannon found by divers in July 1990 and obtained by the National Museum may have come from this wreck. The cannon has been identi-fied as Danish, circa 1700.

Maigue

The 456 ton Limerick SS Co vessel,

Maigue, grounded in fog at the Quay on the inlet on the south side of Clear Island on 6-1-1940. She was badly damaged and was scrapped at Dublin the same year. A portion of her mast still lies at the south Harbour. She had been purchased by the Limerick SS Co in 1919. (166)

Hourtien

The Hourtien or Hourtin of La Rochelle ran aground in fog on Tim Rocks just north of Carraig na Reidh on 15-9-1931. This was just east of the old lighthouse on the highest point of Cape Clear. Skipper Guaider and his 17 crew stayed aboard until dawn and landed on Clear Island. (166) (168)

Rendlesham

On 5-11-1940 the 166 ton Lowestoft steam trawler, Rendlesham, was wrecked a mile from the Harbour on a submerged rock on the NW point of Cape Clear. Though the wind was moderate the sea was very rough. About two hours later the news reached the harbour and three local boats put out. They found the trawler submerged but five of the eleven crew were clinging to the mast. The other six were lost. The survivors were transferred to the patrol boat, Fort Rannock, and taken to the mainland. Built in 1902 by Cook, Welton & Gemmell she was named Rosareno until 1939. She was owned by Consolidated Fisheries Ltd. (149). A brass plate marked with the builders name and job no 323 is on display at the Baltimore House Hotel.

O'Driscoll Fleet

The O'Driscolls were the leading family in the Baltimore area in the Middle Ages. In 1537 a Waterford fleet came to Baltimore to punish O'Driscoll piracy. At Dun na Long anchorage 53 pinnaces were burned and three sunk. During dredging in 1988 cannon balls were found in Baltimore Harbour.

Dispatch

The Dispatch of Margate was wrecked at Baltimore on 4-1-1782. The ship was en route from New York to London. The captain was Mr Hurst. (234)

Christopher

The Amsterdam vessel Christopher was wrecked at Spanish Island, Baltimore on 6-11-1758. The cargo of cotton, coffee, sugar and tobacco was saved. The master was Terence Complate. (155)

HMS Looe

Loo Rock at the entrance to Baltimore Harbour was struck by the British Man O War, HMS Looe, on 30-4-1697. The Looe was a fifth rate 32 gun vessel built at Plymouth in 1696. The warship was turning out of the harbour when she struck. Her men, most guns and sails were saved in a salvage operation conducted by Lethbridge. In 1698 a Captain Townsend was court martialled for selling two of her guns possibly salved by himself. A green wreck buoy marks the spot. (108) (147)

Thomas Joseph

The Thomas Joseph was built at Arklow with sails and became the first local powered trawler when she was fitted with an engine at Baltimore. She sank on 11-10-1918. She struck Cathalogues rocks NW of Sandy Island at the west end of Baltimore Harbour. The trawler had put out from Baltimore for Schull on the Friday evening on a trial trip and was returning at 9 pm with 11 aboard. The owner and skipper, John Daly of Cape Clear, two engineers from Pearsons of Dublin who had fitted her engine and Mr Shipsey, the fish buyer of Baltimore and his two daughters were with the crew. When the vessel struck some clung to the mast and others managed to hold onto the rocks on the shore. One of the engineers attempted to take a rope ashore but was dashed on rocks. The cries for help were heard aboard the Marie Annie whose engine had broken down suddenly. The crew launched a small boat into the fog and for no clear reason took 100 yards of rope with them. The rope was vital as it allowed one of the crew to swim to the wreck and take off those remaining aboard. After the rescue the engine of the Marie Annie started without hesitation. Only five survived and the body of the skipper was recovered by Messrs Collins and Daly, divers of Queenstown about a week later. John Daly had been awarded a Royal Humane Society medal for his part in the rescue of two men from the Nestorian wrecked at the west end of Cape Clear in 1917. Baltimore boatyard was an important influence on the locality. It was opened on 17-8-1887 due to the efforts of Fr Charles Davis, parish priest of Rath and the Islands and the financial help of Baroness Burdett Coutts. In 1891 the railway was extended to Baltimore with a grant of £70,000. By that time there were 75 Baltimore boats and a further 150 from Kinsale to Cape. (71,92)

Helvellyn
The Helvellyn sank near Cape Clear on 17-12-1867. She was carrying a cargo of coal and iron. The captain and crew were shipped to Waterford by T.P. Trecker. Trawlermen frequently find coal at a fishing ground called the Fourth Island, nine miles off the Cape which may be from this collier.

Ocean Gem
Wreckage from an unknown vessel was recovered on 21-2-1910. It is presumed that it came from a ship which struck the Fastnet or the Mizen in the storm. (67).

During the storm the 37 ton lugger Ocean Gem was wrecked a quarter mile E of the Schull coastguard station. The 3 ton cutter, Shamrock, was also wrecked in the same place.

Wreck off Schull
Nine crew were drowned when a boat from Skibereen was wrecked at McCarthy's Island off Schull. The wreck was foretold by a mysterious lady who begged a lift on horseback a few nights before the wreck. (135, 49,p202)

St Briget
The cargo ferry, St Briget, ran aground on Anima rock between Calf Island and Hare Island on 26-4-1922. The cargo was removed.

Enoch Bonner
The 698 ton barque, Enoch Bonner, was lost on the west point of Cape Clear on 7-9-1867. The crew of fourteen were all lost. She was outward bound from Liverpool for Boston with general cargo. (36)

Nestorian
The 6000 ton, 400 foot Nestorian was wrecked on the Bullane Rock at the SW tip of Cape Clear Island on 2-1-1917. She was carrying cotton from Galveston to Liverpool. Steel and shell heads were amongst the cargo. Built by Hawthorn Leslie in 1911 she was owned by F. Leyland. She struck amidships and broke in two. Cape Clear fishing boats reached the scene quickly and the Daly and O'Driscoll families saved 79 of the crew of 80. They were taken by fishing yawls to a sloop offshore. One man was killed when he fell from the rigging. Some large steel bars were lifted in 1988 by salvors. They measured about eight feet long by six inches square. Another wreck is described alongside. (l0) (67) Position 51 25 24N, 09 31 18W.

Ailsawald
Photo: Wigham Collection via Bill Swanton taken for Ensor

Ailsawald

The 4,500 ton Newcastle on Tyne ship, Ailsawald, went aground on rocks at the rope walk on the north side of Sherkin Island on 19-12-1900. The vessel was en route from Penarth near Cardiff to Bermuda in water ballast with 600 tons of coal aboard. During a severe SW gale she was caught broadside by the wind and driven aground. Capt. Muir and his crew of 24 were rescued by the islanders. The propeller was broken and the bottom damaged and it was presumed that the ship was a total loss. Mr Ensor of Cobh negotiated with the owners, Lunn & McCoy and the insurers and as a result sent his salvage steamer, Adelaide to the scene on 23 December. A storm the next day shifted the stricken vessel a further 30 feet onto the rocks. Ensor sent to Cardiff for three extra salvage pumps and these arrived with a Mr Dickenson on the first week in January. Each of the five pumps could clear 3000 gallons of water per hour. A coffer dam weighing 30 tons was built at the Baltimore fishing school. This was placed by Ensor and three other divers on the largest hold of the Ailsawald. A pump was sunk into the hold and as it was pumped out the ship floated. The first attempt was made on January 10 and the next day four tugs pulled the ship off the rocks. They towed her to Whitehall Level in Baltimore Harbour where only her bow could be beached due to the excess draught. The stern slipped off the bank and was submerged with 23 feet of water over her deck. The divers stopped the leaks and further pumping continued. Eventually she was moored at the NE point of Hare island for further repairs. Ensor's ingenuity had saved the 320 foot ship built in 1895. Not everyone was happy. The Royal Irish Constabulary were dispatched with search warrants to Sherkin to recover the crew's property on 29-12-1901. A special court was held at Skibbereen and some islanders were charged with looting the wreck. Ensor's company operated several specially equipped salvage ships at various times and was quite a large operation. These included the Leonesse and the Sea Salvage. (71) (93)

General De Scabon

The General De Scabon sank off Cape Clear on 4-11-1849. The ship was bound from Sligo to Trieste.

Lady Charlotte

On 23-10-1838 the Liverpool brig, Lady Charlotte, was wrecked on the Dromadda rocks at the west entrance to Long Island channel in Roaring Water Bay. Her cargo was hides, wool, bark and specie including silver plate and dollars. She was en route from Callao near Lima to Liverpool. Captain Bartingale and eight crew were lost. One man was saved by the coastguard under Henry Baldwin when he was washed onto the rocks and became attached by his handkerchief to some sharp points on the rock. The main description of the wreck is in a letter published in the Cork Standard and copied in the Freemans Journal of 29-10-1838. The wreck was extensively salvaged. The coastguard salved $36,000 in silver plate. A report on 1-5-1839 described the work of the underwriter's divers. They recovered £70,000 at 1838 prices. After they had finished their official work the two divers stayed on the site working for themselves for eight years. (135, 49, p202) (181) (65)

Arnon

The 241 ton brig, Arnon, was wrecked in Long Island channel on 21-11-1881. The cargo was deals from Halifax to Caen. the crew of eight survived.

Nuovo Zelante
The 211 ton brig, Nuovo Zelante, struck the Targ rocks between Crookhaven and Long island on 21-3-1852. Six of the crew of ten were lost. The voyage was from Galletz to Queenstown with corn.

Rood Rech
The Poole ship, Rood Rech, was wrecked at Long Island during a storm on 31-12-1807. The ship was en route from Newfoundland to Waterford. Of the 14 aboard Captain R. Daw and six perished. (155)

Christian Wilhelm
On 24-4-1894 the 386 ton barque, Christian Wilhelm, was wrecked between Sherkin and Sandy islands at the entrance to Baltimore harbour. The ship was bound from Norway to Swansea with pitwood. She approached the island in haze and dropped her anchors but they dragged and she went on the rocks on the north of Sherkin Island. The crew of ten were rescued by Mr Calhane of Sherkin who put out several times in a four oared boat. (67)

Florence
The Kilkeel fishing boat Florence foundered off Sherkin on 24-4-1894. A gale threatened the fleet fishing for mackerel off West Cork. Several boats were overdue. Wreckage was found including nets, a punt and a lifebuoy with her number, 46, about a mile West of the Kedge rocks. The crew of eight were all lost. (67) (166)

Alfred and Emma
On 29-12-1900 the fishing schooner, Alfred and Emma, was driven ashore at Baltimore. She was owned by Captain J Bourne. (168)

Campodonice
The Italian owned vessel Campodonice was en route from Sulina to Cork with a cargo of maize when she encountered a SE gale. She sank in three fathoms off Crookhaven on 9-2-1874 Capt. Lagna and his crew were rescued by rocket line. (67)

Eliza Young
In the same storm the 530 ton Eliza Young put into Crookhaven for supplies. The SE gale caused her to drag her anchors and she was driven aground on 10-2-1874. She was en route from Dubios, Granda to Barrow, Inverness with timber and had sailed on 18-12-1873. The crew were put up at the residence of Mr Nanty at Crookhaven. The ten man crew arrived at the sailors home in Cork a few days later, joining many other survivors. (67)

Sir Richard
The 68 ton schooner, Sir Richard, was wrecked between Alderman rocks at Crookhaven and Streek Head on 9-10-1893. She was bound for Newport from Bantry with pyrites. The three aboard survived.

Charles
The Nova Scotian barque, Charles, sank outside Baltimore harbour on 10-2-1874. Her masts showed when the storm abated. There was only one survivor. (67)

William Penn
The William Penn was wrecked at Barlogue Bay, Crookhaven on 26-8-1848. Her voyage was from St John NB to the Clyde.

Calder
The 226 ton Calder was lost at Crookhaven on 26-12-1852. She was en route from New York to Liverpool.

Boaunius
The brig Boaunius was driven on rocks at Castle Island in Schull harbour on 4-2-1802. The master, Bernardo Jose Dios, and crew were saved. The cargo of 760 chests of oranges was plundered by locals. (155)

La Solidada
The Spanish frigate sank at Crookhaven on 25-1-1780. The ship had been taken as a prize by a Liverpool privateer. (35)

Sailor Prince
After the storm of February 1874 the barque, Sailor Prince, was offered for sale as a wreck on 3-3-1874. The 445 ton vessel was built at St John New Brunswick in 1862. She was offered for sale as seen at anchor at the coastguard station at Crookhaven. In addition 2,000 Havana sugar boxes were for sale. (67)

Huntingdon
The Huntingdon was wrecked on rocks at Spanish Island, Baltimore on 6-11-1758. The ship had come from Zante with a cargo of currants which were saved. The master was Thomas Erasmus. (155)

CORK MIZEN

Broad Oak
The 274 ton sailing ship Broad Oak was wrecked at Dunlough Bay on 29-12-1852. She carried cotton and sugar from Pernambucco to Liverpool. The captain and fifteen of the crew were lost as they tried to scramble ashore onto the rocks or were washed away. The mate and four sailors were saved by Mr Simmons, a local magistrate who rushed to the scene with the police. (68).

Taurima
On 3-8-1985 the pleasure trawler Taurima owned by the then leader of the opposition Mr Charles Haughey was wrecked when it struck just below the lighthouse at Mizen Head. All aboard were saved with the help of the light-keepers. Some wreckage lies at 15 metres in the deep inlet in the Head. As the vessel was wooden, little is left.

Prudence
On 13-2-1881 the 148 ton schooner Prudence was wrecked on the south west coast. She was built of oak at Bedford and owned by Mssrs White Bros of Waterford. She was carrying oats from Limerick to London. Her master Mr Thomas and crew were lost.

Memphis
The 3191 ton 345 foot, Memphis of the African SS Co was wrecked at Dunlough Bay near Mizen Head on 17-11-1896. The Dominon Line had chartered the ship from Elder Dempster Line. She was en route from Montreal to Avonmouth carrying timber, flour, bacon, butter, cattle and general cargo which included lead ingots. She was built by Harland and Wolf in 1890. Nine of the crew were lost. Some escaped by the boats while the engineers climbed the rigging. One boat capsized. A local family the Leary's took out a boat from Aughmina and saved some of the crew. Even Jones (40) of Carnavonshire who lost his life in the shipwreck is buried at the Church of Ireland cemetery at Crookhaven. The remains of the ship lie in 24 metres near a rock outcrop (Carraig na Coose) on the south side of the bay. They are well scattered with only the boiler and anchors readily identifiable. (10) (67)

Iberian
The Iberian was wrecked on 21-11-1885 in Duncannon Bay just on the coat half a mile south of Bird Island near Mizen Head. She was en route from Boston to Liverpool when she encountered thick weather and ran on he rocks. She had obtained no bearing the previous day. The vessel carried a cargo of cattle. The crew of 54 escaped in four boats three of which landed on the rocks while the fourth was found after some time. The vessel broke up in the storm of 15-10-18986. (67) (77)

Oswestry
Photo: Wigham Collection via Bill Swanton taken for Ensor.

Oswestry

The 2419 ton, 300 foot Oswestry owned by Sivewright Bacon & Co was wrecked at Mizen Head on 12-3-1899. She was en route from Newport News and Norfolk Va. to Manchester with cotton, deal, copper ingots, iron plates, bars and indian corn. The ship was built by E. Withy & Co at Hartlepool in 1888. The wreck occurred in fog just south of a rock pinnacle in the small bay on the north side of Mizen Head. Captain Wilson and the crew of 24 landed safely with assistance from locals by scaling the rocky outcrops. The ship broke in two releasing the cargo and only the forepart was visible. (67) Mr Swanton, the Lloyds agent organised boats to salvage the cotton aboard. The Oswestry was built in 1888 by Furness at Hartlepool. A local farmer saved an engineer by carrying him on his back up the cliff. As a mark of gratitude the farmer received gifts from him each time he reached port. (135).

Bohemian

the 3052 ton 400 foot steamer Bohemian left Boston for Liverpool on 27-1-1881 with a cargo of cotton and bacon. On Sunday February 6 she ran into thick weather though the sea was calm. At 8pm she passed the Calf light which was visible, but at 1am on the 7th the ship struck on a reef of rocks running out from Caher Island off Mizen Head. Though the helm was put hard a port and the engines reversed, the vessel sank in 35 metres so that only her masts showed. Captain Grundy and 35 of the crew of 57 were lost. The Bohemian was built at Harlands in 1870 and owned by F Leyland & Co. (10)

Augusta

The Augusta a 136 foot iron steamer of 54 tons was built at Swansea in 1849 and acquired by Messrs Hodder and Co of Cork in 1881. She was totally wrecked in Dunmanus Bay on 5-12-1886.

Mountaineer

On 14-12-1850 the Mountaineer was grounded at Dunmanus Bay. She left Quebec on 9 November with timber commanded by Robert Harisson. A server gale drove her into the bay. She anchored to ride out the storm close to Carbery Island but was close to the rocks at Kitchen Cove. The next day the coast-guards went out to the endangered vessel and she cut anchors and beached on the mud beneath the coastguard station thus saving the crew.

Ranger

The brig Ranger of North Shields was wrecked on the rocks at Dunmanus Bay on 30-3-1850. Commanded by John Robertson she carried Egyptian wheat to Cork or Falmouth for orders.

Caroline

The 40 ton cutter Caroline was wrecked in Dunmanus Bay on 15-10-1886. The six aboard escaped. She was on route from Crookhaven to Dunmanus Bay on salvage work.

Irada

On 22-12-1908 the Irada en route from Galveston to Liverpool with a cargo of cotton was wrecked on Mizen Head. The ship was built by J.H. Wellsford & Co. in 1900 and measured 8124 tons and 501 feet in length. She was one of the largest vessels of her time. The accident occurred during a SW gale and fog. The Bull Light was seen but its distance miscalculated. The Fastnet Light was not visible. The strong ebb tide caused the vessel to strike shore and become wedged between a rock pinnacle and the mainland at the small bay near Mizen Head. As some of the crew scrambled ashore on a rope a sea caught the vessel and the heeled over crushing a stewardess and the mate. The captain who had remained last was not seen after this mishap. Most of the crew escaped in the ships boats and landed at Crookhaven. Captain Arthur Wellesley Roberts of Brikdale Lancs is buried at the Church of Ireland cemetery at Crookhaven. Four crewmen and a stewardess were also lost of a total crew of 69. Two are buried at Old Kilmore graveyard. The survivors were assisted up the cliffs by the Irish Lights workers constructing the fog station at Clohane Island. The cargo valued at £250,000 included 21,000 bales of cotton. The hull was insured for £896,000. It was washed ashore at Paleen harbour two miles west of Castletownbere. The Lloyds agent at Bere, Mr McCarthy contacted Captain Hugh Williams the owners representative. The Perseverance was chartered from Scotts of Queenstown and much cargo recovered and transferred to a larger steamer for transport to Liverpool. (67, 71)

Confiance

On 21-8-1822 the 393 ton brig sloop Confiance was wrecked between Mizen and Three Castles heads. Commander Morgan and all 100 aboard were lost. The fifth rate carried 36 guns. (147) (141) Cannon were located near the small landing at Coosacuslaun during a search for an Austrian drowning victim about 1980. It is believed that these come from the Confiance.

L'Impatiente

One of the 43 ships of the French fleet which accompanied Wolf tone from Brest to Bantry was wrecked near Mizen Head. The expeditionary force commanded by vice admiral Morard de Galle was storm bound in Bantry Bay and set out on its return journey to France. On 30-12-1796 the fregate-bombardiere L'Impatiente was wrecked on the south side of Mizen Head near the spectacular bridge to the lighthouse. Three were only seven survivors from the crew of 560 commanded by captain de vaisseau Deniau. L'Impatiente was armed with 20 or 21 cannon (24 livre) and a mortar. Three anchors, 10 large and one small canon lie at 15-20 metres just out from the rocks near the steps at Coosanisky. Mortar shot, ballast and other wreckage lies about the area. The victims were buried in the sands at Barley Cove. L'Impatiente was built at Lorient in 1794-5. Two further vessels of the fleet were lost, the frigate la Surveillante at Bantry Bay and the ship of the line Scevola foundered out to sea from Mizen Head. (144,87)

Ribble

On 26-5-1906 the 71 ton steam trawler Ribble struck near Mizen Head in fog and sunk. The wreck occurred on Clohane Island under the fog station construction site. The 183 ton trawler was built in 1900 and operated from Fleetwood by Wyre Steam Trawling Co. The captain, crew of eight and two passengers were saved. (67)

Manaos

The 82 ton steam trawler Manaos of Milford struck Clohane Island off Mizen Head on 1-10-1908. She commenced her first voyage in January 1908 having being built at Shields for Hancock and Harris of Milford. The trawler was returning in fog from fishing off the Blaskets when she struck in a cleft on the Island. She became wedged at the foot of a cliff on one side and a shelf on the other. Skipper Salter and eight of the crew reached the rock shelf with the aid of a plank and a rope. The mate Charles McKenna was drowned. After ten hours Thomas Lord the foreman of the workers on the construction of the fog station lead a team of rescuers who saved the surviors. (67)

Cherwell

The 1129 ton, 204 foot iron barque Cherwell struck the rock at Three Castle Head in Dunlough Bay on 31-12-1889. She had carried coal from Newport to Mauritius and loaded nitrate at Pisagua in Chile bound to Cork for orders. The wreck occurred at the rocks under Three Castle Head. After 115 days at sea Captain F. Toole had no sun sight for five days due to fog. A boat was lowered and seventeen of the nineteen crew escaped. The first officer and a seaman were lost when the ship went down head foremost. The survivors landed at Carbery Island and waited the night before they could reach the mainland. She was built at Middlesboro in 1863 and owned by Edward Bates of Liverpool. (67)

Queensmore

On 8-11-1889 the Queensmore ran onto Bully Rock in Dunlough Bay. She had sailed to the U.S. on her maiden voyage and was returning from Baltimore to Liverpool. The ship carried 900 cattle, 2,000 bales of cotton, 850 tons of copper ore, and 1,000 tons of wheat as well as 77 passengers, crew and stowaways. Her cargo of cotton spontaneously ignited which was a common occurrence due to heating. Despite three days of fire fighting the fire still raged. Captain Frenery decided on the normal course of action in these dire circumstances, to run the ship on a sandy shore and flood the holds. Though Cape Clear was sighted a fog descended and he ran into Dunlough

Bay before striking Bully Rock off Three Castle Head. She drifted off the rock and sank in the centre of the bay at a depth of about 50 metres. A11 had safely taken to the boats before she sank. During an inquiry on 16-1-1890 it was observed that her cotton was loosely packed rather than tightly stacked and covered to exclude air. The fire had started at the bottom of an air duct and spread due to presence of air.(67)

Marchioness Abercorn

On 19-11-1849 the 875 ton Marchioness Abercorn was wrecked at Mizen. The ship was bound for Cardiff from Quebec.

Ranger

On 4-4-1850 the Ranger was wrecked in Dunmanus Bay. She was bound for Queenstown from Malta.

Whim

On 30-10-1852 the Whim was lost off Mizen. She was bound from Ayr to Cardiff.

Calypso

On 26-2-1848 the 370 ton Calypso was lost off Mizen.

CORK BANTRY

Bardini Reefer

The Bardini Reefer lies in 15 metres of water with its mast and funnels showing in the channel between Bere Island and the mainland. The 3976 ton Panamanian ship was lying at anchor awaiting a trip to drydock at Aviles. A fire and explosions broke out on 15-12-1982 and she sank at 51.38.77N, 9.51.33W after burning for a few days.

Contessa Viv

This 110 foot Spanish factory ship sank at the entrance to Castletownbere during a gale on 1-8-1986. The 26 year old ship was en route from Falmouth to Castletownbere. She carried a Spanish crew with a British flag to comply with EEC regulations. As she approached the harbour in a severe gale her engines failed. The vessel struck Ardnakilla Point and sank in the eastern entrance to the harbour. Captain Antonio Inglesias and five of the crew were lost. The wreck lies at 25 metres in Piper Sound.

Talay Mendi

The 140 foot Spanish trawler, Talay Mendi, struck Spanish Rock near Castletownbere on the night of 24-3-1988. She went aground less than a mile from the Contessa Viv. The 17 crew were taken off by the local trawler, Draiocht Na Mara.

Monte Izaskun

The 184 ton Spanish motor trawler, Monte Izaskun, sank at the NW point of Bere Island on 18-11-1974. She hit rocks on the approach to Castletownbere. As the tide receded she heeled over and was abandoned by the crew. Built in 1962, she was owned by Felipe Camara.

Reggio.

The English steam collier, Reggio, was wrecked on Dog Rock at Berehaven on 21-9-1908. She was en route from Barry to Berehaven carrying coal for the Atlantic Fleet which was bound for Gibraltar. The Reggio was built in 1903 by R.Thompson and Sons. Owned by Orders and Handford of Newport she measured 1396 tons and 247 feet. Part of the mast of the vessel is incorporated into the structure of Desci's pub on Bere Island. An attempt to salvage her was made, and Mr Ensor arrived in his tug, the Flying Fish. However he learned that the Western Marine Salvage Co had been engaged. Their ship and tug, the Lady of the Isles and Challenge, worked with a diver Mr Williams, for some months. They discovered that they could not pump her out due to the size of the hole and she was abandoned. The wreck was

washed off the rocks in a storm on
26-2-1910.

Garadossa
The 103 foot Nostra Senora De
Garadossa (Gardozta) was wrecked at
the entrance to Castletownbere on 30-1-
1990. The trawler lost power during a
severe SW gale and was driven onto
Roancarrig Mor near the lighthouse.
Captain Harison and 14 crewmen were
rescued by an RAF helicopter from
Wales. A sailor from the L.E. Deirdre
was lost when an inflatable was attempting assistance. Though the lighthouse is
unmanned, a repair worker reported the
position accurately and illuminated the
scene with flares. Though Spanish
owned, the trawler was U.K. registered.
She was the fourth vessel aground in
Bantry in two weeks, the others were the
Spanish vessels Ancaras and Soneiro and
the Irish trawler Dursey. (140)

Moonstone
The bell of a vessel, marked Moonstone,
was recovered from Rerrin Harbour in
1984.

Java
The brigantine, Java, was built at
Grenville, Nova Scotia in 1864 and
bought into Arklow in 1877. She ended
her days in 1900 as a coal hulk at
Berehaven.

Betelgeuse
The 61,776 ton Betelgeuse, a French oil
tanker, caught fire beside the now
defunct Gulf Oil terminal on Whiddy
Island on 8-1-1979. The vessel broke in
three after exploding. It was believed
that stresses due to the weight of the
cargo caused the ship to break and
ignited explosive gases. The mid section
was towed ashore on 30-8-1979, loaded
on a barge and taken to be dismantled.
The bow was towed by Smit Tak out to
sea and sunk at 50.40 N, 12.04 W. The

stern was raised on 1-7-1980. Of the
crew of 49 there were no survivors and
several shore workers were also killed.
(99)

La Surveillante
Trawlers in Bantry Bay recovered copper
sheeting over the years. A sixteen
hundredweight anchor was recovered
and mounted on a plinth on the Cork
road. This confirmed the suspicion of a
French wreck in the Bay. During the
Betelgeuse clearance operation the
remains of a French frigate were located.
The 140 foot La Surveillante was one of
44 ships with 15,000 men which came to
invade Ireland in 1796 during the
Napoleonic wars. The fleet sailed from
Brest on 16-12-1796 and on arrival was
stormbound in Bantry Bay. The fleet
returned on 13-1-1797 without landing
their forces. La Surveillante was
damaged in the storm and her compliment of 600 cavalry were transferred to
other ships before the crew sunk her.
Two of her 40 cannon were raised from
40 metres in 1987 by Tony Balfe of
Aquatic Enterprises and found to be in
good condition. There is a plan to
salvage more of the wreck for a museum.
The wreck is described as in good condition. The expedition had other losses; the
Scevola sank 60 leagues west of Bantry
and L'Impatiente was wrecked at Mizen.
Some other items from the French
expedition are in Bantry House. A
longboat from the fleet is in the Maritime
museum in Dun Laoghaire. As a result of
the French invasion threat 40 Martello
gun towers were built for ten miles North
and South of Dublin, at Galway Bay,
Bantry Bay and along the Shannon. In
addition 81 semaphore signal towers
were built from Lough Swilly to Cork
Harbour and on to Dublin. Forts were
built at Kinsale, Cork, Bere Island and

Waterford. The expedition of General Hoche was not the only visit by a French fleet to Bantry Bay. On 29-4-1689 the British Admiral, Herbert, discovered from his scouts a French fleet of 44 ships at Baltimore. On pursuing the ships the scouts found that the French had entered Bantry Bay. Herbert lay off the bay that night in the Defiance. The next morning the French line under Admiral Perrault formed against the British ships but could not gain the wind advantage. Fire was exchanged but at long range. Capt. Aylmer of the Portland and 94 British seamen were killed and the flagship disabled. It is believed that no ships were sunk.

Sisters of Liverpool

The British ship, Sisters of Liverpool, was chased into Bantry Bay by the French Fleet. They captured the vessel and she was burned and sunk on 20-12-1796.

Fille Unique

The transport ship, Fille Unique, accompanied the French fleet. On 4-1-1797 she was driven on rocks by a gale and was wrecked.

Dominion

On 4-1-1896 the 2032 ton iron steamer, Dominion, burst an injector line which blew a six inch hole below the water line. She was bound from Portland, Maine to Avonmouth with cargo and livestock. The holds flooded almost to the fire bars and the coal was soaked. In order to maintain steam dry coal was selected from the surface of the bunkers and the sheep pens were burned. The Captain steered for the nearest land and entered Castletownbere whistling frantically for a pilot. The order was "run her aground" which the pilot did between the Perch and Cametrigane. Due to her excess draught he could not reach the

beach and the wreck blocked the entrance of the inner harbour. In the days that followed, 38 horses, 80 bullocks 1500 sheep and £80,000 worth of flour, bacon, peas and sugar were unloaded into SS Pervill which came from Glasgow. The salvage ship, Ranger, under Capt. Pomeroy arrived with divers and 100 men to assist in the unloading. Her powerful pumps cleared the water while fitters and divers repaired the damage. Though it was feared that the Dominion would break her back she was refloated on 10-1-1896. The Elder Dempster owned ship was built in 1873. (67)

Irish Girl

The 93 foot three masted schooner, Irish Girl, was wrecked when washed ashore at Bere Island on 16-3-1914. She was built at Dundalk and launched on 21-7-1876. Jointly owned by Mr McClenaghan and Capt. Lambe, the latter owner was in command when the crew abandoned ship in a violent storm. The vessel was bound for Limerick with a cargo of 330 tons of fertiliser.

Derelict

In November 1849 the Admiralty Court divided salvage of a vessel among the crew of the revenue cruiser, Badger, and the crew of the Liverpool. The vessel they salvaged was found floating upside down at Castletownbere. She had left a Canadian port early in 1848 for the West Indies. It was presumed that she had been carried by the Gulf Stream to Irish waters.

Cardross

The Cardross was lost in Bantry Bay in a gale on 11-2-1874. She was en route from Wanks River with mahogany. She reached Queenstown and received orders to proceed to Liverpool. The gale must have driven her west and she came ashore at Bantry Bay. Captain Carter, his wife, child and eight crew were lost. A further three were saved. A poignant advertisement appeared some days later. The advert offered a £25 reward for the recovery of a packet carried by the chief mate. It was consigned by a John Laird of Carrickfergus who was anxious to recover his packet should the body be found. Mr Laird believed the wreck to have occurred between Cape Clear and Dursey Head. (65)

French Privateer
In the storm of November 1692 a French 20 gun privateer was wrecked at Bantry Bay. Her home port was St Malo. (London Gazette 2894)

Rio Formosa
The Clyde company's 163 ton Rio Formosa was wrecked in Bantry Bay in 1878. She had been built in 1870 and bought from Bowdler's of Liverpool. (159)

Syren
The torpedo boat destroyer, Syren, ran onto Dog Rock at Berehaven some years prior to 1908. The bow was cut off and the stern towed to Gairloch. A new bow was fitted. The Syren was a 390 ton destroyer built 1900 and broken in 1920. (67)

Bonnie Lass
The lobster cutter, Bonnie Lass, of Southampton sank when she struck the mast of the Notre Dame on 9-7-1908. The mast pierced the bow and the Bonnie Lass sank in two minutes. Her crew all escaped. (67)

Notre Dame de Boulogne
The 94 ton French fishing vessel, Notre Dame de Boulogne, no 2409B, struck Dog Rock at the entrance to Berehaven on 17-4-1908. She was badly holed. The Irish Lights tender, Ierne, tried to pull her off but she was stuck fast. On May 1

Mr Ensor of Passage West Salvage Co visited the site with a view to salvage but reported that she had been blown off the Rock by SW winds and had sunk on 26-2-1910. She had come from Falmouth for fishing. (67)

Evlyn
The steam trawler, Evlyn, was struck and sunk by HMS Albion on 29-6-1907. The Evlyn had left port and steamed to Whitehorse Point and commenced trawling in a SW direction. After twenty minutes work she was approached by the cruiser, Albion. The trawler presumed that she required fish for the officers mess but she hailed the trawler to warn her that she was steaming into a zone being used for gunnery practice. The Albion struck the Evlyn and sunk her. At a court the owner of the Evlyn, Somers Payne was awarded £393 against his claim of £800 . Captain Pelham of the Albion became an admiral shortly after the incident. (67)

Wizard
The 231 ton, 10 gun brig sloop, Wizard, was wrecked on Seal Rock (Roancarraig Beag) at Berehaven on 8-2-1859. Initially, gun signals were ignored but the coastguard later obtained a large row boat and a small one. Lieut. Helby and 42 crew were rescued despite great risk. A subscription was raised in London to reward the gallantry but no award was received. The Cherokee class brig had been built in 1830 at Pembroke DY. (141)

John and James
The brig, John and James, was wrecked at Ballycrovane near Berehaven on 18-1-1778. She was en route from Lisbon to Dublin with fruit. Her cargo and crew were saved. (155)

N.S. de Palera St John Baptist.
This Opporto ship was wrecked at

Ballycrovane on 29-1-1781. She carried salt, wine and fruit from Lisbon to Dublin. (155)

William and Anne

The sloop, William and Anne, was wrecked at Ballycrovane on 29-1-1781. She was en route from Glasgow to Cork with tobacco, coal and barley. (155)

Infanta

The Spanish galleon, Infanta, sank in Bantry Bay on 14-11-1683.

Bonadventure

In 1665 the Bonadventure sank at Bantry Bay. (29)

Ariel

The 71 ton ketch, Ariel, was wrecked at Pipers Point, Berehaven on 10-11-1904. The vessel carried a cargo of copper ore from Castletownbere to Swansea. The crew of three survived. The wreck which occurred on Faillnabo Rocks was floated with barrels but sank North of Colt Rock.

Petrel

The 108 ton schooner, Petrel, was wrecked on Pipers Rock in the west channel at Berehaven on 18-11-1918. She carried coal from Cardiff to Bere.

Esperance

The 87 ton Boulogne fishing vessel, Esperance, was wrecked at the west entrance to Berehaven on 20-3-1893. The crew of 19 survived.

Fancy

The 23 ton sloop, Fancy, was wrecked at Garnish Island on 6-3-1889. The sloop was en route from Portmagee to Garnish in ballast. Two of the crew of six were lost.

Three Brothers

On 25-9-1884 the 82 ton schooner, Three Brothers, was wrecked at Bere Island. She was bound from Berehaven for Runcorn. The crew of four survived.

Commodore

The 111 ton brig, Commodore, was wrecked on Piper Rocks, Castletownbere on 9-1-1882. The ship carried guano from London to Galway. The crew of five survived.

Feliz

The 406 ton barque, Feliz, was wrecked 8 miles east of Castletownbere, 2 miles from Adrigoole Sound on 31-12-1876. She was bound from Galveston to Liverpool with a cargo of cotton. The crew of 4 survived.

Louisa Christina

On 17-5-1852 the Louisa Christina was wrecked at Castletownbere.

James

The excise sloop, James, sank in the inner harbour of Berehaven in September 1732. The customs officer, Richard Tonson, and the James's crew had seized contraband New England plank and taken it aboard. In addition 80 ankers of brandy were seized. That night the smugglers boarded the James and the Captain and crew fled for their lives. The James was plundered of sails, rigging and cargo and the smugglers sank her.

Doutelle

The noted smuggler, Morty Og O'Sullivan, was captured in a fight on 6-5-1754. He was later executed in Cork. The following Monday, Crown forces moved to secure his ship. This was not possible as all the rigging had been removed and holes bored in her. They burned the vessel to the waterline and she sank, probably at the anchorage of Cleinderry. Morty's vessel was a fast French built brig or sloop with eight swivel guns. Morty fought at Culloden in 1745 and the ship which took Bonnie Prince Charlie to France was the Du Teilly. It is possibly the same vessel. Morty's ship actually was a privateer under letters of marque for the French. In addition to smuggling he transported recruits to France - The Wild Geese for the Irish Brigade. (209) (210)

Indigo Rock

A rock named Indigo Rock lies to the west of Bantry on the south shore of the bay. It possibly was named after the loss of a ship with dye amongst its cargo.

Peter

The Peter was lost at Berehaven on 11-5-1782. She was bound for Jamaica from Cork, commanded by Captain Sheehan. (234)

Canada

In April 1811, the Canada drifted for six weeks without a rudder, before coming ashore at Dunboy. The ship was carrying mahogany from the West Indies. The master was M. Thomas. (229)

Jolly Tar

On 9-5-1851, the Jolly Tar was wrecked on Pipers Rock. The Swansea brig carried coal and pollard for the Castletownbere workhouse. The master and some crew were lost. (229)

Baring

The 820 ton troopship, Baring, lost its rudder and was blown on rocks on the western side of the harbour of Berehaven on 10-10-1814. The ship carried the baggage of the 40th and York Chasseurs. The master, Mr Carter, was awaiting a pilot at the harbour mouth when his ship lost its rudder, was blown across the sound and wrecked on the island. All but 20 of the 300 aboard were saved. The ship had sailed with five others the previous day from Cork. Convoyed by the HMS Sultan, a 74 gun ship. As American privateers were active in the area, all ships were escorted by a warship. It is not clear where the fleet was bound, being variously described as a secret expedition and for the West Indies. The fleet returned to Cork on the 20th and sailed again on 2nd November.

(229) Two years later, a local, Mr Mealy, wrote that a number of local gentry and smugglers had secreted a large quantity of arms from the wreck. He observed that the local magistrate, Morty O' Sullivan, was making little effort to secure the arms and that they could fall into the hands of rebels. The Baring was a former East India ship and made six voyages up to 1818.

Joseph Howe

The Joseph Howe was bound for Cork from Mexico with a cargo of mahogany and was wrecked on the southern shore of Bere Island on 17-2-1876. Four of the eight crew were lost. The 355 ton brig was owned by S. Hill of Islandmagee, Co Antrim. (229)

Leon

The Leon, of Rouen was driven across the Bay and wrecked on 29-4-1842. Captain Esclapon and all the crew were lost in view of Castletownbere. The cargo was brandy and 53 casks were washed ashore. Over consumption caused the death of one man. Another was saved by his wife who forced butter down his throat to make him sick. (229)

Shamrock

On 13-4-1874 the Shamrock was wrecked on Palmer's Rock. The sloop was carrying bricks and wood for the construction of Galley Head lighthouse. The crew were saved. (229)

Unity

On 21-4-1822 the Unity was wrecked near Castletownbere. The ship came from Glasgow and was lost with all hands. (229) The same night the Argo was lost in the same locality.

Eliza

On 13-2-1852 the Eliza put into Berehaven for shelter. The schooner was en route from Liverpool to Limerick with coal. She struck Dog Rock and the master, Mr Larne, and crew were saved. (229)

Earl of Leicester

On 25-6-1835 the Earl of Leicester was wrecked on Dog Rock. The master was named Domity or Dorning. (229) This ship is also described as wrecked on Crow Head on 24-10-1835

Emily

On 7-10-1861 the Emily was wrecked on Dog Rock. The brigantine was en route to Miramichi from Cork in ballast. Owned by George Howe, the master, Beaze and crew were rescued by a seine boat. (229)

Naiad

On 12-3-1867, the Naiad was wrecked in a SW gale probably on Dog Rock. The brigantine was laden with pitwood from Clare for Cardiff. The crew were all rescued. (229)

Kate Dawson

On 15-4-1874 the Cork smack, Kate Dawson, was wrecked, probably on Dog Rock. She was en route from Cork to Kenmare with a cargo of flour and meal. Her master, Mr Murray and crew were saved.

Bessie Younge

On 28-9-1878, the Bessie Younge was wrecked on Dog Rock. The 282 ton Maryport barquentine was en route from Ayr to Limerick with coal. The seven crew survived. (229)

John Casewell

The Plymouth steam trawler, John Casewell, hit Dog Rock on 22-10-1921. The crew escaped in their lifeboat and were rescued by a local pilot boat. Material from the wreck was salvaged by the Adelaide, of Ensors, Passage Salvage Company.

Joseph Shaw

In the 1830s the Joseph Shaw ran ashore at Faill na Gabhar, near a cave. The crew scaled the cliff and were found two days later. (229)

Ina William

The Ina William, a 337 ton drifter on hire to the Admiralty was wrecked at Bull Light, Berehaven on 30-5-1917. (77)

Spanish Trawler

In January 1960, a Spanish trawler sank in the approach to the Sname estuary at Berehaven. She had come in to land the captain who had had a heart attack. Though the vessel was given up as a total loss a Spanish salvage crew raised the trawler in May 1960 after quite a struggle. The Cabo Finisterre was used to lift the sunken ship while air was pumped in to lighten her. The raised trawler was lashed to the lifting ship and towed ashore. Eventually she was towed to Spain for a refit.

Spanish Trawler

In October 1954 a Spanish trawler was wrecked in a storm at Donovan's Point, west of Gearies. The crew were rescued by locals in hazardous conditions.

Josefa Lopez

The 172 ton Spanish trawler, Josefa Lopez, sank after striking rocks at Roancarraig Lighthouse on 31-3-1962. The crew scrambled onto the rocks but one crewman died later of injuries. (238)

Pearl

The East Indiaman, Pearl, was wrecked at the Kilmar (Kenmare) river near Dursey Island on 30-6-1613. Three East India ships had reached the Irish coast in a distressed condition. The Pearl and the Thomas reached Dursey while the Peppercorn came into Waterford. The latter had a cargo worth £300,000. The 200 ton Pearl was reported badly damaged in November. The account says "her bulk was broken or made altogether unprofitable". The cargo was salvaged through the efforts of Sir Richard Bingley. The goods were conveyed on a Kings ship commanded by Captain William Sydney. The Pearl had sailed in 1610 for the East Indies commanded by Captain Castleton. On the return voyage she and the other ships had encountered storms, lost some men and had other accidents. The authorities feared that they would be attacked by pirates on the Irish coast and took measures to secure all three ships. There is a vague reference to acts of piracy in the East Indies by the Pearl which would be left to the East India Company to deal with. The Pearl was probably an interloper and East India Company documentation is vague about the ship. Sutton (205) lists the Pearl but suggests continued service until 1631. This later service must refer to a second ship of the same name, as three voyages was the average life of an East Indiaman. Timbers have been washed ashore in recent years at Tra na Pherle between Allihes and Eyries. (242)

Ocean
The 258 ton Ocean, was wrecked at Dursey Island on 20-10-1849. She was bound for Sunderland from Quebec. Two of the crew were lost.

John Bull
The John Bull was wrecked on 20-11-1850 between Ballydonegan and Bere. The vessel came from Plymouth. The activity at the tiny port of Ballydonegan was due to the copper mines of Alihies, described in the novel "Hungry Hill" by Daphne du Maurier. Losses of vessels in ballast from Swansea seem to have been frequent.

Sophia Margaret
The 82 ton Sophia Margaret, was wrecked in Ballydonegan Bay on

26-11-1880. The schooner carried coal and bricks.

David Jenkins
The 94 ton David Jenkins, was wrecked at Ballydonegan on 26-11-1882. She was bound for Ballydonegan from Port Talbot in ballast. The four crew survived.

John Stonnard
The 79 ton schooner, John Stonnard, was wrecked on Lea Rock off Dursey on 6-11-1893. She carried slates from Aberdovey for Limerick. The four crew survived.

Miner
The Miner was wrecked at Ballydonegan on 7-2-1860. She was bound for Swansea.

Pencalenick
In March 1867 the 88 ton Pencalenick, foundered off Ballydonegan. The cargo was timber from Hale for Ballydonegan.

Florence
The 93 ton Florence, was lost at Ballydonegan Bay on 3-2-1876. The schooner carried coal from Swansea.

Karen Elsie
The 372 ton Norwegian barque, Karen Elsie, was lost at Ballydonegan Bay on 25-1-1888. She was in ballast bound for Cardiff from Limerick.

Valliant
The Valliant was wrecked at Crow Head on 22-11-1830. The day and month are remembered but the year is vague. The ship was commanded by Captain Davis.

Caliph
The trawler, Caliph, was wrecked at Dursey Island while fishing in the 1920s or 1930s.

Arravale
The motor trawler Arravale sank in Bantry Bay on 28-3-1930. The vessel was trawling a mile and a half south of Roancarraig.

Farnborough
Photo; Gordon Campbell

Submarine U83, Farnborough

The U83 was sunk by the Q ship Farnborough on 22-3-1916 in position N 51.54, W 10.53. The Farnborough was a heavily armed "mystery" or Q ship commissioned by the Admiralty to hunt submarines. Disguised as a neutral collier, the Loderer, she cruised on the merchant routes off the south coast. Captain Campbell allowed Farnborough to be torpedoed and a "panic party" abandoned the ship but leaving a substantial crew aboard. The submarine surfaced and was surprised when false deck housings fell to reveal hidden guns. The submarine was sunk with only two crew surviving. The Farnborough was in a sinking condition and was towed to Berehaven by destroyers, tugs and sloops. The ship was beached at Castletownbere and eventually salvaged. (119)

KERRY

KERRY SOUTH

La Bayonesse

The French corvette, La Bayonesse, sank on 25-10-1690 at the entrance to Kenmare River. French naval records do not list La Bayonesse which implies a privateer or merchantman. The ship was bound for France with dispatches for King James I. Col Wilson, the King's messenger, and 11 of the 24 crew and 31 passengers aboard survived to come ashore on the Beara peninsula. (211)

Hollands Melvaart

The Hollands Melvaart ran ashore on 12-8-1781 at the entrance to the Kenmare River. The vessel was being pursued by the Cicero (Capt. Hill) armed with 22 nine pounders and a brig privateer, both of Boston. The privateers boarded the wreck and burnt it. They were prevented from plundering the ship when attacked by a party of "invalids" from the shore. (234)

Hercules

On 31-12-1808 the three masted privateer, Hercules, was wrecked in Ballinascelligs Bay. The vessel was fitted out under letters of marque by the English to attack Spanish ships. Locals were terrified when the ship flying the skull and crossbones entered the loop of Rineen and anchored in the bay. The anchors dragged and the Hercules went ashore at the "water dogs cave". The crew cut the mainmast which fell to form a bridge ashore. Some of the crew escaped by this route. Some years later

during the Famine, Mary Hoare, a servant of Francis Sigerson was attracted to glittering objects underwater. A considerable quantity of plate was recovered and auctioned by Hunting Cap O'Connell, for famine relief. The place was subsequently known as Lios an Airgead and the wreck lies 100 yards offshore. (199)

Spanish Galleon

An unnamed Spanish galleon sank at Ballinascelligs in 1799.

French Privateer

On 26-12-1691 an unnamed French privateer was driven ashore and staved at Ballinascelligs Bay. The ship had 30 guns and carried a crew of 180 of whom 50 were drowned. (106)

Bristol Volunteer

The Bristol Volunteer was wrecked at Ballinascelligs Bay on 22-1-1818. The ship was en route from Bristol to Antigua. (234)

Sea Flower

Five of the crew of the fishing vessel, Sea Flower, were drowned when the trawler sank near Ardgroom Harbour in Kenmare Bay. She was bound for Castletownbere and was caught by a gale on 22-12-1968.

Agate

The 67 ton iron steamship, Agate, was wrecked on Carraig na Roan Beag at Kenmare on 18-2-1911. All eight aboard escaped. She was en route from Cork to Kenmare with general cargo.

Elizabeth Anne

The Glasgow schooner, Elizabeth Anne, left Kenmare in ballast for Carnavon

27-1-1903. She had shipped coal to Kenmare. Due to the storm she anchored in the bay. Her anchors dragged and she was wrecked at the Parknasilla Hotel.

Drake II

The 207 ton drifter on hire to the Admiralty sank on 3-7-1917 at Garnish Bay in the Kenmare River. (77)

Ithuriel

The steam yacht, Ithuriel, was driven ashore at Inny Beach near Waterville on 11-12-1914. She had sought shelter in Ballinascelligs Harbour but had dragged her anchor and when the rope broke she was driven on the beach. She quickly became a total wreck and her crew of six were lucky to escape being dashed on the nearby rocks.

Benin

The 345 ton barque, Benin, was wrecked at Inny Beach on 17-12-1847. The wreck was described as half a mile SE of Inny Fevy. The vessel carried palm oil and ivory from Benin on the west coast of Africa to Liverpool.

Camelia

The 145 ton French brig, Camelia, stranded on rocks on the north side of Ballinascelligs Bay on 6-11-1847. The spot was one and a half miles west of Inny Fevy on property owned by Patrick Trent of Waterview.

Laurell

The 150 ton, ten gun ship, Laurell, was wrecked at Kenmare on 28-1-1693. Under the command of Captain Christopher Lyall she was en route from Jamaica to London. According to the captain's story they found themselves four leagues west of the Bull, Cow and Calf but mistook them for the Scelligs. They entered Kenmare Bay and anchored at Rossmore. The wind then drove them ashore at Capanacush near

the upper end of the river. The cargo consisted of indigo, ginger, cotton, logwood, Roman vitriol, sugar and fustick. In addition, the ship carried pieces of eight and gold wedges to a value of £2,500. The wreck was abandoned by the crew who took the gold ashore and divided it among themselves. Mr Orpen of Killowen and Mr Crump, a Kings officer, arranged the salvage of the cargo and its removal to a Mr Palmer's house. During the night some local raparees descended on the house and set it on fire. The captain of the ship and the son-in-law of the owner, Mr Spyers, and a Jew, Jacob Myers, accused Orpen of wrecking the ship and looting the cargo. In his defence Orpen said that he had taken prudent precautions to safeguard the goods when the ship was deliberately wrecked by its crew. Mr Orpen advised that the ship's guns should be taken ashore but the captain feared French privateers. These were active in the area. A 32 gun ship and 28 gun ship had captured the 240 ton Elizabeth and Ann from Barbados to Bristol and a 40 ton vessel from the Canaries in January 1693. (106) Both vessels were recaptured by the galley Sheerness (Capt. Lance) and the frigate Monk. Orpen thought that a shore battery would be a better defence against the French and sent boats to unload the cargo. He offered carpenters and timber to repair the broken anchor stock. The captain however ran the ship onto some rocks and sent his carpenter to bore holes in the ship's bottom. (107).

Grain ship

A ship with a cargo of yellow meal was wrecked off the point called Eisc Caorach on Inis Seirci near Sneem. She was bound for the mills at Kenmare from

Brooklyn, USA. (135, 960,p99) The remains of a steel hull reputed to have been a flour boat lie off the Perch at Templenoo near Kenmare.

Ithuriel

The 319 ton barque, Ithuriel, was wrecked in Kenmare Bay on 7-10-1889. She carried a cargo of coal from Newcastle on Tyne to Galway.

Fidelite

The 256 ton Marseilles barque, Fidelite, was wrecked in Sneem Harbour on 25-1-1882. She was bound for Sierra Leone from Liverpool with salt. The crew of ten survived. She had sailed from Liverpool on 5-1-1882 and encountered severe weather. She was driven in to shelter because of leaks and the salt cargo fouled the bilge pumps. The coloured crew suffered great hardship when they came ashore in heavy snow. (67).

Fiddle Light

About 1860 the Fiddle Light encountered a NW gale and sought shelter at Garnish Island off Sneem. Her two anchors cables parted and she was wrecked at the cliff at Ros Dochan. She carried general cargo and stout. (135, 960,p99)

Warship

A British ship, possibly a privateer, was wrecked at Carraig Na Loinge off Parknasilla when she was caught in a gale. Some of her crew had come ashore to recruit sailors. (135, 960,p99)

Scariff Island

On 15-12-1379, in the reign of Richard II an expedition from Cornwall was wrecked at Scariff Island. Reinforcements had been gathered at Southampton to be taken to Brittany. The commanders were Sir John Arundel, Calvery, Percy, Sir Thos Banastre and other knights. The force had seized nuns from a Southampton convent where

some of the troops were billeted, in contravention of the Articles of War of that time. The ships put to sea though the sailing master, Robert Rust, predicted a storm. A gale arose and carried them off the Irish coast. Here sixty nuns were thrown overboard by the soldiers to lighten ship. Arundel's ship ran for an island and Rust tried to place her between the island and the mainland. They found themselves in the midst of rocks where the ship struck. Sir John Arundel and most of those aboard were lost. (75) (200). Twenty five other ships following their leader were also lost. Cape Clear and Sherkin, are mentioned as possible locations of the island referred to in the English accounts but Scariff is mentioned in Irish accounts.

Submarine

A Second World War German submarine is reputed to lie in Kenmare Bay. The wreck is off Ardgroom. She had sheltered for three weeks in the bay while repairs were completed, but was sunk on leaving. A FW 200 Condor crashed off Inisbro near Rosdohan also during WWII. A further submarine lies in 65 fathoms 5-6 miles off Black Ball Head. A piece of timber marked U 31 is believed to have come from the submarine and blocks a gap in a ditch on the western tip of Beara.

Ethel B Jacobs

On 25-10-1899 the 148 ton schooner Ethel B Jacobs was wrecked on a rock near Abbey Island, Derrynane. The schooner had come from the USA bound for Castletownbere for fish. An iron ore ship was also wrecked on Abbey Island.

Sailing ship

A sailing ship was wrecked on the coast about a mile south of Caherdaniel Harbour. The remains of the vessel were found in 1989. Nothing more is known about the ship. On 12-8-1781 a ship was wrecked at Cummaklane inside the Scariff Islands about two miles NW of Derrynane Harbour. The captain, David Murray, empowered Maurice O'Connell to salvage the cargo and in particular to recover two barrels of indigo. (207)

Derrynane wreck
In early summer 1991 five cannon and two anchors were discovered near Derrynane. The cannon are thought to be two three pounders and three six pounders dated about 1770. The anchors appear to be pre 1813 pattern. A further cannon and anchor of the same pattern were found in 1992, 100 yards to the south west, suggesting that a ship dragged before a SW wind and was wrecked on the rocks at Derrynane.

Thomas Rua O Suillabhan
A boat carrying this local poet (1795-1848) and teacher, en route from Derrynane to Portmagee, sank in Derrynane Harbour after striking a rock described as Carraig Eibhlin Ni Rathaille. A poem laments the loss of his valuable library of manuscripts and books. (215)

Barque
On 9-11-1887 a three masted 1000 ton barque carrying coal from Swansea to Galway sank near Sneem. During a storm the vessel anchored near Sneem but her anchors dragged and she struck a reef at Rosdohan Island. The vessel stuck for a few hours but then drifted two or three miles before sinking. Her masts showed above water and her crew escaped. (67)

William Stonard
Wreckage from the 100 ton schooner, William Stonard, was washed ashore at Ballinascelligs on 14-10-1889. The

wreck occurred near Puffin Island on 6-10-1889. She had unloaded coal from Cardiff at Caherciveen pier a few days before. All five aboard were lost. (67)

Harriet Amelia
The 143 ton Harriet Amelia was wrecked at Waterville on 18-8-1900. The brig was en route from Westport to Cardiff with pitwood and oats.

Mary
The small sailing fishing boat, Mary, was lost near Horse Island Ballinascelligs in October 1899. All six aboard were lost.

St Pierre
The 50 ton French fishing smack, St Pierre, was wrecked on 19-3-1884 about 9 miles North of Ballinascelligs.

Kate
The 34 ton smack, Kate, was wrecked on 17-10-1882 in Ballinascelligs Bay.

Peace
The 83 ton brig, Peace, was wrecked at Rineen in Ballinascelligs Bay on 8-11-1878.

Anne
On 3-10-1851 the Anne was wrecked on a rock near Ballinascelligs. She was en route from Queenstown to Tralee. The crew were saved but the cargo was destroyed. (69) The wreck broke up.

Hans Nielsen Hauge
The Norwegian barque, Hans Nielsen Hauge, was abandoned at sea 50 miles off Mizen Head during a gale on 29-3-1899. She was en route from Apalachicola to Havre. On 5-4-1899 she drifted ashore at Garriff Point in St Finians Bay. Her crew had been picked up by the Jersey City and landed at Bristol. The vessel was named after a preacher, Hans Nielsen Hauge,p and sailed for the benefit of the Luther mission. She was built at Drammen on 15-11-1872.

Ranga

KERRY DINGLE BAY

Ranga

The motorship Ranga ran aground in March 1982 at the foot of the 300 ft cliffs of Dunmore near Slea Head. The Spanish container ship owned by Naviera Ason SA was on her maiden voyage from Santander to Reykjavik. During a storm she struck the shore after losing power. The local rocket team failed to get a line on the stricken ship. The crew of fifteen were taken off by an RAF helicopter. The wreck remained intact for several years high and dry above low water. Efforts were made by Eurosalve to scrap the ship during 1986 but were abandoned due to the inaccessibility of the wreck. In Summer 1991 the bulk of the wreck was removed to facilitate filming.

Santa Maria De La Rosa

On 11-9-1588 on Stromboli reef between Dun Mor and the Great Blasket Island the Santa Maria de La Rosa of the Spanish Armada was wrecked. The remains were found by English divers led by the professional diver, John Grattan, in July 1968 after unsuccessful attempts by Sidney Wignall and Des Brannigan. The ship lies 200 yards SE of the reef at 35-40 metres. The wreckage consisted of a mound of ballast covering the remains of the ship's timbers. Some artefacts were recovered the following season. These included arquebuses, pewter plate, and shot. It is not known where any of these items are now. A small brass cannon with a coat of arms bearing the device of an uprooted tree was found on the Blaskets about 1840 and removed to Clonskeagh Castle,

Dublin but its present location is unknown. (6) (7) (19) (247)

Success

The 189 ton barque, Success, was wrecked on rocks under cliffs on the NE of Ventry Harbour on 22-2-1862. Rescue was made impossible by the cliffs and nine perished. The captain and one other survived by clinging to an airbed. The Success was built in 1854 at North Barnsley. The owners were W. Askin of Liverpool. (247)

Caroline

On 19-11-1850 the Italian Brig, Caroline, of Genoa was driven ashore on White Strand on the Great Blasket. The cargo was wheat bound from Odessa for Falmouth. The vessel struck far out due to her heavy load and split in two. The wreck was welcomed by the islanders as it relieved the state of near famine which existed. Nine of her crew came ashore but were not generally well treated by the islanders. (1)

Domestic

On 10-1-1854 a Scottish cargo vessel was wrecked on Iolan na nOg near Beginis. The new ship, copper bottomed and bolted, was returning to Glasgow from Genoa having unloaded pig iron. She had loaded a cargo of sulphur at Sicily. She sprang a leak off Gibraltar and was blown with her sails in tatters all the way to Kerry. Her crew of six men and two boys were assisted by the islanders as well as her master, William Beer of Bridgewater. (1)

Commerce

The three masted vessel 449 ton, Commerce, of Liverpool captained by William Hinde Corron Larkam was wrecked on the west of the Blaskets on 3-4-1850. She sprang a leak at sea and the water in the hold reached 12 feet, despite pumping for four days. Her crew

of 26 men including three coloured men who were then a great curiosity in Ireland, abandoned the ship and escaped by the longboat. Her cargo consisted of palm oil worth £15,000 form Bonny in West Africa for Liverpool. She was owned by Stewart and Doyles of Liverpool. (1)

Brass bolts

A ship with a cargo of brass and copper bolts sunk near a seal cave on the shore of Inis na mBro. Many bolts were recovered by Islanders diving for them. This must have occurred about 1850. Another ship may have foundered locally about 1875 as a large quantity of driftwood was found near Beginis. (38) On 1-1-1858 coastguards recovered several bales of leaf tobacco. These were thought to have come from a smuggling vessel wrecked in Dingle Bay.

El Torro

The steam tanker, El Torro, sank 300 yards NW of Clogher Head on Inisteeraght on the Blaskets on 2-1-1917. This is near the lighthouse. The 3621 ton tanker was bound from Port Arthur in Texas with oil. The crew of 35 escaped without casualty. The ship, owned by Lobitos Oilfields and US registered was built by Swan Hunter in 1913 at Newcastle.

Susan

The schooner, Susan, ran on rocks off the Blaskets in September 1853. She was en route from Liverpool to Galway with a cargo of salt. The crew were saved by a passing schooner. The vessel was owned by Middleton and Pollexfen. (235)

Quebra

The First World War saw considerable action at sea near the Blasket Islands and much wreckage came ashore. The Sworno, a 4500 ton collier, was torpedoed 14 miles off the Blaskets on

8-5-1915. One of her crew, a Russian named Rosenthal, was arrested ashore on suspicion of being a German. The Fulgent, owned by Westoll of Sunderland was torpedoed by U23 some 45 miles off the Scelligs around the same time. The 4538 ton, 377 foot British Steamer, Quebra, sunk on 23-8-1916. She was en route from New York to London or Liverpool with a cargo which included cotton, shells, warheads, brass and pipe. The ship struck the north side of the Great Blasket during the night. She grazed Tail Rock shortly before. The location is on the NW shore of the great Blasket Island about two miles from the Harbour . Bearings are Tower 269 degrees, hill 040 degrees, smaller hill 229 degrees. The Quebra is thought to have altered course to avoid a submarine. The crew escaped in three boats, one with a survivor was assisted by the islanders the other two went into Dingle Bay. The wreck lies on a steep slope. The forward hold lies in 45 metres. Ammunition from the wreck was blown up by the Navy during the summer of 1986 and 1987. A description of this work appeared in the Cork Examiner p8 25-8-1986. (38)

Lochar
The sailing ship, Lochar, en route from Halifax with a load of wheat sank after striking the rock on the Great Blasket subsequently called Lochar Rock. She had been three months at sea and had been damaged by storms. The crew of five seamen swam ashore and climbed the rocks. This must have occurred about 1820 . (38)

Unknown vessel
An unnamed vessel was assisted by Blasket Islanders about 1910. The vessel was found adrift with her captain, two seamen and a boy. The crew were taken

off and lodged on the island but the captain, called Alec, died and was buried at Castle Point near the site of Ferritear's Castle. It was beyond the power of the islanders to bring the ship ashore and only part of the cargo was saved. The vessel was swept away. (38)

Nora Creena
A trawler the Nora Creena fished out stocks around the islands about 1910 and the islanders had a bad season. This trawler sank at Edge rock when the bottom dropped out of her while returning to Dingle loaded with fish. The crew escaped using a boat tied to the trawler.

Sydnelsie
The Sydnelsie sank just north of the Blaskets on 26-6-1935. The 264 ton steel steam ketch was fishing from Fleetwood.

Three Brothers
The 30 metre Dingle trawler, Three Brothers, sank on 23-5-1990 when it struck rocks off Black Head on the Great Blasket. The vessel backed off and went down rapidly after being holed in the engine room. The five aboard escaped by life raft and were picked up by another trawler. The vessel had formerly been owned in Norway and had been recently purchased by Mr Flannery of Dingle. Despite efforts to raise the wreck from 20 metres, rough weather caused the trawler to slip into 25 metres with further damage. (99)

German Bomber
On 8-11-1940 a German bomber came down in the sea not far off the pebble beach on the east side of Inisvickillaune. The crew came ashore in two rubber dinghies.

Medusa
In the great storm which affected the west Kerry area on the 23-11-1850 the Medusa was wrecked near the old church at Smerwick Harbour. The remains of

the wreck were auctioned on the beach a few days later. She carried a cargo of wheat. (247)

Bride of Abydos

The brig, Bride of Abydos, of Hartlepool was driven ashore by a NE wind at Smerwick in the same spot as the Medusa on 20-11-1854. She was bound from Limerick to London with a cargo of oats.

Hiate Fiel

On 24-12-1855 the Portuguese schooner, Hiate Fiel, bound from Opporto to Cork was wrecked near Ventry. The ship hit rocks on the east side of the harbour about half a mile west of Rev Thomas Moriarty's house. The cargo was fruit.

Fairland

On 6-12-1929 the 900 ton Liverpool coaster, Fairland, went ashore at Smerwick Harbour. She was en route from Limerick to Liverpool. She sheltered in Smerwick Harbour and Ballydavid coast lifesaving service fired rockets out to her but the captain signalled that he was safe. The next day she was high and dry on the beach, undamaged (140). The storm continued and on 10-12-1929 the crew of the Volumina were taken off by the Manchester Regiment off the Scelligs. The Lancastrian Prince was also in trouble in the same area.

Manchester Merchant

The Manchester Liners ship, Manchester Merchant, was destroyed by fire in Dingle Bay on 15-1-1903. The 5,657 ton, 452 foot vessel was built in 1900 by Palmers. While en route from New Orleans to Manchester the cargo caught fire. It was not uncommon for baled cotton to ignite spontaneously and the Manchester Merchant carried 13,000 bales. The rest of the cargo was no less flammable, being 100 barrels of

turpentine, soap, pitch pine and some maize. The fire started out in the Atlantic and Captain Couch took the vessel into Dingle Bay, to a mile off Inch Bar to fight the fire. In this course of action he was probably prompted by recent loss by fire of another vessel in the Atlantic with heavy loss of life. However his efforts were to no avail and he scuttled the ship in shallow water at 41 feet at the stem and 36 feet amidships heading WSW, upright and with the decks awash. Salvage was anticipated and the Lloyds agent, Mr Ensor, of Queenstown (Cobh) arrived to supervise the work assisted by the captain and first officer Mr Rich. The Liverpool salvage steamer, Ranger (Capt. Pomeroy) commenced work. Divers closed the hatches and portholes but the work was hopeless. The vessel was declared a total loss at the end of February. The wreck lies at Lat N 52 05 26, Long 10 03 15.

Florence Graham

The 379 ton barque, Florence Graham, was wrecked at Inch Strand on 24-1-1861. Owned by Haloran and Cookson, she was bound for Liverpool from Braha River, Vento, West Africa with palm oil. The pumps were in operation for ten days before she went ashore. The captain and six crew launched a boat which capsized. The mate was lost taking a rope ashore. The wreck broke in two and seven were cast ashore on one portion of the ship. Five more were lost. Two men were saved by the coastguard. Of the 17 aboard only seven survived. (21)

Giardiniera

The 400 ton barque, Giardiniera, with a cargo of bones and marble was wrecked on Inch Strand on 30-1-1865. All the crew of seventeen were lost. (35)

Maria Anna

The brig, Maria Anna, was wrecked on

Inch Bar on 18-2-1885. She was bound from Swansea to Ballinakill near Cleggan with coal.

Veronica

The 350 ton brig, Veronica, was en route from Belfast to Charlestown, USA with a cargo of salt and coal. On 6-12-1828 she entered Dingle Bay and went ashore at Inch Bar. A woman was lost but the coastguard rescued the remaining crew and passengers. (21)

Frederick Symons

The Falmouth vessel, Frederick Symons, was wrecked at Dunmore head on 23-11-1850. In February 1840 four vessels were lost off the Dunquinn Headland. (247)

Ellen Sophie

On 14-1-1865 the Ellen Sophie was wrecked on Ballydavid Head with the loss of her crew of eight. She carried rum and sugar from Demerara to Liverpool. (35)

Elisa Woods

The top of two masts, close to the cliff about half way between Ventry Harbour and Blasket Sound were observed by the Dingle Pilot on 9-2-1871. Some bottles of brandy were found floating at the wreck. The supposed name of the casualty was the Elisa Woods. This was ascertained from some love letters found floating nearby, addressed to the chief officer of the Elisa Woods of Liverpool. (67)

Mary of Glenally

During the Famine the ship, Mary of Glenally, was chartered to carry a load of wheat to Ireland. The wheat had been donated by the Irish in the U.S.A. She was bound for Queenstown but lost her rudder in a storm and was driven against the cliffs at Kinard. Though a number of people were there they were unable to assist. The mast was as high as the cliff

top and swayed close to the crowd assembled there. The crew climbed the mast and one attempted to jump but fell to his death. Only one body was recovered and buried at Kinard graveyard. (88) (1158,p24)

Giralda

The French ketch, Giralda, which had come to Ireland to collect lobsters was entering Dingle Harbour on 28-5-1906 with a pilot aboard. She misstayed and went on the rocks about 70 metres beyond the lighthouse. She sank after five minutes. The crew of six escaped in a yawl. (67)

Seaweed ship

In 1806 a ship with a cargo of seaweed was wrecked at Baile Uachtarach Thiar in Dingle Bay. She was transporting seaweed from Beginish to Ceann Clochar near Ballyferriter. Captain McDonnell was in command. Seven of the crew were drowned. (135,22,p507)

Emanuel

The Emanuel of Bridgewater was part of an expedition from England to Baffin Island off Canada. Frobisher was searching for the North West Passage and mounted three expeditions to the north coast of Canada. The third expedition set out with 12 ships from Deptford on 26-5-1577 to exploit minerals, especially gold, on Baffin Island. When returning the next year the Emanuel, commanded by Captain Richard Newton became separated from the fleet. On 25-9-1578 they sighted Galway but were driven up and down the west coast of Ireland by storms for six or seven weeks. Finally they reached Smerwick Harbour without masts or sails and beached in the shallows off the western shore. The 100 tons of ore was unloaded into pinnances and transferred to Dingle. Eight tons of large rocks were left and transferred to

Dun an Oir. The ore was however worthless because the gold content had been erroneously calculated. The Emanuel was beyond repair and was an abandoned wreck at Coosbaun Cove when Admiral Winter sketched the area in November 1580 at the start of the siege of Dun an Oir. (162) (163)

Jenny Lind

The schooner, Jenny Lind, of Maine was wrecked at Bealban, Smerwick on 24-11-1898. She was built in 1883 and owned by J.E. Mitchell. The cargo was coal.

Dewey Lass

The barque, Dewey Lass, of Bridgewater went ashore at a creek near Smerwick Harbour on 6-10-1889. She carried a cargo of brick bound for Clarecastle. Her crew of five were saved by fishermen. (67)

Ruth Hickman

The large schooner, Ruth Hickman, of Halifax, Nova Scotia was damaged in a gale in January 1920. She dropped anchor near Esk and the crew were taken off by a British naval vessel. The chain broke and she drifted ashore at Minard. She was refloated after a time and towed into Dingle for repair. The cargo of wheat or maize was sold but cattle would not consume it. The ship remained on the shore until the Second World War when her timbers were taken for firewood. The Ruth Hickman, built in 1918 was known locally as the White Schooner. (23)

Swiss sloop

A 30 ton Swiss sloop was wrecked at Black Point, Castlegregory on 17-3-1863. The cargo was staves. The crew of three were lost. (35)

Henry

The homeward bound, 400 ton, 20 gun, East India ship, Henry, of London commanded by Captain Hudson sheltered in Ventry Bay on 12-7-1685.

She was attacked and boarded by a 20 gun French privateer commanded by Neagle. Captain Hudson and his men managed to clear the decks twice but 100 Frenchmen boarded a third time. The defenders blew up the round deck house, causing a fire and ran the ship ashore on the cliffs. The French ship made off leaving the boarders to their fate. Most of the Englishmen were saved but only 30 of the French. The Henry burned to the middle deck but the goods in the hold were undamaged. The following February the Foresight (Capt. Walker) took the salvaged goods to Kinsale. (110)

Nautilus

The Nautilus foundered in Blasket Sound on 8-1-1833. She was bound from Dingle to Cork.

Active

The Active was wrecked near Dingle on 22-2-1818. The vessel was bound for Limerick from Philadelphia.

Ellen

The Ellen was wrecked in Dingle Bay on 22-1-1818. She was bound for Liverpool from New Orleans.

Recovery

The Recovery was wrecked near Ventry in December 1818. She was en route from Limerick to Liverpool.

Phenix

The Phenix of Cardigan was driven ashore at Inch Bar on 20-2-1833. Captain Jones and his crew were saved. (174)

Joseph Hutchenson

The 350 ton Joseph Hutchenson was wrecked near the Blaskets on 28-9-1851. The vessel was en route from Alexandria to Liverpool.

Evangalista

On 24-12-1852 the Evangalista was wrecked on the north of Dingle Bay. The vessel carried general cargo.

Sulina

The 228 ton brig Sulina was lost at the entrance to Dingle Harbour in October 1868. All eleven aboard were lost. The cargo was indian corn.

Stanfriel

On 16-5-1933 the 290 ton steel ketch, Stanfriel, sank off Dingle. The fishing crew were picked up by the SS Caldavia. The position was given as 52.18, N 11.37.W

Hind

The 100 ton schooner, Hind, was wrecked at Ballymore in Ventry Harbour on 12-3-1905. She was bound from Dingle to Cardiff in ballast. The four aboard survived.

Sunbeam

On 27-1-1904 the 74 ton Arklow schooner, Sunbeam, was wrecked at Rosbehy Strand. She was bound from Kinvara to Cork. The vessel grounded and the crew went below to avoid the falling masts. At low water they were able to walk ashore. The Sunbeam was built at Brixham in 1868 and owned by Richard Kearon.

Jane Herbert

The 134 ton brig, Jane Herbert, was lost at the mouth of Dingle Harbour on 26-3-1891. The cargo was coal for Dingle from Liverpool.

KERRY NORTH

Oranmore

The Oranmore, owned by the Limerick SS Co was wrecked on Kerry Head on 21-2-1970. The 180 foot, 650 ton vessel built in 1962 lost power during a WNW gale and anchored on the Kerry Head shoal. She was in danger of being driven on the rocks and the crew abandoned ship. The lifeboat rescued ten but one died. The chain and anchor held for five days before it snapped and the ship drifted onto Banna strand. The tug, Friesland which had stood by but had departed to assist a vessel near Galway returned and towed her off on 5-3-1970. (59)

Golden Lion

While en route from Copenhagen to Tranquebar the Danish East India frigate "Gyldenlove" was wrecked in Ballyheigue Bay on 28-10-1730. The ship beached at the north side of Ballyheigue Bay during a storm. Captain John Heitman, the chaplain, officers and 60 crew were rescued by locals led by Thomas Crosbie from nearby Ballyheigue House. Twelve chests were salvaged containing £16,000 bullion. The sailors and the bullion were housed in a house adjoining Crosbie's. Thomas Crosbie died shortly afterwards from a chill caught during the rescue. His wife, Lady Margaret and Arthur Crosbie of Tubrid claimed £4,300 salvage. In April 1731 a conspiracy of the local gentry and peasantry to rob the bullion had been hatched. An instruction was sent from Dublin to the Custom House at Tralee ordering that the Danes be protected from extortion. The Collector, Mr Chute suggested that assistance be obtained from the soldiers. A huge mob attacked and overpowered the Danes on 4th June. They drew away the bullion on a herd of pack horses. Colonel Denny of Tralee arrested some of the conspirators who were tried in Dublin. A web of perjury followed. The Danes (John Heitman and J. Osdorf) as late as 9-12-1735 in a letter to their embassy in London complained of their poor treatment by the authorities. At this time the English Channel was blocked to continental ships because of the war between England and Holland. Vessels were obliged to take the hazardous longer passage around Ireland to reach their destination. Apart from the twelve chests of silver, the Golden Lion (Gyldenlove) carried sixty tons of iron and corn. (98) (224)

Wind Trader

About 1729, the Wind Trader, engaged in the Baltic-Bristol-American trade was wrecked near Ballyheigue. A five Kopeck coin dated 1725 or 1727 was recovered along with some bottles. (118)

Mary Anne

In 1677 this Limerick trader was wrecked on the rocks at Ballyheigue en route from Queenstown to America. (118) Some years prior to 1756 a ship was cast high upon Kerry Head by a freak wave. Some of the crew escaped over the bowsprit. The wreck fell back into the sea and was smashed before the others could escape. (223)

Catherine Richards

This 167 ton Portmadoc schooner struck Kerry Head with a cargo of grain on 30-12-1891. (157) The vessel was abandoned by her crew in Brandon Bay but all six aboard were lost when their boat was dashed against the ship. They are buried at Killiney. The ship was then blown across the bay and driven ashore near Ballyheigue. When locals were unloading the cargo a pulley fell and killed a boy. (135, 744,p46) When the cargo was being salvaged the ship's cat was found alive.

Port Stanley

The Port Stanley had only a dog and cat aboard when she ran aground near Kerry Head. (118)

Salamander

The 16 ton fishing steamer, Salamander, was wrecked on Ruper Rocks, Garrywilliam on 18-4-1900

Debbie

The Debbie, bound from America to England was wrecked on Kerry Head in 1867 in heavy fog. The cargo included golden ornaments. Only three of the crew survived. She was guided into a sheltered cove (Tiduff) and a rescue attempted at a point now known as "Lough Debbie"(118)

Schooner

At Doon near Ballybunnion a foreign schooner was wrecked in the storm of 23-11-1850. The crew all perished. Wreckage was washed ashore in the Maharees from this or yet another vessel.

Highland Maid

The two masted ship, Highland Maid, was driven ashore on Maharees Strand on 5-12-1874, she carried a cargo of oil (157). A Swedish sailor was washed ashore and buried at Killiney graveyard.

Charger

The three masted Charger of Belfast was wrecked on the back of Carralougha in Brandon Bay on 24-11-1890. She carried a cargo of deal bound for a match factory in Belfast or Liverpool. Her anchor remained on Carralougha beach up to the 1940s. (135, 744,p46)

Hannah Maria

The Hannah Maria of Greece was wrecked at Maharee Point in Spring of 1860. She struck a rock on the Point and all the crew climbed ashore safely. (135, 744, p46)

Maria

On 23-3-1873 the Greek vessel, Maria, grounded at Mucklochbeg and became a wreck. She carried indian corn.

Concessione

The Concessione was wrecked on Bua Bank, Tralee on 4-7-1851. She was en route from Constantinople to Tralee.

Rival

During a gale the Rival was wrecked on Donoughmore Island in Tralee Bay on 20-1-1850. She was carrying oats from Limerick to Liverpool.

Fitzhenry

In the same gale the Fitzhenry went ashore in Tralee Bay. She was en route from Tralee to Limerick.

Tartar

The Tartar was wrecked on 22-11-1850 in Tralee Bay. She was en route to Liverpool.

Derelict

A Tralee report described a schooner from British America driven ashore at Canoe Cove on 14-10-1851. The cargo was 300 batons. The vessel went to pieces rapidly. It appeared that the schooner was abandoned for some months. (69)

Hornet

The 186 ton ship Hornet was wrecked in Tralee Bay on 8-5-1852. She was bound for Liverpool in ballast.

Llanthenry

The 148 ton steel steamer Llanthenry under the command of Captain Brooke foundered on 27-12-1902. She went aground on Beale Bar opposite Scattery Island on the Kerry side of the Mouth of the Shannon. The 10 crew escaped and were lodged at Ballybunnion. The Lloyds agent inspected the ship and considered it a total wreck. The steamer was en route from Garston to Limerick with coal.

Port Yarrock

The 2175 ton iron-clad barque Port Yarrock was wrecked in Brandon Bay at Kilcummin Strand on Monday 29-1-1894. The Glasgow vessel left Santa Rosalia, California in July 1893 with Captain Forbes in command and met a severe storm. After 22 days she had lost all her canvas and she reached Brandon Bay and anchored. The captain went ashore and telegraphed from Tralee for instructions. He refused a tow from any Irish boat and decided to await a tug

which arrived the day of the disaster. He had been advised by the Lloyds agent that his anchorage was insecure. This proved correct and when another gale arose the ship dragged for 5 miles. She was driven aground a quarter mile from the low water shore. A large local crowd assembled to assist. The Tralee lifeboat was sent by the Lloyds agent. Coastguards from Dingle brought rockets but were too late to assist. An attempt was made to reach the ship on horseback. The crew were swept away and none of twenty two survived. Seven were buried at Killiney where a memorial stands in the Church of Ireland. One was buried at Cloghane and three at Stradbally. The court of inquiry (68) at the end of March revealed some surprising details. There were several complaints from letters written by the crew regarding bad conditions. A boy wrote that many of the crew were sick with scurvy, due to bad food though 15 cases of lime juice had been loaded. Their letters were posted from Tralee before the ship sank. The compliment of 22 including 6 apprentices was considered inadequate. The owners, Robert Rowatt, were censured because they did not take action to safeguard their ship. The Lloyds agent's advice was ignored while the captain awaited a tug in an unsafe anchorage. The cost of the ship as new was £13,000 and her then current value £11,000.

Part of the wreck can be seen off Kilcummin Strand at low tide. The cargo of 2200 tons of high grade copper ore was a considerable salvage prize. About 700 tons were recovered soon after the wreck. There remained £17,000 worth when the Queenstown salvor T.H. Ensor worked on the wreck from August 1910. A shed at Cappagh was constructed in 1912 for Thomas Henry Ensor. He was a professional diver and he salvaged copper ore from the Port Yarrock until 1914. An anchor used to lie on the strand near the secondary school but was removed about 1974. The skeleton of a barge lies near Cloghane and this was used in the salvage of the ore. (112) (135, 1158,p24) (175)

Port Charlotte

There have been several shipwrecks in the area of the Seven Hogs. A pirate ship was said to have been lured onto the rocks of Reennafardarrig by fishermen. Searchers for its treasure were said to have met serpents as big as horses. Wrecks include the Laura, Nellie, Port Charlotte and Quickstep. (118)

Ioli

The 900 ton Greek coaster Ioli left the Shannon estuary on 29-2-1971. She carried 1000 tons of barytes drilling mud from Silvermines which had been loaded at Foynes. She had been built at Bremen in 1957. The pilot observed that the engines were troublesome before she left the Shannon. No trace of the vessel was heard until wreckage was found at Kilbaha. Bodies were washed ashore at Spanish point and Quilty. There was speculation as to where the ship foundered. The wreck was found at Mahony's Banks in the Maharees Islands 2 miles N of Brandon Point.

Beal Tairbeart

On 9-6-1964 the trawler, Beal Tairbeart, sank on rocks off Kerry Head. Her engines failed while she was en route from Aran to Dingle. One of the crew of two was drowned.

Monique et Maryvonne

This Concarneau trawler was wrecked to the NE of Inistuisceart on the Maharees on 22-2-1979. The trawler was returning from fishing off the Aran Islands when she struck a rock about three miles off

Brandon point and sank in ten minutes. After four hours in their boat the crew were picked up by the Telestar, another Concarneau trawler. (238)

Darling

On 12-11-1839 the Darling of Maryport was wrecked on a rock at the point of Fenit. She had sailed from Wexford to Fenit to load corn for Cork. She sailed from Fenit with her master, Mr Atkinson, skippered by Charles Mc Mahon of Blenerville. The cargo of corn was worth £1200. The wreck was sold by auction. At the same time an unnamed vessel was wrecked at the Beeves near Tarbert.

Seaward

During a great gale on 12-2-1874 the barque, Seaward, (74 tons) of Glasgow grounded on Samphire Island in Tralee Bay. Her master was Archibold McAllen and she carried iron for Donovans. Divers caulked her bottom and she was refloated along with two other casualties, the Margaret McCaul and Jane McCaul. (67)

Alessandris

In the same place during the same storm on 12-2-1874 the Russian barque, Alessandris (242 tons) was lost. She had delivered iron at Tralee and was commanded by master Morates. (67)

Orient

The 456 ton Russian brig, Orient, en route from Glouster to Limerick with salt went on the rocks at Ballydavid Head on 11-9-1908. During a NW gale she had lost her three masts off Loop Head and was helpless outside Smerwick harbour. Her anchors were dropped but broke. When she struck, Captain Merkis and his crew launched a boat but it was swamped. The survivors reached the bottom of the 400 foot cliffs. After 8 hours on the rocks a coastguard, Albert Warm, climbed down the cliff to rescue them. The four survivors from the crew of ten were taken to Ballydavid. (176)

Notre Dame de Victoires

The 500 ton French trawler, Notre Dame de Victoires, of Etel ran ashore in fog on Black Rock at Smerwick Harbour on 3-5-1956. A man looking for sheep heard voices and saw men on the rocks at the foot of the cliffs. He raised the alarm and a Garda and some men in a small boat rescued the two men by towing them to the boat with a rope. Despite a search by the Valentia and Fenit lifeboats only one dead man was found in a lifeboat. The captain, Andre Gloec, and five crew were lost. (59)

Weasel

The engine of the Weasel blew up and she sank at the pier at Tralee on 23-10-1858. Efforts were made to raise her as she was in shallow water.

Anne

The 77 ton schooner Anne ran ashore on Fermoyle Strand at Brandon and was wrecked on 15-5-1881. She carried bonemeal from Ipswich to Liverpool. The crew of four were safe. Her home port was Inverness.

Eliza

The 27 ton sloop Eliza was lost at Brandon Bay on 14-3-1871. She was en route from Kilrush to Castletown with potatoes. The crew of three were lost.

Alpine Crag

The Alpine Crag sank at Learys Island on 6-9-1870. All aboard were saved.

Vigilante

On 22-12-1857 the French schooner, Vigilante, was wrecked at the same place as the Lexington on Brandon Strand. The wreck was sold to Mr Lunham of Tralee.

Lexington Kennebunk

On 25-8-1857 the 841 ton 8 year old American barque was wrecked at Killiney on Brandon Strand. During the work to make her light a labourer was killed when a bale of cotton fell on him. She was then towed off the beach by a tug for a Liverpool merchant named McCarthy. The towline parted while she was under tow and the ship sank with the loss of two lives. The 22 others aboard were safe. Her cargo was oak staves and cotton. (157)

Martha

On 2-2-1870 the ship, Martha of New Brunswick was wrecked at Carralougha. She carried fish oil. The master was Jas Downey.

Industry

On 24-12-1847 the sloop, Industry, en route to Tralee was wrecked at Scarth, Kilshanig. She carried flour and meal bound for Tralee. The wreck occurred at the height of the Famine and was reputed to have been "arranged" from the shore. (157). According to tradition, wrecking in Kerry was widespread in the 18th century. Though wreckers are reputed to have operated from Kerry Head, Brandon Head and the Iveragh area no documentary evidence survives. (224) Two locals, Tom Scanlon and Maurice McElligot went to America to avoid giving information.

Erricheta

The 263 ton brig Erricheta of Naples was wrecked on the west side of Kilshannig a little north of the church on 19-11-1850. One of her crew was lost and is buried outside the west gable of the church. The brig carried a cargo of wheat. (157)

Hebe

The Hebe was wrecked at Leary's Island in November, 1846. She was bound for Limerick with general cargo. All her crew escaped ashore on a rope. (157)

Other Wrecks

In addition to those described, wrecks were mentioned in the Cork Examiner

(157) recorded by Mr Francis O'Flaherty of Maharees. None appear in the Bord of Trade return. All were described as wrecked in Brandon Bay. In the 40 years to 1894 23 wrecks occurred near Brandon. Among these were : 1857, French schooner, Vigilante; 1870, brig, Alpine Craig; 1873, Greek ship, Maria; 1890, Charger; 1894, Daggere. Information on Mr O' Flaherty's list was supplied by Pat Dowling of Stradbally and Sheila Mulcahy.

Ileen
The Liverpool schooner Ileen was wrecked at Ballybunion on 6-10-1889. Her crew were saved with difficulty. (67)

Coal Steamer
On 3-1-1880 a steamer believed to be one belonging to a local merchant, Mr Eager, was seen to enter Tralee Bay. The observer from Fenit saw no trace of her later and presumed that she foundered in the bay during the storm. The ship was en route from Glasgow to Tralee with coal. (67)

Siddarthur
On 30-11-1880 the 459 ton British barque, Siddarthur, went ashore at Tralee Bay. The cargo of timber was scattered widely. Captain Moore and the crew survived. (65)

Heroine
The 60 ton Heroine was wrecked at Fenit on 3-10-1900.

Irene
The 94 ton schooner, Irene, was wrecked at Ballybunion on 7-10-1889. The cargo was coal from Liverpool for Clarecastle.

Alice
The brig Alice was wrecked at Foynes Island on 30-3-1814. She carried wheat and provisions. (237)

Diamantis
The 8000 ton Greek ship, Diamantis, was sunk by a German submarine NW of Scellig Rock on 3-10-1939. The wreck was recently found on sonar by the trawler, Atlantic Fisher, at a depth of 120 metres. The 29 crew of the Diamantis were landed by the submarine at Baile Mor near Dingle. The ship was en route from South Africa to Barrow on Furness. (236) The U-35 which torpedoed the ship was sunk off Bergen by British destroyers on 29-11-1939.

York
The East India Company ship York was wrecked at Kilshannock on 29-10-1758. Commanded by Captain Peter Lascelles, the York sailed from Deptford on 20-2-1757 and arrived at Bombay on 28-12-1757. The receipt book documents the sums paid for goods traded and after four months the vessel set out on the return trip on 9-4-1758. As well as the crew she carried a convict and seven slaves bound for St Helena, and an East India company deserter and a European being sent home by the East India Company Governors. The entire trip is documented in Captain Lascelles' log. (240). On 7-10-1758 the ship encountered gales which lasted two weeks. The York drifted to a point west of the Blaskets and since the sails were in poor condition it was decided to shelter in the Shannon. Captain Lascelles describes his difficulties in finding the Shannon as his chart was not accurate. A small ship was seen and a gun fired to attract attention. After speaking they agreed to lead him to the Shannon. Soundings were taken and they showed 17 fathoms but the ship suddenly struck at the Maharees with only two fathoms forward. They tried to back off but the tide receded and they were stuck fast. An anchor was taken out by the pinnance and longboat with a warp through the great cabin ports but to no avail. The captain ordered the masts

cut away as they were straining the ship. All aboard escaped ashore.

It transpired that the smaller ship was a cartel ship from Rochelle bound for Plymouth. Irish prisoners aboard had seized the ship off Scilly. They thought the Indiaman was a warship and wanted to run both ashore to escape.

No local assistance was available initially as there were no boats in the area. A large number of people gathered in the hope of plunder. Captain Lascelles commenced a salvage operation which lasted three weeks. The pepper in the cargo was quickly washed away but some 4500 bales of striped and check cotton along with yarn were taken ashore. Other material salved included 5 boxes shellac, 2 chests sticklack, one leager, a cask of arrack, a box of china, six barrels of indigo, 101 chinks, 122 blue gurracks and many personal possessions. The lee gun wall fell out on 18 November due to the weight of the guns and the whole ship disintegrated in a wind four days later. (205)

Sea Lark
The Limerick vessel, Sea Lark, was thrown ashore at Ballybunion on 25-11-1846. The vessel was keel uppermost. The crew were presumed lost.

Senator
The Limerick & London Co screw steamer, Senator, stranded near the mouth of the Cashen not far from the point where the Sea Lark was cast ashore.

Carmanian
The Norwegian three masted ironclad barque, Carmanian, was sunk by submarine gunfire on 25-4-1916 off Kerry. She carried 3000 tons wheat from Buenos Aires to Queenstown. Though described

as Norwegian she is not listed as such in their records.

Three Brothers
The 98 ton Cork Schooner, Three Brothers, was wrecked on 28-6-1850 off Cromane Point. The schooner was built in 1845 by Jones & Co. The cargo was wheat.

Mountaineer
The brigantine, Mountaineer, was driven ashore between Ardfert and Ballyheigue on 9-1-1864. The vessel had a cargo of coal.

City of Limerick
The City of Limerick was wrecked at Ballybunnion on 28-11-1833. She was en route to London from Limerick.

Ann
The Ann was wrecked in Tralee Bay on 2-2-1833. She was en route from Liverpool to Limerick.

Glad Tidings
The 113 ton schooner, Glad Tidings, was wrecked at Fenit on 13-4-1874. She carried wood from Clarecastle to Cardiff. Four of the five crew were lost.

Erin
The 53 ton iron steamship, Erin, was wrecked at Fenit on 21-12-1888. The vessel was built in 1861 and carried general cargo from Tralee to Dingle. The crew of five were safe.

Dronningen
The 837 ton Norwegian barque Dronningen was wrecked at Leek Point near Ballybunion on 20-11-1882. The 16 crew survived. The vessel carried coal from Glasgow for New York.

Norway
On 10-11-1850 the Norway was wrecked on the south point of the entrance to Tralee Bay. The brig was bound for Limerick from Falmouth with wheat.

CLARE

CLARE

Edmund

The emigrant barque, Edmund, (built c 1840) of 400 tons (Capt. Wilson) left the roadstead of Carrigaholt, Co Clare on the evening of Sunday 18-11-1850 bound for New York or Quebec. The next day the vessel was 30 miles out in the Atlantic. A WNW gale was encountered which carried away two of her masts and she became unmanageable. She was driven to the Clare coast and at 11.00 on the night of Tuesday, 20th, she struck on the Duggerna Rocks at Edmund Point in Kilkee Bay. The force of the seas washed her off the rocks and drove her further inshore. The captain had the foremast cut and it fell to the land before she broke in two. The mast provided a bridge from the ship to the rocks and by clambering over it 111 persons, mainly women, were saved. Ninety six of the passengers who had boarded at Limerick were drowned. She had been chartered by Mr John McDonald, TC of Limerick. The bow came to rest on the ledge where she struck but the stern drifted down the bay to a bridge over a streamlet. She had entered the bay by the normal passage but had not let out her anchor. Otherwise she would have beached in relative safety.

At the same time the ferryboat from Kilrush to Tarbert was upset by the gale. The vessel was sunk and 19 cattle jobbers aboard were lost. The Henry and Anne was also washed ashore on the island opposite Kilrush.

Unknown ship

A wooden wreck lies in very shallow water at the Bridges of Ross near Loop Head. Nothing is known about the wreck.

Elbmarchen

The 500 ton German Coaster, Elbmarchen, grounded at Cregga Mor near Ballylaun, Liscannor on 7-9-1973. She was en route to Galway when her engines gave trouble during a storm. Her crew were taken off by helicopter as they could not ascend the cliffs. Her captain, Herbert Khoenatsch, stayed with the ship and on a spring tide the next day he managed to refloat her and was escorted into Galway. (99)

Intrinsic

Near Loop Head is Intrinsic Bay. The Intrinsic was wrecked on Bishop's Island in the bay on 30-1-1836. She was en route from Liverpool to New Orleans with general cargo. She was driven ashore in a severe SW gale and wrecked under the high cliffs. Captain Quirke and his crew of fourteen were lost. The cargo of iron and steel was recovered in an early deep sea salvage operation. Her anchor was recovered in August 1979 and is on display at Kilkee.

Ellen

The Arklow brigantine, Ellen, went ashore at Liscannor in 1923. She was badly damaged but was refloated and brought to Arklow where she was broken up in 1940. She was built at Bridgewater in 1882. Her owner, John Kearon, purchased her for £210 in 1898.

Leon XIII
Photo: John Gill

Leon xiii

The French sailing ship, Leon xiii, was wrecked at Sarsfield Point in Mal Bay near Quilty, Co Clare on 1-10-1907. She was carrying wheat from Port Pirrie to Limerick. Her home port was Nantes. The wreck occurred in full view of the shore and all the crew were landed over two days. Local fishermen braved a terrible storm to bring off the first thirteen survivors. A coastguard party bringing rocket apparatus travelled from Valentia on the gunboat Skipjack and were met by a special train at Ennis. They could not reach the ship with a line despite their efforts. The cruiser, HMS Arrogant, was detached from the Atlantic Fleet and rushed to assist. Her boats took off Captain Lucas and the remaining nine crew. The crew in gratitude raised a subscription for the construction of a new church at Quilty. It has a steeple in the form of a round tower and contains the ship's bell. Another ship may have been lost at Quilty in the early years of this century. (184)

Ballyvaughan wreck

The gale of 9-2-1988 removed about five feet of sand from the beach at Rhine Point in Ballyvaughan. This uncovered the remains of an oak built ship measuring 70 feet by 30 feet. About 80 years ago this wreck was visible on the strand. Local speculation is that the vessel is an Armada wreck. This view is discounted and the National Museum believe that it is a post medieval sailing ship.

Puddog

A small local vessel sank at Carraig Puddog near Quilty Point. The vessel carried a cargo of sausages hence the applied name from the Irish for sausage.

San Marcos

An Armada ship, the San Marcos, of Portugal was wrecked on 15-9-1588 at Bad Bay on the reef between Mutton Island and Lurga Point near Spanish Point. The captain was the Marquis of Penafiel. The vessel (790 tons) had 33 guns and a crew of 409. Some of the crew are buried at Kilfarboy. A table reputed to be from the wreck was at Drumoland Castle and is now at Bunratty. A door from the ship was in Ennis museum at Spanish Point at the turn of the century. (6)

San Estaban

At Doonbeg the Armada ship, San Estaban, of San Sebastian, was wrecked on 20-9-1588. The 736 ton vessel carried 26 guns and 409 men. She was part of the Squadron of Guipuzcoa. Sixty survived from a 264 man crew only to be hanged at Cnoc na Crocaire near Spanish Point. (6)

Island of Yellow Men

A small island off White Strand at Ballyvaughan is called in Irish the Island of Yellow Men. This was a name applied to the Spanish. This may indicate the location of the wreck of a further smaller Spanish vessel.

Annunciada

This Armada vessel was burned and sank at Scattery Island on the Shannon. Her crew and stores were off loaded by the other six vessels which accompanied her. This 700 ton Ragusan vessel was a converted merchantman and carried 24 guns and 275 men. (6)

Undine

The Limerick schooner, Undine, went ashore east of Moyne on 6-1-1839. She was driven by the SW gale, "the big wind," above the high water line and became a total wreck. She was the finest and newest vessel of the Limerick Shipping Company built at a cost of £3,500. She had anchored at Scattery to ride out the storm but was threatened when another vessel, John Of Leith, dragged her anchors. Captain Patterson slipped his anchor but found that his helm was washed away. Two of the crew were washed overboard and Captain Patterson and another were found aboard, dead from exposure. (67)

Tar

The seven month old Tar also of Limerick was washed ashore at Moyne on 6-1-1839. Nine vessels were ashore at Kilcairn Battery. At Labasheeda Bay, Welcome, Isabella, Charity and Albion were high and dry.

Garryone

The steamer, Garryone, was cast on the beach at Kilrush in the storm of 6-1-1839. She was not badly damaged and was expected to be refloated. The revenue cruiser, Hamilton, also went ashore at Kilrush and lost her copper bottom.

Grecian

The Hull vessel, Grecian, was driven on her beam ends at Kilrush on 6-1-1839. Of her crew only three boys who clung to the rigging were rescued the next day. A terrific SW hurricane which affected Ireland, was the occasion of the famous Grace Darling rescue at the Farne Islands on the coast of Northumbria. In addition the Menai bridge was badly damaged. The gale is always referred to in Irish Folklore as the Big Wind.

Inistrahull

The Glasgow Steam Packet Co vessel, Inistrahull, was lost on 2-1-1895 during a gale. She was en route from Glasgow to Limerick and was reported overdue. The ten year old screw steamer carried coal, but no passengers. The port bow of a boat was washed ashore at Kilkee. At

Ross Bay, hatches were found and more wreckage was found on Bishops Island. Captain Whipple and all his crew of 21 were lost. The most likely location of the sinking was regarded as eight to ten miles north of Loop Head. A passenger on a previous sailing recounted a tale of walking the deck with Captain Whipple one night and when passing the cliffs of Moher he remarked that this was the spot where he would be wrecked. Captain Heatherington of the Inistrahull's sister ship Aranmore, surmised that the Inistrahull would have hove to when the light on Loop Head was not seen. He believed that the vessel was swamped rather than driven on rocks as the wreckage was all floating material from the decks. A foul area in 38 metres 700 yards off Donegal point, Co Clare could be the location of the wreck. (67)

Daniel O'Connell
Upriver nearer Limerick a large sail boat, called Daniel O Connell, was lost. On 6-1-1839 thirty small boats which had sailed with turf or oats were presumed lost. (225)

Helene
The iron barque, Helene, en route from Limerick to San Francisco with grain went ashore on Scattery Island on 28-12-1894. It was thought that she might be towed off by a tug. At the same time a schooner with a load of flagstones was driven ashore at Liscannor.

Elizabeth McLean
The 100 foot Arklow brig, Elizabeth McLean, was wrecked near Lahinch on 18-12-1894. The wreck was uncovered during the gale of 9-2-1988 when sand was removed from the beach. She was built by Robt Steele at Greenock in 1860. The wreck occurred near Liscannor Harbour where she had loaded a cargo of Luagh stone.

Brothers
The Kenmare schooner, Brothers, was wrecked when driven ashore east of Isleveroe Point on 14-3-1857. She was en route from Askeaton to Kenmare when caught by a storm.

E.D.J.
The motor vessel, E.D.J., was blown on the rocks at Islevaroo, near Kilrush in 1940 or 1941. Formerly owned by Glynn's of Kilrush she was sold to Mr P O'Keefe for dredging aggregate in Bantry. At the time of the wreck she was owned by O'Sullivans of Ballylongford and engaged in turf transport from Kilrush to Limerick. The hull was patched but the ship only reached Tarbert, where she was sold as she lay, for scrap.

Okeanos
On 13-1-1947 the 7000 ton, Greek crewed, Panamanian owned steamship, Okeanos, grounded near Carraigaholt. She became wedged on two ledges 30 feet from the shore at Kilcreaden Point. She was outward bound, having delivered 5,000 tons of grain from the River Plate at Ranks in Limerick. Her compass had been adjusted in Scattery Roads just prior to the accident. Captain Lambriados and the 27 crew went ashore in three lifeboats and sheltered in an old fort at the Point. As the bottom was badly damaged she was declared a total loss. She was bought as scrap by the Hammond Lane Company. (184)

Aurora
The brig, Aurora, sank near Loop Head in October 1814. She was en route from Belfast to America. Those aboard escaped in two lifeboats which reached shore at Kilkee and Carraigaholt. (95)

Atlanta
The brig, Atlanta, was wrecked at Dunaha on 17-3-1836. (95)

Morven
Photo; Rees

Morven

On 4-12-1906 the 1,900 ton four masted barque, Morven, ran ashore and was wrecked in a bay in the Shannon estuary between Horse Island and Kilbaha. The vessel had left Portland, Oregon 106 days previously with a cargo of 3,500 tons of wheat for Ballantynes of Limerick. The ship was waiting for a pilot when wind and tide drove her too close to Loop Head. The sails were put aback in an effort to slow the ship but she went ashore. Though the vessel was a total wreck Captain Rees and 26 crew escaped by climbing from the bowsprit onto the cliff at Horse Island. The Morven was bought in 1899 from Cairds of Glasgow by Mr Lewis, a Welshman. (72)

Perseverance

The West Indiaman, Perseverance, was wrecked on 3-12-1800. She carried a cargo of cotton. Three of the eight crew were drowned. Another wreck is described in a book in Irish on the shore of Mattle Island. The ship was also bound from the West Indies. The wreck occurred prior to 1830. The masts were observed above water.

Waterlily

The schooner, Waterlily, went down near Kilkee in October 1836. She carried a cargo of musical instruments. The shore from Loop Head to Dunbeg was strewn with guitars and violins. (95)

Mercator

The Mercator went aground at Dunbeg in January 1837. She was en route from St John, New Brunswick to Belfast with a cargo of timber. (95)

Ranger

The brig, Ranger, was wrecked at Coosheen on 1-8-1863. She was bound for Quebec from Liverpool. (95)

Fulmer

The Cardiff steamship, Fulmer, went down between Kilkee and Farrihy, on 30-1-1888. The 418 ton screw steamer was built in 1868 at Middlesboro for Msrs Harris Dixon of London. She carried 800 tons of coal from Troon for Limerick. Her master, Captain Webb, was drowned and is buried at Farrihy Graveyard. (95)

Guiding Star

The Guiding Star, a small schooner, was driven off course by a gale and wrecked on the Duggerna Reef in Kilkee Bay on 23-4-1888. She carried a cargo of salt from Liverpool to Iceland. The crew of five survived (95)

Martin Gust

The sailing ship, Martin Gust, drifted from her anchorage at Scattery in the gale of 27-2-1903. She went onto the rocks at Belvue and was badly holed. Her crew escaped to safety ashore.

Barge

The barge, M64, being towed by the trawler, Mollia, broke loose and was wrecked on the rocks at Liscannor on 19-6-1963. She was owned by Cementation Ltd and was en route to Galway.

Georgina

The schooner, Georgina, was sunk in a collision in the Shannon on 9-5-1884. She was leaving Limerick bound for Greenock when she was struck amidships by the SS Vale of Calder, bound for Liverpool. Though the Georgina sank immediately Captain Montgomery, his wife and all five crew escaped. She was owned by McMorland of Greenock.

Treenaglass

On 1-8-1883 the 1513 ton steamer, Treenaglass, grounded on the rock known as Bridges Bank near Palaskenry on the south side of the Shannon Estuary. When the tide receded the vessel broke amidships and was a total loss. Commanded by Captain Giles she carried maize consigned to Mr S Paiget of Limerick. The ship was valued at £50,000. The Treenaglass was built by Edwd Hain & Sons in 1882.

Spilling Rock

On the 7-10-1889 a great SW gale caused havoc in the Shannon region. The Spilling Rock was driven ashore. In addition a small schooner carrying oats from Lowner & Sons broke from its moorings at Foynes. She was driven ashore at Cains Island 18 miles upriver. A pleasure boat belonging to Mr Lynch was wrecked at Wellesley Bridge. (65)

Topaz

The 196 ton Topaz was wrecked on 28-12-1900 half a mile below Glin Pier on the Shannon.

Paraffin wax

During the storm of 17-1-1925 a quantity of paraffin wax was washed ashore on the Clare coast between Liscannor and Lahinch. A ship may have foundered near the coast.

Hepzibah

The 90 ton schooner, Hepzibah, of Glouster was wrecked at Kilcredane Point, Carrigaholt on 1-10-1912. She was bound from Kilrush to Aran in ballast.

Killydysart wreck

In the storm of 15-10-1886 a vessel was wrecked beyond Beeves lighthouse between Killydysart and Tradaree. One of the crew was lost and four rescued by a fishing smack. Wreckage was also found between Kilbaha and Loop Head. (65)

Rinanna Wrecks

An article in the Clare Champion of 18-1-1947 described the location of the crash of the aeroplane, Star of Cairo, on 28-12-1946. In addition two wrecks were mentioned. A large sailing turf boat was wrecked about 1847 on Lurga Rocks. The nine crew and passengers aboard were lost. An attempt to save them was unsuccessful when a lighter was driven past the wreck and ashore at Trummera. The oak ribs were still visible in the mud around the rocks. About the same time a schooner was wrecked between Rinanna

Point and Feenish Island. Those aboard were saved.

Owen Glendower

In 1851 the crew of the Russian barque, John, of Odessa were saved when it was driven ashore at Galway Bay. They had saved fifteen from the yacht Owen Glendower a few days before. Capt. Heine of the John was given a lifesaving award. The abandoned yacht was towed into Kilkee in September 1851. The Owen Glendower left the Kenmare River after the party aboard had visited Killarney and were bound for Bolands Bay in Clare. A storm arose and they were driven past the Blaskets at 14 knots. Five of the crew were disabled when the mast fell. The distressed vessel encountered the John and with great difficulty the crew and passengers were saved. During the rescue the John made twelve circuits of the stricken yacht while the John's mate and boatmen made three trips to and from the Owen Glendower. The survivors were added to the 200 aboard the John and landed at Kilrush where they were treated hospitably at the Vandaleur House. (69)

Diana

The Diana went ashore at Ballinacurra Creek on 31-12-1811. The vessel was en route from Limerick to Bristol. The master, Mr Jameson, managed to save the cargo. (234)

Inverness

On 19-2-1817 the Inverness was wrecked in Reinvilla Bay while en route from Limerick to Liverpool.

Mary Ann

The Mary Ann was wrecked at Kilrush on 8-11-1817 en route from Limerick to Galway.

Premier

The 537 ton steel steamer collided with the Waterford paddle steamer Mermaid on 26-11-1898. She sank between the Beale Bar buoy and Kilcreadine light. She was bound for Cleeves of Limerick from Hamburg with sugar. The Premier was built in 1894 by J. Shearer at Glasgow and owned by Simpsons. Though the Premier went down in 20 minutes all the crew escaped. The wreck is known locally as the Sugar Boat. It was rediscovered during sonar surveys associated with larger ships using the Shannon.

Bridgewater

The Bridgewater was wrecked at the mouth of the Shannon on 6-1-1818, she was bound from Limerick to Liverpool.

Quereda

The Sunderland vessel Quereda struck the Beale Bar on 27-1-1834. She was en route from Limerick to London and drifted 2 miles up the Shannon. She sank off Carrig Island.

Eliza

The Eliza sank in Scattery Roads on the Shannon on 24-12-1852. She was en route from Sligo to London.

Maria Jane

The 74 ton schooner, Maria Jane, struck the rocks off Liscannor on 27-12-1898. She had been moored having loaded a cargo of flagstones.

Mary of Milford

The 75 ton schooner, Mary of Milford, was wrecked on Boland Rocks in 1875.

Mary

The sloop, Mary, sank off Dunlee Castle on 1-4-1821. All aboard were lost. The vessel came from Drogheda.

Mary

The 84 ton ketch, Mary, sank on 14-8-1913. She went down 3 miles north east of Loop Head.

Mary Collins

The Mary Collins sank on 8-12-1817 at Cappa near Kilrush. Her cargo was

Luagh stone bound for Galway. The crew escaped.

Thetis

The Thetis was lost when she stranded on the Beale Bar on 30-11-1834. She was bound for Limerick.

Rose

The 87 ton schooner, Rose, sank at Seafield pier on 13-12-1889. She was bound for the Clyde with kelp.

Anna Belle

The Anna Belle, a 153 ton brig, sank at Boland Bay, Kilrush on 21-11-1881. She was en route from Limerick to Penrith with oats. The crew of five survived.

Ariosto

The 278 ton brig, Ariosto, was wrecked at Little Creek, Miltown Malbay on 9-3-1861. Of the crew of 10, the captain was lost. The ship was built in 1855.

Andrew White

On 20-11-1849 the 241 ton brig, Andrew White, was wrecked at Malbay.

Cyrus

The Cyrus, en route from Newcastle to Limerick, was wrecked at Malbay on 23-12-1816.

Maria

The Maria was en route from Liverpool on 30-11-1833 when wrecked at Malbay.

Rose Adelaide

On 27-12-1898 the Rose Adelaide was wrecked at Liscannor.

United Kingdom

While en route from Galway to London, the United Kingdom was wrecked at Kilrush on 24-1-1834.

Triton

The Triton was en route to Limerick from Clare and was wrecked near Clare on 12-3-1834.

Columbus

The Columbus of Sunderland sank at Harold Rock at Limerick on 5-12-1851. She had come from Odessa.

Successor

Five crewmen were lost on 20-11-1850 when the 294 ton Successor was wrecked between Seafield Point and Mutton Island.

Ganges

The 67 ton Ganges, of Aberystwyth was lost off Loop Head in 1848.

Thomas & Jane

The Thomas & Jane was wrecked at Liscannor on 4-2-1822. Though insured for £1000 and despite a claim for £1300 no insurance was paid.

Martin

The 18 gun sloop, HMS Martin, was wrecked in Kilkee Bay on 8-12-1817. The 399 ton vessel was driven ashore at Lough Donnell in a severe gale. Commander Mitchell and the crew of 120 were all safe though some accounts state that four were lost. The ship was built in 1809. (141)

Magpie

The 236 ton, wooden screw gunboat, HMS Magpie, was wrecked at Doolin on 3-4-1864. The Magpie was a former tender to the cruiser, Hawke, based at Queenstown and was supplying coast-guard stations around Galway. The ship was negotiating the sound between Inisheer and the Clare coast in thick weather at 2am. She went ashore on Crab Island just south of the cliffs of Moher. An Atlantic swell drove the vessel high on the shore. The coastguards called the Atlantic Steamship Company tug, Rover, from Galway and at the next tide an unsuccessful effort was made to tow off the Magpie. During this operation the guns, including a 68 pounder, were thrown overboard. Two gunboats, Advice and Racer, along with the tugs, Rover and Pilot, made a vain attempt to release the wreck four days later. The engines were removed to help lighten the

Magpie. A few days later the remains of the ship were smashed by the same gale as sealed the fate of the grounded City of New York stranded on Daunts Rock. Lieutenant Bell and the crew of 33 survived. (141) The hull, engines and gear were purchased for £585 by Mr Wilson of Queenstown. It was intended to burn the wreck to extract the copper. (226)

Wentworth
The 254 ton brig, Wentworth, of Beaumont was wrecked on 30-9-1873 at Carraigaholt, a mile west of Kilcreadane Lighthouse. She was bound from Limerick to Shields in ballast.

Erin Go Bragh
The deserted, large three masted ship, Erin go Bragh, came ashore at Cregga near Ballyvaughan. The ship with a cargo of timber had come from Liverpool. This was the occasion of a fierce storm in which many ships were lost.

Melantho
The entire crew of 17 were lost when their ship, Melantho, was wrecked at Malbay on 18-3-1816. She was bound for Barcelona from Limerick.

Pacific
The 320 ton ship, Pacific, was abandoned when she came ashore at Miltown Malbay on 10-12-1821. She carried a cargo of timber.

Unknown vessels
An unnamed schooner was lost in 1886, A large sail boat was lost on 20-11-1816 at Whelp Rock in the Shannon. A further wreck occurred on 1-1-1871 at Carraigaholt. Two vessels are believed to have been wrecked at Mutton Island. There remains an anchor of the first and two small cannon survived from the second. The wreck of a ship bound for Galway from Cardiff was auctioned at Aranview House. She had been wrecked at Ballaghaline near Doolin on 13-10-1821. A further wreck occurred on 12-2-1821 at rocks off Kilbaha. A wheat ship owned by Mr Fawl of Limerick, leaving Carraigaholt was lost on 26-2-1816 near Achenish. Two large turf boats were lost on 31-8-1815 and 26-11-1815. One was at Kilcredane, the other at Poulmangane near Kilrush.

Kelp
In 1908 a vessel called the Kelp was wrecked at Spanish Point. The compass was recovered and is in the Heritage Centre at Corofin. She carried a cargo of mahogany.

French Longboat
After the siege of Limerick in the Williamite wars the remains of the French army were evacuating the city. An overloaded longboat capsized on 4-11-1691 and sank while transferring men to a waiting ship in the Shannon. Twenty two officers were drowned. The French paymaster's chest, money and plate belonging to Count Lausun and cash belonging to King James were lost. Altogether £50,000-£90,000 were estimated to have been lost. (Egmont MSS) The French fleet consisted of 18 men o war, 6 fireships and 20 transports. All anchored on 6-11-1691 some 2 leagues below Scattery Island. Another account (23-11-1691) described the loss of 100 men when a French ship with 400 aboard overturned, having struck a rock. (110)

French frigate
On 14-11-1690 a French frigate with ammunition and arms for the Jacobite army was cast away at the mouth of the Shannon. The 28 army officers aboard as well as the crew were lost. (110) The National Museum has two cannon which were found in the Shannon.

French Brig

Two cannon are reported on shore near Quilty and are believed to have come from a French brig wrecked in 1796 or 1798.

Jane

The Jane sank half a mile west of Kilcreadane lighthouse on 26-2-1879. The 98 ton schooner carried a cargo of coal from the Mersey for Askeaton.

James

The James, a troop transport, sank after hitting rocks at Killimer on 18-1-1782. Her master was Mr Dunlop. Killimer is described as being in the north of Ireland, but the Shannon is the only such placename. (234)

Industry

The Industry was wrecked at Liscannor on 27-1-1781. The ship was bound for London from Jamaica. Part of the cargo was saved. (234)

Lake Patos

On 28-5-1904 the 99 ton schooner, Lake Patos, sank 500 yards east of Liscannor pier. The cargo was coal from Limerick for Liscannor. The crew of four survived.

GALWAY

Plassy
Photo: T. Conlan

GALWAY

Plassy

The Plassy, a motor coaster owned by Limerick Steamship Co was wrecked in March 1960 on Finis Rock at the southern tip of Inisheer. The refrigerated cargo ship had engine trouble and was washed on the rock in a gale. A series of photos of the rocket rescue are on display in the Maritime Museum and were published (182). The wreck lies high and dry on flat rocks to this day. The Plassy was built in 1941 as a trawler for the RN and converted to a cargo

vessel in 1947. The Limerick SS Company acquired her in 1951. (228)

Woodbine

In 1835 the 195 ton Woodbine was wrecked on Inismore. The crew were assisted by Padraig O'Flaitherta. (84)

Timber ship

In a great gale on 21-7-1823 a ship with a cargo of timber was wrecked on Iolan an da Bhrannog. The masts had been smashed and the vessel was out of control when she struck the rocks. The crew were saved. The coastguard prevented locals from removing the cargo. (84)

Providence
On 28-10-1835 the sloop, Providence, was wrecked on the Aran islands. She was on route from Galway to Liverpool. Her crew were saved. (84)

Rambler
The 55 ton Bristol schooner, Rambler, was wrecked at the lighthouse on Iolan an da Bhrannog on 13-9-1861. A passenger and one of the crew were drowned. (84)

Craig Gowan
The schooner, Craig Gowan, en route from Kinvara to Bristol was wrecked at Carraig na Fianaise on 24-5-1876. Her crew were all saved. (84)

Don Quixote
On 14-1-1879 the 425 ton brig, Don Quixote, was abandoned by the crew west of Aran. Her captain and four of the crew had been washed overboard and the ship had been badly damaged in a storm. A passing German ship put two officers and two seamen aboard to navigate and assist. She reached the west side of Inismore and was unable to weather the lee shore. Her anchors were dropped but the crew gave up the struggle and abandoned ship. The steamer, City of the Tribes, put out to seek her but to no avail. She was en route from New York to Limerick with petroleum. (84) (66)

Ocean Tramp
The 33 foot trawler, Ocean Tramp, sank a mile and a half SW of Inisheer on 1-2-1992. The crew of three were rescued by helicopter. The vessel was en route from Fenit to Westport.

Ocean Scout
The 200 ton drifter, Ocean Scout, on hire to the Admiralty sank off Inisheer Lighthouse on 21-12-1917.

Boy Pauric
The 80 foot Clogherhead trawler, Boy Pauraic, sank on 25-2-1987 near the lighthouse on the north tip of Inis Mor. The vessel was driven onto the rocks at Rock Island when caught by a 45 knot gale as it made for the shelter of the Aran Islands. The skipper, Ronan Gill, and crew were saved by an Aer Corps helicopter from near the automatic lighthouse. Another trawler was lost in the sound between Inismean and Inisheer in December 1986. One of the crew was drowned.

Nogi
The steam trawler, Nogi, of London went ashore on 16-8-1938 about 300 yards NW of the lighthouse on Straw Island near Inismore. A strong WSW wind drove the vessel ashore. The lifeboat took off 11 of the crew and transferred them to a sister trawler Hatano. The remaining man was washed overboard but was found safe on Straw Island. Built at Smiths Dock M'boro, she was completed in February 1923 and sold to Jenkenson and Jones of London in 1932. The vessel was probably salvaged as a Nogi was used as a minesweeper from 31-8-1939 until lost on 23-6-1941.

Hatano
The 297 ton trawler, Hatano, ran ashore on 16-8-1938 near Galway. The crew were rescued by the Kilronan lifeboat. She was built at Smith's dock for Neave and West of Cardiff in 1925 and sold to Jenkenson & Jones in 1932. It appears that she was salvaged as she served as a minesweeper from 5-9-1939 through the war. She was broken up in 1956.

Royalist ship
During the Cromwellian Wars, Galway was besieged and the population reduced to near starvation. Limerick surrendered in October 1651 but Galway held out until April 1652. Two grain ships attempted to relieve the distress on 16-2-1652. They were pursued by

Parliamentary frigates. One was captured. The other was wrecked on rocks off Aran Mor. (33) (172)

Tobacco ship

In the mid 19th century the wreck of a sailing ship was driven ashore at Poll na Loinge on Aran Mor. Poll Na Loinge lies between Killmurvey beach and Oatquarter (Fearann na Coirce) on the east shore of Aran Mor. Bales of tobacco washed ashore from the cargo were concealed from the coastguard by the islanders. Bodies from the wreck were buried among the limestone rocks about 80 metres along a side road from where the wreck occurred. (33) A sailing ship was caught on a lee shore at An Sunda Caoch in the Aran islands and dashed on the rocks. (33)

Angmerling

The 1045 ton coal boat, Angmerling, sank on 25-1-1975 in Galway Bay about two miles off Blackrock at the end of the Salthill promenade. The wreck is badly broken and lies in about 20 metres. The cargo of 2450 tons of coal was mostly salvaged by dredger.

Karel

On 7-12-1964 the Dutch coaster, Karel, ran aground on Mutton Island in Galway Bay. She was badly damaged.

Thomas Gray

The 70 ton ketch, Thomas Gray, was wrecked half a mile W by S of Mutton Island lighthouse on 2-10-1916. She carried manure from Plymouth to Galway. The crew of four survived.

Moyalla

The 684 ton Limerick Steamship Co vessel, Moyalla, was lost in fog on the Marguerite Shoal in Galway Bay on 17-2-1946. She struck Black Head and Captain O'Sullivan and his crew left the ship four hours later. She carried tar, soda, ammonia and copper pipes. The

Galway Harbour commissioners in their commiserations noted that the Limerick SS Company ships did not usually avail of the services of a Galway pilot.

Janet and Ann

The 77 ton schooner, Janet and Ann, was wrecked on Straw Island on 13-5-1903. She carried flagstones from Liscannor to Manchester. The crew of five survived.

June

On 16-1-1962 the motor vessel, June, of Groningen ran ashore on reefs at Mutton Island. The crew of eight were rescued by the Kilronan lifeboat. Another vessel grounded beside her a few days later. She had assumed that the June was entering the harbour and tried to follow. The second vessel was towed off.

Razani

The crew of eight of the 3500 ton ore carrier, Razani, of Piraeus were rescued in Galway Bay on 25-10-1967. This vessel which carried the first load of ore from the Tynagh mines grounded 400 metres from the shore at Black Head. The incident occurred when a gale arose as the ship left Galway. The hatches were blown off and the engine room flooded. The lifeboat saved the crew of eight. In 1968 three were charged with the theft of goods from the vessel. The ore was salvaged and the Galway oyster beds thereby saved. The vessel was raised, towed to Passage West, and broken.

Barrister

On 4-1-1943 the 6348 ton, 445 foot Barrister built by Lithgow in 1939. Ran ashore and broke in two on Inishark Island, Co Galway. The vessel was in a convoy in ballast from North Africa to the Clyde. The convoy was dispersed by a submarine threat and went off course in mist. The Barrister was seen drifting about 7 miles offshore at dawn and struck a reef west from Inishark about 8.30. The ship's bell was presented by Captain Copeland to the bar at the Renvyle House hotel where it now hangs. The ship was the third of that name owned by the Charente Steam Ship Company (T&J Harisson). The previous two were torpedoed in 1915 and 1918. The wreck is well scattered. (10)

Reformer

The 145 ton brig, Reformer, was wrecked on the southerly point of Inishark on 24-3-1856. She carried a cargo of wheat. Four of the eight crew were lost.

Royal Oak

A shipwreck prior to 1839 seems to be the origin of the name Royal Oak cove on Inisboffin.

Britannia

An account by Reddington (50) derived from unnumbered papers at the Record Office, London, relates the tale of the Britannia. In October 1779 Captain Robert Protton of the Orange Rangers and Lt Hector Maclean of the 2/84th rgt were recruiting in Newfoundland. They raised 196 recruits and hired an unnamed vessel to transport them to New York or Halifax. They sailed from St Johns on 17-12-1778 and encountered a gale which drove them out into the Atlantic. They decided to continue to England. However on 27-1-1780 the vessel ran aground on Inisboffin. Sixty of the soldiers were drowned and the rest made their way ashore. The Islanders refused to feed them except for exorbitant prices. Fifteen died on the island. Eventually thirty six reached Galway to report a further thirty one as sick on the island and sixteen deserters. Even then the officers had difficulty in arranging pay and assistance. A ship with a cargo of nails was wrecked on Inisboffin at a spot known as Nails Rock. Some daggers were found near the island some years ago from yet another wreck.

Kitty Brig

On 8-2-1741 the Kitty Brig was sheltering in the harbour of Inisboffin. The vessel was in distress. Having guided the ship into the harbour, several islanders slipped the anchors and cut the ropes so that the vessel would be driven ashore. The vessel, commanded by Thomas Stamper was bound from Antigua to London with a cargo of sugar, cocoa and other valuable goods. The Royal Exchange insurance company offered a reward of £30 for the arrest of Edmund Flaherty, his son also called Edmund, Anthony Flaherty, a priest and John Flaherty. (204)

Inisboffin Mailboat

On 1-4-1908 the mailboat to Inisboffin which was an ordinary sailing boat was lost in a storm. Among those lost aboard was Sergeant McCarthy, the policeman of Inisboffin. Four islandmen were lost on 1-6-1942.

Cleggan Disaster

On 29-10-1927 a fleet of fishing currachs from Cleggan were caught in a sudden gale. They had sailed to catch a large shoal of herring and mackerel. The Rose of Lacken was lost near Crevagh Head. Skipper Pat Kearney and eight aboard were lost. Five other craft and crews numbering ten from Rossadilisk were drowned. One hundred years before 10 fishermen were lost at nearby Tarmon point. (122)

Verity

The 1000 ton American barque, Verrity, was washed ashore near Clifden on 8-1-1880. Reports conflict as to whether the wreck occurred on High Island or Omey Island. She left Waterford on 17 December for New York in ballast for grain. Captain Corning had seventeen crew and three passengers aboard. A gale was encountered, the mast fell and four men were lost overboard. The ship drifted for six days. When the vessel was 700 yards offshore the crew abandoned ship. The Verity was built at Quebec in 1878. (67)

American Ridge
The clipper, American Ridge, was wrecked at Crow (Cruagh?) island on the Galway coast.

St Patrick
During the great gale of 6-1-1839 the true Atlantic force of the gale was felt in Galway Bay. The barque, St Patrick, with a valuable cargo was driven out of the dock and onto the shore. The brigs, Glenora and Lively, went high and dry. The Lelia, with a cargo of timber went ashore to the west of the town. The Courier and Albion were lying in the roads. They were driven ashore in Murragh Bay and on rocks at Hare Island, respectively.

Union
The schooner, Union, was lost two miles from Slyne Head on 3-2-1836. She carried a cargo of oats en route to Glasgow. Her bulwarks were cast ashore.

Ard Angus
The trawler, Ard Angus, lost power in Galway Bay on 13-11-1968. She was assisted by the Star of Faith and towed to Aran Islands. However she sank between Inis Mean and Inis Mor when she was driven ashore. Her crew escaped. The wreck occurred in the same spot where 15 fishermen were drowned in 1948.

Dash
During a storm, year unknown, the Dash was wrecked at Cleggan. The captain went ashore in a small boat. While he was ashore a storm arose and the ship was driven ashore. The captain was the

only survivor. The wreck was still visible in 1934 at Sceaca about half a mile west of Cleggan. She carried a cargo of butter. (135, 77,p265. 113,p73)

County Clare
The steamer, County Clare, went ashore at Cleggan Bay on 19-11-1906. She was owned by Watson of Liverpool, the owners of Liscannor slate quarries.

Constance
The armed tender, Constance, was driven ashore in Roundstone Bay on 17-1-1805. The vessel was pounded by breakers and became a total loss. Locals assembled to plunder the remains. Lieut. Menzies lost two of his crewmen. (141)

Fishing boats
As a mechanism for the relief of famine, people on the western seaboard were assisted in the acquisition of fishing boats by the Congested Districts Board. The Aran fishing fleet was at anchor on 28-12-1899. Many of the fishermen had taken the opportunity of sleeping aboard to ensure an early start. A storm arose during the night. Several boats were torn from their anchorage and dashed ashore. Six men were drowned. (33)

West Indiaman
In the storm of 7-12-1833 a West Indiaman was wrecked at Ardfry. She was en route from London to Barbados. Another vessel was lost with six lives in a collision in the mouth of Finvara Harbour. Eight were lost on a vessel which sank in Cleggan Bay, including the sons of three coastguards. (173)

Coal boat
During the storm of 24-12-1924 a sailing boat with coal from Kinvara sank in Galway Bay.

Conception Delcano
The 418 ton Armada ship, Conception Delcano, of the Biscay squadron was wrecked on 25-9-1588. The wreck is

believed to have occurred at Durling na Spaineach at Ards near Carna. She carried 225 men and 18 guns. (6) At Doohar point near Carna a millstone, cannon and coal were found in 1988. Local legend suggests that these came from a ship carrying a cargo of sugar, possibly a West Indiaman. A large anchor was found at the base of the Skeard Mor, one of the Skeard rocks about 4 miles off Carna.

Falco Blanco Mediano
The Armada urca (hulk) Falco Blanco, struck a reef WNW of Freaghillaun South in Ballinakill Harbour on 25-9-1588. She carried 103 men and 16 guns. The Captain, Pedro de Arechaga, was captured and taken to Galway. Another Armada ship may have been wrecked on Davillaun, east of Inisboffin. However, despite the tradition there is no hard evidence. (6) About 1980 a 5 metre anchor and a pile of stone ballast were found near Inisboffin. An early anchor with a 2 metre shaft and one broken fluke was found between Davillaun and Inisboffin by a trawler in 1992.

Barna Wreck
Legend suggests that timbers projecting from the beach at Barna were the remains of an Armada ship. No record exists of the loss of a vessel there; however, an Armada vessel anchored off Barna and landed 70 men who were captured. As comprehensive official reports exist for Galway they would have recorded a wreck. The timbers more probably belong to a French trading barque wrecked about 1680. (6)

Rapid
The 328 ton Rapid was wrecked on 4-5-1900 on Carrigfada Point on Aran Mor. The ship was being used by the Congested Districts Board as an ice hulk for the Aran fishing fleet.

Betty Canahan
On 23-1-1753 the Betty Canahan was wrecked on the Aran Islands. The vessel was bound for Newry from Galway with kelp. Most of those aboard were lost. (69)

Margurite
The Margurite shoal buoy was lighted in former years by a carbide light. A vessel struck the buoy (year unknown) and was sunk by the exploding carbide.

Heros
On 7-10-1889 the 599 ton barque, Heros, was wrecked on Hare Island in Galway Bay. Having delivered coal to Galway the ship was bound for Newport in ballast.

Lily
The 223 ton brig, Lily, sank at Mutton Island on 30-11-1889. She carried coal to Galway from North Shields.

Olga
The 316 ton Norwegian brig, Olga, was wrecked a mile east of Cloghane Point on 21-12-1889. She carried deal from Canada to Galway.

Edward
The Edward, a 98 ton schooner was wrecked a mile from Galway docks on 1-9-1891. She was en route from Tralee to Newport. The crew of four survived.

Albion
On 26-11-1835 the Albion was wrecked in Connemara. She was en route from Limerick to Liverpool. All the crew were drowned.

Sarah Margaret
The Sarah Margaret was wrecked at Galway on 20-10-1833. She was bound for London from St John NB.

Friendship
The 83 ton Cardiff schooner was wrecked near Spiddal on 22-1-1850.

Isabella
On 4-1-1834 the Isabella was wrecked

on the Galway coast. She was en route from the Clyde to Clare.

James
The James was wrecked at Slyne Head on 17-1-1834. She was bound for Galway from the Clyde.

Gem
The 98 ton Gem was wrecked in Galway Bay on 21-11-1848. She was bound for Liverpool from Limerick. Three of the crew were drowned.

Susan
The Susan was wrecked at Hare Island on 24-12-1848 while en route from Galetz.

Bonnie Marie
The Bonnie Marie was wrecked on Mason Island, Connemara on 15-11-1848. She was bound for Galway from Nantes. All the crew escaped.

San Spiridone
In February 1850 the San Spiridone was wrecked on Hare Island. An Austrian brig was lost in the same storm at Clifden.

Thoburn
The brig, Thoburn, was wrecked at Omey Island near Clifden on 22-10-1854. One of the crew of eight was drowned.

Lirope
The 303 ton barque, Lirope, was wrecked seven miles SW of Clifden on 4-12-1863. All eleven aboard were lost.

Kate
The 112 ton schooner, Kate, was wrecked on Black Rock in Galway Bay on 8-6-1885. She was bound for Galway from Runcorn with salt and pipes.

Marion
The Marion was wrecked near Roundstone on 31-12-1852. The vessel was bound for Greneda from Glasgow.

Nordlyset
The 1593 ton steel barque, Nordlyset,

was wrecked on Mutton Island on 10-11-1914. The cargo was deal bound for Galway from Rimouski. About 1928 the ship was scrapped on the spot and the wreckage conveyed to Summers wharf at Shotton. (13)

Austrian brig
In February 1850 an Austrian brig was lost in a storm at Clifden.

Thetis
The 217 ton schooner, Thetis, was lost at Black Rock on 12-1-1882. She carried coal from Garston to Galway.

Capitaine Plevin II
The 2,600 ton French factory trawler registered at St Malo, Capitaine Plevin, ran aground on Loo Rocks off Black Head in Galway Bay early on 5-4-1991. Due to a falling tide the ship stuck fast on the reef and the crew of 60 were taken to safety by Irish and RAF helicopters. The ship had entered Galway Bay to land a sick crewman. The captain, Jean Marc Le Borgne, and some of the crew stayed aboard for some hours and pumps from the Galway Fire Brigade were airlifted out to the vessel. A salvage operation, involving the United Towing Company of Hull and their salvage tug, Salvageman, refloated the wreck at the high tide on 16-4-91.

Nancy
The Nancy was wrecked at Slyne Head on 4-3-1795 en route from Bristol to Westport. The master was Captain Jones.

Tom
The Tom was wrecked at Galway Bay on 16-3-1799. Captained by Mr Gibson she was en route from Liverpool to Limerick.

Friendship
The Friendship of Dublin, captained by Mr Cosgrove was wrecked in "Galway river" on 1-9-1750. The ship was en route from Norway to Galway. (110)

Mollia

The BIM owned motor trawler, Mollia, sank 6 miles off Mutton Island on 12-6-1965. The trawler had caught fire and the crew escaped into a dingy. They were picked up the following day.

Elizabeth

The 128 ton brig, Elizabeth, was wrecked at Gollen Head on 30-12-1865. Four of the nine aboard were lost. She was en route from St Paul de Loano to Queenstown with general cargo.

Flash

The Flash, a 122 ton brig was wrecked on Shark Island (Inishark?) on 1-3-1870. All five aboard were lost. The Flash was built in 1860.

Helen

The 100 ton brig, Helen, was lost at Roundstone on 24-11-1889. She carried kelp from Clare for Scotland.

Water Nymph

The 61 ton schooner, Water Nymph, was wrecked at Bayleek near Clifden on 2-8-1884. She was on route from Clifden to Dunowen.

San Dionigio

On 25-11-1852 the San Dionigio was wrecked at the Galway Bank. She was en route from Galetz.

John Toole

The 822 ton John Toole was wrecked near Galway on 1-2-1852. Nobody was saved. The vessel was bound for Liverpool from New Orleans.

Progressor

On 20-11-1850 the brig, Progressor, was lost at Mutton Island. The cargo was oats. Six of the eight crew were lost.

MAYO

MAYO

Roussalka
The 1400 ton yacht, Roussalka, sank on 1-9-1933 at Killary Harbour. The vessel under Captain Laidlaw had landed some guests in Killary and was leaving the inlet when he took a wrong course in mist. She struck Bloodslate Rock near Fraebl Island and sank in seven minutes. All aboard, including Lord Moyne, his guests and crew of 25 escaped without injury. When the captain and some crew returned the next day not even the mast was visible. Originally named the Brighton she was built by Denny in 1905 as a railway steamer. Bought by Lord Moyne of the Guinness family in 1930, she was refitted and had a 500 ton oil tank installed to enable her owner cross the Pacific. In 1931 her turbines were replaced by Diesels. A porthole from the ship is on display in Diamonds Pub at Tully near Letterfrack. (175)

Charles Stuart Parnell
The wooden ketch rigged sailing vessel, Charles Stuart Parnell, was lost by fire in Ilanmore Harbour, Westport Bay in June 1928. The 200 ton vessel was used to carry supplies and coal to lighthouses in the area. The wreck which is charted lies between Island Mor and the channel between Inisgort and Collanbeg. The wreckage is considerably broken on a sand and coral bottom at 12 metres.

Aghia Eirini
The 4,330 ton steamer, Aghia Eirini, foundered on the western shore of Achill Island on 10-12-1940. The wreck lies in 15 metres on a rocky bottom. The cove is surrounded by high cliffs surmounted by a salvage derrick which was used by a local man, Mr J Sweeney, in the salvage operation in 1941. The diver was also a local, Mr J. Gorman.

Jenny
The 492 ton Norwegian barque, Jenny, was wrecked on Achillbeg Island on 13-1-1894. She was bound from Jamaica to Hamburg with a cargo of logwood. The crew of ten escaped.

Lios Cara
On 13-2-1979 the 30 foot half decker, Lioscarra, sank off Doeega Head on the west of Achill Island. The three fishermen aboard were lost. At first it was thought that they had sheltered on Clare Island as the LE Grainne was in the area monitoring salmon fishing. After 17 hours the significance of a lifebuoy found on the beach was realised and a search commenced, but to no avail. (99)

Sentry
The 41 ton steel steamer, Sentry, was wrecked at the entrance to Keel Harbour on Achill on 4-5-1911. The ship was bound from Keel to Westport with a cargo of stones. The four crewmen survived.

Neptune
The barque, Neptune, en route from Demerera to London was wrecked below Meenaun Cliffs on Achill on 21-1-1860. Two of her crew of thirteen were lost. She carried sugar, coconut and rum in her cargo. Her anchor was raised in 1988 and is to be placed on a plinth at Dookinella.

Santiago, San Nicholas, Grand Grin

Tradition places these three Armada wrecks on the north Mayo coast. One in Tirawley located somewhere between Benwee Head and Dunpatrick Head. The best estimate is that this was a large ship carrying about 400 men and probably named the Ciervo Volante. Tradition places two wrecks in the Broadhaven area; one at Kid Island was possibly a tender or other minor ship as no records support the oral tradition; the other may have been the urca(hulk) Santiago of 600 tons with a crew of 86. This wreck occurred near Poulatomish. One account locates an Erris wreck of 900 tons at the sands of Ballycroolie. On the Curraun Peninsula a vessel was wrecked near Toorglass. This may have been the San Nicholas Prodaneli. This was a Ragusan vessel of 834 tons and carried 355 men and 26 cannon. The previous identification assumes that the Grand Grin was wrecked on Clare Island. El Grand Grin of the Biscay squadron was an 1160 ton vessel and carried 329 men and 28 guns. La Rata Encoronada of the Levant squadron was an 820 ton ship carrying 419 men and 35 guns. She sunk on 21-9-1588 at Fahy strand Ballycroy, Blacksod Bay. Jacob the diver worked and recovered a cannon in Blacksod bay from an Armada wreck on 1-6-1633. (170) It was taken by the local chief to Cormick's castle. (6) A large anchor with the stock measuring four metres was found in 1960 with a pile of stones similar to ballast under a cliff at Davillaun by Mr O'Halloran. However it was thought to be of English design and pre Armada.

Mae

In June 1910 the hooker, Mae, was caught by a gale en route from Westport to Inisboffin. The crew of three were washed overboard and lost. Kiladoon

people saw the plight of the vessel from their church but were unable to assist. Eventually the vessel was washed onto Cross Strand. The vessel survived and was taken with its cargo to Inisboffin. In keeping with tradition it was not used again and was broken there for firewood.

Black Eyed Susan

The Black Eyed Susan was wrecked in 1879 at Killala Bay. She was carrying flour from Santander, Spain. The cargo was salvaged by the tug Maid of the Moy. (122)

Arcania

The Arcania was wrecked at Ross Coastguard Station in 1879. The cargo was guano. (122)

Thames

The 295 ton London steamer, Thames, struck St Patrick's Reef off Kilcummin Head on 5-3-1893. She backed off into deeper water and sank. She struck the rock in fog, en route from London to Sligo with guano. The 12 crew were all saved. The ship was built in 1860. (122) The wreck was discovered by Castlebar SAC on 14-9-1984 in 13 fathoms at St Patrick's Rock.

Maid of the Moy

A 37 ton wooden Tug of this name was built by Victor Coates of Belfast on 23-9-1860. A bye law passed in 1866 or 1867 allowed her to trade with other ports. In 1873 she towed a barge from Essex Quay to Ballina. This barge spent her last years on a mudbank at the Quay at Ballina. A new Maid ten feet longer with a steel hull was built at Glasgow. The engine from the old Maid was transferred to the new hull and the old hull towed home. She worked in the Moy and on runs to Belmullet and Sligo. On a stormy night in 1899 she dragged her anchor and was wrecked at Porturlin. (123)

Eureka
In 1901 the Eureka ran aground and disappeared in two days in quicksand at West Bartra. (122)

Maren
In 1923 the Maren of Sundswell, Sweden sank off West Bartra. She carried a cargo of timber. (122)

Sine
On 6-12-1927 the Sine, a 140 foot, 500 ton three masted barque of Marsdal, Sweden sank. She had anchored in shallow water off Ross and was driven onto Kilalla Bank off Bartra in a northerly storm when her anchor cables broke. She carried a cargo of timber from South America for Beckets of Ballina. Captain Christofferson and seven crew were rescued by a party of locals and Gardai, led by Sergent Kelly. They launched a 14 foot boat which had to be plugged with sods of turf. When they reached the Bartra Island they waded out with lanterns and managed to float a lifebuoy to the ship. The crew were brought ashore by a rope. The cargo of timber was saved. The wreck is still visible. (122)

Lady Washington
The Lady Washington was wrecked on Bartra about 1867 at the same place as the Sine in 1927. (122)

German Vessel
A German vessel with tea from Trieste was wrecked in Blacksod Bay in 1828 or 1829. Some of the crew were drowned. A Minister, Mr Dawson, accused William Bingham of looting the wreck (125)

Maria
The Norwegian vessel, Maria, was wrecked near Eagle Island on 24-9-1830. She had taken 28 days to carry a cargo of stock fish from Bergen. Six of the nine crew were saved but were robbed. The ship ran into a track between Eagle Island and the cliffs and drifted and dragged into timber cove under 300 foot cliffs. (125)

Mansfield
The 155 ton brig, Mansfield, was wrecked at Iniskea on 26-11-1834. She was en route from St John's, New Brunswick to Ballyshannon with a cargo of timber. She was abandoned by the crew north of Iniskea and boarded by South Iniskea men who then fought a battle with the coastguard under Captain Nugent. The vessel was driven into a narrow rocky cove on Iniskea and stripped. The master, Thomas Moon and his eight crew were wrecked in their lifeboat between Erris Head and Broadhaven. They were robbed by the locals. (126)

Spring Flower
The Spring Flower from Odessa was wrecked at Pullaheeny on 16-12-1864.

Killala wrecks
In the Great gale of 12-1-1839 four vessels were wrecked at Killala. Their crews were saved by Andrew Burke of Ross.

Tuskar
On 6-9-1917 the Clyde Co steamer, Tuskar, was sunk by a mine three miles west of Eagle Island. Ten of the crew were lost. The 1159 ton vessel was built in 1890 by Thompson of Dundee.

Ivy Rose
On 3-6-1988 the Westport trawler Ivy Rose went on rocks in Clew Bay. The four man crew were rescued by another trawler. An RAF Nimrod flew low over the vessel in response to the distress call, to direct the rescue effort.

Clew Bay Disaster
On 14-6-1894 a hooker capsized in Clew Bay. She carried passengers from Achill bound for Glasgow. The Laird line

steamer, Gardinia which ran a Westport to Glasgow service was awaiting transfer of the Achill passengers. The hooker was caught by a gust of wind and overturned. Thirty two of those aboard were drowned. Their bodies were brought back to Achill by special train on the new railway. This fulfilled a sombre prophecy that the first and last trains on the line would carry corpses as its cargo. The last train on the line was also a funeral special carrying the 18 bodies of the victims of the Kirkintilloch bothy fire disaster.

Wreckers

In the Kilgalligan area of the Erris peninsula wreckers were active in the early years of the nineteenth century. They would light fires at a spot known as an Ball Doite. These fires lured ships between Broadhaven and Inver onto the reef Ton Rin na nEan. Including a wreck which occurred at Bun a Gleanna as a result of their work. A Spanish ship was wrecked near Swallow Rock about 1810. She carried a cargo of silk and had been lured by a fire at Rinroe. A family called Rooney had a great chest of women's attire salvaged from the wreck. At Shanks Cave a Mr Shank was murdered by a wrecker about 1805. Despite the absence of roads the murdered man's parents are reputed to have travelled to collect the body. Mr Shank was thought to be the mate of the ship and a person of some substance. (135, 1395,p48,70,337) At Inver Bay a ship bound for England was wrecked. She carried gold bars which were salvaged by local people and buried in the vicinity. Many were not recovered as the hiding places were not accurately marked. All the crew were lost. (135, 1405,pl42). A wreck occurred at a place since known as Imleach na Muc near Tra na hAoine because two

black pigs were the only survivors. (135, 146,p200) A two masted ship was wrecked at Inver harbour. She had a local pilot aboard who was lost with the crew. (135, 227,p400)

Sorcha an tSneachta

During the Famine in 1847 the Sorcha an tSneachta was lost when she struck between the two Iniskea Islands. Local fishermen saw the incident and put out their boats. Three aboard who were below were lost and one survived. The ship carried flour in barrels from the USA. (135, 227,p421-3)

Ballina wreck

Prior to the Famine a vessel was holed during a storm. On the approach to Ballina she struck on the Carraig Baite. Her cargo was timber. A body recovered from the sea was buried at Teampail na Croise near Beal an Murtid. (135, 227,p418)

Margaret

In November 1798 the navy tender, Margaret, was caught by a severe westerly gale near Achill. She was driven on a reef between the mainland and Inisboffin. Lieutenant Pollexfen and all 25 aboard were lost. The vessel was built in 1785 and was totally broken up. (141)

Arab

On 18-12-1823 the 390 ton brig sloop, Arab, of the Cruiser class was wrecked in Broadhaven near Belmullet. Commander Holmes and his crew of 100 perished. The vessel was built in 1812 at Pelham's Freundsbury. (141, 147)

Inisbiggle wreck

During a gale (year unknown) a ship was wrecked on Inisbiggle between Achill and the mainland. Most of the crew had left the ship when she struck on a rocky point on the north side of the island. Those aboard were the captain who was lame, his wife and a sailor named Milne. The sailor jumped overboard and was drowned. He is buried under a stone cairn on the beach. The captain and his wife waited until the tide receded and they waded ashore. He buried a boot filled with money but due to snow it was not found. (l35, 1405,p3)

Sutherland
The Sutherland touched a rock at the tip of Clare Island and crashed into the north side of the island.

Lee
On 5-10-1909 the 365 ton 210 foot destroyer, Lee, was wrecked at Dolagh Point at the entrance to Blacksod Bay. The ship stuck fast only six yards from the shore and the rocks went through the ship's bottom. Lt Duncan Carmichael and his crew survived. The repair ship, Assistance, removed all the portable gear but the wreck was broken up by heavy seas. The Lee was one of six destroyers based at Queenstown. Built at Doxford in 1899, she was armed with 1x12 pdr and 5x6 pdr guns as well as two torpedo tubes. The wreck was high out of the water for many years until it was removed by the Hammond Lane scrap company in the early 1950s. (147) (150)

Ocean Witch
On 30-4-1894 the Ocean Witch foundered on Eagle Island. Captain Holden and the mate with three crewmen landed at Dunaff Head in an open boat. She carried artificial manure from Plymouth to Limerick. (67)

Unknown vessel
On 14-12-1833 the body of a woman and some firkins of butter were found in Blacksod Bay. A wreck is presumed to have occurred during a recent storm. (l73)

Otter
The 327 ton barque, Otter, was wrecked at Mulrany on 30-12-1865. The cargo was petroleum bound for Havre from Philadelphia. One of the crew of nine was lost.

Sophia
The 13 ton Sophia was wrecked on 22-11-1901 at Clare Island.

Tommaseo
The 645 ton wooden barque, Tommaseo, struck Claggen Head on 17-11-1888. She carried coal from Newport to Capetown. The crew of 12 escaped.

Teresina Stinga
On 11-9-1887 the Teresina Stinga, an Italian barque, went ashore and was lost at Lacken Bay. She was bound for Buenos Aires from Leith with coal.

Leopard
The wreck of a Dutch East Indiaman lies at Poulatomish. The wreck was identified and approximately dated 1640 by presence of a belamine jug and leaf shaped ingots. The wreck lies in 6-10 metres mixed with the remains of another wreck, perhaps the Santiago of the Armada. In December 1665 there was a Dutch ship reported ashore at Mayo. In August 1666 efforts were made to salvage the vessel. A ship was sent from Crookhaven to Sligo to recover anchors and cables. (29) The date tends to point to the outward bound 400 ton Zeepard (Leopard) which left Wielingen on 28-10-1665. The ship was reputed wrecked west of the Shetlands but the details seem to fit the Mayo wreck. (220). At Rinroe point near Belmullet a location is known as Crann Casta (twisted masts). Here searchers found lead ingots; clay pipes which were dated about 1675 and cannon. (22) A mile south east of Erris Head there is a cave called the Danish Cellar with a possible association with a Danish ship. The museum at Beleek Castle Ballina

contains timbers and three small brass cannon from local wrecks. The material was recovered about 1965 by the owner, Marshall Duran.

Sinai

The 339 ton brig, Sinai, was lost at Inver, Broadhaven on 1-1-1877. The collier was bound from Troon to Demerera

Fancy

The Fancy was a man o war formerly the Charles II of the 1694 Spanish expedition from Corunna. She was taken by Henry Everly (Long Ben) and used for piracy. After unspeakable cruelty and robbery in the seven seas the crew broke up. The last record of them is the arrival of 20 pirates in Mayo in June 1696. Several were arrested. It is not clear what became of their ship which must have been wrecked or abandoned where they landed. (241)

Thomas and Rebecca

The Thomas and Rebecca was wrecked on 23-1-1752 at Clew Bay near Westport. (69) A report (101) indicates that it was wrecked at Chewland Bay near Wexford but this appears to be an error. Though described as an East Indiaman, the ship is not listed in the records. (205)

East Indiaman

About 1709 a large East India ship with a rich cargo was lost attempting to enter Killala bay. The ship struck the sandbar at the mouth of the river. (206).

Steintje Mensinga

On 4-12-1961 the 900 ton Dutch coaster, Steintje Mensinga, struck a submerged rock a mile and a half NE of Eagle Island. The Aran lifeboat put out and a German coaster, the Maria Schulte, stood by. At first light a British Naval helicopter took off six of the crew and landed them at Aughadoon near

Belmullet. The captain and three men stayed aboard. The seas became rougher and it was decided to take off the remaining crew. A lifeboat from the Maria Schulte was launched with five aboard which succeeded in taking off the captain and the three men from the Dutch ship. The lifeboat capsized on the return trip and all aboard were drowned. The bodies were washed ashore at Ellybay between Belmullet and Blacksod.

Annie

The 175 ton brig, Annie, was wrecked at Broadhaven on 14-1-1893. She was en route from Limerick to Bristol with a cargo of oats. The crew of six survived.

Otter

Cannon balls were found in Clew Bay and thought to come from a ship called the Otter.

Earl of Caithness

During the Big Wind on 6-1-1839 the Earl of Caithness was at anchor in Killala Bay. When the wind struck, the crew of five lashed themselves to the ship. The vessel capsized spilling her cargo of salt. Locals observing the crew's plight, launched a boat and rescued the five crewmen. (225)

Wellington

In the same storm the Wellington was blown from her anchorage in Killala Bay and driven on rocks. The crew were able to walk ashore. She carried barley and oats bound for Belfast. (225)

Smuggler

In the 18th and 19th centuries there was a smuggling trade from Toin na Dumca harbour with Flushing in Holland. Captain O'Malley and Paudin Ban MacCann were the local smugglers. While transhipping goods for Newport,

Captain O'Malley's vessel was sunk at Poll na Raite by a revenue vessel. The date is not clear and the revenue vessel is known locally as Sloopeen Vaughan I255I, doubtless a sloop commanded by Mr Vaughan. (233)

Margaret Bannister
The 66 ton schooner Margaret Bannister was wrecked at Lenadoon Point, Killala Bay on 1-10-1894. She was bound from Ballina to Mumbles with oats. The crew of five escaped.

Desire
On 10-5-1835 the Desire was lost at Ballina. The vessel was leaving port bound for London.

Union
In May 1835 the Union was wrecked on the Moy Bar. She was bound from Ballina to London.

Volunteer
On 30-3-1833 the Volunteer was lost near Louisberg. The ship was bound for Quebec from Cork.

Love
The Love of Scarboro was lost near Louisberg on 26-6-1833.

Hope
On 5-5-1818 the Hope foundered near Achill Head. She was bound for Newport from Liverpool.

Draper
The Draper stranded near Kilalla on 6-11-1818. She was bound for Sligo from St Andrews, New Brunswick.

Lady Mackenzie
The 92 ton Lady Mackenzie was lost near Ballina in 1829.

Magdala
The 183 ton brig, Magdala, was wrecked at Broadhaven on 14-4-1882. She was bound from London to Galway with a cargo of bran.

Alexander
The schooner, Alexander, was wrecked

at Broadhaven on 18-10-1854. All six aboard were lost.

Shepherd
The 64 ton schooner, Shepherd, was lost at Killala Bay on 18-12-1854. The cargo was oats. All five aboard were lost.

Princess Marie
The 81 ton schooner, Princess Marie, sank at Ballina on 30-3-1856. The crew of five were lost.

Solicito Borghese
In March 1850 the Solicito Borghese was wrecked at Achill. At the same time a brig and barque were wrecked at Achill Head.

Maria
On 10-1-1849 the Maria was wrecked at Westport Bay. The vessel was en route from Liverpool to Galway.

Gem
On 18-1-1849 the Gem was wrecked at Killary. She was en route from New York to Galway.

Unity
The steamer Unity was wrecked at Moy Bar, Killala on 17-9-1848. She had just left Sligo.

Nono
The 250 ton brig, Nono, was lost at Gubban Sand, Ballina Bar on 20-11-1850. She was en route from Constantinople to Ballina.

Mary Wilson
On 9-10-1884 the Mary Wilson was wrecked at Belderrig. The 94 ton schooner was bound for Galway with coal from Newcastle on Tyne. One of the crew of four was lost.

City of Limerick
The City of Limerick was lost at Broadhaven on 20-11-1850. She was en route from Limerick to Glasgow.

Sommand
On 29-9-1886 the 646 ton Norwegian barque, Sommand, sank at Achill Head.

The cargo was deal from Pugwash, Nova Scotia for Belfast. The 13 aboard were safe.

Elizabeth and Anne

The 132 ton schooner, Elizabeth and Anne, was wrecked at Bartra Island on 10-1-1887. The vessel carried bog ore from Ballina for London.

Tallyho

The 216 ton iron steam ketch, Tallyho, sank 12 miles SE by E of Bull Lighthouse on 29-5-1933. The crew took to the boats and were picked up by the Cotsmuir. The ketch was built in 1918.

SLIGO

SLIGO

Juliana

The Juliana of the Spanish armada was wrecked at Streedagh Strand along with La Lavia and Santa Maria de La Vision. They were found under shifting sand by English divers in 1985. Among the items recovered from the Juliana were three large cannon which are now at Dromahair undergoing restoration. Five guncarriage wheels have also been located. A rudder with nine pintails has been found but not lifted. The finding of a main anchor was quite a surprise as the Armada slipped anchors at Calais when the fleet was in danger from fireships. The three ships were described by Bingham as being at anchor in Sligo harbour before the storm and they must have dragged and lost further anchors when driven ashore. (6) A further wreck seems to have occurred at Kildoey. De Cueillar relates that at a big strand there were many bodies and a lot of wreckage. He was travelling from Streedagh to Ballyshannon.

Isaac

The Isaac was lost near Sligo on 21-11-1758. The master was Mr Clotworthy. (234)

New York

The New York stranded and was lost at Sligo on 23-12-1816. The vessel was bound from New York to Sligo.

Speculator

The Speculator was wrecked in Sligo Bay in December 1816. The vessel was bound for Sligo from Glasgow.

Friends of Sligo

On 10-3-1820 the Friends of Sligo went ashore at Deadman's Point. The vessel was bound for Greenock with goods from local merchants. Several people were charged with taking goods from the wreck. (235)

Britannia

The Britannia was driven on the beach at Kildoney on 25-7-1840. The Sligo vessel was en route from St John, new Brunswick. The cargo was saved but the vessel was a wreck. (235)

Tolagazone

The 170 ton Tolagazone struck the Bomore Rocks off Inismurray in February 1853. The captain and crew were rescued by the Mullaghmore coastguard. The vessel carried maize for Cuthbertsons of Sligo and Ballysodare. (235)

Delta

The schooner, Delta, of Liverpool went aground at Seal Rock and was wrecked in January 1856. Captain Gillen and the crew were rescued. The vessel carried general cargo. (235)

Thistle

The iron paddle steamer, Thistle, ran aground on Bird Rock and was wrecked in December 1858. The remains were lifted and scrapped. She was returning to Sligo from Glasgow. (235)

Naslieduk

The Austrian brig, Naslieduk, was wrecked on the Bungar Bank in December 1859. She carried maize for Pollexfen's.

Diamantis Pateras
Photo: R. Kirwan

Diamantis Pateras

The Diamantis Pateras was entering Sligo Harbour on 23-2-1925 when a snow storm blotted out visibility. The pilot lost his marks and the 2776 ton ship grounded amidships on a sandbank off Ballincar. There was deep water fore and aft and as the tide ebbed the ship broke her back due to the weight of the 5,000 tons of maize in her four holds. The grain was bound for Pollexfen's from the River Plate. The cargo was discharged into lighters and landed. The Belfast salvage company, McCauslands commenced work using their steamers, Milewater and St Anthony. They beached the ship in two halves at Ballincar and cut her up for scrap. The Diamantis Pateras was built in 1905 as the Arosa, renamed Glenrosa in 1917, sold to D.J. Pateras of Chios in 1924 and renamed. (230)

Marianopolis

On 8-10-1869 the Marianopolis ran aground at Rosses Point. The ship was being towed by the tug, Hope, and her keel was damaged when passing between Elsinore and the Island. The vessel filled with water and became a total wreck. The cargo was 800 tons maize for Pollexfen's.

Barbara

The Barbara was wrecked at Ballinabbey on 5-11-1817. The ship was en route to Glasgow from Sligo.

Butter Boat

The ribs of a boat are visible at Streedagh Strand and are presumed to belong to an Armada ship. This wreck is known locally as the butter boat.

Breezland

The collier, Breezland, ran aground on the sandbars at Raughley Point on 6-12-1952. She stranded half a mile offshore and failed to free herself. A tug from the Clyde was summoned but it is not clear if she was freed. (134)

Olive

The 1000 ton steamship, Olive, was driven ashore at Sligo in the gale of 27-2-1903. She carried a cargo of Indian corn for Pollexfen & Co., her owners, bound for Ballina. While moored at the deepwater quay her cables parted and she was blown across the bay and stranded high and dry on Catron shore. A tug was sent from the Clyde and the salvage efforts seem to have been successful.

Fancy

The Marquis of Drogheda's 140 ton schooner rigged yacht, Fancy, was wrecked at Sligo Bay on 26-11-1859. A pilot was aboard when the vessel struck the Dungar Bank. The buoy which should have marked the hazard had been missing for two years. At five a.m. she grounded on the bank. There was no alarm and the party breakfasted aboard at nine. However the sea blew up and the vessel was pounded on the bank breaking her to pieces in two to three hours. The Marquis, the Marchioness and their aide de camp, Captain Foster, with 16 servants escaped ashore taking their plate. Considerable quantities of valuables were lost along with the vessel which was worth £8000. The locals were criticised for pillaging the goods washed ashore. (68)

Tampico

The schooner, Tampico, was wrecked in Sligo Bay on 5-2-1843. Captain Gregg and two crewmen survived out of a crew of seven. (235) The following story was told and is linked by location and the captains name, though it was thought to have occurred about 1822: a sailing ship with a cargo of indigo dye was off the port of Sligo during a storm. The ship

was attempting to enter the harbour when people ashore lit a decoy fire which Captain Gregg took as a route to safety. The ship was lured onto a rocky part of the shore at a creek now known as Poll Gorm near Aughris Head. The creek was so named because of the effect of the dye. The crew were murdered when they came ashore and their fingers cut off to remove rings. Two mounds of stones mark their graves. (90)

Idwal

The 69 ton schooner, Idwal, was wrecked on the Red Brae rock on the portion of Leitrim coast north of Mullaghmore on 25-1-1868. A headstone in the old graveyard at Kinlough with a Welsh inscription marks the grave of one of those lost. The vessel carried stakes from Sligo to Wales.

Submarine

Local fishermen indicate the presence of the wreck of a German submarine dating from 1942 or 1943 between the Duff and the Drowes Rivers on the Leitrim coast. The wreck is fairly close to the shore. There is no official record of any loss in this area. A story also relates the seeing of the wreck from a helicopter. The story is unconfirmed.

Imperator

The 549 ton barque, Imperator, was wrecked at lower Rosses Point, Sligo on 1-12-1898. The Norwegian vessel was bound from Sligo to Hull with timber.

Dwina

The 328 ton Swedish barque, Dwina, was wrecked in Sligo harbour in May 1896.

Narayana

The 384 ton Norwegian barque, Narayana, was wrecked in Sligo Bay on 29-11-1886. She was en route from Shediac, New Brunswick to Ayr with a cargo of deal and put in to shelter. The anchor dragged and broke and she was driven ashore on the west side of Coney Island. The captain and crew were rescued. A small cannon remains on the island while a nameplate from a lifeboat is in Austies pub at Rosses Point.

Rathlee

The 137 ton iron steamer, Rathlee, was wrecked at Enniscrone on 15-11-1883. Her crew of 14 survived. She was bound for Liverpool from Ballina with general cargo. Parts of the iron superstructure remain buried near the Enniscrone Bath House. (122)

Rose

The 283 ton steamer, Rose, was wrecked on 16-7-1867 at Horse Island, 8 miles N of Ardbowline, Sligo. She was en route from Sligo to Glasgow with general cargo and cattle.

Norfolk

The 247 ton vessel, Norfolk, was wrecked on a rock in Blennick Sound on 13-1-1850. She was en route from Glasgow to Sligo.

Albion

The Albion was wrecked on 23-2-1851 in Sligo Bay. She was en route from Cardiff to Sligo.

Sligo

The 248 ton iron steamer, Sligo, sank at Ardbowline Island on 5-2-1912. She ran aground while carrying coal from Garston to Sligo. Captain Devaney and

the 13 aboard escaped ashore at low water by ladder from the bow.

Mediaeval wreck

The Annals of the Four Masters record that in 1105 Flaithbeartach Ua Canannain, lord of Cinel Conaill, his wife and a ship load of their people were drowned. Their ship was lost at sea opposite Cairbre near Drumcliffe.

London Galley

A large London galley grazed the isolated rock pinnacle, a mile south of Inismurray in 1732. The bottom was torn out of the vessel and she sank in deep water. Though the night was bright the rock was not apparent to the crew. (206)

Horizon II

The trawler, Horizon II, sank on 28-12-1992. The vessel was trawling four miles south west of Inismurray when she went down. The crew were rescued by another trawler.

Frederick Langley

The Frederick Langley was wrecked near Sligo on 16-1-1835. the ship was en route from Sierra Leone to Liverpool.

Culloden

The Culloden was wrecked near Sligo on 6-10-1835. She was bound for Sligo from Newcastle.

Dumbarton Castle

On 28-1-1834 the Dumbarton Castle was lost near Sligo. She was en route from Norway to Ballyshannon.

DONEGAL

DONEGAL

Hawkerman
The Norwegian ship, Hawkerman, was wrecked on Ballyshannon Bar on 27-3-1812. The captain was Mr Throw. (110)

Benjamin Nickelson
The Benjamin Nickelson was wrecked at Ballyshannon on 10-12-1835. She was en route to Ballyshannon from Liverpool.

Betsy
The brig, Betsy, was wrecked on the rocks at Kildony while entering Ballyshannon Harbour on 28-9-1839. Under the command of Captain Hall she was carrying a cargo of deal from St John, NB to Ballyshannon. Control of the vessel was lost crossing the Bar and she struck on the rocks.

Rose
The Rose from Liverpool was wrecked at Ballyshannon on 17-1-1833.

Ada Letita
The 96 ton Ada Letita was lost on Ballyshannon Bar on 16-9-1880.

Widow
The 90 ton brig, Widow, was lost at the Ballyshannon Bar on 10-8-1884. The ship was bound for Barrow with a cargo of timber. The crew of four survived.

Rockabill
The 136 ton iron steamship, Rockabill, was wrecked in the channel to Ballyshannon on 25-7-1884. The Rockabill sailed from Liverpool. She may have been built by Wingate in 1878, formerly owned by the Clyde Company and sold to JJ McFarlane in 1883.

Anne
The 73 ton schooner, Anne, was wrecked on Ballyshannon Bar on 12-11-1874. The cargo was china clay from Charlestown for Ballyshannon.

Prussian vessel
A Prussian vessel was lost on Ballyshannon Bar on 5-10-1849.

White Abbey
On 29-10-1934, the White Abbey was wrecked on Ballyshannon Bar. The 263 ton steel 2 masted barque was carrying coal from Whitehaven to Ballyshannon. Formerly called the Lockibar she was owned by Kellys and built by Scotts in 1915. Little of the wreck is left as a local yachtsman arranged to have it dispersed with explosives as it was a danger to navigation.

Texa
On 30-4-1932 the 186 ton Texa, was lost on the South Rock at Ballyshannon. The iron steam schooner was carrying a cargo of coke from Preston to Ballyshannon. The boiler can be seen from the shore at low tide. The Texa was built in 1884.

Thrushfield
On 28-4-1936 the 243 ton Thrushfield, sank six miles SE of Rathlin O'Byrne Island off Carrigan Head. She was built as the Eller in 1896 by Fullerton of Paisley. She was renamed in 1927 on being acquired by Wilson, Reid & Co of Belfast.

Strathmore
On 8-2-1922, the Strathmore struck a submerged wreck and sank 10 miles W of Inishowen Head. The 394 ton ship carried a cargo of maize for Kellys of

Belfast. She was built as the Yorkshire in 1892 by Fullertons at Paisley and renamed on acquisition by Kellys in 1916.

Connaught Ranger

The steamer, Connaught Ranger, was lost on 19-10-1851 when she struck a rock off Buninver. A report from Dunfanaghy describes her striking a rock off Inis Irrer Sound. She came off with her rudder unshipped and making water. She was driven ashore off Buninver. It was hoped to save the cargo. (69)

Connaughtman

The Connaughtman was wrecked when she struck a rock, afterwards known as the Connaughtman, off Creevy Pier, year unknown. She carried a cargo of china possibly Wedgewood.

Twilight

The 756 ton barque, Twilight, was wrecked in Trabrega Bay west of Inishowen on 25-11-1889. She had sailed from St John N.B. with a cargo of deals. Her ribs are still visible on the north shoreline.

Mary Anne

The 136 ton schooner, Mary Anne, was wrecked at the entrance to Strabrega Bay on 9-11-1882. The crew of eight were all safe.

Danube

This 652 ton barque was wrecked at Roland Bay, Strabrega Lough on 8-3-1878. The vessel was en route from Liverpool to New Brunswick. The crew of twelve survived.

Danish Ship

On 8-11-1588 a report (16) described the loss of a Danish ship in O'Boyles country which would be between Ardaragh and Aranmore. There were only five survivors including a Scot and all went to Scotland. The cargo was masts, tar, pitch, flax, hemp and cordage.

Though not of the Spanish Armada, the ship was bound for Spain.

Killybegs wreck

In 1739 Rev William Henry (206) described the double dangers of the Horn Head area as those of being dashed ashore and being plundered by the wild Irish who inhabited the area. A ship was wrecked on a single rock which breaks at low water about 100 fathoms off McSwynes Gun. The vessel struck at night and was a total loss. A Spanish whale fisher was wrecked at Rosguill (Downings) when the anchors dragged while sheltering in Sheephaven. He notes a visit by an Ostend East India ship to Rathmullen in 1736 with a cargo reputedly valued at over a million pounds.

Galley

HMS Tremontana cruised from May to July 1601 off the west coast to intercept Spanish ships with supplies for the Irish soldiers who had fought at Kinsale. She encountered a galley of 38 oars with 100 shot on board. This was forced onto the rocks between Teelin and Killybegs. The galley had fired on a McSwiney boat and the Tremontana ended the affray. Capt. Plessington of the Tremontana believed that the galley belonged to Grace O'Malley and that with another galley manned by the O'Flahertys had come north to plunder the McSwineys. (227)

Sheila

The wooden motor yacht, Sheila, was burned at the Clady River, Bunbeg on 6-5-1929. She was bound from Ballycastle to Sligo.

Nancy

On 2-3-1796, the Nancy was wrecked in Donegal Bay. The vessel was carrying cotton from Savannah to Lancaster.

Viktor Lyagin

This 10,000 ton Russian factory ship was driven ashore in McSwyne's Bay on the rocks at St John's Point on 13-4-92. During the storm 41 of the crew were lifted off by helicopter while 17 remained aboard. Diesel oil was removed and the Russian tug, Murman Ryer, arrived to assist. The vessel was towed off on 18-4-1992.

Venus
The schooner, Venus, was driven on the Inch Bank at Rathmullan in the "Big Wind" on 6-1-1839, along with the fishing wherry, Patrick. The crew clung to the rigging although the Venus fell over on her beam ends with the masts just above water. The coastguards succeeded in rescuing the crew. Part of the cargo of whiskey and sugar was salvaged. One of the wherry crew was drowned when he tried to swim ashore. (225)

William the Fourth
On the same terrible night, the brig, William the Fourth, was driven on rocks at Buncrana. She was torn from her anchorage in Lough Swilly. Four locals reached the wreck and rescued seven. She carried oats bound for Liverpool. (225)

Albatross
Near the Broomhall light off Moville, the Albatross collided with the Mayflower. The Mayflower sank about 150 metres from the lighthouse.

Gute Hoffnung
In December 1814, the Gute Hoffnung sank at the Tuns Bank off Moville.

Earl of Derby
The Glasgow ship, Earl of Derby, was in distress off the Donegal coast in 1862. Captain Forbes of the Schomberg was dispatched to act as agent for the owners. (138)

Strathmore
This 56 ton drifter caught fire and sank off Buncrana on 20-8-1918. The vessel was being used by the Admiralty for war work.

Nathaniel Cole
The 275 ton trawler, Nathaniel Cole, sprung a leak and sank off Buncrana on 6-2-1918.

Rostellan
The puffer, Rostellan, of Downings was chartered by Msrs Woldey of Glasgow to service lighthouses on the west coast. On 9-6-1934 she had 300 tons of coal aboard and was landing supplies at Rathlin O'Byrne Island when she sprang a leak. She sought help but no vessel was nearby. After two hours, Captain McGettigan and his four crewmen took to the lifeboat. They landed safely at Teelin. The ship sank in 30 fathoms. (148)

Yawl
A yawl loaded with seawrack sank near Innishinny Island off Bunbeg on 14-4-1934. The crew had loaded the craft full of the seaweed. A SW wind washed a wave onto the cargo adding extra weight. The yawl overturned throwing the four crewmen into the sea. Another yawl returning to the island rescued two men but the other two were lost. (148)

Emilie Marie
The 580 ton Norwegian barque, Emilie Marie, was wrecked at Port Salon on 18-1-1905. The vessel carried coal from Greenock bound for Barbados. The crew of twelve survived.

Venerable
The 68 ton ketch, Venerable, was lost 4 miles NNW Glengad Head on 27-4-1904. She was bound for Ramelton from Siloth with coal. The crew of three survived.

Boniface
The 3799 ton Booth line steamer, Boniface, was torpedoed and sunk on 23-8-1917. The position was given as 7

miles NE by N of Aran. One of the crew was lost when the ship was torpedoed without warning. An expedition to salvage the cargo of copper was mounted in 1963 and an area off Inisierra Island near Bunbeg was investigated.

Friendship
The Friendship was lost on the coast of Ireland on 3-10-1758. The ship was en route from the Leeward Islands to Derry captained by Mr Cockran. (234).

Carraig Una and Evelyn Marie
Both these trawlers were lost in stormy weather on the south side of Rathlin O'Byrne Island. The Carraig Una tragedy occurred on 7-1-1975 and her crew of five were lost. The 65 foot Evelyn Marie sank on 23-11-1976 with the loss of seven crew.

Tory
The 61 ton schooner, Tory (Troy), of Sligo was wrecked on a reef at Rathlin O'Beirne Island on 14-1-1856. She was en route from Sligo to Liverpool. The owner John Hodgson, was on business in Donegal and boarded her for the passage. He jumped ashore onto the rocks but neither the captain nor crew of five followed and they were drowned.

Mary Parsons
The luxury yacht, Mary Parsons, sank off Gola. She was owned by a cripple reputed locally to get about on golden crutches when he landed at Bunbeg harbour.

Boy Sean
The trawler, Boy Sean, was lost in 180 feet of water a mile off Malin Head on 20-9-1987. Efforts were made to drag the wreck to shallower water to retrieve bodies. The skipper and three of the crew were lost. One survivor was rescued after clinging to wreckage for several hours.

Gaelic
The iron barquentine, Gaelic, was wrecked on Frenchman Rock at Melmore Head on 25-2-1952. She was on passage from Ards, Co Donegal to Garston with a cargo of silica sand. The 224 ton 127 foot ship was built at Amlwich in 1898. During the First World War she operated as a Q ship out of Gibraltar for the Admiralty, like her sister ship, the Cymric. She was bought by Capt. O'Toole of Arklow in 1923. Twin motors were fitted for her war service in 1916. She sank after a collision in the Mersey in 1939 but was raised and her masts removed. Captain Hagan and all the crew were saved. (185)

Stipey
The wooden vessel, Stipey, lies at 10 metres outside Moville. According to local legend her crew went ashore leaving her at anchor. The ship caught fire and sank.

Florence
The wreck of a vessel which sank in 1900 was located close to the shore at Dunfanaghy. She carried a cargo of flagstones from Galway to Derry. Bert Robinson, skipper of the Girl Eileen found the wreck on 26-8-1973. She lies opposite the hotel. A wreck is also reputed to lie under the "customs post" at Dunfanaghy.

Catherine Roberts
The 54 ton ketch, Catherine Roberts, was wrecked on 10-2-1893 on the sandy beach of Trabeg Bay at Sheephaven near Rosapenna. She carried coal from Workington to Dunfanaghy. Her crew of three survived. (196)

Lock Ryan
The 200 ton three masted schooner, Lock Ryan, was wrecked on the shingle beach on the north side of Inisdooey on 7-3-1942. She had unloaded timber at Bunbeg and was heading to Sheephaven for her next cargo. A SE gale arose

suddenly and caught her without ballast. As the ship negotiated the sound she was caught and driven on the beach. The crew were saved by the lifeboat. She was owned by her master, Capt. Nolan, and was registered at Skibbereen.

Laurentic

The armed merchant cruiser, Laurentic, was commandeered by the Royal Navy at the outbreak of the First World War. She was one of 150 vessels which had been pre selected as suitable to be armed in wartime. Initially 15 vessels were equipped with 4.7 inch guns and placed at sea as the 10th cruiser squadron, to intercept vessels and determine their destination. The Laurentic was built by Harland & Wolff in 1908 and was operated by White Star line. The 14,950 ton liner was 500 feet long. The Laurentic landed some naval ratings at the base at Buncrana and sailed at 5 p.m. on 23-1-1917 in fine but very cold weather under the command of Capt. Norton. The cargo was gold bound for Halifax from the Treasury to pay for American munitions. An hour out from Buncrana in Lough Swilly she struck a mine on the port side. A second explosion occurred to port abreast the engine room. Though the vessel sank within 45 minutes, 130 officers and men were saved. Another 350 died due to exposure to the very severe weather. A memorial over the grave of those lost can be seen in Fahan Church of Ireland cemetery. The wreck is located in 35 metres. Initial salvage work was done by HMS Racer, with Commander Damont and a team of naval divers in a seven year period during and after the First World War (78,97). Initially the wreck was intact and some gold was removed from the strongroom. A storm however collapsed the decks of the ship and the forty tons of gold sank through the mass of debris and silt. The wreckage had to be systematically searched by hand and this went on until 1926. During the operation the divers worked in a strong current and were buffeted by the blast of exploding wartime mines up to two miles away. They observed that dogfish alone survived the shock of the explosions they used to break up the wreck. The operation recovered 3,186 out of 3,211 gold bars worth £5m. Its present value would be £300M. After the salvage operation the Laurentic's bell was presented to the Protestant church at Portsalon. (80) Eleven of the divers were awarded the OBE for their work and they shared £6,000- a reward of half a crown per £100 salved. (114) (10) (187) A further salvage operation was carried out on the wreck in the summers of 1986 and 1987.

Saldahna

On 4-12-1811 the 38 gun frigate, Saldahna, accompanied by the sloop of war, Talbot, were caught in a northerly gale. It seems that the Saldahna struck the Swilley rocks. They had sailed west the previous day from their base at Lough Swilly. On Thursday 5th the concern was mounting for the vessels. The worst fears were realised when 200 bodies were washed ashore near the entrance to Lough Swilly at Ballymastoker Bay. There were no survivors. Captain Packenham's body is buried at Rathmullen (79). The only relic of the disaster was a parrot with a silver collar inscribed "Saldahna" (80). Captain Packenham of the Saldahna was a brother in law of the Duke of Wellington. The Hon. Captain Jones commanded the Talbot. The wreck of the Saldahna is marked on the southern end of the bay on the old fathom charts. The lighthouse at Fanad Head was erected as a result of this incident. The fifth rate Saldahna was built by Temple of South Shields in 1809 and measured 145 feet and 951 tons. The Saldahna's mast formed the support for the roof of the former Chapel now a museum, in Ramelton. (128)

Trinidad Valenciera

On 16 September 1688, the Trinidad Valenciera, of the Levant Squadron of the Spanish Armada sank at Glenagivney Bay near Kinnagoe on the Inisowen peninsula. This 1100 ton vessel carried 360 men and 42 guns. The wreck was found and excavated by a group from Derry. The bell of the Church of Ireland at Carndonagh is reputed to be from a wreck at Glenagivney, probably the Trinidad Valenciera. (137) In the 1890s there was an Armada gun at Lochadoon, near Glenties. Two brass cannon were on the island at Kiltoorish from the wreck at Trymore Strand. Lead ingots and 1588 coins were found at Gola.

Barque de Hamburg

At Mullaghderg (Kincaslagh) near Arranmore, the 860 ton Barque de Hamburg, also of the Levant Squadron was wrecked. She carried 395 men and 32 guns. In the Spring of 1895 the vessel, Harbour Lights, investigated this site for a fortnight without results (81). A few brass cannon had been found by Rosses men, including Mr Boyle of Farrmore about 1795 (79). It took 60 people to haul the cannon up the beach. These were heated over a fire, broken and sold to a Donegal merchant. Triangular lead ballast was also found in six metres of water. (135,1118,p3) Two miles to the south of Castleford Bay, inside Aran Island, the coastguards of Rutland Island raised an anchor in 1853. This artefact was placed outside the United Services Club in Parliament Street London. (81).

The anchor is now on display at the museum at Rossnowlagh. In early 1793 a large wreck was discovered three feet below low water near Rutland Harbour. Four massive bronze cannon were found and from their markings they were thought to come from the Armada. Nearby at Cloughglass Beach at a place known as Cul Tra, an unknown vessel, perhaps a zabra was wrecked. Some artefacts were recovered in 1975. Cannon were drawn away by tractor and removed to Armagh.

Duquesa Santa Ana

The Duquesa Santa Ana, a 900 ton ship of the Andalucian squadron, is believed to lie at Rosbeg in Loughros Mor Bay. She sank on 26-9-1588 carrying 357 men and 23 guns. Two unidentified zabras were wrecked outside Killybegs harbour. (6)

Sydney

The 1118 ton Sydney, built in 1860, carrying timber from Quebec to Greenock was wrecked on an indentation in the cliffs at Camas Binne just north of Glen Head on 16-10-1870. She was driven off course in a NW storm and struck the shore. Of a crew of twenty one only two managed to cling to timber and scale the 1600 foot cliffs to reach Glencolmcille. Captain Hamilton and the others were lost. (132) (135,143,pl836)

St Patrick

The 21 foot trawler, St Patrick, was lost when it drifted onto rocks at Toralayden Island off Port Hill near Glencolmcille on 8-5-1988. The trawler's engine broke down and a stiff breeze drove her ashore. Two of the crew reached the shore in safety but the skipper, Mr Maher, of Ardara was drowned. (140)

Cambria

The iron steamer, Cambria (1997 tons, 324 feet), was en route from New York and Quebec to Lough Foyle and Glasgow with 170 passengers and crew, commanded by Capt. George Carnahan. Built by R Duncan & Co in 1869 she was owned by Anchor Line. On approaching the Irish coast, the weather was foul and spray obliterated the light on Inistrahull, 10 miles north of Bloody Foreland. At about 11 p.m., on 19-10-1870 while under canvas and steam, she struck the rocks near Inistrahul. A boat was lowered with 16 passengers but capsized. Only one man succeeded in getting back on board when it righted. During the night this passenger, McGartland, was rescued by the steamship Enterprise. Despite a prolonged search no further survivors were found. (67) (10)

Racoon

During the First World War the destroyer, Racoon (920 tons, 266 feet), built in 1910 by Cammel Laird was wrecked on 9-1-1918. She struck the Garrives Rocks between the islets of the Garvans, situated in the sound formed by Inistrahull and the mainland. The accident happened during a snowstorm and none of the 100 strong crew survived. Lt George Napier was in command. One crew member is buried on Rathlin while two more are buried at Culduff churchyard. Twenty bodies were taken to Rathmullen for burial. This closing period of the Great War was very active around the Irish coast. On the 30-1-1918 the liner Audania was torpedoed and 200 survivors brought ashore. (10). A foul area lies close to and north of the middle island and is believed to be a wreck.

Argo Delos

The Pireus registered Argo Delos (10392 tons), went ashore on Torbeg islet, a mile N by E of Inistrahull on 22-11-1960. The

Portrush lifeboat arrived to find the bow and stern ashore and the midships awash. The destroyer, HMS Leopard, was standing by. A navy radio party landed on the bow but were unable to communicate with those on the stern. The lifeboat took off 14, while a helicopter lifted off a further 15. The master and two more were saved in the following days. The vessel was a total wreck. The forward portion was beached but the stern sank while under tow in position 55. 23 . 36N, 07 .03 . 24W.

Fleur De Lys, Sunburst

The 74 gun French ship, Hoche, was captured in battle with a British fleet in 12-10-1798 about 15 miles off the Rosses. Commodore Bompart was met by a more powerful fleet commanded by Sir John Borlasse Warren. Six French frigates were captured in the battle and during the following days. The Fleur de Lis and Sunburst were sunk. The Hoche was taken to Lough Swilly in a damaged condition. Her guns were mounted on batteries at Fort Dunree. She was later repaired and fought at Trafalgar as HMS Donegal. The British vessel, Robust, was badly damaged in the battle and was repaired at Lough Swilly. A memento of the French fleet is the 1.5 ton 15 foot anchor of the Romaine. She sailed from Brest 16-9-1798 and anchored in Donegal Bay on 13-10-1798. The ship is reputed to have cut her cable when the presence of militia discouraged a landing. The anchor was found off Doon Rock about 1850 and brought to Donegal Bay. It was placed on a plinth in Donegal Town in 1951 . (79)

Wave

The Wave was wrecked at Rutland Harbour on 30-7-1848. She was en route from Westport to Liverpool.

Audacious
Photo: The Great World War

Audacious

The new 23,000 ton battleship, Audacious, built in 1913, carrying ten 13 inch guns struck a mine off Lough Swilly on 27-10-1914. She was turning in formation with the 2nd battle squadron when a detonation flooded the port and centre engine rooms. As a submarine had been sighted earlier by the Monarch the larger ships were kept clear. Destroyers, tugs and small craft rushed from the base at Lough Swilly to assist. The collier, Thornhill, brought towing hawsers and the Cambria provided an escort. The hospital ship, Soudan, stood by in case of casualties. The tow commenced but the Audacious was sinking by the stern. When the tow parted Captain Damoier and his officers left the crippled ship at 7.15. She blew up mysteriously at 9.00. (179) (10)

Pandion

On 30-1-1941 the 1900 ton Pandion reached Lough Swilly in a badly damaged condition, following an air attack out in the Atlantic on 28-1-1941. On entering Lough Swilly she struck the Swilly Rocks and sank. During the salvage attempts the Admiralty tug, Salvonia, came under sniper fire. (133)

Caliope

On 7-10-1943 the Greek ship, Caliope, was torpedoed by a submarine at 54 N, 26. 35 W and reached the Donegal coast with severe damage. She was wrecked on the rocks at Port na Blagh near Downings, between Long Burn Rock and the shore. This is inshore of Frenchman's

Rock. The wreck is scattered at a depth of 20-25 metres. Another source says that the wreck is at the NE tip of Tormore. She was en route from Halifax to London with grain.

Andrew Nugent

The sailing trader, Andrew Nugent, was wrecked on Rutland Island on 6-1-1839. Captain Crangle put into Aranmore Sound for shelter during the "Big Wind". When he took a wrong course, a light was displayed on Aranmore to guide him. After he tacked, a pilot from Poulawaddy was put aboard. The vessel was anchored between Rutland and Aranmore and appeared safe. During the night her anchors dragged and she was damaged on Duck Island rocks. She sank with the loss of her crew and the pilot. One of the owners, Scott and Patrickson, of Sligo speculated that she had been struck at sea by another vessel, as some strange timber was found wedged on her deck. It was thought that some of her crew had been washed overboard as only two or three men of a crew of sixteen were seen by the pilot's crew. This would have left insufficient men to work her. She was built at Gelston's yard, Portaferry in 1826. Captain Crangle is buried at Templecrone. The cargo was 992 casks of butter and 182 casks of provisions. The wreck settled on the beach west of Rutland and could be seen in the 1950s (139)

Harold

The brig, Harold, of Dublin was wrecked on the SW shore of Rutland Island on 14-1-1895. She was en route from Kilrush to Liverpool when caught in a severe gale and snowstorm. Her crew were saved by local fishermen. Rutland Island was developed in 1785 as a major fishing station and its harbour was very active. The island was known locally as Inis Macduin. The development was partially covered in a sandstorm.

Fanad Head

At Fanad Head west of Arryherra crossroads a group of standing stones mark the graves of bodies washed ashore after a shipwreck (116)

Gortahork

After a storm and spring tide the sea went out a considerable distance from Gortahork. The hull of a wreck which was full of candles was seen.

Pride of Glenties

The fishing boat, Pride of Glenties, from Owey sank on 19-11-1947. She had been caught by a SW storm off Magherorty. Her crew of five were rescued by the St. Ann. (149)

Anna Marina

The 400 ton Danish coaster, Anna Marina, struck a rock at the entrance to Burtonport on 5-2-1972. She had arrived to collect a cargo of salted herring. The wreck blocked the harbour mouth and was removed by salvors. (148)

Copper Boat

A ship with a cargo of copper was wrecked on the west shore of Aranmore near Poll Dhun. The wreck occurred in 1798. The crabs found in this area have a green colour as a result.

Acacia

On 17-11-1879 the 168 ton brig, Acacia, was wrecked on Aranmore Island. The Acacia was en route from Tralee to Ardrossan. The crew of seven survived. (196)

Mango

The 250 ton SS Mango was wrecked on the south shore of Aranmore in Cladaghlahan Bay on 6-2-1933. The skipper and crew of 8 were saved by the lifeboat. The steamer was owned by the Newry company, Frontier Town Steamship Co (Fisher & Co). The ship ran aground in fog while on route from Sligo to Coleraine in ballast. The ship was badly holed and ended at an angle of 45 degrees on the rocks. (148)

Cotton ship

A ship carrying a cargo of cotton was wrecked on the west of Iniskeeragh near Aranmore about 1914.

Aranmore disaster

On 9-11-1935 a ferry carrying passengers from Burtonport to Aranmore struck the rock near the pier on Aranmore. The islanders were returning from the potato harvest in Scotland. Their boat struck in darkness and 19 of the 20 aboard were lost. The sole survivor of the Gallaghers aboard saw his family slip off the upturned boat during the sixteen hours, before he was saved. This was the worst Donegal marine disaster since the wreck of the Wasp on Tory in 1884.

Eleftherios M Tricoglu

The charted wreck near the pier at Aranmore was a Greek ship, the Eleftherios M Tricoglu. The 2633 ton ship was stranded and wrecked on 29-1-1926. The wreck occurred during a severe storm. For a time the captain and officers remained aboard while the 23 crew were taken ashore. She carried a cargo of maize from Bralia for Sligo. This was unloaded into fishing boats and taken to carts on the mainland. She was built in 1894 by Palmers. (99)

Dublin

The 240 ton iron steamship, Dublin, was wrecked on the SE corner of Aranmore inside Calf Island. The wreck occurred on 11-2-1877. She was bound for Troon from Killybegs in ballast. Her crew of eleven survived. (196)

Sacharan

A vessel known by the name "Sacharan" was wrecked three or four hundred years ago on the east side of Aranmore. She

was off course and lost when she foundered; hence the locally applied name-the Irish for "astray".

Greenhaven

On 2-3-1956 the 488 ton MV Greenhaven, of Newcastle was wrecked on Roninis Reef in Gweebara Bay, four miles south of Aranmore. She was en route from Ballina to Belfast when she got into difficulties during a storm and was driven onto the reef. The Limerick coaster, Galtee, attempted a tow. The destroyer, HMS Wizard, stood by. The Aranmore lifeboat made three attempts to rescue the crew. Captain Balmain and ten crew with two pilots were taken off, two at a time by RAF helicopters from Eglington near Derry. A Shakelton aircraft dropped flares to illuminate the scene. The helicopters refuelled at Nairn where one crashed during the operation. The Greenhaven which was owned by Anthony & Bainbridge of Newcastle on Tyne was later salvaged for scrap. (101) The wreck turned upside down and was dry at low water.

God's Tear

The God's Tear, was wrecked on a rock in Barney's Bay on the west of Aranmore on 25-3-1983. Wayne Dickenson, the single handed sailor climbed the 300 foot cliffs to safety. He had crossed the Atlantic alone but his record was not acknowledged as no trace of the 9 foot boat was found. After a stay on the island he returned to Florida. (99)

Skifjord

The 128 foot trawler Skifjord lies off the beach at Arland Strand. An isolated rock, Bullignamirra, which is barely covered at high tide lies near the channel leading to Burtonport. On Halloween night 1-11-1981 the Skifjord struck the rock. Despite the closeness of the lifeboat only three of the crew of eight who were washed ashore survived. The skipper, Francis Byrne, and his son were amongst those lost. The wreck lies intact in 30 metres about 100 yards SE of the rock. The owner was Aloysius Bonner of Burtonport. (99)

Carlingford
The SS Carlingford, was anchored at Burtonport on 20-10-1935. In a NW gale her anchor dragged and the Carlingford went ashore. The crew were rescued by the lifeboat. (149)

California
The Anchor liner, California, en route from New York to Glasgow went ashore in fog near Tory. The accident occurred on 28-6-1914. No lives were lost, the passengers were taken off by the Cassandra. After assistance by the salvage ships, Ranger and Linnet, she was refloated in August. The California was later torpedoed on 7-2-1917 38 miles off Fastnet with the loss of 43 lives. (10)

Wheat Plain
On 27-3-1930 the Wheat Plain was wrecked on Tory. She struck rocks on the east side of Tory, 100 yards from Portadoon while en route from Birkenhead to Westport and Kilrush. Captain Glendinning and his crew of 14 escaped in the ship's boat. She was owned by Spiller and Tanker. The ship broke into three parts within a few days. Her boiler is still visible on the rocks. She carried 420 tons of flour for Spillers of which 50 tons were saved by the islanders. (4) (70)

Corrib
On 7-9-1921 the Belfast steamer, Corrib, ran ashore on small boulders 3/4 mile SSW of the lighthouse at the West End on Tory. She was en route from Ballina to Ayr in ballast. The Salvage Association made an attempt to free her

but the 506 ton vessel was abandoned. Her boiler remains visible at low tide. (99)

Rose
The 41 ton smack, Rose, of Ipswich was wrecked on Tory on 10-12-1876. She was en route from Ballyshannon to Plymouth with potatoes. She ran ashore in fog about 6pm. Her master, Wm Wilcox, and two crewmen survived. (115)

Elizabeth Ray
The Elizabeth Ray was wrecked at Scoilt Nell on Tory in 1889. Her captain was McSparain. Two crew were saved. (115)

Chestnut
About the same time or possibly 1886, Chestnut was also lost on Tory. She carried timber from St Johns. She lost her masts and was turned over at Loch Doire. (115)

Chester
A derelict, the Chester, was encountered by the islanders in 1853. Two boats went out to the ship to sell fresh food but when they boarded her they found her deserted. They told their story and returned to the derelict. The Thoir Mor boat won the race back and she was brought in. The islanders broke her up despite threats from the coastguards. The coastguards were not available to give evidence at the salvage trial. They had departed to serve in the Crimean War. (115)

Lusby
On 16-2-1925 the Lusby was wrecked on Tory. (115) Other Tory wrecks include Fair Holland 1875, Press Home 2-5-1886 and the Rothsay bound for Greenock on 18-2-1902, Livelyhood pre 1918, Our Monica and Malaga off Tory. Queen of the Sea 15-8-1893, Jacinth 6-9-1886, Isabella 18-10-1851, Peace 11-7-1849 en route from Liverpool to Sligo. Osprey,

bound from the Clyde to Westport was
wrecked on 1-3-1833. Hazard was on
route from Ballina to Liverpool and was
wrecked on Tory on 23-12-1833.

Wasp
The gunboat, Wasp (455 tons and 145
feet), struck the isolated rock "an
Feadan" under the lighthouse on Tory
Island on 22-9-1884. She was en route
from Westport to Moville in Lough
Foyle. The gunboat was powered by
steam and had schooner rigged sails. She
was armed with two 64 pounder, two 20
pounder and two machine guns. While
sailing at 3.30 am in clear weather she
passed too close to the island and struck.
As the fires were banked the order for
full steam could not be obeyed. Seeing
that the position was hopeless the boats
were ordered out. Rough waves however
pounded them in the davitts. The
doomed vessel slipped off into deeper
water until only her masts showed. The
commander, Lt J.D. Nicholls, and fifty of
the crew were lost. Some are buried at a
small cemetery near the lighthouse. Eight
survivors were conveyed to Lough
Swilly by H.M.S. Valliant. The Wasp
was built at Barrow by Vickers in 1880.
The wreck was sold in November 1910
by the Cornish Salvage Co. (10) (141)

Whitehaven
The 14 gun Whitehaven, caught fire and
was lost off Tory in September 1747.
Captain Matthews, later Admiral
Matthews, was courtmartialled on
15-10-1747. (101)

Stolwijk
On 7-12-1940, while en route from
Corner Brook, Newfoundland to
Glasgow, the Dutch steamship, Stolwijk,
went aground on the NW side of
Inisdoey Island. The ship was in a
convoy which was caught in a gale. She
was built by NV Stoom Maats Wijklin in

1920 and measured 2489 tons, 285 feet.
Of the crew of 28 ten were lost. The
difficult rescue was accomplished by
breeches buoy to the lifeboat. During the
operation the line parted on three
occasions. (10) The Northern Approaches
was the only route open to Britain at this
stage of the war.

Viknor
The armed merchant cruiser, Viknor,
formerly SS Viking, of the Viking
Cruising Company was wrecked on
13-1-1915. The 5386 ton vessel was built
in 1888. The details are not quite clear
but it is assumed that she struck a mine
in a newly sown minefield during stormy
weather. The location "off Tory Island"
is vague as there were no survivors from
her crew of 22 officers and 273 men.
Wreckage and bodies were found all
along the north coast of Ireland. Some of
the bodies were recovered and buried at
Rathlin. At the time the Viknor was a
unit of the 10th cruiser squadron under
the command of E. O. Ballantyne. (10)

Filey
On 2-10-1916 the 226 ton trawler, Filey,
was wrecked at Camusmore Bay on
Tory. The 226 ton vessel was on hire to
the Admiralty for war work. (77)

Flying Hurricane
The Clyde company paddle tug, Flying
Hurricane, was wrecked on the south
side of Tory on 14-2-1879. Her crew of
seven were saved. The 17 ton tug was
built in 1874. (159)

Augusta
The iron steamer, Augusta, was also
wrecked at the same place on Tory as the
Flying Hurricane and on the same day.
The 188 ton vessel was on tow from
Sligo to Belfast in ballast. Her crew of
seven survived.

Isabella
The Isabella of Belfast, was wrecked on

Tory on 18-10-1851. The ship carried a cargo of oats. All the crew were lost, one body was found aboard lashed to the pump. (69)

Speculation

The Speculation, en route from Opporto to Sligo was wrecked on 5-12-1798 on Tory. (68)

Jacinth

The 100 ton schooner, Jacinth, was wrecked on Tory on 6-9-1886. She was bound for Widnes from Sligo with railway sleepers.

Mary Snow, Evir Allen

The Mary Snow was en route from Virginia to Britain with tobacco and rum. Captain Wallace took aboard an Inistrahull pilot, Barney Duffy. He was a noted wrecker and the ship went ashore at Glenagivney. The Glen men assembled and looted the ship. A watch was found and the wrecker did not know what it was. He thought it said "Mick, Mick,Mick" and crushed it with his boot heel. It was local banter that Glen men afterwards had the mark of a watch on their heels and a common insult was "nigger, show me your heel". The Glen wreckers were known as niggers. Fuldarach MacLangain, another local wrecker, was reputed to have slain sailors for their boots. (135, 1404,p313,p357) About 1841 the Glen men lured a vessel, the Evir Allen, ashore. (135, 1118,p3)

Iris

The 276 ton iron steamer, Iris, was wrecked on 2-9-1883. She went ashore in a gully a mile east of Inistrahull lighthouse. (135, 1404,p272) A wooden hulk (possibly Isabella of Mulray 10-12-1835) was described as being driven onto Inistrahull between Gull Island and the East Port. This was thought to be an attempt to collect insurance and the event

was credited with introducing rats to the island. (5) The wreck lies from 3 to 30 metres in a canyon near Gull Island. Another wreck occurred on the rock, Barna Mor, at Inistrahull in May, year unknown. It gave rise to the local wreckers sentiment "save the ships but drown the crew" expressed in a local rhyme. (135, 1404, p272) The Orion of Picton was lost at Inistrahull. The Brothers en route from Galway to Belfast was wrecked at Inistrahull on 22-9-1835. The smack Amity was also lost on Inistrahull on 9-9-1870.

Ada

The 59 ton iron steamer, Ada, was wrecked on Torbeg near Inistrahull on 1-1-1890. She carried bog ore from Ballina to the Clyde. The crew of seven escaped.

Agnes Lovatt

The 679 ton barque, Agnes Lovatt, was wrecked at Inistrahull on 31-3-1870. Four of the 13 crew were lost. She was en route from St John with a cargo of deal.

U-Boats

A U-Boat UB 109 was scuttled between Inistrahull and the Mainland. A U-Boat is charted between Glasheedy Island and the mainland near Tullagh Point. This boat was scuttled during operation Deadlight after the Second World War when captured craft were scuttled. During the First World War the German submarine U-110 was depth charged and sunk by HMS Moresby and HMS Michael on 15-2-1918 about a mile and a half off Fanad Head.

Agnes

The 98 ton schooner, Agnes, sunk at the SW corner of Inistrahull on 15-11-1850. She was bound for Belmullet from Liverpool via Glasgow with general cargo.

Schooner

During February 1833 a schooner with four aboard was caught in a NW gale off the Gweedore coast. She was driven on the rocks at Inis Irrir. One man drowned and the three survivors reached relative safety on a perpendicular rock where they held on for two days. The seas had not abated much, but local men decided that they could not survive another night. Six islanders set out in three currachs and the three sailors were rescued. (142)

Fishing disasters

On 16-12-1815 the Donegal fishing fleet was caught in Bruckless Bay by a sudden storm. Many boats were overturned and over eighty persons were drowned. A vast herring shoal had accumulated in the bay. The price of herring was very high due to a salt shortage and the rewards were substantial for all involved. From Teelin came 120 boats. Two hundred boats assembled at Fintra. The shoal moved out to sea and was followed by the boats. A sudden storm caught the fragile craft overloaded with fish with disastrous results.

The Downings fishing boats were similarly caught on 9-2-1848. Twenty currachs were fishing between Horn Head and Melmore. A storm front was seen approaching and some fled for the safety of the shore. The bay of Sheephaven was filled with whitecapped waves which caught the remaining boats. Several were driven ashore at Dooey and Black Rock with the loss of eight lives. In Mulroy Bay on 7-12-1906 a storm caught a fishing fleet. Thirteen men were drowned.

The Malin peninsula was the scene of a disaster on 1-3-1941. Six men put to sea in a 28 foot fishing yawl. After some time it was realised that they were overdue. Inistrahull was contacted by semaphore but there was no sign of the men. Niall Hutton and his five comrades were lost.

Maria

On 22-11-1960 the 50 foot half decker, Maria, was lost between Owey Island and Cruit Island. While fishing her net fouled the rudder. The trawler sank after striking a rock about 100 yards from Owey while returning to Kincaslagh Pier. Men from Owey heard cries and launched currachs. Two were picked up and a trawler rescued another. Three of the six aboard were lost. (148)

Saoirse

On 1-6-1989 the Downings half decker, Saoirse, struck rocks on Dooey Point at Sheephaven. Her nets may have been entangled in her propeller. Two of the four aboard were lost, including a son of the owner, Mr Doherty. The boat was recovered and towed to Downings.

Rathcormac

The 50 foot Downings trawler, Rathcormac, sank on 9-4-1989 off Malin Head. The trawler began to take in water after structural damage about 20 miles NW of Malin Head. An American nuclear submarine surfaced and stood by until the lifeboat arrived. A salvage pump was taken out by an Air Corps helicopter. After a four hour tow towards Lough Swilly the Rathcormac sank. Skipper McBride and his crew of three were taken to safety by the Portrush lifeboat.

Ann Falcon

The 108 ton brig was wrecked at Inis Doagh near Malin on 17-2-1852. She was en route from Limerick to Glasgow.

Lady Octavia

The 199 ton barque, Lady Octavia, was wrecked at Malin Head. She carried a cargo of sugar.

George
On 10-9-1816, the George was wrecked at Malin Head. She was en route from Limerick to Sligo.

Elizabeth
The 70 ton schooner, Elizabeth, was wrecked at Malin Bay on 19-11-1890. She carried coal from Irvine to Killybegs.

A C Bean
On 18-11-1893 the 553 ton barque, A C Bean, was wrecked near Malin Head. She was bound for the Clyde from Mirimuchi with a cargo of timber lathes.

Malaga
The Fleetwood steam trawler, Malaga, disappeared in Donegal Bay on 18-10-1935. Skipper Albert Novo and the crew were presumed lost when a lifebelt was washed ashore at Castlerock. (148)

Orient Star
The motor fishing vessel, Orient Star, was homeward bound for Killybegs on 29-10-1940. Her engine failed in a strong S.E. gale. The stricken vessel was blown to Carrigans Head. Before the vessel sank her crew of seven were rescued by the fishing boat, Naomh Colum.

Helen
Rockall lies almost 100 miles off the Donegal coast which is the nearest land. On 19-4-1824 the Helen of Dundee was wrecked on what is known as Helen's reef near Hasselwood Rock. The Helen was bound for Quebec. (117) (188)

Norge
The Norge of Copenhagen was wrecked in fog on Helen's Reef at Rockall on 28-6-1904. She left Copenhagen for New York with 700 emigrants and a crew of 71, commanded by Captain Gondall. Among the emigrants were, 68 Swedes, 79 Danes, 15 Finns, 296 Norwegians and 236 Russians. Rockall is an 80 foot high isolated rock, miles from the nearest land in Donegal. A reef extends for five miles from the main rock. When the Norge struck the engines were reversed and the ship began to sink rapidly. Eight boats were launched but smashed and five boats got away. There was considerable panic. The first boat with 27 aboard was picked up by the trawler, Salvia, of Grimsby. Two days later another boatload of 17 was picked up off St Kilda and taken to Aberdeen. The Cervonia of Dundee landed 129 at Stornoway. The Energie found 70 more along with the captain and brought them also to Stornoway. Of the 765 aboard 517 were lost. The 3318 ton Norge was built by Stephens at Glasgow in 1881. (188) (140)

Lockatif
The 64 foot trawler, Lockatif, got into difficulties 8 miles SW of Rathlin O Byrne Island on 8-3-1990. The trawler was en route from Burtonport to Belmullet when the engine gave trouble. A distress signal gave a position in error off Aranmore and eventually a Dauphin helicopter was directed to the vessel by flares. With the assistance of the lifeboat, the crew were lifted off. On 10-3-1990 the Lockatif drifted ashore at Shalwy and an oil slick floated into Fintra Bay. (140)

Smuggler
A Rush smuggler, Matthias Gede, is commemorated by a memorial stone at Kenure Church. His ship was lost on the Donegal coast in October 1820. (193)

Nellie M
The 954 ton coaster, Nellie M, was sunk off Moville by bombs placed aboard by the IRA on 7-2-1981. The wreck was cleared of explosives by Irish Navy divers and she was refloated on 12-7-1981. The ship carried 1260 tons of coal from Blyth to Colraine. (201)

St Bedan

The 1251 ton St Bedan was also sunk by bombs placed aboard by the IRA on 23-2-1982. She sank at 55.10.30 N, 7.03.00 W. The ship was en route from Blythe to Derry with 1626 tons of coal. After clearing the residual explosives she was raised on 16-7-1982. In December 1990 during a particularly poor season mussel fishermen from Moville used their dredges to raise coal from the wreck. This was sold to Thompson's, a local coal merchant. (201) The wreck was raised and broken at Liverpool.

Anchor

A large anchor with a wooden stock was recovered on 15-3-1983 according to a report in the Derry Journal. The divers, John Davidson, Brian Thompson and Garret Canning were photographed with the 14 foot anchor. It was found 1.5 miles off the Tuns Buoy in Lough Foyle. The inscription on the anchor was CIAVI. It is not clear what vessel lost the anchor.

Alceste

The 676 ton ship, Alceste, was wrecked between Culduff and Glengad Head on 15-6-1869. One of the crew of 19 was lost. The vessel was en route from Greenock to Mauritius.

William & Jane

The American vessel, William and Jane, was wrecked on a rock in the Rosses of Donegal on 3-3-1805. The ship was en route from New York to Belfast with flax seeds and cotton wool. Captain Hale was in charge. Part of the cargo was salved. (69)

Entreprise

The 194 ton barque, Entreprise, sank at Ballyness Pier on 16-8-1879. The vessel had loaded oxide bound for Liverpool.

Woolton

The 194 ton barque, Woolton, sank near Moville on 1-10-1882. The vessel was bound for Kingston from Newcastle on Tyne with coal.

Everestine

On 26-4-1865 the 1048 ton Everestine was wrecked on the Swilly Rocks.

Lady Arthur Hill

The collier, Lady Arthur Hill, was wrecked at Inisowen Head on 7-1-1901.

Assurance

The Admiralty tug, Assurance, struck Bluick Rock and sank on 18-10-1941. The wreck, north of Greencastle is regularly dived, .

Lady Maxtwell

On 26-4-1860 the Lady Maxtwell sank at "Teeling" Head. She was en route from Liverpool to Belmullet.

Other losses

Vessel	Tons	Lost	Location
Lady Cathcart		Aug. 1816	Lough Swilly
Mary Anne		11-11-1816	Near L. Swilly
Farie		24-9-18₁7	Killybegs
Golden Fleece		5-11-1817	Swilly Rocks
Nancy		2-1-1833	Foundered Donegal
Mary & Anne		11-10-1835	Stranded Dunfanaghy
Florence		1-1-1853	Donegal
Orchard	43t	20-9-1852	Horn Head
Dorade		27-7-1849	Narrin

Vessel	Tons	Lost	Location
Augusta Jessie	382	6-2-1856	L. Swilly
Ida Gessina	145	10-2-1853	Donegal Bay
Bee	22	2-3-1881	Near Fannet L.H. Lough Swilly
Melfort	36	3-3-1881	Knockallen, Lough Swilly
Ocean Child	51	1-10-1882	Off Rathmullen Lough Swilly
Fred	78	1-10-1882	Close to C.G. Moville
Elizabeth	18	22-9-1883	Near Malin Head
Fayaway	85	19-3-1884	Gweedore Bay
Agricola	97	4-9-1884	Duck Island
Star of the Sea	66	16-9-1878	Near Rathmullen
Chrysolite	54	8-11-1879	Tory Island
Blue Jacket	12	18-4-1880	Inisboffin Island
Leslie	58	26-2-1886	Inistrahull
Presshome	99	2-5-1886	Tory Island
Lady Bute	66	15-10-1886	near Dunfanaghy Bar
Beatrice	84	14-12-1886	Rossan Point
Scale Duck	20	17-9-1889	Portsallagh
Slieve Donard	28	3-2-1890	MacSwines Bay
Rob Roy	10	21-12-1894	Lough Swilly
Willie Menia	10	22-12-1894	Ballyboyle Island
Tees Packet	49	31-3-1896	Farmer Rock, Lough Swilly.
Three Brothers	57	29-7-1896	Rinboy Rock Ballyhorisky Pt
Eclipse	67	18-4-1897	Ards Bay
Zeus	65	15-10-1897	Kilultan Cove, St Johns Pt
James & Jessy		5-9-1848	St John s Point, Killybegs
Emily Maria		19-5-1849	St John s Point
Edel Cathraine	68	30-1-1898	Ards Bay
Elizabeth	87	15-11-1899	River Swilly, near Letterkenny.
Rothesay	79	18-2-1902	Tory Island.
Maria	64	10-12-1861	Doaghbeg
Lotus	165	22-10-1864	Ballyhorisky
Unknown	180	20-1-1863	Gola
Caroline	98	9-9-1870	Pollin, Castleport
Thrasher	69	12-7-1874	Bunbeg River
Christian	72	8-10-1874	2m W Culaduff Bay
Sealer	93	10-3-1875	Moville
Eringo	67	28-2-1876	Dunfanaghy bar
Elizabeth	57	11-11-1877	Burnsfoot, L Swilly

WARTIME WRECKS

The following merchant ships were listed as lost near the Irish Coast during wartime. Details are sparse because Irish newspapers were severely censored in all matters relating to shipping. The data is derived from sources 77 and 197. Surprisingly no US ships were lost near the Irish Coast according to data supplied. Some Greek ships were traced. Details of these and some of those listed below appear in the main text. Naval ships both British and German are listed in the main text. The circumstances of loss are abbreviated: M=mined, SMT=torpedoed by submarine, SMB=bombs placed aboard by submarine, SSM=shelled by submarine, AT=torpedoed by aircraft, AB=bombed by aircraft. * = Details in main text.

British losses near Ireland in the First World War

Name	Tons	Date	How lost	Location
Manchester Commerce	5363t	27-10-1914	M	20 miles N, 1/4 E Tory.
Tritonia	4272t	19-12-1914	M	22 miles NNE of Tory
Cherbury	3220t	29-4-1915	SMB	27 miles WNW Eagle Is.
Fulgent	2008t	30-4-1915	SMB	20 m WNW Blaskets
Earl of Latham	132t	5-5-1915	SSM	8 m SW of Old Head Kinsale
Centurion	5858t	6-5-1915	SMT	13 m SE 1/4E Coninbeg
Candidate	5945t	6-5-1915	SMT	15 m S Barrels LV.
Luisitania*	30396t	7-5-1915	SMT	15 m S Old Head Kinsale
Glenholm	1968t	21-5-1915	SMT	16 m WSW Fastnet
George & Mary	100t	4-6-1915	SSM	15 m SW Eagle Is
Sunlight	1433t	6-6-1915	SMT	20 m SW Galley Head
Trafford	215t	16-6-1915	SSM	30 m WSW Tuskar
Iberian	5223t	30-7-1915	SMT	9m SW Fastnet
Osprey	310t	12-8-1915	SSM	40m NE by E Inis Teraght
Maggie	269t	17-8-1915	SSM	8m E S Arklow LV
Bonney	2702t	17-8-1915	SSM	16m SE Tuskar
Africa	1038t	16-9-1915	M	1.5 miles off Kingstown
El Zorro*	5989t	28-12-1915	SMT	10m S Old Head Kinsale
Aranmore	1050t	21-3-1916	SMT	24m ENE Eagle Is
Englishman	5257t	24-3-1916	SMT	30m NE Malin Head
Manchester Engineer	4302t	27-3-1916	SMT	20 m W by S Coningbeg LV
Zent	3890t	5-4-1916	SMT	28m W By S Fastnet
Cardonia	2169t	16-4-1916	SMT	20 m S of Fastnet
Lilian H	467t	19-1-1917	SMB	15 m SE Old Head Kinsale
Neuquen	3583t	20-1-1917	SMT	20m NW by W Sceligs
Ava	5076t	27?-1-1917	SMT	? off South of Ireland
Ghazea*	5084t	4-2-1917	SMT	2m SSW Galley Head
Cliftonian	4303t	6-2-1917	SMT	4.5 m S 3/4 E Galley Head.
Hopemoor	3740t	14-2-1917	SMT	20 m NW of Scelligs
Kincardine	4108t	3-3-1917	SMT	20 m NE Teeraght

WARTIME WRECKS

Name	Tons	Date	How lost	Location
Westwick*	5694t	7-3-1917	M	1 m S Roche Point
Mediterranean	105t	10-3-1917	SSM	13 m S Hook
T Crowley	97t	10-3-1917	SSM	12 m S Hook
Folia*	6705 t	11-3-1917	SMT	4 m ESE Ram Head
Brika	3549t	13-3-1917	SMT	13 m SE by S Coninbeg
Northwaite	3626t	13-3-1917	SMT	14 m WNW Blaskets
Norwegian*	6327t	13-3-1917	SMT	4 m SW of Seven Heads
William Martin	104t	16-3-1917	SMT	9 m SW by W Ram Head
Ennistown	689t	24-3-1917	SMB	10 m SE of S Arklow LV
Howe	175t	24-3-1917	SMB	4 m NE from N Arklow LV
Adenwen	3793t	25-3-1917	SMB	6 m SE by E from N Arklow LV
Holgate	2604 t	27-3-1917	SMT	10 m NW of Scelligs
Gafsa*	3974t	28-3-1917	SMT	10 m SE 1/2S Kinsale Head
Ardglass	778t	28-3-1917	SMB	4m E from S Arklow LV
Wychwood	1985t	28-3-1917	SMT	4 m SSW S Arklow LV
Harvest Home	103t	28-3-1917	SSM	4m NE S Arklow LV.
South Arklow LV		28-3-1917	SMB	10 m SE 1/2 S Arklow
Lincolnshire	3965t	29-3-1917	SMT	8m SW by S Hook
Gold Coast	4255 t	19-4-1917	SMT	14 m S Mine Head
Arethusa	1279t	23-4-1917	SMB	15 m NW Eagle Island
New Design	66t	4-5-1917	SMB	15 m E by S Tuskar
Pilar De Larenga	136t	4-5-1917	SMT	2 m SE by S Tuskar
Greta	297t	5-5-1917	SSM	11 m SE Mine head
Lodes	396t	5-5-1917	M	4 m SE Ballycotton
Feltria	5254t	5-5-1917	SMT	8 m SE Mine Head
Calchas	6748t	11-5-1917	SMT	5m W by S Teeraght
Barrister	3679t	11-5-1917	SMT	7m SW Mine head
Silverburn	284t	13-6-1917	SSM	4m SE Cove Bay
Dart	3207	14-6-1917	SMT	6m SSW Ballycotton LH
Carthaginian	4444t	14-6-1917	M	2.5m NW Inistrahull LH
Raloo	1012t	17-6-1917	SMT	6m SE by E Coninbeg LV
Violet	158t	18-6-1917	SSM	9m SSE Coninbeg LV
Kangaroo	76t	18-6-1917	SSM	20 m S Tuskar
Batoum	4054t	19-6-1917	SMT	6m S Fastnet
Miami	3762t	22-6-1917	SMT	11 m ESE Fastnet
Lady of the Lake	51t	30-6-1917	SMB	15 m SSW Hook
Iceland	1501t	3-7-1917	SMT	10m SW Galley Head
Coral Leaf	428t	7-7-1917	SSM	18m NW by N Teeraght
Tarquah	3859t	7-7-1917	SMT	10 m SW Bull Rock
Garmoyle	1229t	10-7-1917	SMT	14 m SE Mine Head
Kioto	6182t	11-7-1917	SMT	20 m SW Fastnet
Ludgate	3708t	26-7-1917	SMT	2 m S Galley Head
Akassa	3919t	13-8-1917	SMT	3 M SE Galley Head
Athenia	8668t	16-8-1917	SMT	7 m N Inistrah
Roscommon	8238t	21-8-1917	SMT	20 m N Tory
Devonian	10435t	21-8-1917	SMT	20m N Tory
Cymrian	1014	25-8-1917	SMT	13m SE by S Tuskar
Lynburn	587t	29-8-1917	M	1/2m SW by W Arklow LV
Cooroy	2470t	29-8-1917	SMT	10m SW by W Hook

Name	Tons	Date	How lost	Location
Tuskar	1159t	6-9-1917	M	3m W Eagle Island
Minnehaha	13714t	7-9-1917	SMT	12 m SE Fastnet
Zeta	2269t	14-9-1917	SMT	8m SW Mine Head
Sandsend	3814t	16-9-1917	SMT	6 m SE by S Mine Head
Etal Manor	1875t	19-9-1917	SMT	7m SW Hook
Carrabin	2739	1-10-1917	SMT	10m S Daunt Rock
Bedale	2116t	6-10-1917	SMT	25m SE by S Mine Head
Aylevaroo	908t	7-10-1917		off S coast
Richard De Laringa	5591t	8-10-1917	SMT	15 m SE Ballycotton Is
Memphian	6305t	8-10-1917	SMT	7m ENE of N Arklow LV
Greldon	3322t	8-10-1917	SMT	7m ENE N Arklow LV
Rhodesia	4313t	11-10-1917	SMT	7m SE by S Coninbeg LV
WM Barkley*	569t	12-10-1917	SMT	7m E Kish LV
East Wales	4321	14-10-1917	SSM	8m SW Daunt Rock
Carlo	3040	13-10-1917	SMT	7m SW Coninbeg
Ardmore	1304	13-10-1917	SMT	13 m WSW Coninbeg LV
Elsena	335	22-10-1917	SSM	16m SE 1/2S S Arklow LV.
Copeland	1184t	2-12-1917	SMT	15m SSW Tuskar
Hare	774t	14-12-1917	SMT	7m E Kish LV
Formby	1282t	16-12-1917	SMT?	Irish Sea
Coninbeg	1279t	18-12-1917	SMT?	Irish sea
Canova	4637t	24-12-1917	SMT	15m S Mine Head
Daybreak	3238t	24-12-1917	SMT	1m E, S Rock LV
Birchwood	2756t	3-1-1918	SMT	25m E Blackwater LV
Rose Marie	2220t	5-1-1918	SMT	13m SE N Arklow LV
Auriana	13936t	4-2-1918	SMT	15m NW Inistrahull
Cresswell	2829t	5-2-1918	SMT	18m E by N 1/2N Kish LV
Pinewood	2219t	17-2-1918	SSM	15m S Mine Head
Wheatflower	188t	19-2-1918	SSM	10m SE by S Tuskar
Rockpool	4502t	2-3-1918	SMT	12m NE by N Eagle Is
Castle Eden	1949	4-3-1918	SMT	4m SSE Inistrahull LH
Nanny Wignall	93t	9-3-1918	SSM	14m SE by S Tuskar
Tweed	1777t	14-3-1918	SMT	15m SSE Tuskar
Glenford	494t	20-3-1918	SSM	24m E 1/2 S Rockabill
Kassanga	3015t	20-3-1918	SMT	23m SE by S of S Arklow LV.
Trinidad	2592t	22-3-1918	SMT	12m E Codling LV.
Lough Fisher	418t	30-3-1918	SSM?	12m SSE Helvick
Myrtle Branch	3741t	11?-4-1918	SMT	9m NE by N Inistrahull
Ladoga	1917t	16-4-1918	SMT	15m SE of S Arklow LV.
Fern	444t	22-4-1918	SMT	5m E by N Kish LV.
Johnny Toole	84t	29-4-1918	SSM	off Carnsore
Christiana Davis*	86t	29-4-1918	SSM	8m SE by S Tuskar
Iniscarra	1412t	12-5-1918	SMT	10m SE Ballycottin Is
Inisfallen	1405t	23-5-1918	SMT	16m E 3/4 N Kish LV
Mesaba	6833t	1-9-1918	SMT	21m E 1/4 N Tuskar
City of Glasgow	6545t	1-9-1918	SMT	21 m E1/4 N Tuskar
Joseph Fisher	79t	15-9-1918	SSM	16m E by N Codling LV
Energy	89t	15-9-1918	SSM	18m E by N Codling LV
Downshire	368t	21-9-1918	SSM	8m ESE Rockabill

Name	Tons	Date	How lost	Location
Hebburn	1938t	25-9-1918	SMT	14m S Mine Head
Baldersby	3613t	28-9-1918	SMT	9m El/2 S Codling LV
Eupion	3575t	3-10-1918	SMT	10m W Loop Head
Leinster*	2646t	10-10-1918	SMT	7m ESE Kish LV
Salvia	1250t	20-6-1917	SMT	off West coast sloop
Stephen Furness	1712t	13-12-1917	SMT	in Irish sea
Marmera	10509t	23-7-1918	SMT	off South coast (AMC)

British losses near Ireland in the Second World War

Name	Date	Tons	How lost	Location
Vancouver City	14-9-1939	4988t	SMT	51.23 N, 07.03 W
Hazleside*	24-9-1939	4646	SMT&G	51.17N 09.22W
Arandora Star	2-7-1940	15501	SMT	55.20N 10.33
W Frances Massey	6-6-1940	4212	SMT	55.33N 8.26W
Scottish Minstrel	16-7-1940	6998t	SMT	56.10N 10.20W.
Pearlmoor	19-7-1940	4581t	SMT	55.23N 9.18W
Troutpool	20-7-1940	4886t	M	54.40N 5.40W
Jamaica Progress	30-7-1940	5475t	SMT	56.26N 8.30W
Jersey City	31-7-1940	6322t	SMT	55.47N 9.18W
Boma	5-8-1940	4586t	SMT	55.44N 8.04W
Cumberland	23-8-1940	10939t	SMT	55.43N 7.33W
Pecten	25-8-1940	7468t	SMT	56.22N 7.55W
Har Zion	30-8-1940	5027t	AT	56.20N 10.00W
Stratford	26-9-1940	4753	SMT	54.50N 10.40W
Manchester Brigade	26-9-1940	6042t	SMT	54.53N 10.22W
Mardinian	9-9-1940	2434t	SMT	56.37N 9.00W
Aska	16-9-1940	8323t	AB	55.15N 5.55W
City of Mobile	16-9-1940	6614	AB	54.18N 5.16W
New Sevilla	20-9-1940	13801	SMT	55.48N 7.22W
City of Simla	21-9-1940	10138t	SMT	55.55N 8.20W
Kerry Head*	21-10-1940	825t	AB	5m S Blackball Head
Empress of Britain	28-10-1940	42348t	SMT	55.16N 9.50W.
Osage	18-12-1940	1010t	AB	4 m NE Arklow LV
Isolda	19-12-1940	734t	AT	Near Barrels LV
Diplomat	27-11-1940	8240	SMT	55.42N 11.37W
Ringwall	27-1-1941	497	M	Irish Sea S Isle of Man
Pandion*	28-1-1941	1944	AB	55.34N 10.22W
Kyle Rona	17-2-1941	307	CU	Irish Sea
Port Townsville	3-3-1941	8661	AB	52.05N 5.24W
Empire Frost	12-3-1941	7005	AB	51.36N 5.40W
London II	21-3-1941	1260	AB	51.23N 4.30W
Brier Rose	26-3-1941	503	CU	Irish Sea
Olivine	28-3-1941	929	CU	Irish Sea
Olga S	6-4-1941	2252	AB	55.48N 9.45W
Baron Carnegie	11-6-1941	3178	AT	51.55N 5.34W
St Patrick	13-6-1941	1922	AB	52.04N 5.25W
Botwey	26-7-1941	5106	SMT	55.42N 9.53W
Empire Gunner	7-9-1941	4492	AB	52.08N 5.18W
Daru	15-9-1941	3854	AB	51.56N 5.58W
Empire Heritage	8-9-1944	15702	SMT	55.27N 8.01W
Pinto	8-9-1944	1346	SMT	55.27W 8.01N

Name	Date	Tons	How lost	Location
Maja	15-1-1945	8181	SMT	53.40N 5.14W
Norfolk Coast	28-2-1945	646	SMT	51.58N 5.25W
King Edgar	2-3-1945	4536	SMT	52.05N 5.42W
Sea Sweeper	20-11-1939	345	SMG	25m NW Tory
Delphine	20-11-1939	250	SMG	18m NE Tory
Thomas Hankins	20-11-1939	276	SMG	14m NW Tory
Respondo	11-9-1940	209	CU	Off Old Head Kinsale
Bass Rock	24-9-1940	169	AB	Off Old Head Kinsale
Exeter	29-3-1940	165	AB	5m SW Ballycotton
Whitby	4-4-1940	164	AB	3m SSE Blackwater LV
Caliph	2-11-1941	226	AB	12m S Old Head Kinsale
Duquesa	7-1-1941	8,600	frozen meat torp off Ireland German report	

Norwegian losses near Ireland in the First World War

Name	Tons	Date	How sunk	location	Voyage and cargo
Cambuskenneth	1924t	29-6-1915	M	26m SW Fastnet	Portland - Queenstown wheat.
Caprivi	2932t	23-4-1915	M	16m NNW Tory	Baltimore - Kristiania.
Hitteroy	1914t		SMB	30m s Fastnet	Skrien - Nantes Saltpetre.
Songdal	2090t	3-2-1917	SSM	50.10N 10.15W	Buenos Aires - Falmouth maize.
Tamara	453t	3-2-1917	SSM	50.26N 12.15W	Jamaica Fleetwood logwood.
Songlev	2064t	3-2-1917	SMB	50.05N 11.15W	Buenos Aires -Falmouth maize
Wasdale	1856t	3-2-1917	SMB	50.22N 11.53W	Buenos Aires -Dublin maize.
Dukat	1408t	20-2-1917	SMB	off Ballycotton	Barry -Fayal coal.
Storenes	1870t	1-3-1917	SMB	off Kinsale	Buenos Aires -Queenstown maize.
Mabella	1637t	1-3-1917	SSM	22 m SSW Kinsale	Galveston - Kolding oil.
Adalands	1577t	8-3-1917	SSM	9m SW Fastnet	Senegal - Hull ground nuts
Storstad	6028t	8-3-1917	SSM	51.20N 11.50W	Buenos Aires - Rotterdam maize.
Spartan	2286t	9-3-1917	SMT	50.26N 10.45W	New York - Liverpool petroleum.
Lars Fostenes	2118t	9-3-1917	SSM	lled 51N 7.5W	New York - Rotterdam piece goods
Blenheim	1144t	22-2-1917	SMB	30m SSW Fastnet	Pensicola - Greenock timber.
Malmanger*	5671t	22-3-1917	SMT?	20m off Fastnet	New York -Avonmouth petroleum.
Dagali	742t	28-3-1917	SSM	at Arklow Bank	Hennebout - Glasgow ballast.
Os	900t		?	20m NN Loop Head	Llanelly - Kristinsand coal.
Snespurven	1409t	2-4-1917	SSM	25m SSW Tuskar	New York - Dublin petroleum
Vestlev	1728t	22-11-1917	SMB	14m off Tory	Mobile - Liverpool textiles.
Anne Marie	441t	23-4-1917	SSM	Atlantic off Ireland	Fray Bentos - Silloth guano.
Teie	1973t	28-5-1917	SMB	50.28N 9.20W	South Georgia - Liverpool whale oil.
Asheim	2147t	8-7-1917	SSM	30m off Inistrahull	Dublin - New York ballast.
Falkland	4877t	12-8-1917	SMT	10 m off Mine head	Philadelphia -Liverpool oil.
Majoren	2747t	3-9-1917	SSM	25m off Tory	Philadelphia- Glasgow oil.
San Andres	1656t	11-5-1918 S	MT	51.23N 7.53W	Spain - Norway piece goods

Norwegian losses near Ireland in the Second World War

Touraine	5811t	7-10-1940	SMT	55.12N 10.18W
Rask	613t	19-10-1941	ACB	near Tuskar
Galatea	1152t	21-1-1945	M	52.00N 5.00 W
Vigsnes	1599	23-1-1945	M	53.32N 4.19W
Solor	8262t	27-1-1945	SMT	52.20N 5.19W
Novasli	3204	18-3-1945	SMT	52.04N 5.42W
Norwegian Vessel		7-2-194	16/15 seamen landed at Dingle after 6 days afloat	

BIBLIOGRAPHY

1. The Blasket Islands, Joan & Ray Stagles, O'Brien Press, Dublin, 1980.
2. The Saltees, Richard Roche & Oscar Merne, O'Brien Press, Dublin, 1977.
3. Skellig, Des Lavelle, O'Brien Press, Dublin, 1976
4. The Islands of Ireland, Thomas H. Mason, Mercier Press, Cork, 1967.
5. Sailing Round Ireland, Wallace Clarke, B.T. Batsford Ltd., London, 1976.
6. The Armada in Ireland, Niall Fallon, Stanford Maritime Ltd., London, 1978.
7. Graveyard of the Spanish Armada, T.P. Kilfeather, Anvil Books, Tralee, 1967.
8. Irish Passenger Steamship Services, Vol. 2, D.B. McNeill, David & Charles Ltd., Newton Abbot. 1971.
9. Wreck and Rescue on the East Coast of Ireland, John De Courcy Ireland, Glendale Press, Dublin, 1983.
10. Dictionary of Disasters at Sea During the Age of Steam (1824-1962), Vols. 1, 2. Charles Hocking, Lloyds, London, 1969.
11. Lusitania, Colin Simpson, Longman, London, 1972, or Penguin, 1974.
12. Seven days to Disaster, Des Hickey and Gus Smith, Collins, London, 1981.
13. Schooner Captain, Norah Ayland, Bradford Barton Ltd., Truro, 1972.
14. Achill, Kenneth McNally, David & Charles, Newton Abbot, 1973.
15. The Aran Islands, Daphne Pochin Mould, David & Charles, Newton Abbot, 1972.
16. Callender of State papers Ireland.
17. Islands of Ireland, Kenneth McNally, Batesford, London, 1978.
18. Shipwrecks of the Ulster Coast, Ian Wilson, Impact-Amergin, Colraine, 1979.
19. Treasures of the Armada, Robert Stenuit, Newton Abbott 1972.
20. H.M.S. Colossus, Roland Morris, Hutchinson, London, 1979.
21. Emergency, Kerry Coast, Dick Robinson, 1989.
22. In search of Spanish treasure, Sydney Wignall, David and Charles, 1982.
23. Irish Shipping, published by Belfast branch of World Ship Society.
24. Deep Sea Treasure, Mark Williams, Heinemann, London, 1981.
25. The Irish Lighthouse Service, T.G. Wilson, Hodges Figgis, Dublin, 1968.
26. Rathlin, Disputed Island, Wallace Clarke, Volturna Press, Portlaw, 1971.
27. Valentia, Portrait of an Island, D.C. Pouchin-Mould, Blackwater Press, Dublin, 1978.
28. Lloyds Casualty Return, Lloyds, London, annual.
29. The Automobile Association, Motoring Guide to Ireland, 1976.
30. Lifeboat Ireland, published by RNLI 1953-1983.
31. Subsea, published by Comhairle Fo Thuinn, the Irish Underwater Council.
32. Down the Quay, A history of Dundalk Harbour, 1987
33. The stones of Aran, Tim Robinson. Viking Press, London, 1986.
34. Journal of the Cork Historical and Archaeological Society. Vol. 1 second series 1895 No 4 April, Port of Cork Steamships from 1815 to 1894. William J. Barry. Ibid no 10, October 1895.
35. Hibernian Chronicle, Cork, contemporary account.
36. Tales of the Wexford Coast, Richard Roche, Duffy Press, Enniscorthy, 1993.
37. History of Kinsale, John R. Thulier.
38. Twenty years a growing, Muiris O'Suillabhain.
39. The Islandman, Tomas O'Crothain.
40. Maritime Arklow, Frank Forde, 1988 Glendale Press Dublin.
41. Bright Lights, White Water, Bill Long, New Island Books, 1993.
42. History from the Sea, Peter Trockmorton, 1988 Mitchell Beasley.
43. A History of Seafaring Based on Underwater Archaeology, 1972, George Bass.
44. Archaeology Underwater, an Atlas of Submerged Sites, 1980, Keith Muckelroy.
45. The World Atlas of Treasure, Derek Wilson, Pan Books, 1981.

46. European shipwrecks over 3000 years, Colin Martin. Pgs94-97
47. Sailing ships of war, Howard, Publ Conway 1979.
48. Paddy's Lament Ireland 1846-1847, Thomas Gallagher, Ward River Press, 1982
49. Diving for Treasure, Peter Trockmorton, Thames & Hudson, 1977.
50. Journal of the Galway Archaeological and Historical Society, 1917, vol. 10, p.156
51. The Long Watch, Frank Forde, Gill & Macmillan 1981.
52. Ballycotton Wrecks and Rescues, 1800-1855, ditto 1855-1900, Fr B. Troy. published privately.
53. The Campaign of the Spanish Armada, Peter Kemp, Phaidon.
54. The voyage of the Spanish Armada, David Howarth, Collins 1981.
55. Griffiths Co Wexford Almanac 1872, 1875, 1876, 1877, 1880. Chronicles of Co Wexford.
56. Gentleman's magazine vol. 36 1766 p.150. vol. 35 1765 p545-6-7.
57. Robt Frazer Dublin 1807 Statistical survey of Co Wexford by order of RDS.
58. Songs of the Wexford Coast, ed Rev Joseph Ranson. 1948. Reprinted 1975, John English & Co, Wexford.
59. The Kerryman Newspaper, contemporary account.
60. Wexford Herald, contemporary account
61. Ardmore Journal, no 5 1988
62. Ardmore Journal, no 2 1985
63. Decies, The Journal of the Old Waterford Society Sept. 1982, p32-35
63. Ennis Chronicle, contemporary account.
64. Decies, Sept 1977, p17-18
65. Freemans Journal, contemporary account.
66. Waterford Mail, contemporary account.
67. Cork Examiner, contemporary account.
68. Times, London, contemporary account.
69. Belfast Newsletter, contemporary account.
70. Derry Journal, contemporary account.
71. Cork County Eagle, contemporary account,
72. Clare Journal, contemporary account.
73. Wexford Constitution, contemporary account.
74. Decies, September 1979, pages 46-50.
75. A fortnight in Kerry, in Short Studies on Great Subjects, 2nd series, 1871, J.A. Froude.
76. History of the Town and County of Wexford, Vol. 4. Hore.
77. British Vessels lost at sea, 1939-45, 1914-18. Patrick Stephens Ltd., Wellingborough, 1988. Facsimile of four HMSO publications.
78. Masters, D. Divers in deep seas, 1938.
79. Harkin, Scenery and Antiquities in North West Donegal, 1893 , Irvine, Derry.
80. Romantic stories and Legends of Donegal, Swan.
81. Highways and Byways in Donegal and Antrim. Hugh Thomas, McMillan, 1895.
82. Decies, Autumn 1985 pages 31-34.
83. The Sea Thine Enemy, Jarrolds, London.
84. Oileain Arann, Antoine Powell, Wolfhound Press.
85. History of Port of Dublin, Gilligan 1988.
86. U-Boats Destroyed, the effect of anti submarine warfare 1914-18. Robert M Grant Putnam London 1964.
87. Bandon Historical Journal No 1 Nollaig 1984.
88. Irelands Own 22-1-1955 p17
89. Irelands Own 31-12-1955 p17
90. Irelands Own Vol. 39 1922 p347

91. Irelands Own 3-9-1938
92. Irelands Own 15-5-1954
93. Irelands Own 10-12-1955 p6
94. Deep sea diving, Masters, D. 1935
95. All About Kilkee, Kilkee Development Association,
96. When ships go down , Masters D., Eyre and Spottiswood , London , 1932.
97. Wonders of salvage, Masters, D. John Lane Bodley Head, 1924.
98. Discovering Kerry, T.J. Barrington, 1976.
99. Irish Independent, contemporary account.
100. Decies, The Journal of the Old Waterford Society, September 1979 pp46-50.
101. Shipwrecks of Great Britain and Ireland, Richard Larn, David and Charles, 1981,
102. Dungarvan, a Maritime and General History 1690-1978, John Young. Published locally.
103. History of Waterford, Charles Smith publ 1812.
104. History of Cork, Charles Smith, publ 1812.
105. In search of Spanish treasure, Ian Wilson, David & Charles, 1980.
106. London Gazette, 25-29 January 1693 no 2944.
107. Journal of the Cork Archaeological and Historical Society 1903, vol. 9, pp 1-20. ibid 1902, Vol. 8, 205-230. "The London Master or the Jew Detected."
108. London Gazette, 30-4-1697, no 3288.
109. London Gazette, 1711, no 4935.
110. London Gazette, Contemporary account.
111. Cork Holly Bough Christmas 1974 Cardiff Hall
112. Cork Holly Bough Christmas 1978 Port Yarrock
113. Palmer's Official Index to the Times (London)
114. Rambles round Donegal, Patrick Campbell, Mercier Press, 1981.
115. Toraigh na dTonn, Eoghan O'Colm, Foilseachan Naisiunta, 1971.
116. Hidden places in Donegal, John M Feehan, Mercier press.
117. The way that I went, Robert Lloyd Prager, Figgis Dublin, 1980.
118. Irish Times, 16-5-1975, p12
119. My Mystery Ships, Gordon Campbell, Houdder & Stoughton, London, 1928
120. Derry Journal, 3 February 1987.
121. The Kowloon Bridge Disaster, Unanswered questions, Earthwatch Research report, February 1988.
122. Western People 12-11-1927
123. Western People 5-11-1977
124. The Past, Wexford, vol. 9, p54.
125. North Mayo Archaeological and Historical Society, Blianiris 1982, p44.
126. North Mayo Archaeological and Historical Society, Blianiris 1983-4, p46.
127. Waterford News 24-10-1930 pp4, 8, 9.
128. Narratives of shipwrecks of the Royal Navy between 1793 and 1849, W.O.S. Gilly, Parker, London, 1851.
129. A companion to the Royal Navy, David A. Thomas, Harrap 1988.
130. Bantry Bay, Brendan Bradley, Williams & Norgate 1931.
131. Shipbuilding and repairs, John Smellie, McCorqudale, Glasgow, 1935.
132. Wexford Independent or Independent Wexford, contemporary account.
133. Irish Naval Service, Thomas H. Adams, World Ship Society Monograph No 4, 1982.
134. Sligo Champion, contemporary account.
135. The Main Manuscripts Collection, Volume no, Page no, held at Department of Irish Folklore, University College Dublin.
136. The Western Ocean Packets, Basil Lubbock, James Brown, Glasgow, 1935.

137. Inisowen and Tirchonnaill, Doherty.
138. The Colonial Clippers, Basil Lubbock, James Brown, Glasgow 1925.
139. Derry Journal, 4-7-1955, 8-7-1955.
140. Irish Times, contemporary account.
141. The Lost Ships of the Royal Navy 1793-1900, W.P. Gosset, Mansell, London, 1986.
142. Facts from Gweedore, 1887, Lord George Hill.
143. The Munster Express, contemporary account.
144. Subsea, Journal of The Irish Underwater Council, Spring 1989.
145. The Navy in the English Civil War, J.R. Powell, Archon Books, Hamden, London, 1962.
146. Ireland and the Irish in Maritime History, John De Courcy, Glendale Press, Dublin.
147. Ships of the Royal Navy, J.J. Colledge, Greenhill Books, 1987.
148. Donegal Democrat, Contemporary account.
149. RNLI, Annual Report.
150. Connaught Telegraph, Contemporary account.
151. Howth, a history, unknown c1988.
152. Malahide, Donebate and Portrane, Peadar Bates, Anglo, Drogheda, 1988.
153. Illustrated guide to Historic Malahide, Tom O'Shea.
154. Blenerville Gateway to Tralee, Kelly, Lynch, O'Sullivan, Publ. Blenerville Windmill Project, 1989.
155. Harbour Lights, no 1 1988, Journal of Cobh Historical Society, Colman O'Mahony & Tim Cadogan.
156. Historical Manuscripts Commission Report.
157. Cork Examiner, 19-5-1932, The Kingdom of Kerry, xxiii by Rambler.
158. Kerry Evening Post, Contemporary account.
159. Clyde Shipping Company, a history, Alan Cuthbert, University Press Glasgow, 1956.
160. History of Rosslare Port.
161. People Wexford, Contemporary account.
162. Kerry Magazine Vol. 8, No 1, pp113-114.
163. American Neptune, pp14-20
164. Down the Quay, a history of Dundalk Port. Published locally 1988.
165. Seanachas O'Chaibre, Sean O'Croinin, Ed Donnacha O'Croinin 1985
166. Aisti O'Chleire, Donnacha O'Drisceoil. Publ. An Clochomhar 1 987.
167. The Irish Sword VII, no 26, 37-57, 1965.
168. Southern Star, Contemporary account.
169. Memoir for the Wasp, Enda McLoughlin, Glendale Press, Dublin, 1989.
170. Mariners Mirror, Vol. 62, no 3, August 1976. Alan Roddie.
171. Archaeology Ireland, September 1989.
172. Edmund Ludlow, Memoirs 1625-72, Ed C.H. Firth 1894, Vol. I, p303.
173. Galway Free Press, Contemporary account.
174. Wexford Freeman, contemporary account.
175. Sea Breezes, January 1955 , p4-13.
176. Kerry Weekly Reporter and Commercial Advertiser, Contemporary account.
177. Irelands Own, 15-12-1989.
178. The Mystery of the Casement Ship, Capt. Karl Spindler, Anvil Press, 1965.
179. The Great World War, Vol. 9 , publ. Gresham c1920.
180. Great Sea Rescues, E.W. Middleton, New English Library, 1976.
181. Ireland's Own, July 1988.
182. Inisbeg Revisited, John C Messinger, Sheffield Publ. Salem Wisconsin,
183. The wreck of the Killarney, contemporary pamphlet by Baron Spolasco, in National Library, Dublin.

BIBLIOGRAPHY

184. Clare Champion, Contemporary account.
185. Arklow Last Stronghold of Sail, Jim Rees and Liam Charlton, 1985.
186. J. of the Cork Historical and Archaeological society, Vol. 11, 201-2 1905. History of Port of Cork Steam Navigation.
187. Men Under the Sea, Commander E. Ellsberg, Geo Harrap, London, 1940.
188. The Beam, house publication of Commissioners of Irish Lights.
189. Wexford Guardian, Contemporary account.
190. Disaster at Sea, John Mariott, Arrow, London, 1989.
191. Maritime Ireland, No 25. 1990.
192. History of Wexford Port.
193. Irish Sea Book, 1989, Smuggling in the Irish Sea.
194. J. Cork Historical and Archaeological Society Vol. 7, p43-6, Vol. 1 236-7, 1895.
195. J. Cork Historical and Archaeological Society, Vol. 8, 53-5, 1902. Vol. 9, 131-2, 1903.
196. Board of Trade wreck returns published in various volumes of House of Commons papers.
197. Pertes de Guerre, subies par la Marine De Commerce Norwegienne, Kobelske Bok OG Kunsttrykkeri, Kristiania. circa 1920.
198. A.A. Bestic, article in Irish Independent 7-5-1956.
199. Sceligside, Michael Kirby, Lilliput Press Dublin, 1990.
200. The Royal Navy, Wm Laird Clowes, Sampson Low 1897.
201. Modern Shipping Disasters 1963-1987, Norman Hooke.
202. Lloyd's War Losses, The First War, Publ facsimile 1990 Lloyds.
203. Lloyd's War Losses The Second World War, Publ facsimile 1990 Lloyds.
204. Catholics and Catholicism in the Eighteenth Century Press, John Bradley, Maynooth, 1965.
205. Lords of the East, Jean Sutton, Conway, 1982.
206. Hints towards a Natural and topographical History of Counties Sligo, Donegal and Fermanagh, Rev Wm Henry, 1739, manuscript 2533 in National Archives, Dublin.
207. The Last Colonel of the Irish Brigade, Mrs Morgan O'Connell.
209. The True Story of the chiefs of Dunboy, A.J. Fetherstonhaugh, J. Royal Society of Antiquaries of Ireland, 4, 1894.
210. J. Cork Historical and Archaeological Society 1a 1892, John O'Mahony.
211. Finch Mss Historical Manuscripts Report, 2, 1922, p491.
213. U-Boat Intelligence 1914-1918, Robert M Grant, Putnam, London.
214. Some Experiences of an Irish RM, E.O.E Sommerville, 1923.
215. Amhrain Tomas Rua O'Shuilleabhain, Ed Maire Ni Shuilleabhain, An Sagairt, Maynooth, 1985.
216. Cork, Daphne D.C. Pochin Mould, Brandon Books, Dingle, 1991.
217. Egmont Manuscripts, Historical Manuscripts Commission, 1909, 2, pp23, 37.
218. Off beat Ireland, Des Moore, Nomad Books, c1976.
219. Danger Zone, The story of the Queenstown Command, E. Keeble Chatterton, Rich & Cowan, London, 1934.
220. Bruijn J.R., Dutch Asiatic Shipping in 17th & 18th centuries. Martinus Nijhoff, the Hague, 1987.
221. Shipping Wonders of the World, ed. Clarence Winchester, Amalgamated Press, London.
222. Book Of Cloyne, ed. Padraig O'Loinsigh, Cloyne Historical and Archaeological Association, 1977.
223. The Ancient and Present State of Kerry, Charles Smith, 1756. republished Mercier 1979.
224. Old Kerry Records, Mary Agnes Hickson, 2nd series 1874.
225. The Big Wind, Peter Carr, White Row Press, Belfast, 1991.
226. Galway Vindicator, 6-4-1864, 23-4-1864.
227. The history of County Mayo, H.T. Knox, 1908, republished, De Burca 1982.

228. Ships Monthly, March, April 1982, Limerick Steam 1893-1970. R.J. Scott.
229. Bere Island, Ted O'Sullivan, Inisgreagy Books, Cork, 1992.
230. Sea Breezes, June 1964, p461.
231. Egmont MSS, Historical Manuscripts Commission Report, 1905, p260.
232. Drogheda Independent, contemporary account.
233. Achill 5000BC-1900, Theresa Mc Donald, IAS Publishing, 1992.
234. Lloyds List, from 1741 (except 1745, 1746, 1754, 1756, 1759, 1771-1778, Facsimile reprint, Greg International Publishers, 1969. Also Lloyds List to date (indexed 1838-1927)
235. Memory harbour the Port of Sligo, John C. McTernan, Drumlin Avena, Publ. 1992.
236. Limerick Chronicle 1-12-1992.
237. History of Limerick, Maurice Lenihan.
238. Irish Press, contemporary account.
239. Register of ships of the East India Company, Charles Hardy, publ c1850.
240. Log of the York, manuscript held at British Library, Oriental and East India Collection, 197 Blackfriars Rd., London.
241. The Ocean Almanac, Robert Hendrickson, Hutchenson, 1992.
242. Chichester letter book, State Papers Ireland James I.
243. Tracton Community Newsletter 1969.
244. Inisboffin, ed Kieran Concannon, 1993.
246. Annals of Dublin, O'Donnell, Wolfhound press, 1987.
247. Romantic Hidden Kerry, Tómas O' Suilleabhain, Kerryman, 1930.

HMS Mignonette
Photo: Di Silva via D. Woosnam

INDEX

INDEX

INDEX

INDEX